LOYALTY

Dr. Richard Reusch, 1891-1975

*"Even as St. John was loyal unto death, so the men of our regiment.
Loyalty is what counts in life."*

LOYALTY

Richard Gustavovich Reusch

Imperial Russian Cavalry Officer

Oriental Scholar

University Professor

Lutheran Pastor

Political Refugee

East African Missionary

Mountaineer

Ethnographer

Builder

Spy

Linguist

Historian

Honorary Masai Warrior

Raconteur

*His exploits read like adventure stories out of the past — Beau Gest,
Kipling, Lawrence of Arabia, the Crusades.*
— Gareth Hiebert

Daniel H. Johnson
©2008

ABOUT THE AUTHOR

Daniel Johnson graduated from Gustavus Adolphus College and did graduate work in Communication Studies at the University of Massachusetts, Amherst. He taught at the University of Minnesota, Duluth, and the College of St. Scholastica where he was awarded a Fulbright Scholarship, developed a debate exchange program with two Russian universities, taught in St. Scholastica's service learning program in Cuernavaca, Mexico, and received the Max A. Lavine Award for Teaching Excellence. He is presently retired and lives in Mexico. Email address: **toosentak@gmail.com**

Text © 2008 by Daniel Johnson

First published by SunRay Printing, *St. Cloud, Minnesota*
First United States edition 2008

Editor: Patra Sevastiades
Proofer: Kirsten Johnson

Cover and inside design by Joan Henrik, *Duluth, Minnesota*

Printed in the United States

ISBN-13: 978-1-934478-17-2
ISBN-10: 1-934478-17-2

In Acknowledgement

Reusch Family Members
Betty Anderson, Neil, Richard and Mark Anderson; and Aurelia Reusch (†1996),
who generously shared recollections of their father, grandfather and brother.

Galina Tioun
my friend at Petrozavodsk State University whose encouragement, assistance and
criticism are integral to this project.

J. William Fulbright Foreign Scholarship Board
for the opportunity to teach and follow Dr. Reusch's trail through
Russia, Europe and Tanzania.

Chester Johnson
Lutheran Church Archivist, Folke Bernadotte Memorial Library,
Gustavus Adolphus College.

. . . .

Archivists and Individuals
whose assistance and hospitality I treasure:

Denmark
Danish National Archives
Knud and Marianne Filt
Trygve and Merethe Grann
Knud J. V. Jespersen, Ølstykke Library and Archive

Estonia
Estonian State History Archive
Eero Medijanien, History Faculty, Tartu University
Tartu City Museum
Tartu University Museum and Library Archive
Dmitri Udras

Finland
Archive of the Foreign Ministry
Mannerheim Museum
National Archive of Finland

Germany
Bundesarchiv, Berlin
Deutsche Bücheri, Leipzig
The Evangelisch-Lutherische Landeskirchliches Archiv, Schwerin
Evangelisch-Lutherische Missionswerk Archiv, Leipzig
Rev. Dr. and Mrs. Ernst Jäschke, and Martin Jäschke
Uta Lunkenheimer
Anja Ruhe

Latvia
Rev. Harijs and Mara Grigoli
Latvian State History Archive
Lutheran Consistory Archive

Russia
Vera Artesevich, Director, Saratov State University Library
Vjatcheslav V. Bogdanov
Vladimir Bolgov, Ataman, Vladikavkaz Terek Cossacks
Central State Archive of North Osetia
Eleanora Chevyenova
V. V. Digoev, North Osetia State University
Federal Security Bureau, Petrozavodsk, and Central Archive, Moscow
Vadim Goloubev, St. Petersburg State University
Anatoli Isaenko, North Osetia State University
Rev. Georg Kretchmar, Bishop,
Evangelical Lutheran Church in Russia and Independent States
Leonid Kuznetsov
Henri Kusov, North Osetia State University
Ivan Malygin
Museum of the Osetian Republic
Evgeni Okunev
Vadim Pavlov, Karelian State Pedagogical University
Sergei Ruseen, Principal, School No. 5, Vladkiavkaz
Sergei Starkov
Valeri and Olga Teto
Vladikavkaz City Library and Archive
Colonel Yerzhan Yusupov, Retired
Professor Rudolf and Tatiana Yanson
Anatoli, Galina and Sergei Zhivoglyadov
Alexander and Galina Zubokov
Andrei Zhukov, African Studies, St. Petersburg State University

Tanzania, East Africa
The Right Reverend Paul Akyoo, Bishop, Usa River
Ludovik Gtilya
The Right Reverend Erasto N. Kweka, Bishop, Moshi
The Right Reverend Thomas Laiser, Bishop, Arusha
Jeremy LeFoy
Agnal Malunda
Northern Diocese Archives, Moshi
Rev. David and Eunice Simonson

United Kingdom
Public Record Office, Kew, London

United States of America
American Historical Society of Germans from Russia
Rev. Stanley and Marie Benson
College of St. Scholastica Librarians:
Karen Ostovich, Susan Walkoviak, Barb Warner and Todd White.
Joan Henrik
Elsa C. Johnson, my mother
Julie Johnson, my sister
John and Joyce Johnson
The Library of Congress
John and Sandra Lipke
Luther Seminary Library and Archive
Sharon Lund and Robert Falls
MINITEX Library Information Network
Tom Morgan, Russian Studies, College of St. Scholastica
New York Public Library, Slavic Collection
Mayme Sevander
Fr. Philemon and Patra Sevastiades
Sisters of the St. Scholastica Monastery:
Mary Catherine Shambour, Joan Braun and Mary Richard Boo.
Lary Skow
Paul and Ruth Tillquist
Elizabeth Whitman, Archive of the Evangelical
Lutheran Church in America.
Pastor Kermit and Dorothy (Magney) Youngdale
University of Minnesota Libraries

*And the many other individuals on three continents whose recollections
are noted in the following pages.*

Table of Contents

PART I: IMPERIAL RUSSIA

PART II: EAST AFRICA

PART III: MINNESOTA

PHOTOGRAPHS

MAPS

INDEX

KEY TO ARCHIVE ABBREVIATIONS

AELCA . . . . Archives of the Evangelical Lutheran Church in America, Chicago

AELML . . . . Archives, Evangelical Lutheran Missionswork, Leipzig

AFFM . . . . Archives of the Finnish Foreign Ministry, Helsinki

ANDTL . . . . Archives of the Northern Diocese, Tanzanian Lutheran Church, Moshi

BArch . . . . Bundesarchiv, Berlin

CSANO . . . . Central State Archive of North Osetia, Vladikavkaz

DNA . . . . Danish National Archives, Copenhagen

ESHA . . . . Estonian State History Archive, Tartu

FSBA . . . . Federal Security Bureau Archives, Moscow

GACA . . . . Lutheran Church Archives, Folke Bernadotte Memorial Library, Gustavus Adolphus College, St. Peter, Minnesota

LHAO . . . . Local History Archive, Ølstykke, Denmark

MOR . . . . Museum of the Ostetian Republic, Vladikavkaz

NAF . . . . National Archives of Finland, Helsinki

PRO . . . . Public Record Office (Kew), London

TUA . . . . Tartu University Archives

Author's Foreword

JANUARY 1948

A blizzard had blown into Minnesota from the Dakotas. The storm was winding down, and already nighttime snowplows were beginning to clear the township roads. Local farm families who belonged to the West Union Augustana (Swedish) Lutheran Church had braved the weather to assemble in the parish hall to hear a special speaker. But would the famous missionary from Africa make it through the storm all the way from St. Peter? It was already twenty minutes past eight.

Suddenly, the door swung open and in a swirl of wind-driven snow two men came into the hall, stamping their feet and taking off coats, caps and gloves. One was a neighbor who had driven to St. Peter to pick up the speaker. The other man was the famous Dr. Richard Reusch.

He introduced himself as a former officer in the Imperial Russian army who had fought the Bolsheviks before going as a missionary to Tanganyika Territory, East Africa. But I was seven years old, and it was his story about the lion (or maybe it was a leopard) that I remember most vividly.

A man-eating lion had killed some cattle and badly mauled a Masai warrior. So Dr. Reusch went hunting. He was tracking the animal through the bush when all of a sudden he heard a roar. Lo and behold, across the clearing only twenty or thirty feet away he saw the lion, already crouching, which, he hastily explained, signaled its intention to leap — on him. But he had foolishly left his rifle leaning against a nearby tree, so what could he do? In only seconds he would be in paradise!

He glanced at his rifle. Then at the lion. Time stopped. Suddenly, with a roar the lion was airborne, those hideous teeth hurtling toward his neck!

It was not humanly possible in those few seconds to reach for his gun, bring it to his shoulder, take aim and fire. And yet that's what happened. The voracious beast shuddered in mid-leap and — dropped at his feet. Dead. With a single bullet. (Pause.) "My friends," intoned the former Russian cavalry officer, "it was not my doing, but that of an angel sent by my Heavenly King!"

His was the best-told story I'd ever heard.

SEPTEMBER 1960

Swedish American Lutheran immigrants founded Gustavus Adolphus College in 1862. A century later, first year students were still required to enroll in a two-semester Bible history course. And so on the first day of the fall semester in 1960, the freshman class gathered in the Little Theater for the first lecture in Old Testament studies. A short, bald man stood on stage next to the proscenium dressed in a green and tan checked sport coat over a maroon vest, black tie, British cavalry twill trousers and cordovan plain-toed shoes. According to my class schedule, his name was Dr. Richard Reusch.

As we settled into our assigned seats, the professor studied our faces as if he were a drill sergeant assessing new recruits. Our babble and silly laughter died away as he strode with military gait to the lectern positioned stage-center. There he stood in the spotlight, his intense dark eyes gazing at us from behind heavy dark framed glasses. He spoke in an unusual and heavy accent that was not immediately easy to understand. The other professors in the Christianity Department were Swedish Americans with names like Engberg, Erling, Esbjornson and Johnson. Who was this Reusch? He seemed vaguely familiar.

In time we adapted to his accent but often forgot to take notes when he departed from his prepared lecture to tell stories of ancient Israelites, the Caucasus Mountains, the bloody Russian Revolution or his adventures in East Africa. That's it! He's the guy who shot the lion! He was a student of ancient history, fluent in Arabic, Hebrew and Aramaic as well as several other obscure Middle Eastern languages. He had actually crossed the Sea of Reeds, climbed Mt. Sinai and gathered manna in the wilderness. Like Moses, he had struck a limestone outcropping in the hot desert with his staff so that he and his Bedouin guide could drink cool water.

Dr. Reusch was unlike any other professor on campus. He puffed on a pipe with a foul-smelling cigar jammed into the bowl, and in his cluttered office he smoked a Turkish water pipe. It was rumored that at sixty-nine years of age he still bench-pressed 220 pounds. He taught fencing, not with foils but real sabers. He seldom wore a winter overcoat, not even when striding across campus in a blizzard. However, none of us realized that our professor of Old Testament had sparked the interest of reporters in the world beyond our campus:

> Dr. Richard Reusch is a short, slight Lutheran missionary who chose to work among one of the fiercest tribes in Africa — the blood-drinking, spear-wielding Masai. — *Time* Magazine (1950)

> The Tanganyika Government has named Kibo's inner crater for Dr. Richard Reusch. He was presented with a gold medal on his 25th ascent and it was decided that a diamond medal be made to commemorate his 50 climbs and long service to the Mountain Club of East Africa. — *Tanganyika Standard* (1954)

> One of Lutheranism's most fabulous missionaries, lion-shooting, mountain-climbing Richard Reusch, is back in Minnesota, supposedly to retire. — Minneapolis *Star* (1954)

> His life sounds like something out of Richard Harding Davis, and maybe it is, although his Lutheran colleagues vouch for him from Cossacks to Kilimanjaro. — Los Angeles *Times* (1954)

For some reporters, Reusch's stories brought to mind Crusader knights, Beau Geste, Rudyard Kippling, Lawrence of Arabia, or an epic Russian novel. But in 1960 few college freshmen knew much about East Africa, the Crusades, or had read *The Seven Pillars of Wisdom* by T. E. Lawrence much less Tolstoi's *War and Peace*.

SEPTEMBER 1993

Shortly after the collapse of the USSR, I visited Kem, a small town on the White Sea, that had served as the administrative center for the Soviet Karelian gulags and the notorious Solovetski Island prison. Two days later, while waiting with some Russian friends for the train from Murmansk, we passed the time by describing the most memorable characters we had ever met. When it was my turn, I described Dr. Reusch. When my modest storehouse of memory was exhausted, one of the Russians exclaimed, "Dan-eel! You must tell his story because about such Russians we were never permitted to learn!"

"Richard Reusch was one of those zesty and melodramatic people who flowered in the intrigues of the Central Europe of World War I and later the African bush," Jim Klobuchar wrote in *The Cross under the Acacia Tree*. "In truth, not a whole lot about Richard Reusch is explainable."

Most people who interviewed Dr. Reusch or heard him speak regarded him with admiration and respect, even awe. To others he was an unforgettable, colorful and eccentric character. But there were a few who suspected that he skillfully manipulated the facts in order to promote himself. It was true, for example, that the crater of Kibo Peak bore his name. But could this Lutheran pastor and missionary have actually known Joseph Stalin, escorted the Grand Duchess Anastasia to a winter ball in St. Petersburg, and single-handedly held off a Red armored train with an empty sub-machine gun during the Russian civil war?

When I returned from Russia, I decided to search for clues that might establish the facts of his life and thereby gain insight into his unique character. Thus began an odyssey that was to span thirteen years and three continents.

OCTOBER 2006

Dr. Reusch's personal papers include documents, letters, hundreds of sermons (1916-1975), manuscripts, ticket stubs, vouchers, permits, lecture notes and photographs. I have searched for his traces in libraries, archives and homes in Russia, Kazakhstan, Estonia, Latvia, Finland, Germany, Denmark, England, Tanzania and America. In addition, scores of people who knew Dr. Reusch welcomed me to their kitchens, living rooms, offices and farmsteads to share their recollections and impressions of this unusual man.

Physically and mentally disciplined, enthusiastic, melodramatic, energetic, a weightlifter, culturally adaptable, recklessly daring, stubborn, empathetic — all these character traits describe Dr. Reusch. His is a story of Imperial Russia, the Bolshevik revolution, colonial East Africa, the American Augustana (Swedish) Lutheran Synod, the rise of the indigenous African Lutheran Church in Tanganyika (Tanzania), and the tribe with whom he shared mutual affection, the Masai.

After sifting through an enormous collection of data and testimony, it is clear that two primary beliefs shaped his worldview and behaviors. The first was the motto of his Caucasian regiment, which he adopted as a young man: "Loyalty for Loyalty, Blood for Blood, Life for Life." "*Loyalty* is what counts in life," he said in his seventieth year, a premise that echoed the Book of Revelation: "Be you loyal unto death and I will give you the crown of life."

The second premise, first articulated in his ordination sermon, became the theme he preached throughout his lifetime: "He that loveth not knoweth not God; for *God is love*."

To understand Richard Gustavovich Reusch, one must appreciate the historical contexts and cultures that shaped him. Upon his death in 1975, the local *Chisago County Press* published this eloquent tribute: "A man who was involved in one of the most awesome revolutions in history, he walked with African natives, American college students and Minnesota farmers. His life reads like some sprawling Russian novel."

His story begins in a rural village, the fifth generation born in Russia of German colonists who had settled near the Volga River more than a century earlier. The year is 1891.

PART I

Imperial Russia

(1891-1923)

European Imperial Russia, 1900

Aurelia Reusch

Five-year-old Richard stands between his parents. Left to right: Emil, four years old, Gustav Ivanovich, Albert, two years old, Ottilia Filipovna and baby Olga.

Chapter One

RICHARD THE LION-HEARTED
Baratayevka, Russia, 1891-1897

Your Imperial Majesty!

We Germans in South Russia pray that our Lord and Emperor may graciously believe that we are prepared always and everywhere to protect your throne with our lives, and regard it as a sacred duty to be grateful to our dearly beloved Emperor and our great Fatherland.
— L. G. Lutz, telegram, 30 September 1910

I read your telegram with pleasure. I express my thanks.
— Nicholas II[1]

Baratayevka is a village situated on the flat eastern side of the Volga River about 800 kilometers southeast of Moscow. At the invitation of Catherine II, German Lutheran colonists settled there in 1767. Some 170 years later, two months after the Germans invaded Russia in June 1941, Stalin banished the descendants of the original colonists to Siberia. The Russian agricultural community is still not indicated on most maps.

A government inspector from Moscow intent on visiting the Lutheran settlement in the 1890s would first have taken a train to Saratov. This city, situated on the western bank of the Volga River, the cultural center of the sprawling German colonies, boasted the largest flour mills in Russia. At the Saratov city wharf the inspector would have either headed north up the Volga to Katherinenstadt (a city named in honor of the colonists' patron, Catherine II, later renamed Marx) or crossed the river by ferry to Pokrovsk (Engles) and continued on horseback northward along the eastern shore of the river about fifty kilometers to Katherinenstadt. Riding through the center of town, the official would have passed beneath the shadow cast by the spire of the largest Lutheran church in the Russian Empire.[2] Baratayevka is less than ten kilometers to the east where some trees cluster on the undulating steppe. That is where Gustav Otto Richard Reusch was born on the last day of October 1891.

Today, the late afternoon visitor to Baratayevka can watch from the slope behind the sprawling village as the steep hills on the far western bank of the Volga turn from hues of pink to purple and then to gray. In the foreground on this flat eastern "meadow" side of the great river the visitor looks out over single-story houses of log or brick that face onto broad dirt lanes laid out in an orderly grid. Vegetable gardens and an animal shed or two cluster in spacious yards. Ducks waddle out of the way while fat geese stand their ground in front of a gate and raucously scold the passersby. In the next yard a red rooster struts among a dozen hens. A tethered brown cow looks up from munching the grass along the dirt street and cautiously comes forward, straining against her rope, and from behind a fence on the right a horse whinnies and tosses his mane. The animals and gardens are privately owned, but the land has been farmed as a collective since the late 1920s when Soviet commissars put an end to private enterprise.

The village hall, a two-story rectangular stone building, still serves its original administrative functions. A Russian Imperial flag flaps in the breeze from its pole over the front door just as it did a hundred years ago when children gathered there for classes. The village has since expanded northward, and the village center is now marked by a monument with the simple inscription "1941-1945" etched in flaking red paint below a massive statue of a heroic Russian soldier.

The manager of the collective farm has heard about a stranger wandering about the village with a camera, and so the friendly and engaging middle-aged man drives up in a small van to check on the visitor. He is surprised and pleased to learn that a foreigner has come in search of records that might illuminate the life of an unknown village son whose achievements are admired elsewhere in the world. No, he knows of no one living in the village by the name of Reusch or Riehl. Neither do any of the older women passing the time at the village store.[3] No longer do any descendants of German colonists live in Baratayevka.

GERMAN IMMIGRANTS

Had a government inspector arrived in Baratayevka on the 31st of October 1891, he would have found the inhabitants wearing their Sunday best. Lutherans worldwide were celebrating the 374th anniversary of the Reformation, and so were the German Russian Lutherans.[4] However, a more private event was taking place in Baratayevka. In the modest schoolmaster's dwelling, twenty-one-year-old Ottilia Filipovna Reusch, née Riehl, labored to give birth for the first time.

Ottilia Filipovna had been born in a German colony on the west side of the Volga, near Volsk. She was a descendant of Prussian Junkers, military officers who accompanied Princess Sophia of Anhalt-Zerbst to Russia in 1744. Eighteen years later, in 1762, the German princess was crowned Empress, Catherine II, Autocrat of All the Russias. The following year she issued a proclamation inviting war-weary Europeans, especially industrious Germans, to settle the expanding Russian frontier in the hope that Russian peasants would adopt Western European farming techniques and the work ethic of her countrymen. Special privileges were offered to the settlers as inducements, including transportation, land, freedom to practice their religion, and exemption from military service.[5]

The first 4,000 German families arrived on the Volga River a few years later.[6] As on any frontier, life beyond the pale of civilization was difficult. The environment was unfamiliar. Weather was unpredictable. Settlers fell victim to disease and injury. And until 1808 the western Volga colonies were subject to raids by nomadic Kierghiz and Kalmyk warriors, who resisted the invasion of the farmer-colonists. Settlements were looted and burned and captives taken.

Among the groups who sought a new life in Russia were seventy-four people who settled on the eastern side of the Volga River along the Little Karaman River. The primitive dugout village they began building in August 1767 was initially known as the Bettinger Colony.[7] Two years later the colonists gave up on the "too arid, salty and miserable" site and moved the village closer to the Volga.[8] The settlement was renamed for the Georgian prince, Melkhisedek Baratayev, who, hounded by Caucasus Mountain tribes, appealed to Catherine II for permission to bring a thousand "brothers and relatives" to safety in the Kizlyar region.[9]

Ottilia Filipovna's husband, Gustav Ivanovich Reusch, had been born to a family of three brothers and two sisters in the Neu Boaro colony on the Big Karaman River, some 50 kilometers to the south. His ancestors emigrated from Württemberg in southern Germany. Gustav Ivanovich, like his father, became a Lutheran schoolmaster and deacon.

Ottilia Filipovna's mother had died when Ottilia was a child, and her father had quickly remarried. The pensive young girl was unhappy in the household of her stepmother and at the age of seventeen made her escape by marrying the schoolmaster from Baratayevka, the settlement on the opposite side of the river.[10] Her older brother, Konstantin Filipovich, followed family tradition and was enrolled as a military cadet.[11]

THE FAMINE OF 1891-1892

The Russian winter that followed the wedding of Ottilia Filipovna and Gustav Ivanovich was one of the worst in memory. Bitterly cold temperatures of -40°F enveloped the Volga River region in late autumn and held the land in an icy grip well into March. But a lack of snowfall caused the greatest worry because the fields surrounding the villages lay unprotected from sub-zero temperatures. At the end of February the sun rose earlier and set later, but otherwise there was no other hint of spring, and the Volga German farmers, huddling in their log villages north and south of Saratov, were gravely concerned.[12]

In the middle of March, the season's snowfall came, all at once, driven by ferocious winds into every crevice. Everyone was thankful for the moisture, but the damage had already been done: Without a blanket of snow in December and January to insulate the autumn-seeded fields, the winter wheat harvest would fail. The month of April remained in winter's grip, and so the spring planting was delayed. Occasional bad seasons were expected, but one following upon another was a forecast of disaster.

Spring turned into summer without significant rainfall, and the farmers of Baratayevka resigned themselves to their fate as temperatures soared and crops withered on the Russian steppe. Government officials in far-off St. Petersburg became alarmed and began making plans to cope with yet another famine. Streams and ponds and wells went dry. Farmers began selling off their livestock. Hot summer winds blew gritty clouds of topsoil across the landscape, and trees dropped their leaves more than a month before the first frost. Conditions were far worse than the previous year when a poor harvest had driven up food prices and caused unemployment in cities as well. The prospect of another famine was enough for some Volga Germans with sufficient resources to pull up stakes and sail for the Americas.[13]

September reports confirmed the fears of summer. From Archangel in the north to the Astrakhan and Don regions in the south, the bad news piled up on the desks of the bureaucrats in St. Petersburg. The autumn harvest was off by 75 percent in Voronezh, 67 percent in Kazan, and 34 and 45 percent in the Saratov and Samara regions.[14] The specter of recurring famine began to lurk in the lengthening shadows.

Despite this threat, the end of October 1891 was a joyful time for Gustav Ivanovich and Ottilia Filipovna as they awaited the birth of their first child. The indomitable papa had made up his mind that, if blessed with a son, his firstborn would be named after kings: *Gustav*, for Gustavus II Adolphus "Lion of the North, Defender of the Lutheran Faith in Northern Europe" (1594-1632); *Otto*, for Otto I (The Great), Emperor of the Holy Roman Empire, "the Charlemagne of Germany" (912-973); and *Richard*, for Richard I, Coeur-de-Lion, King of England, leader of the Third Crusade (1157-1199).[15]

The Riehls had always served in Prussian armies, and Ottilia Filipovna understood that her first-born son was destined to become a military officer.

REFORMATION DAY

At nine o'clock in the morning of October 31, 1891, Ottilia Filipovna delivered a baby boy. A month later, Pastor Keller, a clergyman from Saratov, whose circuit included Baratayevka, baptized the Reusch baby and signed the certificate, No. 168. The rite was conducted in the schoolhouse where the Baratayevka congregation also met for worship, with Ferdinand Keller and Rosina Schmidt Reusch serving as sponsors. The baptism was later filed in the city of Samara, where the clerk added the boy's Russian patronymic: Gustav Otto Richard *Gustavovich* Reusch.[16] His family called him by his third name, Richard. The proud papa would soon begin infusing the little boy with heroic tales of Crusader knights, emperors and kings.

Eleven days after Richard was born, Grand Duke Nicholas Alexandrovich was put in charge of a hastily announced Special Committee on Famine Relief, and summoned the governors of Saratov and Samara to St. Petersburg.[17] Three years later the Grand Duke would be crowned tsar, Nicholas II.

The famine turned out to be the worst in sixty years. Desperate farmers removed the thatch from roofs to feed starving cattle[18] as disease spread among people weakened by starvation. "The first thing that tells you this," reported a traveler, "is the appearance of the population. Everywhere, you encounter crowds of people. They look you in the eye; they literally seize upon every glance, every step you take. . . [with] a kind of dumbfounded expression; all are emaciated, defeated." The children, however, left the deepest impression: "You can talk with the adults, discuss matters; but the children — that is the most terrible thing of all."[19] The American Red Cross Society, said Clara Barton, "made this state of affairs known to the citizens of the United States," and mobilized "the charitable work of the people" by sending ships loaded with Iowa corn, Minneapolis flour, and potatoes and salt pork to the Russian famine victims.[20]

Despite international aid, the loss of life — people and livestock — was terrible. Conservative estimates place the death toll in European Russia at 400,000 persons. Another 100,000 perished from a cholera epidemic during the same year.[21]

No one recalls how the Reusch family survived the famine, but somehow Gustav Ivanovich managed to provide the necessities for his family, which continued to grow: in 1893, Emil was born. Albert was born two years later, in 1895, and Olga in 1897.

FAMILY LIFE IN THE COLONIES

Richard was too young to remember the famine, but he did recall this feature of his early years: "I was not yet five years old when I began to learn under the instruction of my pious, God-fearing father. In my parents' house I was always kept to prayer."[22] Indeed, the Ten Commandments were taken seriously, including the Fourth, which bids children to "Honor thy father and thy mother, that thy days may be long in the land which Jehovah thy God giveth thee." That injunction had an effect on behavior not only at home but also in school where discipline, it was said, was not one of the issues with which teachers had to contend. In the colonies there was no spoiling the child because of sparing the rod, not in communities where, generation after generation, strict Lutherans subscribed to the notion that

> All good schools in proper measure
> Are a town's important treasure;
> But the switch that parents wield
> Bears the fruit of greatest yield.

The patriarchal command, "That's enough!" silenced an argument even with an adult son.[23]

DIE FAMILIE REUSCH

The family name is thought to derive from the Latin, "ruscus," the name given by the Romans for the low, bushy evergreens they found growing in swampy areas in Southern Germania. By the year 1200 a few families were known by the name of *Riust*; by 1392 the name had become *Ruisch*; and after Guttenburg printed Luther's translation of the Bible, which in 1534 fixed the spelling of words, the *ui* became *eu*: Reusch. The family name marks the German landscape: the towns of Reuschendorf, Reuschenfeld, Reuschenhagen, and Reuschwerder; a river and waterfall, Reuschenbach bei Niedermohr; Reuschberg Mountain; and Reuschenberg Castle near Cologne.[24]

Family members did not hesitate to emigrate in search for new opportunities abroad — and foreign missionary service. During the last half of the eighteenth century several Reusches emigrated to Hungary and Switzerland. Early in the nineteenth century the brothers Jacob (1793), Johannes (1796) and Bernhardt (1798) left for foreign lands. Jacob died while serving as a soldier in France, and the other two emigrated to the Russian Caucasus. Perhaps the brothers volunteered to serve in the Russian Imperial Army, which in the early 1800s was ordered to subjugate all of the Caucasian tribes.

Three Reusches emigrated from Germany to Brazil, and forty to North America. From the town of Winnenden alone came twelve clergy and missionaries who served in China, Surinam, India, and Australia.[25] An exasperated parent sometimes invoked a particularly potent threat to correct an errant child. Recalling the tribes who had threatened the colonies in past decades, they would warn: "Unless you behave, the Kirghiz will get you!" Said a Volga German, "I had never heard of their raids and massacres, but the word ['Kirghiz'] itself had become analogous to catastrophe, terror, and abduction."[26]

Gustav Ivanovich was a conservative and strict head of the family, but he was also an enthusiastic and energetic patriarch to whom people of various nationalities and religious traditions were happy to bring their children for instrution.[27] One of Richard's sisters, Aurelia Gustavovna, who was born in 1899, remembered their paternal grandmother as "very strict, severe, even mean," whose harsh words sometimes made her mother cry; however, the elderly woman adored her grandson, Richard.[28]

Saratoff *(Sar-âh'toff)*, a city exactly 500 miles by rail SE of Moscow [with] broad streets and fine squares. There are a handsome new cathedral (1825), an old cathedral (1697), and the museum with its art gallery and a library. Manufacturers of brandy, liqueurs, flour, oil, and tobacco are carried on. Fishing is prosecuted in the river, and market-gardening (especially fruit and the sunflower) in the vicinity. The population is about 200,000. [The province] has a pop. of over 3,000,000, including several flourishing German colonies which settled here in 1763-65.

— *Chambers's Concise Gazetteer of the World (1914)*[29]

Grandmother Reusch operated a little store in Saratov, Aurelia Gustavovna recalled, and Grandfather Riehl was middleclass. A few uncles and aunts counted themselves among the professions, but most were farmers in the colonies around Saratov and Volsk. As children, both Richard Gustavovich and Aurelia Gustavovna looked forward to the family reunions in Volsk and Saratov.[30]

Saratov was the eleventh largest city in Russia, a busy Volga River port and railroad terminus. Many of the city's businessmen were of German origin, men who turned Saratov into a grain-milling center whose product, ground from high quality hard wheats, was distributed from Helsinki to Vladivostok.[31] The bourgeoisie promenaded along German Street, where, according to a city guide published in 1911, they shopped in elegant stores "just like in the capital."[32] Uniformed Terek Cossacks paraded on horseback along Great Cossack Street and their stories thrilled little boys like Richard and his cousins.[33]

Saratov may have been one of Russia's larger cities, but intellectuals from St. Petersburg and Moscow regarded it as a dusty and depressing provincial capital city of "gingham, retired generals, and flour kings."[34] To the little boy and his family from Baratayevka, however, Saratov must have seemed the very cradle of civilization.

LUTHERANS IN ORTHODOX RUSSIA

German colony schoolmasters like Gustav Ivanovich also served as parish deacons. Since the average Lutheran district numbered more than 6,000 persons, nearly all clergy rode a circuit among a number of villages. Remote parishes saw their pastor only once a year when he came to administer Holy Communion and conduct the Rite of Confirmation.[35] Pastor R. Keller served the large congregation in Saratov and also ministered to colonies on the east side of the Volga, including Baratayevka. In his absence Deacon Gustav Ivanovich read the Sunday sermon provided by church authorities and tended to the spiritual needs of the faithful.

The clergy shortage seems to have produced two benefits. First, the laity had to take an active role in the life of the congregation. Second, it wrought an ecumenism born of necessity. In the absence of a priest, a Lutheran pastor sometimes married a Roman Catholic couple, and a Roman Catholic priest sometimes baptized a Lutheran baby. However, the first generations of Lutheran and Reformed colonists had not forgotten the violent theological disagreements of the 17th century. A Lutheran pastor sometimes refused to give communion to Reformed members, and in an emergency some Reformed members sought the services of a Roman Catholic priest rather than a Lutheran cleric.[36] By the 1830s, however, the two Protestant groups had forgotten their differences and decided to share pulpits and a common hymnal.[37]

A senior cleric in a large, prosperous parish could earn up to 3000 rubles a year in contrast with teachers' salaries, which averaged only 120 rubles a year. The enormous salary disparity between the only educated men in the colonies, clergy and teacher-deacons, was said to have produced "enmity, jealousy, and bitterness." It was also reported that some of the clergy who served the larger Lutheran parishes "despised, belittled, and publicly ridiculed" the farmers for their peasant ways and eighteenth century dialects.[38] However, such enmities evidently did not spoil the relationship between the faithful and loyal Gustav Ivanovich and the clergy with whom he closely worked.

The Russian Orthodox patriarchate was suspicious of the foreign colonists and their Western heretical faith traditions. For example, Ivan IV, "The Terrible" (1547-84), regarded Martin Luther as "a false prophet, a thief and a hireling," and he prayed that "our face may be protected so that the darkness of this [Lutheran] unbelief may not overwhelm us."[39] Non-Orthodox Christian denominations — Lutheran, Roman Catholic, Mennonite, Reformed, and Baptist — labored under stringent constraints.

In 1832 Nicholas I recognized the Russian Evangelical Lutheran Church as one of the Christian Churches of the empire, but the Imperial government and Orthodox Church were determined to prevent the spread of Western theological heresies because they seemed linked to radical political theories. Official quotas limited the number of clergy, and evangelism and the publication of religious literature in the Russian language were prohibited; as well, the colonists could provide social services to their own members — but not to their Slavic neighbors.

During the reign of Nicholas II (1894-1917) as many as 20,000 Russians a year were sentenced to terms in Siberian labor camps. Some were Lutherans, and several of their clergymen traveled from camp to camp bringing "the light and comfort of the Gospel to those poor souls."[40]

By the nineteenth century it was only a small exaggeration to say that one could travel by ox-cart from the Baltic to the Black Sea and stop each night in a German village.[41] The population of Imperial Russia (including Finland, the Baltic provinces and part of Poland) before the First World War was approximately 140 million,[42] but the number of Russian Lutherans is difficult to establish. S. G. Youngert claimed 7 million,[43] but John Morehead estimated only 4 million who, prior to the 1917 revolution, worshiped in 770 churches served by 560 clergy.[44] The only Lutheran seminary in Imperial Russia was affiliated with Dorpat (Tartu) University in Estonia. From 1802 until its closure in 1918 it graduated some 1600 clergymen who served congregations across the eleven time zones of Russia.[45]

Excluding Finland, the Baltic provinces and Poland, an 1893 estimate put the number of ethnic German, Finnish, Estonian, Latvian and Swedish Lutherans living in communities scattered from St. Petersburg to Vladivostok at 3.3 million.[46] Römich reported a figure at a million-plus in 1909.[47] Koch and Scheding put the number at two million,[48] an estimate generally regarded to be more accurate.[49]

Urban Germans acculturated to Russia more readily than did their rural relatives living in insular colonies. Annette M. B. Meakin, who traveled extensively through Russia in 1906, reported that the Lutheran church in Sevastopol had closed because most of the Germans had converted to Orthodoxy.[50] They had become Russians. But conversion was the exception, not the rule. Most German colonists remained apart, separate from their Orthodox neighbors. Meakin wrote,

The German colonies have been compared to a kingdom within a kingdom, a world apart from, yet surrounded by and sharply contrasting with, a larger world, from which it differs in religion, in speech, in type of feature, in character and in dress. A large proportion of their families cannot speak a word of Russian and have not the least desire to learn it, consequently they have neither sympathy nor intercourse with the Russians.[51]

One Volga German insisted that the colonists "not only bore a deep allegiance to their Romanov rulers, but they also had come to love Russia, the nation, as their own land." However, he admitted they "did not want to become Russian in creed or character."[52] As one of Richard Gustavovich's Slavic contemporaries put it, the Germans in Russia were loyal to the throne but not to the Motherland — only to their own land.[53] What is the soul of Russia if not the Slavic soul? And how can there be a Slavic soul unless it is Russian Orthodox? More than any other factor, that was what caused Slavic resentment toward German Russians to sometimes flare into violence.

However, the colonists did adopt some of their host culture's artifacts and behaviors. Not only did Russian words naturally became a part of their speech, but also in the words of one historian, "The long sheepskin coat and high felt boots became standard winter survival garb; kvas was adopted as a beverage en route to the colonies; vodka supplanted Rhine wine and beer as a stronger household drink; and Russian borsch soon took its place with the Hessian and Palatine fare."[54]

Nevertheless, many Germans assiduously refused to forsake their language and customs. Even after five generations. Galina Nikolaievna, a Muscovite and a member of the aristocratic von Meck family, admitted that her aunts never learned a word of Russian. Her parents, however, adopted the Russian language and lived like their Russian peers. And yet a fundamental difference remained: Her entrepreneurial father enthusiastically embraced new ideas and methods. The Russian aristocracy, in her words, "refused to accept that times had changed." Moscow nobility, therefore, "regarded my father as a bit of an upstart because he was never wholly 'one of them' and his German surname made him somewhat alien." A child during the 1905 revolution, she cowered in her classroom as she watched anti-German mobs set fire to a German Russian's furniture factory nearby.[55]

Vladimir Lenin once wrote, "We [Russians] are a predominantly talented people, but we have a lazy mentality."[56] However, his mother, Maria Aleksandrovna, who worshipped at the Lutheran church in Simbirsk, was anything but lazy and ran a disciplined household. Of Swedish, German and Jewish ancestry, her parents, according to one historian, regarded sloth as "a cardinal sin."[57]

A Russian aristocrat, Elizabeth Kutaissova, noted that Catherine the Great had hoped "that the Russian peasants would imitate the German example, but they didn't." She went on to characterize a wealthy German Russian neighbor as "an improver," someone who "used to ride around on a big white horse inspecting things." Said she, "My father was suspicious of them."[58] So were Dostoevski and Tolstoi. Both writers peppered their novels with insensitive and boorish characters who speak Russian in heavy German accents.

Despite Slavic antipathy, energetic Germans gravitated to positions of economic and military power in Imperial Russia. "For reasons I could never understand," Andrei Kalmykov wrote, "monarchical Russia was largely represented by Germans — nine-tenths of the Russian diplomats were of Russo-German origin."[59] Perry and Pleshakov estimated that one-third of high government officials were of German descent, "even more in the ministries of war and foreign affairs."[60] A Slavic critic of the monarchy grumbled that Lutherans were almost equal to the Orthodox in status because the Imperial family, infused with German blood, "remained sympathetic toward the Church of their ancestors and their living co-religionists in Russia." When Alexander I asked General Yermolov how he might honor the hero of the Caucasus, the General is said to have quipped, "Could I be made a German?"[61]

By the end of the nineteenth century German Russians had been stripped of many of the privileges and benefits granted by Catherine II. The colonists' exemption from military conscription was revoked in 1874, and in 1887 all schools in ethnic communities were required to use Russian as the language of instruction.[62] Many German Russians understood the need to learn and use the Russian language, but at the same time they worried that their children would turn into Russians; that is, adopt Russian Orthodoxy.[63] The first Russian-speaking Lutheran congregation was not organized until 1922 — in Soviet Petrograd — and grew rapidly, attracting German, Estonian, Latvian and Finnish Lutherans who no longer spoke the language of their parents and grandparents.[64]

Ambivalence toward foreigners was not a new phenomenon in Russia. Decades before Catherine the Great promoted immigration, Peter the Great (1672-1725) invited foreigners from Europe to live and work in Russia, but during a period of political instability a mob marched on the foreign quarter in Moscow and torched the community. During Richard Gustavovich's childhood, too, public sentiment turned against the ethnic Germans. In search of a scapegoat, said George Kennan, the press "attempted to arouse Russian society by declaiming that all Germans living in Russia posed a grave threat to national interests."[65] "Russia for the Russians!" cried the more xenophobic newspapers. Wasn't it true that 60 percent of the industrious colonists have made for themselves a comfortable life and some have become wealthy? [66] Why, like the Jews, do they remain faithful to their ethnic and religious traditions? Why haven't they become Orthodox Russians? Troubled times always heightened xenophobia, and Russian Jews braced for another round of pogroms.

Despite cycles of famine and anti-German sentiment, Gustav Ivanovich had no thought of emigrating because he felt duty-bound to serve Lutheran communities in Russia as teacher and deacon. He did consider volunteering for service in Africa with the Basel Mission Society. Although he ultimately remained in Russia, the Lutheran layman was an advocate for foreign missions, and his eldest son grew up hearing about the adventures of Leipzig Lutheran missionaries in the German African and Asian colonies. But it was a picture of Mount Kilimanjaro in East Africa that arrested his attention.[67]

In 1897 Pastor Emil Bonvitch asked Gustav Ivanovich to take charge of the Lutheran parochial school in Nikolayevskaya, a German colony on the outskirts of Pyatigorsk in the

Northern Caucasus. It was an exciting prospect because the Caucasus was a colorful and occasionally incendiary mixture of tribes, religions and ethnic groups — so different from the pietistic and plodding life in the Volga colonies.

Richard was nearly six years old when his family moved to Southern Russia. He had been formed and nourished by a closely-knit extended family that was conscious of its heritage and traditions and surrounded by strict role models who worked diligently and valued education. The centering influence for the Reusch family, as for most Volga colonists, was the church. "The Lutheran faith permeated every facet of life from the time I was a baby," said a German Russian who grew up in one of the colonies. "Our lives revolved around it much the same as the Russian's life was centered about the Greek Orthodox Church."[68]

Moving to the Caucasus meant a promotion for the father, and everyone was glad for his good fortune. For the proud papa's eldest son, however, the move would mean separation from his family and the metamorphosis of the German lad into a Russian Cossack.

CHAPTER 1

1 Telegram sent on the 100th anniversary of the Beresan Colonies (celebrated in Landau) and the Tsar's response, reproduced by Conrad Keller, *The German Colonies in South Russia*, Vol. II, 2nd edition (1983), 85-87.

2 *A Light in the Darkness*, Envoy Productions, distributed by Visions Video (1996), 48 min. The video documentary reports the experiences of German Russian Lutherans who, after Stalin's order in 1941, were sent to the far reaches of Siberia and the Southern Republics such as Kazakstan, places where some of the Gustav Reusch family spent the remainder of their lives.

3 Author's description of Saratov, Marx and Baratayevka, 11-15 June 1996.

4 According to the Julian calendar, the date was October 18th.

5 "Manifesto of Catherine the Second, 22 July 1763, concerning the Invitation of Foreign Colonists to Russia," document reproduced by Gottlieb Beratz, *The German Colonies on the Lower Volga: Their Origin and Early Development* (3rd ed., American Historical Society of Germans from Russia, 1991), 23-29. Beratz was a Roman Catholic priest and an amateur historian who gathered data and preserved an important record of the early colonist period.

6 Beratz, 39.

7 Fred C. Koch, *The Volga Germans in Russia and the Americas, from 1763 to the Present* (1977), 307. Koch was born in one of the German colonies.

8 Beratz, 63.

9 Roger P. Bartlett, *Human Capital: The Settlement of Foreigners in Russia, 1762-1804* (1979), 37.

10 Aurelia Reusch, Richard's sister (d. 1996), from notes of an interview by the author and Galina Tioun in Alma Te, Kazakstan, 17 October 1995.

11 Betty Anderson, Dr. Reusch's eldest daughter, from the author's notes of an interview, 4-5 July 1997.

12 The conditions that led to famine, and the government's response, are described by Richard G. Robbins, Jr., in *Famine in Russia, 1891-92* (1975), 1-13.

13 Koch, 205.

14 A. S. Ermalov, *Neurozhai I narodnoe bedstvie* (1892), 19; cited by Robbins, 2.

15 Author unknown (perhaps Emeroy Johnson), "Son of Kibo" (undated manuscript, ca. 1954), in the uncatalogued papers of Richard Reusch, GACA.

16 Baptismal Certificate, document 6, Richard Reusch file (2100 1/13219), Estonian State History Archives (ESHA). The document was not filed in Samara, the capital of the *oblast* (province), until 28 July 1900.

17 Robbins, 70.

18 Y. Barchatova and others, *A Portrait of Tsarist Russia: Unknown Photographs from the Soviet Archives*, trans. by Michael Robinson (1989), 214.

19 P. L. Korf, "Poezdka v neurozhainye mestnosti Kurskoi gubernii," *Trudy IVEO* (1892), II, 110, cited by Robbins, 10.

20 "Bread for the Millions," Washington, D. C. *Evening Star*, clipping, 12 March 1892.

21 Robbins, 170-172.

22 R. Reusch, "Mein Lebenslauf," undated (ca. 1920), 2 (404, East Africa, Richard Reusch file), ELMLA.

23 Koch, 154.

24 Johannes Reusch, *Die Familie Reusch* (Reutlingen, Württemberg: C. Killinger, 1935), 3-6.
25 *Die Familie Reusch*, 60-61.
26 Koch, 108.
27 Aurelia Reusch, interview.
28 Aurelia Reusch, quoted by her daughter, Elinora Chevyenova, letter to the author, 15 February 1996.
29 *Chambers's Concise Gazetteer*, 628.
30 Chevyenova, letter.
31 Koch, 62.
32 Cited by Donald J. Raleigh in his book, *A Russian Civil War Diary: Alexis Babine in Saratov, 1917-1922* (1988), 5.
33 Raleigh.
34 Soviet author, Konstantin Fedin's characterization of Saratov, cited by Raleigh, xiv.
35 James W. Long, *From Privileged to Dispossessed: The Volga Germans, 1860-1917* (1988), 42,
36 Beratz, 249.
37 Koch, 112-13.
38 Long, 44.
39 John Moorhead, "The First Convention of the Evangelical Lutheran General Synod of Russia," pt. 1, *Lutheran Companion*, vol. 32 (6 September 1924), 574-75.
40 John Woodward, "Glimpses of Siberia," a two-part article in *The Illustrated Home Journal*, a publication of the (German American) Lutheran Church — Missouri Synod, February 1 (33-37) and 15 (58-60), 1896.

Woodward drew from information reported by Rev. Henry Lansdell and George Kennan who had traveled throughout Russia. Events in Imperial Russia were widely reported in the U. S., and American public opinion sided with Russia's victims of tsarist autocracy.
41 Michael Balfour, *The Kaiser and His Times* (1964), 5.
42 Sheila Fitzpatrick, *Stalin's Peasants: Resistance and Survival in the Russian Village after Collectivization* (1994), 19.
43 S. G. Youngert, "Persecution in Soviet Russia," *Lutheran Companion*, vol. 39 (2 May 1931), 558.
44 Morehead, 574.
45 Moorhead, 575.
46 J. N. Lenker, *Lutherans in All Lands*, vol. 1 (1893).
47 H. Römich, *Heimatbuch* (1961), 2; cited by Ingeborg Fleischhauer and Benjamin Pinkus, *The Soviet Germans: Past and Present* (1986), 49.
48 Koch, 11, and W. L. Scheding, unpublished manuscript for a history of the Russian Lutheran Church, 19 (PA 142), AELCA.
49 The estimate of 2 million was also also cited by *The New York Times* (*Current History*, 18 October 1918), 93.
50 Annette M. B. Meakin, *Russia: Travels and Studies* (1906), 25 and 31.
51 Meankin, 28.
52 Koch, 202.

53 Gregory P. Tschebotarioff, *Russia, My Native Land* (1954), 32-33.
54 Koch, 50.
55 Galina Nikolaievna von Meck, "The Death of Stolypin," *The Other Russia: The Experience of Exile*, ed. by Glenny and Stone (1991), 40.
56 Cited by Robert Service, *Lenin: A Biography* (2000), 29.
57 Robert Service, *Lenin: A Political Life*, vol. 1 (1985), 13.
58 Elizabeth Kutaissova, "On the Estate," Glenny and Stone, 46, 48.
59 Andrew D. Kalmykov, *Memoirs of a Russian Diplomat: Outposts of the Empire, 1893-1917* (1971), 74.
60 John Curtis Perry and Constantine Pleshnakov, *The Flight of the Romanovs: A Family Saga* (1999), 31. Koch (195) reported that during the reign of Alexander II (1855-1889) 40 percent of higher-ranking military officers were of German extraction and nearly all the members of the St. Petersburg Academy of Sciences had German last names.
61 Victor A. Yakhontoff, *Over the Divide: Impersonal Record of Personal Experiences* (1939), 40.
62 Patrick L. Alston, *Education and the State in Tsarist Russia* (1969), 120.
63 Koch, 145.
64 Kurt Muss and five other clergy, letter to the Executive Committee of the Lutheran World Confederation, ca. 1927 (LWC-7-22), AELCA.
65 George Kennan, cited by Long, 58-59.
66 Long, 58.
67 R. Reusch, "Mein Lebenslauf."
68 Long, 41.

The Soviet government suppressed Cossack culture, but in 1991 a remnant of the Terek Cossacks elected Ataman Konyakin to serve the traditional three-year term as their leader. Cossacks gained official recognition by the post-Soviet government in 1994.

AMONG THE COSSACKS
Pyatigorsk, Northern Caucasus, 1897-1904

*And as Allah hovered between the Caspian and the Black Sea, the Evil One slipped up
beside his sack, slit open the cloth, and all the mountains fell down into the plain
between the two seas. Thus began the Caucasus, the Land of Mountains.*

— Essad-Bey[1]

Early in the summer of 1897 the Volsk relatives helped Gustav Ivanovich and his wife bring
their children and household baggage down to the wharf to be loaded onto a riverboat. Gustav's
brother, Feofil Ivanovich, lived in the Land of Mountains, so they were not sending the young
family to live among strangers.[2] But that was small comfort when it came time to bid farewell.

At Tsaritzen (Stalingrad, then Volgograd), some 400 kilometers due south, the schoolmaster
and his wife hauled their four children and earthly possessions from the riverbank to the city's
railway station to begin a zigzag journey through the southern steppes toward the Northern
Caucasus. They boarded a train for Tichoreck, more than 500 kilometers to the southwest,
where they changed trains and traveled in a southeasterly direction for another 300 kilometers to
Pyatigorsk. *Pyat'* means "five" in Russian, and *gori*, "mountains."

Pyatigorsk, a town in Russian Caucasia, at the southern foot of Mount Beshtau
(4587 feet), facing Mount Elbruz, and 124 miles by rail NW. of Vladikavkaz, with warm
sulphur-springs (88.7 to 117.5 F.) Pop. 47,000.
　　　　— *Chambers's Concise Gazetteer of the World (1914)*[3]

As the family approached their destination they looked out onto a foreign landscape.
Occasional cone-shaped mountains popped up on the plain to the south, laccolithic bulges
of igneous rock that had separated from the Great Caucasus Range.[4] On the horizon some 60
kilometers to the south they caught a glimpse of the magnificent snow-capped twin peaks of
Mt. Elbruz in the central Caucasus range where, according to Greek myth, Prometheus was
chained as punishment for stealing the heavenly fire and giving it to mortals. Pastor Bonvitch and a
delegation from the Nikolayevskaya colony probably welcomed the Reusch family and helped
load their possessions into a cart and brought them over dusty lanes to their new abode.

The Caucasus was home to an unusual mix of peoples, religions and cultures. In the bazaar of Tiflis (Tbilisi, Georgia), a linguist inventoried upwards of sixty languages and dialects. Caucasian cultures derived from the ancient Egyptians, Phoenicians, Scythians, Jews, Assyrians, Medes, Persians, Greeks, Romans, Arabs, Genoese, Mongols, and Russians; here lived Kurds, Armenians, Georgians, Turkomen, Circassians, Ossetians, Kabardinians, Chechens, Daghestanis and Lezgins. "The traveler," said a visitor to the region in 1906, "has not to look very deeply to find that he is still in the very heart of the East."[5]

The Reusch family settled at the northern edge of a region drenched in violence and alive with the stories of regimental heroes who had fought and died to subjugate the Caucasus. Peter I ordered such a campaign, but the region's Kahns rode after the Russian invaders, cheetahs poised on their saddles and trained to leap on the fleeing Russians as if they were wild game. Asiatic chieftains caught and flayed one of the generals, Prince Bekovitch, and used his skin to make a drum. Peter I ultimately set aside his plan to take the Caucasus. Neither did Catherine II succeed in claiming the region for her empire. After wresting the Crimea from the Ottoman Turks, she turned her energy toward more fruitful objectives rather than subjecting her armies to further torture in the Caucasus.[6]

Nicholas I initiated a campaign in 1826, one that drained men and resources until finally achieving a measure of success. But a dispirited General Tornau left this vivid account of an engagement with Chechen rebels:

> We can hear their yells, as they surround and press on the rear guard from all sides; they rush in, flourishing their swords, driving our men onward, towards the last clearing, where the rebel sharp-shooters await them with a deadly hail of bullets. . .One day is like another; yesterday's happenings will be repeated tomorrow — everywhere, the mountains, everywhere, the forests, and the Tchetchens (sic) are a ferocious tireless enemy.[7]

In this contest between Russian emperors and Asian sultans, between the cultures of the cross and the crescent, the Russian tsars slowly subjugated Caucasian mountain villages and pushed back the northern borders of Persian Shah and Turkish Ottoman. In 1839, for example, a battle raged for eighty days in Daghestan, the region between Chechnya and the Caspian Sea, and when it was over the Russians counted 500 dead, 1,722 wounded, and 687 "badly bruised by stones."[8] In the 1820s Kazi Mullah, a Muslim imam of the Murid sect, proclaimed a *jihad* against the Russian foreigners. In 1838 the loyal warriors of another charismatic Muslim leader, Shamyl, on one occasion left 3,000 Russian casualties on the field. In 1844 Viceroy Vorontsov went after the Chechens with a force of 18,000 men, but his command suffered 4,000 casualties before retreating to safety in the fort at Grozni.[9]

Shamyl surrendered in 1859, and four years later the Russians were victorious in the Caucasus.[10] Mop-up operations continued until 1878, only twenty years before the Reusch family moved to the region.

"To obtain possession of the Caucasus," General Kuropatkin wrote, "we had to fight twice with Persia in the nineteenth century, and were at war for sixty-two years with the mountaineers of the Caucasus." But, he warned, despite the sacrifices spanning two hundred years "we have, perhaps, so placed our neighbors that it may be their object in the coming century to regain the territory of which they have been deprived. If so, the danger will not have been removed; it will have been changed in nature from that of an offensive to a defensive struggle."[11] Indeed, a Russian historian has counted 127 Chechen uprisings and rebellions, from the first skirmishes with Russian troops in the eighteenth century to the bitter and massive conflict that erupted once again at the end of the twentieth century.[12]

Caucasian Proverb

Question: *When shall blood cease to flow in these mountains?*
Answer: *When sugar canes grow in the snows.*[13]

Richard absorbed the stories of Kazi Mullah and Shamyl even as "most wicked and dangerous" Chechen bandits continued to disturb the peace south of Pyatigorsk. Criminals of all kinds were welcome in Chechen villages and joined in robbing travelers, raiding military depots and plundering Russian frontier settlements.[14]

In the secure northern Caucasus, the Reusch family settled into the schoolmaster's house in Nikolayevskaya, and Gustav Ivanovich set to work planning for the coming academic year. But later that summer he made a difficult decision that had a traumatic effect on the little boy already counting the days until his sixth birthday.

AMONG THE COSSACKS

Ottilia Filipovna's ancestors were Prussian officers who served the Russian imperial autocrats. In keeping with Riehl family tradition, the eldest son was expected to serve as a military officer, the second a clergyman, and the third an estate manager. Grandfather Riehl expected his eldest grandson to follow in his family's tradition, and like his own son, Konstantin Filipovich, be commissioned an officer.

Gustav Ivanovich had named his son for heroic kings and imbued the boy with tales of the Teutonic Knights of the Sword and the Crusades; but career military officers in the real world were notorious as heavy drinkers and libertines. The devout Reusch side of the family preferred that Richard be firmly grounded in the spiritual tradition of Martin Luther and serve as a pastor, perhaps a missionary. Moreover, Gustav Ivanovich wanted a better material life for his children than what he could earn as a schoolmaster. His daughters might choose to become schoolteachers, but not his sons. A university-educated cleric earned a salary substantially higher than a pedagogue and could anticipate a pension equal to that of a retired major general.[15] By virtue of a university diploma, he knew that his sons could one day be counted among the nobility, a factor important to class-conscious Germans and Russians.

In this battle of values, the tradition and force of the Riehl side of the family prevailed: Richard would be educated at a military school; graduate as a second lieutenant; and apply for admission to a military academy where, after two years, he would be commissioned a first lieutenant and posted to a regiment. But this career path carried a heavy price tag. A young lad who was not proficient in the Russian language could not become an officer.[16] And so Gustav Ivanovich had little choice but to send his eldest son to live with a family in the dusty Terek Cossack *stanitsa*, Goryachevodskaya, a village at the southeastern edge of Pyatigorsk. There the boy would learn Russian and live in a community where the boys and men constituted a reserve military unit, ready at an instant to defend Tsar, God and Mother Russia.

His eldest son might become "russified," but Gustav Ivanovich was determined somehow to preserve his son's religious heritage. Most Cossacks were Russian Orthodox, but it was not uncommon to find families in their ranks of disparate ethnic and religious origins. It just so happened that the elderly wife of the grain miller in Goryachevodska was an ardent Lutheran. Richard Gustavovich later confessed that "[in] this foreign environment, it was the old miller's wife who kept me praying," a ritual, which "under the influence of the somewhat wild Cossacks, I was in danger of neglecting."[17]

But there was another reason the boy was sent to live with another family: Gustav Ivanovich was finding it difficult to feed his growing family. From the age of fourteen Richard had to make his own way in the world. But separation from his family left a psychological wound. In a rare instance of self-disclosure he penned these mournful lines: "Wholly alienated from my family, so that my younger brothers and sisters took me for a 'foreign uncle,' I followed Him [God] with the ardor of a child's soul which searches for — but cannot find — love."[18]

Richard attended the *stanitsa* elementary school and quickly adapted to his new surroundings. His serious attitude, discipline, and aptitude for learning earned him an early transfer to the intermediate school in Pyatigorsk, where he boarded in the Russian Orthodox home of the school's director, an officer in the Terek Cossack Reserve. Meanwhile, in Nikolayevskaya, Richard's mother gave birth to her fifth child, Aurelia.

No documentation exists to verify that Richard was initiated as a Terek Cossack. However, he marked his tenth birthday in Pyatigorsk, the age when a boy sent to live with a Cossack family was automatically taken into the circle.[19] Richard had seen Cossacks parade in Saratov but now he lived with them, absorbing their traditions and history. For fourteen years he was educated in their institutions. If the boy didn't find unconditional love among the families with whom he boarded, at least he found a social structure that accepted him, recognized his abilities, and gave him an identity.

Cossacks were the "sons of Mother Russia," it was said, "sired as it were, by the Tartars of the steppe."[20] Mongolian Tartars from Asia had swept across Russia and taken the Byzantine city of Kiev in 1240. After the collapse of the Mongol Empire, groups of Tartars remained camped at the edges of Muscovy, Lithuania, and Poland. There they continued to raid, pillage, and kidnap and sell their captives into slavery. Borders had to be secured, and therefore "frontier guards" were recruited, men who came to be known as "Cossacks." Volunteers, especially those who had cause to leave home — serfs seeking freedom from a landowner, members of a religious sect persecuted by intolerant Orthodox clergy, convicts, army deserters — responded to the call. So did Polish and Lithuanian peasants, and even Frenchmen, Germans, Greeks, and Turks. Renegade Tartars, too, were enticed to join with the promise of land and other perks. Most were Orthodox, but religious affiliation did not matter as long as the candidate was willing to take the oath of loyalty.

Cossacks from the Saratov region had settled along the lower Terek River in the mid-1500s.[21] This "advance guard of the advance guard," men who were in the saddle by the time they were twelve years of age, and in the words of Leslie Blanch, rode "like centaurs on the small vigorous horses of the steppes."[22] Imperial Russian troops were trained to meet the enemy head-on and press forward without retreating — but not Cossacks. "To evade the enemy, by any means whatever, they regard as a good deed and not a disgrace," said a Russian officer, because the Cossack knows "that as long as he is alive he will think up a thousand ways to harm the enemy, and hence he saves himself assiduously."[23]

Such was the heroic ethos that fired the imagination of the boy who no longer played with the sons of stolid German Lutheran farmers but with a Cossack comrade whose father "was a soldier by the time he was twelve" and whose grandfather "stunk of vodka, sweat, gunpowder and blood."[24]

By 1875 Cossack regiments accounted for half the Russian cavalry. A young Cossack was trained for three years, served twelve years on active duty (four of them at home), and then was put on active reserve for five more years.[25] Commanding officers were graduates of military cadet corps and academies.[26] However, they fought on the battlefields like their forebears. For example, during the civil war Alex Babine saw three boxcars near Saratov filled with the bodies of Red Army soldiers badly cut up and mutilated by Cossacks who "simply drove the panic-stricken defenders of the Bolshevik revolution for over twenty miles, belaboring them with cold steel."[27] In the Second World War, after the battle near Kushtschevskaya, with flashing sabers the Cossacks slashed away at the Germans for almost four hours. Said a Cossack veteran, "It took them [the Germans] eight days to bury their dead."[28]

Cossacks were often implacable warriors, but they sometimes gave vent to a demonic side. When Bogdan Khmelnitski led Ukrainian Cossacks in revolt over grievances with Moscow in 1648, he and his troops slaughtered anyone dressed like a Pole and lynched rich Roman Catholic merchants, stringing the heads of their wives and children around their necks. Others they flayed or burned alive. As for the Jews who had "insulted our religion," Khmelnitski's Cossacks pounded nails into their bodies and hacked off their limbs.[29] It is estimated that 100,000 Jews perished in Ukraine between 1648 and 1656.[30] Pogroms, some led by Cossacks, occurred elsewhere in Russia during the years that Richard lived with the Terek Cossacks, but not in the Caucasus.[31]

Pyatigorsk was home to the 151st Infantry Regiment, and small boys relished the opportunity to watch the soldiers drill. Richard especially admired the *djigitovka*, Cossacks who performed spectacular feats: horsemen standing upright on their saddles, the troop gallops past; then two horsemen race past a comrade who has dismounted, and carry him off the field between them; another dismounts and waits for his comrade to gallop near, and in one graceful leap takes his place behind his partner; others somersault from one side of their horses to the other, one sergeant all the while clenching a saber between his teeth; handkerchiefs are thrown on the ground, and at a gallop the fabled horsemen lean down far enough to pick them up, one rider snatching the cloth from the ground with his teeth.[32]

Shenanigans at the Cadet Corps

A story often told by Dr. Reusch, the main character was often himself or, depending on the audience, his uncle, Konstantin Filipovich:

Late one night Konstantin Filipovich was returning with his comrades to the barracks after a night on the town. It was past curfew, and they knew they would face severe disciplinary action if they were caught. The moon was so bright that shadows were cast across their path. As they passed a cemetery one of them lurched to a halt and stammered in fright, "Look! A vampire!"

Konstantin, not too steady himself, whirled to look. Seeing a figure moving toward them, he drew his pistol, fired several times and joined his buddies as they ran for their lives.

The next morning the hooligans were summoned to the commandant's office. "Last night you reprobates desecrated the cemetery by using the statue of an angel in the cemetery for target practice!" thundered the general. "You ought to be dismissed from the Corps! What do you have to say in your defense?"

A heavy silence filled the room. "But — Your Excellency," Konstantin Filipovich finally stammered, "I thought it was a werewolf or a vampire — and I only reacted according to our training."

"A — what?" the incredulous officer exclaimed, never before having heard such an excuse. "A vampire? Why, that is utter and complete foolishness!"

After a tense interval the boys' tutor stepped forward and with a hint of a grin said, "Well, Your Excellency, the boy did get off a dead-shot before the 'enemy' destroyed the entire company."

And so the boys' careers were saved. Konstantin Filipovich and his friends were not dismissed, but they were fined the cost of replacing the bullet-scarred "vampire" — a gravestone angel that had seemed to move in the moonlight when the shadow of a branch moved across its marble features.[33]

Cossack legends infused European popular culture. After Sunday liturgy at the chapel in the Winter Palace, in St. Petersburg, Irina Skariatina played "Cossacks and robbers" with her friends.[34] Volga German parents may have threatened to call the Kirgiz, Kazakhs or Kalmyks when their children misbehaved, but exasperated Muscovite parents invoked the assistance of Cossacks.[35] As Longworth noted, to Russian youth the Cossack "was recognized as the personification of courage, audacity — and debauch," and Cossack heroes "came to fill the niches occupied by Robin Hood, Raleigh and Richard the Lionhearted in the pantheon of English schoolboy heroes."[36] Since Richard's mentors were officers in Terek Cossack regiments and institutions, it is hardly surprising that he was influenced by their customs and behaviors.

During Richard's occasional visits with his family, his father began to notice the changes in his son and feared that, despite the attention of the old miller's wife, his eldest was slipping from the faith of his fathers. He therefore removed Richard from the Cossack village and sent him to live with Pastor Bonvitch in the Nikolayevskaya colony on the other side of Pyatigorsk. There, Richard Gustavovich explained, "daily devotions were held and the children were kept to prayer and diligent attendance of church services, and received religious instruction from the pastor himself."[37]

The young Cossack from Pyatigorsk looked forward to the occasions when he could visit his brothers and sisters. During one such visit in March 1902, he held brother Erich for the first time. He treasured the infrequent visits to Saratov and Volsk, especially for the opportunity to spend time with his maternal uncle, Konstantin Filipovich, fifteen years his senior, who attended a military academy.

When Richard was twelve, in the spring of 1904, the senior pastor of the Lutheran Church in Vladikavkaz was searching for a qualified director to take charge of his parochial school, one large enough to have employed a second teacher, Elaine Michalovna Engle. Gustav's brother, Feofil Ivanovich, taught German philology at the city's Technical School No. 6,[38] and perhaps it was he who suggested his brother for the post. Pastor Aksim inquired if the teacher from Nikolayevskaya might consider the job.

Gustav Ivanovich happily accepted the position, pleased with the promotion and the opportunity to move to the capital of the Northern Caucasus. Vladikavkaz was a regional government and military center, and the hardworking schoolmaster was relieved to find two additional part-time positions as a German teacher, one at a secondary school and another at his brother's technical school. And so, during the summer of 1904 the family moved from Pyatigorsk to the former Mittelsdorf colony, Mikhailovskaya, the German Russian suburb of Vladikavkaz.

Richard left the Pyatigorsk gymnasium with the rank of Head Boy, first in his class,[39] and a recommendation for admission to Kron's Military Gymnasium in Vladikavkaz.

"I was born in the Caucasus," Richard Gustavovich always said. In a sense that was true, because in those black mountains he came of age and gained the military élan, discipline and skills that prepared him to keep his balance in an unstable world.

CHAPTER 2

1 Essad-Bey, *Twelve Secrets of the Caucasus* (1931), 6.
2 Richard Reusch, "Mein Lebenslauf," 2; also, Aurelia Reusch, interview; and *Terski Kalendar na 1911 god* (Vladikavkaz, 1910), 57, 60.
3 *Chambers's Concise Gazetteer of the World* (1914), 555.
4 Paul E. Lydolph, *Geography of the USSR*, 2nd ed. (1970), 213.
5 Annette M. B. Meakin, *Russia: Travels and Studies* (1906), 413.
6 Leslie Blanch, *The Sabres of Paradise* (1960), 17.
7 Blanch, 92.
8 John Shelton Curtiss, *The Russian Army Under Nicholas I* (1965), 162-63.
9 Hugh Seton-Watson, *The Russian Empire* (1967), 293.
10 *The Cambridge Encyclopedia of Russia and the Former Soviet Union*, ed. by Archie Brown and others (1994), 535.
11 General Kuropatkin, *The Russian Army and the Japanese War*, ed. by E. D. Swinton, vol. 1 (1909), 33-39.
12 Anatoli Isaenko, North Osetian State University, from notes of author's interview, 21 June 1995.
13 A popular saying cited by Blanch, 6.
14 Thomas M. Barret, "Lines of Uncertainty: The Frontiers of the North Caucasus," *Slavic Review*, vol. 54 (no. 3, fall, 1995), 578-601 (on-line journal, 1).
15 Mark Conrad, "Generals' Pension," online posting, H-Russia *[RYLE@ urvax.urich.edu]*, 3 February 1997, notes that a retired major general earned an annual pension of 2,000 rubles. According to Long (42), Lutheran pastors were paid between 1,500 and 3,000 rubles per year.
16 James W. Long, in *From Privileged to Dispossessed: The Volga Germans, 1860-1917* (1988), 32-33, describes the problems faced by Volga German boys drafted into the army after 1874 who could not speak Russian. Long also cites conscription as a factor motivating that generation's adoption of the Russian tongue (36-37).
17 R. Reusch, 2.
18 R. Reusch, 2-3.
19 Vladimir Bolgov, Ataman of the Vladikavkaz Terek Cossacks; from notes of an interview by the author and Galina Tioun, 20 June 1996.
20 Philip Longworth, *The Cossacks* (1969), 12.
21 Chantal Lemercier-Quelquejay, "Cooptation of the Elites of Karbarda and Daghestan in the Sixteenth Century," *The North Caucasus Barrier: The Russian Advance Towards the Muslim World*, ed. by Marie Broxup (1992), 36-37.
22 Blanch, 104.
23 "Otryvki iz pokhodnykh zapisok," *Voennyi Sibornik*, III (1860), 49; cited by Curtiss, 142.
24 Longworth, 20.
25 Longworth, 262.
26 Longworth, 251.
27 Donald J. Raleigh, *A Russian Civil War Diary: Alexis Babine in Saratov, 1917-1922* (1988), 56.
28 Maurice Hindus, *The Cossacks: The Story of a Warrior People* (1945), 4.
29 Hindus, 105.
30 Martin Gilbert, *Atlas of Russian History* (1972), 69.

31 Gilbert, 69-70.
32 Longworth (267) cites a 1915 Djigitovka performance described by an American,
    Robert McCormick.
33 This narrative has been fashioned from Dr. Reusch's various notes and the memories of those
    who heard him tell the story.
34 Irina Skariatina, *A World Can End* (1931), 56.
35 Hindus, 27.
36 Longworth, 2.
37 R. Reusch, 2.
38 R. Reusch, 2. Gustav and Feofil Ivanovich Reusch and Elaine Michalovna Engle are named,
    and their positions described, in *Terski Kalendar na 1911 god* (Vladikavkaz, 1910), 57, 60.
39 R. Reusch, 2.

The Imperial Cadet Corps, Vladikavkaz (1901)

Chapter Three

MILITARY CADET
Vladikavkaz, The Caucasus, 1904-1911

The Cossack steeds paraded, shine.
The regiments fall into line . . .
And lo! across the plain resounding
A deep "Hurrah!" rolls from afar.
The regiments have seen the Tsar.

— Alexander Pushkin[1]

By the time that Gustav Ivanovich moved his family south to Mikhailovskaya, the German colony at the edge of Vladikavkaz, twelve-year-old Richard had grown to be a self-sufficient lad. Although he was an outstanding student and spent much of his time reading, living among Cossacks had made him physically strong, a gutsy little kid. He had earned the admiration of his peers because of his physical strength, loyalty, and a capacity for empathy unusual in a boy his age.[2]

A strategic fort had been constructed along the Terek River in 1784, and as the Russian army gradually gained a foothold in the region, the settlement that grew up around the fortress was named Vladikavkaz. This military presence was vital to the security of Russia's southern borders: the Caucasian tribes were intractable; the Turks and Persians wanted to reclaim territories the Russians had wrested from them; and the Russians were in competition with the British, who were based in India, for influence in Persia and Afghanistan.

The train carrying the Reusch family steamed into the small Mikhailovskaya station after traveling a distance of less than 200 kilometers south from Pyatigorsk. Uncle Feofil Ivanovich Reusch greeted them, and Richard helped to transfer his family's possessions from the baggage car into the waiting horse-drawn cart.

The entourage made its way through the tidy village of brick houses with roofs of orange tile. Each residence boasted well-tended gardens that yielded a profusion of flowers, vegetables, grapes, strawberries, cherries and juicy melons. Clouds of gray and deep blue mist lay stacked and motionless against the steep and jagged contours of the mountains. Suddenly, the sun broke through, and in an instant the emerald plain and boulder-strewn gray and muddy Terek River were mottled in pools of golden light. But Richard saw only the mountains that towered beyond the river, dark purple in hue, streaked with black crevasses beckoning upward into the clouds. They soon arrived at No. 5 Beslanovskaya Street,[3] and Ottilia Filipovna set about the business of organizing her new household.

Vladikavkaz is one of the most beautiful places in the Northern Caucasus. It lies on both banks of the Terek River, 21 kilometers from its rising in the Black Mountains. Vladikavkaz is the administrative center of the Terek Oblast, with a population of 50,000.

— *Illustrated Practical Guide to Vladikavkaz (1906)*[4]

Caucasus, a great mountain-range that forms the backbone of the well-marked geographical region. . . . [Sometimes] treated as the boundary line between Europe and Asia, the region is really Asiatic in character . . . The higher and central part of the range is formed of parallel chains, not separated by deep and wide valleys, but remarkably connected by elevated plateaus, which are traversed by narrow fissures of extreme depth. The highest peaks are in the central ridge or chain, at least six of them well over 16,000 feet, much exceeding the highest Alps.

— *Chambers's Concise Gazetteer of the World (1914)*[5]

The Lutheran church and school were not located in Mikhailovskaya but in Vladikavkaz, two blocks from the city center on Mozdokskaya (now Tolstoi) Street. As he walked to the city center, Richard passed the large Baptist church on Tifliskaya Street, built by a wealthy German baron.[6] Then, several blocks past the Sunni and Shi'a mosques, he could see the spire of the Evangelical Lutheran Church.

Religious Affiliation in the Terek Region (1916)[7]
Russian Orthodox. 660,662
Muslims. 580,368
Old Believers and Sects 52,095
Other Christian Faiths 55,225
Jews 9,767
Other 2,167

The city's population reflected the ethnic and religious diversity of the Caucasus. Twenty-eight religious structures were inventoried in 1904: several Russian Orthodox chapels, shrines, a women's monastery, five parish churches, and a cathedral;[8] two mosques, Sunni and Shi'a; Old Believer, Armenian Orthodox, Georgian Orthodox, German Evangelical Lutheran, Baptist and Polish Catholic churches; and a Jewish synagogue.[9]

As he approached the city center, Richard would have seen an electric trolley for the first time. The modern public conveyance system had been installed the previous year, running along Mariinski and Moscovskoi Streets and then the length of the main street, Alexandrovski Prospect. If he had had a kopek in his pocket, the boy undoubtedly would have taken a ride, but it was not unpleasant to wander up the Prospect's center islands under the leafy linden trees toward Mikhailovski Square. There he would have paused to read the inscription at the pavilion built to commemorate the visit of Tsar Alexander III in 1888. To the left was the great Orthodox cathedral, and on the hill beyond stood the armory where the Terek Cossacks stored their military equipment. The Second Caucasian Army Corps, with headquarters in Tiflis, based one Infantry Division and one Reserve Artillery Brigade at Vladikavkaz, along with 4,000 cavalry and another 4,500 in reserve.[10] Nearby he found Kron's Military Gymnasium, where he would begin classes in the fall.

Vladikavkaz was a holiday destination for the wealthy. Tourists registered at the Imperial Hotel, where they paid from one to five rubles a night for a room with bath and telephone, and dined in the restaurant, said to be the finest in town. "In many parts of the city," gushed the city guidebook, "the panorama of the mountains, especially in the morning when the sky is cloudless, is so beautiful that you cannot stop looking at it for hours." Stretching from the Black Sea eastward to the Caspian Sea, "the picture is majestic, grandiose, and of rare beauty. It is worthwhile coming to Vladikavkaz just to see these mountains."[11]

THE IMPERIAL CADET CORPS

A new Imperial Cadet Corps had just opened, located at the southwestern edge of Vladikavkaz in a facility originally built in the 1880s to train officers for Cossack military units, including the Cossack Pokrovski Regiment that was headquartered in the city. By Imperial decree in 1901, the structure was renovated to serve instead as the thirty-fourth campus in the Cadet Corps system.[12] Grand Duke Konstantin Konstantinovich, the Tsar's uncle and patron of the Cadet Corps, had sent a telegram of greeting on its opening day.[13]

The Grand Duke recognized the need to modernize cadet education and had encouraged the reforms of 1882. The humanities component in the curriculum was retained, but military discipline was strengthened as officers replaced civilian tutors. Courses in mathematics and science were upgraded.[14] In 1904 the War Ministry integrated teaching methods based on learning theory and required the teaching staff to take special courses in developmental psychology.[15]

General Nicholas Alexandrovich Lenyevich, director of the Vladikavkaz Cadet Corps,[16] was responsible for implementing the 1904 directives, but at the moment he faced a more mundane problem. His two sons had done poorly in their German language studies during the previous academic year, and he was determined to find them a tutor for the summer months. The principal and reserve officer in Pyatigorsk recommended his Head Boy who had just moved to Vladikavkaz for the job,[17] and so Lenyevich summoned Gustav Ivanovich and his son to his apartment to discuss the matter.

On the appointed day, Richard set out with his father for the military complex. The June sun was hot and the breeze cool as Richard and his father passed the Orthodox chapel at the left end of the parade ground and continued toward the central entrance of the imposing building, claimed at the time to be the longest structure in Russia.[18]

Father and son stood for a moment in the grand foyer. Parquet flooring gleamed under an enormous chandelier suspended from a ceiling as ornate as the more modest rooms in the Catherine Summer Palace at Tsarskoye Selo. In front of them a grand staircase with finely detailed wrought iron railings drew their gaze upward where the only decoration to grace the wall above the landing was a portrait of Tsar Alexander III. Thus was Imperial grandeur made manifest in Vladikavkaz.[19]

Gustav Ivanovich was instructed to proceed to the apartment complex — just go back outside, turn right, and continue straight on. After seeing his son to the commandant's spacious apartment, Gustav Ivanovich went home to Mikhailovskaya. And so Richard's brief time at home with his brothers and sisters — Olga, Albert, Emil, Aurelia, and two-year old brother, Erich — came to an end. Richard lived on the campus in the home of the commandant for the next seven years.

Seventy new cadets were admitted to the Vladikavkaz Imperial Cadet Corps in the autumn of 1904. The student body numbered about 500 boys, whose term of study lasted from six to seven years.[20] In the previous year, 1903, only 56 sons of the region's nobility chose to prepare for a military career whereas 287 sons of Terek Cossacks were enrolled,[21] 33 of whom received state scholarships.[22] However, it was unusual for the son of a worker or Cossack to pass the exam unless he came from a family in which education was valued.[23]

Definitions

Gymnasium: a secondary school that specialized in preparing graduates for admission to universities. Graduates could apply for admission to a military academy after serving with a regiment for eleven months.

Cadet Corps: a military secondary school that prepared boys specifically for admission to a military academy. Graduates were commissioned as second lieutenants or ensigns, and served for eleven months with a regiment before enrolling at an academy.

Military Academy: a professional military school that accepted graduates of the Cadet Corps and gymnasia. Academy graduates were commissioned as first lieutenants and assigned to a regiment.

According to the Code of Military Regulations, commissioned officers had to be born of the noble class. Since it was their birthright, eleven-year-old sons of the nobility were automatically accepted into the Cadet Corps.[24] However, because an insufficient number of such boys chose a military career, a means was expediently created that opened the doors to a military commission for those of common social rank: Any boy who was nominated by his Cossack ataman or a commissioned officer, and who passed the rigorous entrance examination, was admitted. Nobility was then conferred upon the young men when they had earned their commissions.

A cadet took the oath of allegiance to his Tsar and regiment at age fifteen and became a junior officer known as a *podkhorunzhi*. At age seventeen a successful cadet was promoted to the rank of *khorunzhi*.[25] In the cavalry, these young men served as *cornets of horse*, smartly carrying the colors at the head of a regiment. As well, these junior officers served as sergeants' assistants in drilling peasant recruits, many of whom were illiterate. Cadets who graduated with first-class honors received the rank of second lieutenant; those with second-class honors were appointed as ensigns.[26]

There was an alternate route to a military commission that circumvented the Cadet Corps system. A gymnasium graduate could seek admission to a military academy after passing an examination and serving in a regiment for eleven months.[27] That may have been the route to a commission for Richard.

The German tutor was swept up into the life of the Corps, of uniforms and dress parades, as well as rigorous physical training, including 25-kilometer marches, walking and running in 200-meter segments. They drilled "until the seventh sweat," otherwise known in a popular song as the "black sweat."[28] Cadets also participated in fencing and gymnastics, and learned to ride and care for their horses. As is natural in the cavalry, said a Hussar officer, "the well-being of the horses is much more important than that of the men" because in the cavalry "a man without a horse is nothing, and a horse without hoofs is nothing."[29]

The cadets were also drilled in the basic skills of the *djigitovka*, two of them riding to the rescue of a comrade who had dismounted, leaning from their saddles and lifting him from the ground and carrying him out of danger. "Paradise on earth," Dr. Reusch later told high school students in St. Paul, Minnesota, "is on the back of a good horse."[30] They were taught how to care for and use personal armaments — pistol, rifle, saber and bayonet — and the rules of military and social etiquette.[31] "It was an honour to be enrolled," Dr. Reusch said to a group of U.S. Army officers. "Discipline was severe, but it made men out of boys."[32]

In the autobiographical sketch he prepared in 1920 for the Leipzig Mission Society, Reusch described his life at the Corps and the military high school in which he was enrolled:

> Until my matriculation, I remained in the Cadet Corps. Here, as in the high school [Kron's Military Gymnasium] where I graduated with the Gold Medal, I received a full military education. I lived often in camp, participated in manoeuvres, rode and practiced the use of weapons. I was at the time a bold horseman and did not belong to the worst marksmen or swordsmen. . . . To educate myself to be a good cavalry officer, I took part in many hunting expeditions, participated in nearly all the

expeditions into the mountains, and wandered around there for 2-3 weeks in the summer holidays with 3-4 like-minded companions. We encountered thirst, frequently battling beasts and men. Our teacher was not against this, which encouraged us even more.[33]

Whether Richard Gustavovich was officially enrolled at the Cadet Corps cannot be confirmed because the records, if they survived, have not been located. However, his gymnasium transcript does exist, signed by Director R. Keller and stamped with official seals. Items four and six verify that he completed the full course of study in seven years, 1904-1911; matriculated on August 19, 1911, No. 233985; earned the highest grade, a "5," in all subjects including Russian, Greek, Latin, French, and German, philosophy, mathematics, geography, physics, history, geography, and state law; was cited for "perfect behavior"; earned the rank of *primus omnium*, first in his class, and was awarded the Gold Medallion.[34]

Almost a century after Richard Gustavovich graduated from Kron's Gymnasium (known since Soviet times as School No. 5), a plaque at the entrance reads, "Here, from 1914-1916, the Terek Communist Party was organized and conducted its meetings." The main corridor of the school was still decorated with red banners, and a portrait of Joseph Stalin gazed vacantly at those passing in the main corridor. Sergei Ivanovich Ruseen, the director, sat behind his desk, a relief of Lenin on the wall behind him, and spoke of the institution's past accomplishments. He regretted that no lists of graduates or valedictorians are known to exist prior to 1945, but from the safe behind his desk he took a faded sepia-toned photograph made in 1903 that shows a group of boys in uniform each holding a rifle posed in front of the large portrait of Alexander III. The gymnasium was a military high school, the director explained, and therefore the students wore uniforms and were trained in military drill and etiquette.

Dr. Reusch always identified himself as a Cadet. Was it usual for a student to be enrolled at both the Corps and gymnasium?

The director reached for a history of the school published in 1897. "Of course," he replied, "because the gymnasium provided the liberal arts curriculum for the cadets."[35]

THE FIRST REVOLUTION OF 1905

In contrast to the bright mood conveyed in the city guidebook, a pall of gloom had settled over Vladikavkaz and all of Russia in the spring of 1904. In February of that year the Imperial government went to war with Japan over territorial influence in Manchuria and Korea, suffering loss upon loss. Terek Cossack reserves were mobilized but had not been ordered to the Far Eastern Front, something for which everyone in Vladikavkaz was thankful, but they were placed on alert in case Turkey or Persia took advantage of the moment to regain lost territories.

The war dragged on through the summer of 1904, bringing only depressing news, including the sinking of most of the ships in the Imperial Navy. Demonstrations and strikes against the autocratic and incompetent government in St. Petersburg grew in frequency and nastiness, and officials ordered firm and brutal repression in a futile attempt to restore domestic tranquility. The Cossacks were ordered to ride against Russians, and that brought grief to everyone.

The Tsar continued to rule as if he were God's agent on earth, accountable to no elected body. Some who desired social and political change gathered under the banner of the Social Democratic Workers Party. The most radical elements broke away in 1901 to form the Social Revolutionary Party, and Vladimir Ilyich Lenin was chosen to lead the most radical faction known as the *Bolsheviks* ("majority").[36] In 1905, a year after the Reusch family moved to Vladikavkaz, the Bolshevik's "fighting section" initiated a plan to assassinate monarchist politicians, military officers, policemen, secret agents, and spies. Two years later 116 such "enemies of the people" had been eliminated.[37] The assassins were not active in the Caucasus except Tiflis, but there was strong support for the Bolsheviks in Samara and Saratov. In Vladikavkaz the more moderate Social Democrats, the *Mensheviks* ("minority"), had formed a local organization in 1903 and from 1905 to 1907 led workers in taking an active part in strikes and demonstrations.[38]

Civil disturbances increased as Richard finished his first semester. Then on Sunday, January 22, 1905, a crucial event occurred in St. Petersburg in front of the Winter Palace that provided martyrs for a revolution. Father Gapon, a Russian Orthodox priest, led 200,000 demonstrators, some carrying sacred icons, in a march on Palace Square. There they peacefully demonstrated for labor reform, universal suffrage, and participation in governance. But the "Little Father," as loyal subjects referred to the Tsar, was not in residence. Worried that they might lose control of the situation, the increasingly agitated Cossack Guard fired on the crowd. It is estimated that on this "Bloody Sunday" between 100 and 1,000 people died. A month later the governor of Moscow, Grand Duke Sergei Alexandrovich, was assassinated outside the Kremlin. By the end of the year more than 1,500 government officials had been assassinated.[39]

Americans were sympathetic to the cause of the Russian people, and even in remote towns the press breathlessly published the wire service reports filed in far-away St. Petersburg: "Russian Troops Firing on the People," read the banner headline in the January 23d issue of the Superior (Wisconsin) *Evening Telegram*. "Conflicts Between Military and Demonstrators Resumed in Nevsky Prospect; Czar May Flee From Capital City," ran the sub-head. And in bold type, "Leaders of Strikes Advocate Armed Effort to Secure Rights of Man — Liberty or Death is the Wail of an Oppressed and Outraged People." According to the story, "Emperor Nicholas is completely prostrated by grief. In the meantime everything awaits his decision. All the schools are closed. Every window in Grand Duke Sergei's St. Petersburg palace was broken by the mob during the night."

The Romanov throne nearly toppled in the following months as workers, singing the "Marseillaise" and the "Internationale," went on strike across the empire and demonstrations were staged in most Russian cities and towns — including Saratov, Pyatigorsk and Vladikavkaz. On the Black Sea near Odessa the crew of the Battleship Potemkin mutinied. In nearby Grozni the Terek Cossacks joined in demonstrating against the Supreme Autocrat of All the Russias. From Saratov, Governor Stolypin reported that Cossack units were angry for being ordered to fire on the people and might revolt. And in St. Petersburg the elite Cossack Guard grew disgusted with its reputation as "hangmen of the workers."[40]

Meanwhile, Armenians, Georgians, Estonians, and Ukrainians seized the opportunity to launch movements for independence. In the countryside peasants looted the estates of some landlords and burned their houses. Such was the milieu that framed daily life as the cadets continued their education.

In February 1905 local administrations in every city and town were encouraged to stage a public ceremony in memory of the soldiers killed in the ill-fated and on-going war with Japan. On February 19, 1905, students at Richard's military gymnasium in Vladikavkaz staged a demonstration that turned into a riot. Their demand was simple but bold: honor the citizens who lost their lives on Bloody Sunday in St. Petersburg rather than soldiers killed under the leadership of incompetent generals and war profiteers. The schoolboys left the gymnasium in shambles and marched down Alexandrovski Prospect to the technical institute, where they tried to rouse their peers to join their protest. It was smugly reported, however, that the older technical students "were not inclined to join their juniors."[41]

The Russian nation appears to have gone temporarily insane; government practically helpless to restore order throughout the country; departments at sixes and sevens; also crippled by postal and telegraph strike. Only socialists appear well organized to establish strikes when and wherever they like.

— *Telegram, U. S. Ambassador in St. Petersburg, November 1905*[42]

General P. A. Polovtsoff, a member of the General Staff, admitted that by September 1905 the threat of revolution forced the government to conclude peace with Japan and devote its energies to restoring order in Russia.[43] A peace treaty with Japan was signed in the United States just as Richard put on his uniform for his second year at the Cadet Corps and gymnasium.

In Moscow things almost got out of hand at the end of the year when revolutionaries took control of much of the city; however, their sabers glinting in the sun, the cavalry cleared the streets and the inevitable revolution was stalled. Martial law was declared, censorship imposed, and revolutionary leaders and activists were marched in chains to Siberian exile or hard labor. But despite the best efforts of the *Okhrana*, the state secret police, the radicals continued their subversive activities.

The frustrated Minister of War, A. F. Rediger, tried his best to reform the defeated and badly managed military structure, but that was difficult to accomplish while the army was ordered to quell civilian demonstrations and riots. A further obstacle to effective military reorganization was the attitude of Nicholas II, who grandly declared, "Military doctrine consists of doing everything which I order."[44]

MOUNTAINEERING

Of all the skills taught at the Corps, mountain climbing became Richard's passion. Cadets became proficient in using ropes and ice axes, which, according to contemporary standards, indicate that they reached a Class 4 level of difficulty.[45] Richard and his like-minded comrades spent most of their free time traversing the glaciers and saddles in the high mountain passes. Climbing had become an amateur sport during the 1890s, and the Caucasus range attracted many European climbers. A military alpine unit was based at nearby Mozdok, with whom Richard climbed during training exercises.[46] Sergei Kirov, editor of the *Terek* newspaper in Vladikavkaz, also directed the work of the Bolsheviks in the area from 1909 to 1917.[47] He too was an avid climber, and so it is not impossible that Richard Gustavovich might have encountered the dedicated Bolshevik on the peaks south of the city.[48]

Until the Vladikavkaz Terek Girls Gymnasium opened in 1910, young women were taught practical skills, including how to weave rope nets, which climbers wore over their leather boots to improve traction. Richard's eleven-year-old sister, Aurelia, was taught to make them, and until her brother left for Estonia in 1911, she made many pairs for him.

Aurelia remembered Richard as quiet, shy and obedient, "a wonderful brother and friend." She doubted that her brother was much interested in girls because he spent his free time reading, writing, lifting weights and mountain climbing. The reserved young man was quiet during family conversations, and never spoke about his life in the Corps, Aurelia said; "but without hesitation and for any excuse, how he loved to talk about those mountains!" His brothers and sisters looked forward to his occasional visits, and clustered around him because they loved him, wanted to be close to him and to touch him. When one of his sisters came down with diphtheria it was Richard who carried her in his arms down the street to an emergency medical facility.[49]

The Old Military Road that winds its way south through the Caucasus Mountains begins near the Cadet Corps campus, crosses the Terek River, and continues upward into the crags and peaks of the Caucasus Range until it reaches Tiflis (Tbilisi), the Georgian capital. According to an army officer, it was "one of the world's most magnificent routes, so rare is its beauty and the grandeur of its mountain scenery."[50] Anton P. Checkhov made the trip, and urged a friend to do the same: "I have never in my life seen anything like it. It is sheer poetry — not just a road."[51]

Richard hiked the Road toward the gorge above a rock formation known as Tamara's Temple located just inside the Georgian border.[52] Where the road crossed to the other side of the river, like other climbers he always paused to carve his initials and the date somewhere on the beams of the old wooden bridge. The structure was replaced long ago, but old men still recall the initialed and dated timbers.

Mt. Ararat is part of the Caucasus range. Dr. Reusch said that he twice climbed it and had seen the wooden beams that some enthusiasts believed were pieces of Noah's Ark. Initially he was inclined to agree but later came to regard the claim as nonsense. The timbers, he speculated, were the remains of a large wooden cross that had been dragged up to the summit centuries earlier by devout Georgian or Armenian Orthodox pilgrims.[53]

Lutheran Pilgrims on Mt. Ararat

In 1817 some 1,700 families left Württemberg, Germany, for Mt. Ararat, where the pious Germans believed the Second Coming of Christ would occur in 1834. They reached Odessa, not far from their destination, when tragedy befell them. All but 100 families perished in a plague epidemic. Tsar Alexander I took pity on the German Lutherans and granted them land in Georgia facing Mt. Ararat. While they waited for the end of time, however, the true believers recreated a charming village in the style of their homeland, rich with vines, apricots, and apple orchards. The clouds did not part to the sound of trumpets in 1834, but the colonists and their descendants continued to live quietly and peacefully in Ararat's shadow until 1941, when Stalin sent them and all German Russians into exile.[54]

The census taken just before the world war reported a Transcaucasus population of about 7 million, comprising eighteen distinct nationalities and forty-eight different languages and dialects. "From Biblical times," said Ranald MacDonell, a British diplomat who served in the region during the First World War, "the country has been swept by successive struggles for supremacy by these various races. What a cauldron of trouble!"[55]

Topography and fierce independence of the mountain tribes presented an implacable barrier to invasion. When Marco Polo saw the Caucasus range for the first time he suddenly understood why Alexander the Great's campaign had been stymied there, and why the Mongol invasion could not penetrate its mass or subdue its peoples. Here, in the Caucasus, Dr. Reusch explained,

"I came in close contact with Turks and Kurds, Persians and Tatars, Armenians and Syro-Chaldeans, Georgians, and Osetians who speak a language akin to the ancient German; with Arabs and Circasians; with our Cossacks as well as with the mysterious Khevsours who claim to be descendants of a group of captured knights of King Richard the Lionhearted. And so I became acquainted with the Oriental ways of living and thinking to such an extent that they became as familiar to me as the western ways."[56]

"LOYALTY FOR LOYALTY, BLOOD FOR BLOOD, LIFE FOR LIFE"

General A. K. Benckendorff, chief of state security under Tsar Nicholas I, noted, "For the Russian soldier, war is something sacred. He goes into battle as one entering a church, crossing himself and whispering a prayer."[57] Daily routine at the Cadet Corps included a religious component, and spiritual discipline culminated with the taking of the oath, a solemn moment in the lives of the young cadets.

They memorized a simple prayer: "Holy Mother of God, save us; Saint Nicholas, pray for us." The Corps protopresviter (chaplain) declared, "Without this prayer, do not pull out a sword, do not load your gun, and start no action whatsoever. Everything should start with God's blessing, and a soldier is to be faithful to his Emperor and the Fatherland until his last breath."[58]

The cadets memorized Psalm 91, which every soldier was to recite during heavy fighting. And so the wraiths of Jewish prayers floated upward like incense, laced with Russian fatalism, passing in and out of memory for those trapped in the hell of battle:

> Thou shalt not be afraid for the terror by night,
> Nor the arrow that flieth by day;
> For the pestilence that walketh in darkness,
> Nor for the destruction that wasteth at noonday. . .
>
> A thousand shall fall at thy side,
> And ten thousand at thy right hand;
> But it shall not come nigh thee. . .[59]

According to Prince Lobanov-Rostovsky, the religious component drilled into the regiments was not forgotten on the field:

> "A sudden command, 'Reserves forward,' set the whole field in motion. The entire Fourth regiment and our company knelt down, and four thousand men sang in chorus the beautiful Russian military prayer, immortalized in Tchaikovsky's '1812.' Under the circumstances this was the most impressive song I have ever heard. As the troops rose the priest, holding his cross high, passed among the running men, blessing them on all sides."[60]

A Volga German Roman Catholic priest was also deeply moved when he observed "thousands upon thousands of men with caps in their hands sing aloud the Lord's Prayer."[61]

In the autumn of 1906 Richard turned fifteen, the age when cadets prepared to take the oath of a junior officer, a *podkhorunzhi*. The ceremony was a grand ritual. The adjutant reminded them that an oath is a soldier's holiest vow. There was no pardon or mercy in this world or in the next for the soldier who failed to perform his duty or broke his oath; but, in the archaic language of Tsar Peter I, he "who completes his allotted life without grievances preserves the purity of his soul and remains stable and true to the given oath will reap in heaven from his Omnipotent Creator a worthy reward."[62]

The cadets of various religious confessions stood in separate groups, each facing their own spiritual leader who led them in repeating the oath:

> I promise and swear in the name of Almighty God and in the presence of the Holy Evangel [the Gospels] that I wish to and must serve His Imperial Majesty, the Autocrat of all the Russias, and His Imperial Highness, the Heir to the Russian throne, loyally and truthfully without sparing my life, to the last drop of my blood.[63]

On command the cadets turned from their clergy to face the adjutant, who bellowed the phrases of the regimental motto — which the young men repeated in unison, their deep voices heavy with emotion: "Loyalty for Loyalty! Blood for Blood! Life for Life!"

In 1907 Major General Ivan Gavrilovich Semyenov was appointed director of the Vladi-kavkaz Cadet Corps, a post that he held until 1910.[64] General Semyenov, said Dr. Reusch, became his "military papa" and the regiment his family.[65]

"Katya Semyenov" is a name that often appears in Dr. Reusch's notes about his years as a cadet. Who was she? Probably, imagined his sister, Aurelia, some girl with whom he was infatuated. It was an accurate guess.

The cadets were told that girls were "from another planet," Dr. Reusch once told members of the Fort Snelling Officers Club, and cadets were strictly forbidden to date.[66] One afternoon as Richard returned from classes at the gymnasium he encountered the beautiful Katya, General Semyenov's daughter, on her way into town. She smiled. As required by military etiquette, he clicked his heels, bowed, and kissed her hand. Although it was prohibited, he then escorted her for a stroll. He was observed, and was subsequently put on bread and water for three days. "Cured forever," he grinned.[67]

SUMMER ENCAMPMENTS

"I have purposely not mentioned a few things," Dr. Reusch wrote in an autobiographical sketch in 1949, which "are of little interest for Westerners since they were concerned with military questions and mountaineering." But, he added,

> The students of our military Cosak-schools [sic] were enrolled into different regiments after they completed their fifteenth year. In this capacity they were often called out to fight bandits ("Abreks" in Caucasian) and stop revolutionary bands when they pillaged shops, etc. They had also to stay in the military camps, especially on the Persian or Turkish boundary, from May until the end of August every year. This explains why I took part in different fights at a comparatively young age.[68]

Caucasian bandits made headlines in Russia at the same time that the American public avidly followed the exploits of Butch Cassidy and the Sundance Kid. Cadets were not usually sent on punitive missions, but in 1906 cadets were called into action again against Caucasian bandits and political terrorists.[69] Former Georgian seminary student-turned-Bolshevik, Iosif Vissarionovich Dzhugashvili, Joseph Stalin, had staged at least one successful bank robbery in Tiflis.[70] Years later, Dr. Reusch claimed to have known Stalin, but they could not have been acquainted because the Georgian revolutionary was serving a term in Siberia during the years that Richard Gustavovich lived at the Corps.

In 1908 Cornet Richard Gustavovich, now a *khorunzhi* or senior cornet, was assigned responsibility for training peasant recruits. Recalled Dr. Reusch,

My captain gave me the order to instruct the "green recruits" of how to behave outside the barracks. The majority of them were boys from farms and villages. I began: "You so-and-soes," because in those days, over 70 years ago, a green recruit could be addressed only by his name or as "mister." Noticing an agreeable grin on the face of the drill sergeant, I continued, "You so-and-soes, every Saturday from 6 to 9 p.m. you are free and can go to the beer shop to have a good time. I want to instruct you how to behave there. When you see two men quarreling and beginning to fight, do not mix in but drink your beer and go peacefully back to the barracks. Do you understand?"

"Yes, Sir!" was the unanimous answer.

I looked around and saw the glittering eyes of one of my men. So I said, "Well, Yermolov, how will you act when you see two fellows quarreling in the beer shop?"

The answer was prompt: "Sir, I shall not mix in. I shall wait until those sons of a dog start to fight. Then I shall go to their table, drink their beer, and go peacefully back to the barracks."[71]

In the summers of 1908 and 1909 Cornet Richard Gustavovich's regiment made its way as far as the Persian border on the Araxes River, which rises from the snows of Mt. Ararat. In 1954 Dr. Reusch told a *Los Angeles Times* reporter that a squadron

> was ordered into Persia in 1908 to quell a revolution, which resulted in seating of the present Iranian dynasty. In the course of that venture "our second squadron sacrificed itself to the last man to save the brigade in Teheran.
>
> "We never accepted replacements for that squadron. When each evening at parade they were ordered to report, the call echoed over the ranks: 'They fell true to their tradition!'
>
> "If I had my life to live over again, I could pick no finer beginning than that Army experience."[72]

Along the border during those summers, Richard Gustavovich learned about the Persian followers of the Mahdi, the "Hidden Imam" and final prophet of Islam.[73] Said Dr. Reusch,

> On the border with Persia, people insisted on a constitution. The despotic Muhammed Ali Shah resisted them. Then the Hidden Imam issued an order asking Ali Shah immediately to grant a constitution and summon a parliament. The despotic Shah followed the instructions, but the young parliament refused to support the corrupt Shah's budget. He disbanded the parliament, and when the deputies hesitated to leave Teheran the Shah seized the parliament and held court in the very building. The Hidden Imam sent another message saying that Shah was shah no longer, and so his servants deserted him. The Shah thought he could survive an Imam who keeps himself hidden, but immediately the terrible revolution broke out, which took the crown of the Shah despite Russian help, and brought his dynasty to an end.
>
> All these things happened because of the supposed order of the Hidden Imam, and where ever the troops took part in putting down the revolution, everywhere they heard the same thing: "It happened because of the orders of the Hidden Imam." That is how he became of interest to me.[74]

In Teheran, Colonel Vladimir Platonovich Liakhov shouted to his Persian Cossacks, "Who will die for the brigade?"

"We!" roared the deep-throated response from nine hundred Lancers.[75]

"Brave soldiers and Cossacks!" Liakhov exhorted his men, "May God grant you safety and a glorious victory!"[76]

Cornet Richard Gustavovich was almost eighteen when Colonel Liakhov returned from duty in Persia. The young man thrilled to the stories of intrigue that the senior officers told: the competition between Russia and England for influence in Persia; Turks invading Persia in 1906-07 and threatening Russian mountain passes; the struggle for power between the Shah, described as "a ferocious degenerate whose fitting abode should have been a psychiatric hospital"[77] and the Constitutional Assembly in Teheran; the Shah's threat to burn his enemies' houses to the ground and put their women and children to the sword; several hundred Mujahedin riding on Teheran, together with a thousand horsemen from Tabriz to save the defenders of the Constitution; fierce Bakhtiari warriors under the leadership of their Kahn, Sirdar-i-Asad, who plotted to overthrow the Shah; of the siege and suffering at Tabriz, and the casualties in the Second Squadron whose places in the regiment were left vacant as a memorial to their bravery.

Colonel Liakhov's Persian Cossack regiment did defend the Peacock Throne in Teheran: 800 men in the capital, another 350 stationed at the Karji Bridge some 40 kilometers to the west of the city, and another 200 men dug in along the road from the south. A second regiment was in position at Shahabad, including loyal Bakhtiari troops.[78] But in fact, Colonel Liakhov's command in Teheran was a disaster. Bakhtiari warriors circled around the city during the night, and at 6:30 a.m. on July 12th entered through a city gate without resistance.[79]

RESIGNATION

Not until he returned from duty on the Persian border in 1909 did Richard Gusta-vovich actually complete his preparation for the rite of Lutheran Confirmation, perhaps at his father's insistence.[80] Pastor Aksim asked the junior officer if he ever thought about a different kind of life, for example, a missionary in East Africa — perhaps on the slopes of the highest mountain on the continent. The pastor showed him a picture of a German Lutheran Leipzig Mission deaconess, standing on the plain with the snow-capped and twin-peaked Mount Kilimanjaro looming majestically in the background. In the following weeks Richard Gustavovich could not erase the picture from his mind.[81] "I don't know that he used the term 'conversion experience,'" said one of his former students, "but there was a change in his life, and he decided to proclaim the Gospel."[82] Said Dr. Reusch,

> Two ideals lay side by side in my soul: on the one hand, a smart Cossack officer who serves his Emperor with unswerving loyalty; on the other, a missionary to Africa, faithful to his Saviour to the end. . . . If during the day I contemplated my future as an officer, then in the quiet evening the ideal of a missionary would grow stronger in my

soul. I went so far as to involve myself with such activities that, in my opinion, could be used in either career. For example, I eagerly involved myself for a long time with the Japanese Jiu-Jitsu system.[83]

In 1909 General A. N. Kuropatkin, commander-in-chief of the war with Japan, wrote of the continuing need to "pacify the Caucasus."[84] The next year, in 1910, cadets were among the troops sent to quell another Chechen uprising.[85] That same summer Kaiser Wilhelm's nephew and his retinue were hiking in the Western Caucasus when bandits set upon the party. Someone in the group frantically blew a whistle to raise an alarm. A detail of cadets was nearby, including Richard Gustavovich, and came to the Germans' aid. Kaiser Wilhelm II later sent a letter of appreciation and commendation through channels to the cadet's commanding officer.[86]

Richard Gustavovich was not a financial burden to his father since he lived with the commandant and other officers at the Cadet Corps whose children he tutored. "Later," he wrote, "when I was in the higher classes, I received whole detachments, yes, even whole classes of cadets and school children to whom I gave afternoon tutorials."[87]

Gustav Ivanovich was unhappy that his son had adapted so completely to military life, including the inevitable exposure to Russian Orthodox influence that was an integral part of life at the Corps. Dr. Reusch seldom spoke about the Orthodox Church except for the Pascha (Easter) Vigil, a liturgical experience that remained etched in his memory. Some forty years later he described the event to young Lutherans in Minnesota:

> In my old home country, Russia, we have a wonderful custom Saturday night of Holy Week when the whole congregation gathers in the dark church. The priest in black clothes is in the altar room. Only one little candle is burning on the altar. Deep silence in the church. Exactly at midnight the big bell is beginning to ring, the priest appears before the altar in golden robes with this little candle in his hand and is shouting into the dark church, "Christ is Risen." And the congregation is answering, "Verily, He is Risen." And in the same moment the whole church is flooded with streams of light.[88]

If the Lutheran deacon worried about the influence of Russian Orthodoxy on his son, the notorious, unholy and dissolute lifestyle of career military officers drove him to his knees. Pastors Bonvitch and Aksim and Richard's paternal grandfather joined in the campaign to change Richard's career path; indeed, Grandfather Reusch threatened to revoke his grandson's inheritance unless the young man changed course.[89]

Richard Gustavovich completed his exams and graduated with highest honors from the gymnasium in May 1911.[90] As he later remembered that pivotal moment in his life, he was to have served as a lieutenant in the Cossack regiment for 11 months before going to the Academy. "However, my father had wanted throughout that I should become a pastor. Pastor Aksim tried to persuade me to the same view, and Professor D. A. von Bulmerincq [theology faculty, Tartu University] wrote to my father for the same purpose."[91]

The junior officer's only desire was to apply to a military academy — perhaps the one at

Rostov. He had watched the Terek Cossack colonel from St. Petersburg select the lucky few who would serve in the Cossack regiments as the Tsar's personal bodyguard, a nomination that Richard Gustavovich coveted.[92]

The young man ultimately could not stand against his father and grandfather. "The thought that I could prepare for mission work through theological studies made me give in," he explained. "Thus I took leave from camp life, from the military, from all expeditions, and the academy, and joined the theological faculty [department] of the Dorpat University."[93] Cornet Richard Gustavovich had carried the regimental flag on maneuvers and in parades. However, he left the military with one wish unfulfilled — just once, to have led his regiment into battle.[94]

In the spring of 1911 some 6,000 students were expelled from Russian universities for "provocations" against the state,[95] but Richard Gustavovich had little sympathy for their plight. On July 8th he mailed his application to the rector of the only university in Russia that was permitted to conduct business in the German language. Along with the letter of application he enclosed his military registration identification, No. 5430, and three photographs.[96]

At the end of August the first movie theater opened in Vladikavkaz, the Patz,[97] but Richard Gustavovich no longer walked its streets to witness yet another technological marvel. Born a Volga German and educated to become a Terek Cossack military officer, he was almost twenty years of age when he left for the Baltic university town on the northwestern edge of the Empire.

LOYAL UNTO DEATH

Everyone who knew Dr. Reusch thought of him as a brave and loyal Imperial Russian cavalry officer, a man of his word. He and others of his epoch were the last of their age, men who identified with a chivalric code of behavior in the tradition of the Knights of the Round Table and Teutonic Brothers of the Sword. It is a code that is all but unintelligible to post-modern humankind.

During the Russian civil war, Bolshevik authorities in Kiev demanded that a captured White cavalry officer take an oath of loyalty to the new Soviet government. The Cossack replied, "I have already taken an oath once before in which I swore to remain faithful to my Church, my Tsar, and my Country. As this was an oath for my life, I am therefore not in the least prepared to break that oath, which is sacred to me."[98] Dr. Reusch shared that code, one that was not determined by situational ambiguities.

In his cluttered office at Gustavus Adolphus College during the autumn semester of 1960, Dr. Reusch fussed with his Turkish water pipe. Then he peered at the student who had followed him to his office after his lecture on the Old Testament prophet, Amos. "So, young man, what is your question?" he asked.

"Sir, how is it that you seem to have absolutely no doubt about your faith in God?" Dr. Reusch continued to gaze at the boy, the only sound coming from the bubbling water as he drew on the stem. After an interval the student stammered, "I'm lucky if I believe fifty-one percent of the time."

Peering over the rim of his spectacles, the former Imperial cavalry officer replied, "When I was a young man, younger than you, I gave my word to serve my Emperor, loyal unto the death. But," he added with a shrug of his shoulders, "they have killed him. And so I gave my word to my Heavenly King." He paused, his dark brown eyes gazing intently at the student. "You see, young man, once you have given your word to your Heavenly King there can be no doubt, no question — not when you have given your word."[99]

CHAPTER 3

1   Alexander Pushkin, "Poltava," from Canto III, *The Poems, Prose and Plays of Alexander Pushkin*, ed. by Avrahm Yarmolinsky (1964), 94.

2   Aurelia Reusch, from the author's notes of an interview, 17 October 1995.

3   Document No. 3, Richard Reusch file (2100-1-13219), ESHA.

4   P. N. Ulyanova, *Illustrereovanyi Praktiicheski Pytevoditel no Kavkazu* (Odessa, 1906), 191.

5   *Chambers's Concise Gazetteer of the World* (1914), 164-65.

6   Henri Kusov, Geography Faculty, State University of Northern Osetia, from the author's notes of an interview, 20 June 1996.

7   *Statisticheski Otchyot Glavy Terekskoi Oblasti I Atamana Tereekskogo Kazachestra* (Vladikavkaz, 1916), 14.

8   Document 114, "Svedeniya ob Ekonomicheskom e Kulturnom Razvitii g. Vladikavkaza po Sostoyaniio na 1 Yanvarya 1904 g.," *Istoria Vladikavkaza, 1781-1990*, ed. by E. D. Betosva and A. D. Beryokova (Vladikavkaz, 1991), 136.

9   *Terski Kalendar na 1912 god* (Vladikavkaz, 1911), appendix, 2.

10 Gervais Lyons, *Afghanistan, the Buffer State* (London: Luzac & Co., 1910), 197-98.

11 P. N. Ulyanova.

12 "Vladikavkazu Kadetskii Korpus," Betosva and Beryokova, 128.

13 Keller file, "Vladikavkazku Kadetskii Korpus," 1-3, MOR.
     Grand Duke Konstantin Konstantinovich married a German princess, Elizabeth of Saxe-Altenburg. She did not convert to Orthodoxy, as was the custom, but remained a Lutheran throughout her lifetime.

14 *Great Soviet Encyclopedia*, trans. of 3rd edition (1973), vol. 11, 18.

15 Patrick L. Alston, *Education and the State in Tsarist Russia* (1969), 229-30.

16 Keller file, 14.

17 R. Reusch, "Mein Lebenslauf," 2.

18 The "longest Russian structure" is claimed by St. Petersburg University for its Hall of the Twelve Colleagues, a structure built by order of Peter I.

19 In June 1996 the Cadet Corps was being used as an army base for the war in Chechnya. The structure was in disrepair. The parquet flooring had buckled and the paint was peeling; the Romanov portrait was long gone, replaced with a relief of Lenin — which had recently been pulled from the wall; the wrought-iron balustrade still bore heavy black circles of steel with red stars. The chapel had been torn down long ago, and trees now grew tall around the perimeter of the parade ground, which was partially filled with physical training equipment. Essentially, however, the structure still looked as it did a century ago.

20 *Terski Kalendar*, 156.

21 Allan K. Wildman notes that by 1913 only 43 percent of Russia's military academy graduates had entered as hereditary nobles — *The End of the Russian Imperial Army* (1980), 22-23.

22 *Terski Kalendar*, 156.

23 Anatoly Isaenko, History Faculty, State University of Northern Osetia; from the author's notes of an interview, 21 June 1996.

24 John Shelton Curtiss, *The Russian Army Under Nicholas I* (1965), 180.

25 Vladimir Bolgov, Ataman, Vladikavkaz Terek Cossacks, from the author's notes of an interview, 20 June 1996.

26 *The Modern Encyclopedia of Russian and Soviet History*, vol. 6 (1978), 88.

27 However, it was more difficult for gymnasium graduates to succeed because former cadets and some academy instructors regarded them as "youngsters from the railroad station," a phrase which put them in the same class as beggar urchins. "I was one of those," said Vladimir Littauer, a Hussar in the Imperial Cavalry, "and there were not many of us." Hazing of new candidates could be extremely cruel. Vladimir Littauer, *Russian Hussar: A Story of the Imperial Cavalry, 1911-1920* (1993), 11-12.

28 R. Reusch, "From Cavalry to Calvary," speech notes ca. 1965, p. 1, GACA.

29 P. A. Polovtsoff, *Glory and Downfall: Reminiscences of a Russian General Staff Officer* (1935), 3-4.

30 R. Reusch, "Outline to my speech to N. St. Paul's High School" (circa 1970), 1, GACA.

31 Col. Yerzhan Yusupov, retired, from notes of an interview, 27 June 1996. Yusupov is a member of the board of the St. Petersburg branch of the Union of Suvorov Academy Alumni.

32 R. Reusch, "Speech, Fort Snelling," 12 May 1970, GACA.

33 R. Reusch, "Mein Lebenslauf," 1-2.

34 Gymnasium transcript, R. Reusch file (2100-1-13219), ESHA.

35 Sergei Ivanovich Ruseen, Director of School No. 5, Vladikavkaz, from the author's notes of an interview, 22 June 1996.

36 Yakhontoff, 36.

37 Martin Gilbert, "The Socialist Revolutionaries 1902-1922," *Atlas of Russian History* (1972), 72.

38 *Great Soviet Encyclopedia*, vol. 23, 395.

39 Alan Moorhead, *The Russian Revolution* (1958), 53.

40 Wildman, 63.

41 Document No. 120, "Doseneniia Hachalneka Terckovo Oblastastnovo," 6 February 1905, Betosva and Beryokova, 142-43.

42 Cited by Abraham Ascher in *The Revolution of 1905: Authority Restored* (1992), 9. Ascher describes a most detailed and grim picture of this period.

43 P. A. Polovtsoff, *Glory and Downfall* (1935), 79.

44 Bruce W. Menning, *Bayonets Before Bullets: The Imperial Russian Army, 1861-1914* (1992), 219, 216.

45 Assessment by Rick Kolath, Duluth, Minnesota, a mountaineer.

46 R. Reusch, untitled, undated speech notes, ca. 1960, GACA.

47 *Great Soviet Encyclopedia*, vol. 23, 395. According to Professor Kusov, Kirov remained in Vladikavkaz until 1921. The Bolshevik mountain climber became head of the Leningrad Communist Party and was assassinated in 1934, perhaps by order of Stalin who regarded him as a competitor.

48 Kusov, interview.

49 Aurelia Reusch, interview.

50 Yakhontoff, 24.

51 Document 82, "Iis Pesma A. P. Chekova o Prebvanii v g. Vladekavkazye," Betosva and Beryokova, 106.

52 According to a discredited legend, when Princess Tamara couldn't find a suitable husband she invited knights, potential candidates, one after the other, to spend a night with her at her castle, "Tamara's Temple." She exhausted them to death, and in the morning threw the lifeless knights from her window into the Terek River below.

53 R. Reusch, untitled, undated speech notes, GACA.
54 Negley Farson, *The Lost World of the Caucasus* (1958), 23-24. August von Haxthausen, who toured Russia in 1848, mentioned the Würtemberg Lutherans who had come to witness millennial Mt. Ararat events. — *Studies on the Interior of Russia* (1975), 155.
55 Ranald MacDonell, *And Nothing Long* (1938), 108.
56 R. Reusch, unpublished manuscript, "Let These Stones Speak," undated, GACA.
57 Blanch, 102.
58 Fil' Hryhorji, "Religion and the Russian Army in the 19th Century," *War and Society in the Nineteenth Century Russian Empire*, ed. by J. G Purves and D. A. West (1972), 34.
59 Fil' Hryhorji, 27-29.
60 Prince A. Lobanov-Rostovsky, *Reminiscence of War and Revolution in Russia*, 1913-1920 (1935), 31.
61 George P. Aberle, Msgr., *From the Steppes to the Prairies* (1963), 67.
62 Fil' Hryhorji, 27-28.
63 Littauer 34.
64 Keller file, 30.
65 Ernst Jäschke, letter to the author, 25 August 1995, 3. Missionary Jäschke left Germany for Tanganyika Territory in 1936 and while learning Kiswahili lived in a house next to the Reusches.
66 R. Reusch, "Speech, Fort Snelling," 12 May 1970, GACA.
67 R. Reusch, "Outline of my speech to N. St. Paul High School," ca. 1970, GACA.
68 R. Reusch, "Biographical Data," Augustana Lutheran Church, 12 January 1949, 4, AELCA.
69 R. Reusch, letter to Rev. Koski, undated, GACA. He made the same claim in his "Biographical Data" sheet for the Augustana Lutheran Church, 1949, AELCA.
70 Hugh Seton-Watson, *The Russian Empire, 1801-1917* (1967), 646.
71 R. Reusch, "Memories of an old Cossack Officer," manuscript of a speech prepared for North Branch (Minnesota) Education Association, ca. 1970, GACA.
72 Dan L. Thrapp, "Missionary Tells of Fabulous Feats," *Los Angeles Times*, 27 June 1954, sec. 1-A, 10.
73 N. V. Tcharykov, *Glimpses of High Politics: Through War and Peace, 1855-1929 (1931)*, 179.
74 R. Reusch, "Ich lebte unter Mohammedanern," no. 26 in the series, *Auf den Straßen der Welt* (Evangelischer Missionsverlag, Stuttgart, 1954), 2, GACA.
75 R. Reusch, "From the Cavalry to Calvary," GACA.
76 Cited by Edward G. Browne, *The Persian Revolution* (1910), 256-68. The speech, given on October 11, 1908, was translated from a report of the speech that appeared in a Turkish newspaper, 11 November 1908.
77 Lothrop Stoddard, "How Persia Died: A Coroner's Inquest," *The Century*, vol. 99, no. 3 (January, 1920), 318.
78 Percy Sykes, *A History of Persia*, Vol. II (1930), 415-20.
79 Liakhov later rose to the rank of major general during the civil war in General Denikin's White army and fought against the Reds in the northern Caucasus. In 1919 he was appointed commander of 10,000 troops in the Terek-Daghestan region where 25,000 Whites faced 70,000 Reds, but his leadership was characterized as "incapable" and "tactless." In 1919 General Denikin stripped him

of command because of "sordid extortion schemes" and atrocities committed by his personal bodyguard. Later that year an unknown agent assassinated Liakhov. — *The Modern Encyclopedia of Russian and Soviet History*, vol. 19, 236; and Wildman, 127.

80   R. Reusch, "Biographical Data" (1960), Augustana Lutheran Church, 1, AELCA.

81   R. Reusch, sermon notes circa 1954, GACA.

82   Roger Munson, Bishop, from the author's transcript of an audio taped interview, 23 June 1994.

83   R. Reusch, "Mein Lebenslauf," 2 and 3.

84   A. N. Kuropatkin, *The Russian Army and the Japanese War*, vol. 1 (1909), 58.

85   Isaenko, interview.

86   Betty Anderson, interview. Dr. Reusch also told this story to a reporter. —Donna Kavanaugh, "Novel-like Interview with Church Worker Is Concluded," pt. 2, *Ramsey County Review* (26 May 1965), 1.

87   R. Reusch, "Mein Lebenslauf," 2.

88   R. Reusch, "'The Heavenly Bell," a manuscript for a speech delivered to a Minnesota Luther League group in the 1950s, 6, GACA.

89   R. Reusch, one of several often repeated explanations explaining his decision to leave the military.

90   R. Reusch, "Biographical Data (1949), 1, GACA, and gymnasium transcript.

91   R. Reusch, "Mein Lebenslauf," 2.

92   "When I was in the old days an officer of His Majesty's bodyguard, and when I used to come every year to choose young Cossacks to serve in the Emperor's own escort," said a Terek Cossack colonel, "in all the villages I was greeted most cordially; every family wanted to have one of its members in the Imperial Household squadrons, everybody was anxious to please me, and very often I was even offered bribes." — P. A. Polovtsoff, *Glory and Downfall: Reminiscences of a Russian General Staff Officer* (1935), 329.

93   R. Reusch, "Mein Lebenslauf, 2.

94   R. Reusch noted these details in notes prepared for various lectures, speeches and sermons, GACA.

95   Alston, 200.

96   Document 3, Richard Reusch file (2100-1-13219), ESHA.

97   Betosva and Beryokova, "Kronika," 986-87.

98   Lewis Stanton Palen, *White Devil of the Black Sea* (1924), 9-10.

99   The author's recollection of his conversation with Dr. Reusch, Gustavus Adolphus College, fall semester, 1960.

Richard Gustavovich begins his studies at Dorpat University in 1911.

Chapter Four

FROM STUDENT TO PROFESSOR
Dorpat (Tartu), Estonia, 1911-1917

*There was no malice in him. He was young, sincere, and passionate in his
convictions as the best Russian students always were.*

— Aleksandr Solzhenitsyn[1]

The former junior officer left Vladikavkaz at the end of July 1911 for the university town of
Dorpat. Richard Gustavovich did not intend to prepare for ordination as a Lutheran cleric but
rather to study theology, ancient history, archeology and Middle Eastern (Oriental) languages.

The young man changed trains several times along the route from Vladikavkaz in the south to
Dorpat in the north: first at Rostov, and then perhaps through Voronezh, Kursk, Orel, Bryansk,
Smolensk and Vitebsk to the Russian medieval town of Pskov, its golden monastery and church
spires gleaming in the sun.[2] As the train proceeded toward Dorpat, he looked out on a flat
landscape of forests, small farms and occasional estates and manor houses owned by powerful Baltic German barons. The Russian province of Livonia (a part of which is now Estonia)
was as different from the Caucasus as Vladikavkaz was from Baratayevka. An English diplomat
stationed in the Baltic came to appreciate the muted but lovely hues, Estonia's "dun stubbles,
pale grasses and grey willows; its grey-green corn touched delicately by the passing wind as by the
shadow of passing smoke; the airy lightness of its birch trees, standing among dark pines."[3]

As the train steamed into town from the south, the passenger from the Caucasus could
not have but noticed the twin spires of St. Petri Evangelical Lutheran Church across the
Embach (Emajõgi) River and the single spire of the medieval St. Johannes Church in the
town center. Carrying his one suitcase, he walked out of the small depot and left behind the
acrid smell of locomotive steam and smoke that permeated the rail yard. On the other side of the
park that fronted the station he passed comfortable homes that appeared more German than
Russian in design. He walked up present-day Lossi Street under Devil's Bridge, a memorial
to Tsar Alexander I who in 1802 reopened the university founded by Sweden's Gustavus II
Adolphus in 1632. On Domberg Hill he paused to look at a eighteenth century Swedish
cannon left behind after the Great Northern War (1701-21), and walked around the ruin of
the thirteenth-century Cathedral of Saints Peter and Paul. The historical lore alone must have
fascinated him as he made his way along the cobblestone street down the hill toward the old
European town square. The main university building was a block to the left.

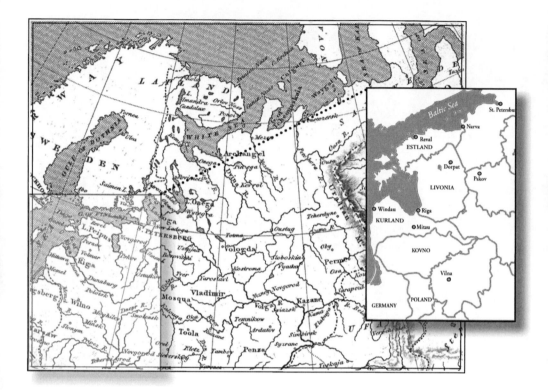

THE RUSSIAN BALTIC PROVINCES, 1809-1917

German Livonian Knights seized the Baltic territory in the 13th century, named it Livonia and made Riga its capital. The northern part of Livonia became the Russian province of Estland with Reval (Tallinn) its capital; the center part the province, Livonia, included the cities of Riga and Dorpat (Yuriev, then Tartu); and the southern province, Kurland. The borders of the modern states of Estonia and Latvia were drawn after the First World War.

Dorpat (or DERPT, Russian *Jurjev*), a town in the Russian province of Livonia, on the Embach, here crossed by a fine granite bridge 165 miles (247 by rail) SW. of St. Petersburg. . . . Dorpat was a Hanse town in the 14th and 15th centuries, and until 1704 was alternately captured by Swedes, Poles, and finally Russians. It possesses large printing establishments, breweries, and manufactories of cigars, tiles, and pianofortes. Pop. 44,000 — 80 per cent. German.

— *Chambers's Concise Gazetteer of the World (1914)*[4]

Native Estonians had named their settlement Tarbatu. But invading thirteenth century German Livonian Knights and "Brothers of the Sword," a religious order after the manner of the Teutonic Knights, renamed it Dorpat, and thus it was known for more than 600 years.[5] In 1893 Tsar Alexander III gave the town a Russian name, Yuriev, and therefore Dorpat University became the Imperial University of Yuriev. Residents of German ancestry, however, ignored the imperial attempt to russify their town.[6]

According to a Russian naval officer who studied at the University in 1911, nostalgic ethnic German Balts referred to Dorpat as the "Baltic Heidelberg," an outpost of Germanic culture in the Russian Empire. Nevertheless, professors dispatched from Imperial Germany to teach at Dorpat were said to keep "painstaking diaries of their adventures as if they were going to Borneo." The Baltic Germans "lorded it over the Estonians," said the officer, and "kept itself very much to itself as far as we [Russians] were concerned."[7]

On September 14, 1911, Richard Gustavovich presented himself to the University bursar, paid the fee of twenty-five rubles, and was registered as student No. 23985.[8] Professor Alexander von Bulmerincq,[9] who had urged Gustav Ivanovich to send his son to Dorpat, recommended the penniless student to Baron Reinhold and Baroness Anna von Liphart, who were looking for a live-in tutor to work with their five children. And so Richard Gustavovich set out for an interview at the Rathshof Estate at the northeastern edge of town.

The attachment *von* denotes a surname of Prussian military origin. Some of the old Prussian families had assimilated into the Russian Imperial establishment, and a few had converted to Orthodoxy.[10] Baron von Liphart raised horses for the Russian Imperial cavalry, but he remained a faithful Lutheran layman. Richard Gustavovich walked across the bridge over the Embach River, passed the Russian Orthodox Church of St. George on his right, proceeded up the hill past St. Petri Lutheran Church along the Narva Road, and then entered the forest of the Rathshof estate.

Excerpts from "The Junkers of the Baltic Country,"
The Living Age (1919)

The Baltic baron is self-confident and proud of his achievements. They are industrious farmers and, for the most part, finely educated men. The refining influence of centuries of old tradition is apparent in their families, and makes intercourse with them a source of constantly renewed pleasure and satisfaction.

The moment one crosses the threshold he finds himself in the midst of an agreeable, liberal, comfortable home life. The lady of the house greets the visitor, and we enter a large living room whose walls are adorned with pictures, with well-selected engravings and paintings. The great room is furnished as were the houses of the wealthier middle classes in Germany a half century ago. Nothing is ornate or brilliant; everything is comfortable and in good taste. The visitor converses and smokes the inevitable cigarette. The whole family joins in the circle, and almost immediately the stranger becomes acquainted with every member. Their circle of interests is remarkably wide.

They appreciate all the motives and all the interests that play a part of the [Russian] Empire. No manor house is without its library, composed mainly of German works. These are carefully selected and range from the classic writers to the latest best seller.

The conversation never lags. An invitation to take a walk in the park interrupts a discussion of Tishbein's Goethe. We stroll out to the stables. The cattle are at pasture, but the horses are there. Among these horse-breeding landlords good riders are universal. Both ladies and gentlemen ride until old age, the ladies riding astride like the men with great poise and dash.

We return for the evening meal, at which we gather around a long table presided over by the master of the house. We discover that our hosts have been wide travelers, and they bring back with them to the retirement of their manor houses and their parsonages material for thought and discussion during the long winter evening.[11]

Betty Anderson

The Rathshof and grounds, which belonged to the von Liphart family at the edge of Tartu.

The Rathshof was not the typical manor house that graced most Baltic German estates. The original sixteenth-century structure had evolved into a palatial mansion, remodeled and expanded in the French style popular in the late eighteenth century, and again in the Italianate style preferred in the mid-nineteenth century.[12] Five generations of wealthy, scholarly, musical and artistic von Lipharts had assembled the greatest private art collection in the province, and guests strolled through galleries hung with 200 works of art: paintings by Aretino, del Garbo, Tintoretto, van Eyck and van Dyck; reliefs by Michelangelo and Donatello; and special collections of glass and antiques.[13] The von Lipharts loved music, especially the works of Mahler and Zeichner, and often invited friends for private concerts. Unfortunately, Richard Gustavovich was tone-deaf.

Perhaps the genial Baron led his young guest to the library. The long corridor led through doorway after doorway, room after room, more modest in scale but similar in design to the great palaces of Europe and Russia. Along the way the Baron briefly noted portraits of his father and uncle, Reinhold Wilhelm and Carl Heinrich. Both were Dorpat University graduates, the former in philosophy and the latter in medicine.[14] The Baron's wife, Anna Mathild Mannteuffell, was born at Castle Talkhof near Libau (Liepaja, Latvia) to a powerful German Baltic family of long service to the Russian Empire.[15] If the Baron and Baroness expected to meet a bright but crude bumpkin from a Volga colony, they were pleasantly surprised when the former junior officer clicked his heels and kissed the Baroness's hand with courtly élan.

Richard Gustavovich was introduced to the von Liphart children: Reinhold, Paul, Karl, Gotthard and little Arved. The parents were pleased that the candidate interacted so easily with their children. And so a cultured German Baltic family of Russian nobility — devoted to literature, art and music — welcomed the russified Richard Gustavovich into their home.

Most of the Baltic barons and their offspring counted Dorpat University as their *Alma Mater* where, as Konstantine Benckendorff recalled, they had joined fraternities and continued the Prussian tradition of "beer feasts and duels resulting in faces marked for life by the stitches of old cuts."[16] Richard Gustavovich witnessed fifteen such duels during his undergraduate years.[17] A Russian student sourly noted that the Baltic German who tutored one of his Russian classmates "continuously wore a typical German student cap with the colors of some student corporation [fraternity] from within the German empire."[18] Those fraternity caps were yet another manifestation of Germanic *kultur,* behaviors that irritated Russians and native Estonians alike.

However, Richard Gustavovich entered the University at a time when Germanic influence was in decline. Of more than 5,000 students enrolled, German Balts numbered 524 and Slavic Russians 1,854. The majority, 2,378, comprised "foreigners," including Armenians, Georgians and students from the Muslim regions of the Empire. Fewer than 400 native Estonians studied at the institution.[19] Non-Russians and anti-monarchists were more readily admitted at Dorpat than anywhere else in Russia because of the institution's administrative autonomy and relatively liberal atmosphere.[20] In 1907 66 percent were listed as members of leftist political organizations, such as anarchists, Social Democrats, and Social Revolutionaries. Eighty-three percent of the students received state scholarships.[21]

The theology faculty, under the supervision of the Riga Evangelical Lutheran Konsistorium, had earned doctorates at such universities as Aberdeen, Erlangen, Kiel, Riga and Uppsala, and prepared their students for careers either as pastors or scholars. Congregations throughout the eleven time zones of the Empire — from Riga in the west to Vladivostok in the east, and from Krasnoyarsk in the north to Tashkent in the south — depended on this one seminary for their clergy.

Rationalists dominated the faculty when the University was reopened in 1802. Pietists briefly replaced the rationalists, but were themselves supplanted in 1850 by orthodox Lutheran professors, the orientation that prevailed until the seminary was closed in 1918.[22] When Richard Gustavovich arrived in 1911 the theology faculty attracted students in number second only to medicine; however, by 1915 the law and engineering faculties drew more students than either medicine or theology.[23]

The Dorpat faculty rejected modern biblical criticism, and two professors in particular influenced Reusch's perspective. According to Professor Rudolf Kittel, "The Prophets are HIS messengers! Your duty is to study the background & language, and to explain this message as clearly] as possible, not to criticize it!" And Professor Theodore Zahn: "My brother, the New Testament is the Proclamation of God's amnesty for all sinners! On bended knee & with folded hands study this Amnesty-message. Don't criticize it but try to understand it, and then proclaim its contents." Said Dr. Reusch,

> That made sense to me, for I must confess that I always had the feeling that the Wellhausens, Prokashes, Gunkels, Gressmanns or Strauss, Feuerbach, Bauer, etc. have too much superfluous brains and not enough common sense! "Let the stones speak, my brother, if the people are silent!" Those were [Zahn's] last words. And the stones of the excavations speak a powerful language in favour of the majestic WORD of GOD.[24]

As a gymnasium student, Richard graduated first in his class, but at the University he completed the first year with an unsatisfactory grade of 2 in Greek, 4s in Latin and Hebrew, and a 4 and 5 in philosophy. He successfully adapted by the second year, however, earning 5s in Old and New Testament Exegesis, Old and New Testament History and his scholarly papers, and boosting his evaluation in Greek to a passing grade of 3.[25]

The tercentenary of Romanov rule was celebrated in 1913. That autumn Emil Gustavovich joined his elder brother at the University seminary to study in a series of courses that led to ordination.[26] Richard focused his studies on ancient and Middle Eastern languages: Monday through Saturday, as well as Sunday afternoon, he went for tutorials at the home of Professor and Mrs. von Bulmerincq. In their comfortable living room he was drilled in the vocabulary of several languages simultaneously — bread and *brot; chlyeb* and *sepik; churek* and *lavash, lekhem* and *dzul, puri* and *panis*. Mentor and student relaxed between intensive sessions by listening to classical music, including Wagner. "The Frau Professorina," Dr. Reusch recalled, "thought the Master and his disciple are both a little crazy."[27]

Von Bulmerincq found in Reusch the qualities he sought in a successor. The two men traveled to academic conferences in Leipzig, and to Berlin for a series of lectures by Dr. Gressmann, the Old Testament scholar, and were appalled to hear the distinguished professor declare that the Holy Scriptures were merely a collection of legends and myths — for example, the story of Moses striking a rock and fresh water gushing forth.[28] Von Bulmerincq directed Richard's studies in Old Testament and Islamic history, and through translating and memorizing sections of the Koran, Richard mastered the Arabic language. He studied Aramaic with Professor Seesemann, New Testament with Professor Dr. Graß, historical theology with Professor Kvacala, systematic theology with Professor Jürgensohn, and practical theology with Professor Traugott Hahn.

But the pleasant and stimulating life at the University and the von Liphart estate came to an abrupt end in August 1914.

THE WORLD GOES TO WAR

World conflagration was the last thing on the mind of Stella Arbinina, the Baroness Meyendorff, when she arranged a "motor reliability trial" to begin at Pskov on July 27, 1914. The route would take the party through the provinces of Vitebsk, Livonia and Kurland, ending in the city of Riga. She was especially pleased when the Tsar's first cousin, Grand Duke Kyril Vladimirovitch and his wife, Grand Duchess Victoria Feodorovna, agreed to take part.

"It was," said the Baroness, "a delightful trip in every respect, and if anyone had prophesied that we were within a week of the declaration of the most terrible war in history, he would have been considered raving mad." Some in the party were uneasy as they drove their luxury automobiles from one palatial estate to another. Archduke Franz Ferdinand and his wife had been assassinated in Sarajevo that June, and the Austro-Hungarian Empire subsequently declared war on Serbia. "Russia has done enough for these small Slav countries as it is," Grand Duke Kyril complained to the Baroness. "We never get any gratitude for it and only a lot of unpleasantness every time."[29]

The aristocrats arrived in Riga on July 31, 1914 where they heard the news of Russia's mobilization, which, said Baroness Meyendorff, "damped our spirits considerably." The next evening, August 1st, everyone gathered at the Majorenhof Resort outside of Riga for a farewell banquet. Toward the end of dinner, just before the dancing was to begin, Baron Palen brought the bad news: Germany had declared war on Russia.

Within days the lines were drawn: the Austro-Hungarian and German empires versus France and the empires of Russia and Great Britain. The *Atlantic Monthly* attributed these words to a wounded Russian soldier:

> By wish of Wilhelm, by the order of Antichrist, war has been let loose over the world. War has eaten the corn in the land, and war has cut down the nations by their roots. From the beginning of time there has been nothing like it. War is more dreadful than thunder, it is sharper than lightening, and is not more merciful than the wrath of God.[30]

When the First World War came to an end four years later, the autocrats had been deposed — Emperor Franz-Joseph, Emperor Wilhelm II, and Tsar Nicholas II. Nine *million* soldiers died. "The world of 1914, as we see it now," wrote Herbert Gibbons seven years later, "reminds us of Humpty-Dumpty."[31]

In the autumn of 1914 Richard Gustavovich watched a regiment of Terek from the First Corps based in St. Petersburg pass through Dorpat on their way to the front. Overcome by patriotism and sense of duty, he went in search of von Bulmerincq to announce his intention to leave the University and rejoin his regiment. He could not continue at the University, not when his regiment was marching to war.

Von Bulmerincq reminded the 23-year-old that a student of theology who enlisted or rejoined a regiment was not permitted to later resume theological studies. And what about his father's and grandfather's wishes? What about Pastors Bonvitch and Aksim, whose prayers have followed him to this place?

The professor went on to cite a third factor, perhaps more compelling than the other two. When Germany invaded Russia in August 1914 vehement anti-German emotions surged through the Russian Empire. The German Embassy on St. Isaac's Square in St. Petersburg was attacked by a mob and plundered, the statues of powerful Teutonic horses over the portico heaved to the sidewalk below. Windows of shops owned by German Russians were smashed, their buildings put to the torch. Fearing for the future of the German Lutheran theology faculty in the months ahead, von Bulmerincq asked his protégé to stand ready to take his place should senior German professors be forced into exile.

Richard Gustavovich reluctantly submitted to his mentor's argument, and soon learned that von Bulmerincq's concern was justified. In the weeks and months that followed, the performance of works by Bach, Brahms and Beethoven were prohibited in Russia. The Holy Synod of the Russian Orthodox Church banned Christmas trees as a German artifact, and the Tsar changed the name of the capital from the Germanic St. Petersburg to the more Slavic Petrograd. "People with German names were hunted down, and some were lynched," said a German Russian whose grandfather quickly arranged to change the family name from Schumacher to Shoumatoff.[32] In Moscow a mob gathered outside the Orthodox Convent of Mary and Martha and hurled stones at the abbess, Grand Duchess Elizabeth, sister of the German-born Tsarina. "Away with the German woman!" they chanted.[33]

German troops beat back the initial Russian advance and marched onto Russian soil. In February 1915, those Baltic German barons, pastors and professors whose loyalty was suspect — including von Bulmerincq — were arrested and exiled to Siberia.[34] Because of his military service as a Terek Cossack, Reusch was left to continue his academic work, and at the end of the year he was nominated to replace his mentor as professor of Oriental languages. One year later, in December 1916, Reusch was appointed to teach Oriental languages.[35]

The Baltic Lutheran Church lost many of its clergy, and therefore, as he was to do so many times throughout his lifetime, Professor Reusch felt compelled to serve where he was most needed. Although it was not his original intention, because of the crisis he agreed to prepare for ordination. The Riga Konsistorium quickly assigned him to begin his probationary year under the direction of Pastor Wittrock at St. Johannes Church in Dorpat.[36] In January 1916 he completed his course work for the *kandidat* degree, received an excellent review of his scientific paper on the Old Testament prophet Hosea, and passed his exams with honors.

Meanwhile, Adjunct Pastor Reusch took responsibility for working with the children of the parish and directing refugee relief while simultaneously completing his dissertation, "The Poetic Testament of King David." Professor von Bulmerincq later remarked that the work would have been published had it not been for the exigencies of the war.[37] Reusch was awarded the *Kandidata Bogoslaviya* Diploma, No. 152, on April 1, 1916.[38]

Machinery of modern warfare was unleashed during the second year of the war and plunged Europe into unparalleled misery, destruction and death. Americans wanted nothing whatsoever to do with the war in Europe. In Russia, meanwhile, the front stretched from present-day Latvia all the way south into Romania. Under incompetent leadership, ill-prepared and poorly equipped Russian troops were sometimes sent into battle without guns, ammunition, food or medical support. Therefore, it is not surprising that one-and-a-half million Russian soldiers deserted in 1916, forming gangs and terrorizing the countryside as they did what had to be done in order to get home. Anti-monarchists and well-organized Bolsheviks seeded discontent and urged the draftees on both sides of the front to throw off their yokes and join together to form an international dictatorship of the proletariat.

Britain and France, and later the United States, did everything possible to keep Russia in the war as a means of diverting pressure from the Western Front. Meanwhile, incompetent Russian generals and ministers dithered as living conditions in the faltering Empire became intolerable. One-half of all Russian farmers had been drafted by the spring of 1916, and agricultural production sharply declined as a result. The foundering Petrograd government requisitioned existing farm commodities, and the effect was a food crisis and lack of fuel on the home front that led to starvation, cold, and disease. The adjunct pastor at St. Johannes alternately preached to frightened and miserable congregations at all three Lutheran congregations in Dorpat: St. Johannes, University Church and St. Petri, which included both German and Estonian members.

Dr. Reusch always wrote or typed his sermons, sometimes producing two or three drafts before he was satisfied with wording, phrasing and cadence. The earliest surviving manuscript is no exception, and it also models the form that distinguishes his homiletic style: a text from Holy Scripture, exposition of a contemporary issue or ancient story, the solution illuminated by the text, and concluding with an evangelical appeal. On Sunday morning, July 16, 1916, Richard Gustavovich ascended the steps of the pulpit at St. Johannes Church, taking his text from Romans, Chapter 10: "The scripture says, 'He who believes in God will not be put to shame.'"

He began by telling a story about the sea captain whose ship was caught in a storm within sight of a French port. The captain considered making an attempt to gain the safety of the harbor, but the entryway was narrow, and the slightest miscalculation or shift in wind would send his vessel onto the rocks. And so he decided to drop anchor and ride out the storm. Immediately, however, the harbormaster signaled him to make the attempt. It did not make sense to the captain, but he did as he was told. The harbormaster later explained that had the captain not obeyed, the ship would have been lost because the seabed would not have held the anchor. Reusch continued,

> Jesus is the good ground which holds our anchors. And so in these days, terror and doubt appear like a frightful and evil ghost, and you feel as if you will perish despite your trust in God. But if in our desperation we freeze under the hand of the gentle Lord and the end comes differently than we expected, our fear only reveals our small-mindedness. Rather, shouldn't we conclude that the Lord does not let anyone perish, that He will put a crown on a life-long work in the moment of dying?

After all, He Himself is crowned with thorns. And with His mild face looking upon us, with His hands he places the crown of life on our heads and will walk with us through the valley of death. So we say with the Psalmist, "Though I walk through the valley of the shadow of death, I am not afraid, for You are with me; Thy rod and Thy staff comfort me."

That gives us courage; that, and the huge cloud of witnesses who have gone before us give us courage because they show us the way. They tell us that it is always worthwhile to put our trust in Him because He does what he promised: whosoever believes in Him will not perish.

Oh, my Christian neighbor, try it again with this thing that hurts you the most, with your sin; turn yourself to the Messiah who died for you. Turn towards Him and ask for forgiveness and help so you can be rescued, that you might know this Jesus who is alive and wants to help you. Then you will have the strength to throw out your anchor for the last time because you'll happily know that you've found the ground that holds your anchor: nowhere else than in Jesus' wounds! Before the beginning of the world, He is the ground that is unmovable. When earth and heaven pass away, this is the eternal truth that overcomes our fear.

Amen.[39]

Richard's brother, Emil, was ordained in December 1916,[40] the month that Rasputin was assassinated in Petrograd. Richard completed his probationary year in January 1917, and he continued to supervise religious education and refugee relief. His ordination was scheduled for Easter Sunday, April 22, 1917.

The winter of 1916-17 brought exceedingly cold temperatures and heavy snowfalls, which brought agony to soldiers in the trenches as well as their families at home. Typhus and cholera epidemics took a terrible toll on the frontlines as well in cities and villages behind the lines. By February 1917 food and fuel had all but disappeared in Petrograd. To die in the streets from starvation or from Cossack bullets, what difference did it make? The same mobs who had cheered the Tsar in 1914 now threatened to depose him. The critical moment came in early March when the starving masses refused police orders to clear the streets and the Cossack Guard was ordered to fire on the people. This time, however, the elite soldiers refused — and turned on their own officers. So it was that after abdicating his imperial power, Nicholas Alexandrovich Romanov and his family were placed under house arrest at the Alexander Palace not far from Petrograd.

Law and order all but disappeared as a "provisional" government lurched from crisis to crisis. The suffering Lutheran congregations in Dorpat could no longer support their clergy and parish staff, and so Baron von Liphart once again was pleased to provide room and board for Pastor Reusch.[41]

Richard Gustavovich prepared for ordination as anarchy spread through the trenches and behind the barricades. He was in his twenty-fifth year, but already the essential nature of his character was clearly evident: He was loyal, disciplined, intelligent, adaptable, an empathetic teacher, and a pastor firmly grounded in the Evangelical Lutheran tradition. In the following months, however, his character would be put to the test in ways that bring to mind the words of William Bell:

I think he had his dream without regretting,

but tonight all men are carried on a freezing stream

or wander weeping in the cold moonlight.[42]

Aurelia Reusch

The Gustav Ivanovich Reusch Family gathers one year before the war began, on August 14, 1913, for Grandmother Reusch's funeral. Richard never again saw his family. From left to right: Albert, Papa, Richard, Vallie, Olga, Mama, Emma, Marie, Aurelia, Erich and Emil.

CHAPTER 4

1 Aleksandr Solzhenitsyn, *August 1914: Knot I*, trans. by H. T. Willetts (New York: Farrar Straus and Giroux, 1989), 123-24.
2 Speculative route derived from Map 12, "Railways in European Russia up to 1917," Hugh Seton-Watson, *The Russian Empire, 1801-1917* (1967), 781-82.
3 Sir Stephen Tallents, *Man and Boy* (1943), 275.
4 *Chambers's Concise Gazetteer of the World* (1914), 230.
5 "Those Dangerous Baltic provinces," *The Literary Digest* (2 March 1918), 21.
6 Arthur Ruhl, *New Masters of the Baltic* (1921), 115. After securing independence from German influence and Russian control in 1919, the Estonians changed the name of the city and university to Tartu.
7 Gregory P. Tschebotarioff, *Russia My Native Land* (1964), 21-22, 32-33.
8 Document 1, Richard Reusch file (2100-1-13219), ESHA.
9 Professor von Bulmerincq (1868-1938) was a published scholar in Old Testament studies, especially the prophets Jeremiah and Malachai. He also taught Arabic, and his co-authored work on Arabic folk literature, *Kitan al-Hikayatal-aj ibah wa-al-akhbar al-gharibah*, was posthumously published in 1956. The professor became Reusch's mentor, and guided his studies in Old Testament and Arabic.
10 Michael Glenny and Norman Stone, editors, in note 1, chap. 2, *The Other Russia: The Experience of Exile* (1990), 445.
11 Excerpts from "The Junkers of the Baltic Country," *The Living Age* (11 January 1919), 80-82.
12 Hubertus Neuschäffer, *Schlösser und Herrenhäuser in Estland* (Heide: Verlag Hubertus Neuschäffer, Plön, 1993), 187.
13 Georg von Rauch, "Ein Baltischer Musenhof im Alten Livonia," in Erik Thomson's *Schloss Ratshof in Estland: vom musenhof zum nationalmuseum* (Lüneburg: Verlag Nordostdeutsches Kulturwerk, 1985), 21-22.
14 Document 5, Reinhold von Liphart file (402-2-15082); and document 2, Carl von Liphart file (402-2-15082), ESHA. It is interesting to note that both brothers earned higher grades in Russian philology than they did in German.
15 In 1919, a year after the Tsar and his family were murdered outside Ekaterinberg, Baron Mannteuffell led a *coup d'état* against the independent Latvian President Ulmanis in a vain attempt to regain power for the Baltic Germans. See Ernst von Salomon, *History of Political Violence: The Outlaws* (1931; Kraus Reprint, 1983), 79.
16 Konstantine Benckendorff, *Half a Life: The Reminiscences of a Russian Gentleman* (1954), 258-59.
17 R. Reusch, "Speech at Fort Snelling" notes, 12 May 1970, GACA.
18 Tschebotarioff, 21-22.
19 F. W. Pick, *The Baltic Nations* (1945), 51.
20 Ela Martis, "The Role of Tartu University in the National Movement," *National Movements in the Baltic Countries During the 19th Century* (1983), 324.
21 Paul J. Novgorotsev, "Universities and Higher Technical Schools," Part II, *Russian Schools and Universities in the World War*, eds. Paul Vinogradoff and Michael Florinsky (Yale University Press, 1929), 138, 141.
22 Tartu University Museum exhibit, historical outline of the Theology Faculty (Department), January, 1996.

23 Toivo Raun, *Estonia and the Estonians*, "Studies of Nationalities in the USSR Series" (1987), 94.

24 R. Reusch, notes for remarks in honor of Swedish Lutheran Bishop Anders Nygren at Gustavus Adolphus College, May, 1962, GACA.

25 Document 4, R. Reusch file (2100-1-13219), ESHA.

26 Documents, Emil Reusch file (22415-1-22416), ESHA.

27 R. Reusch, Nygren notes.

28 R. Reusch, Nygren notes.

29 The automobile trial is described by Baroness Meyendorff in her autobiography, *Through Terror to Freedom* (London, 1929), 10-18.

30 Madame Fedorchenko, "The Russian," *Atlantic Monthly*, vol. 123, no. 1 (January, 1919), 1-2. Although the passages were said to have been authentic statements, there is a similarity of style in all of them, which suggests that Madame Fedorchenko's article may have been created as part of the official U.S. propaganda campaign during the World War.

31 Herbert Adams Gibbons, "The International Whirlpool: The Baltic Sea Republics," *The Century*, vol. 101, no. 3 (January, 1921), 375.

32 Alex Shoumatoff, *Russian Blood* (1982), 118.

33 Greg King, *The Man Who Killed Rasputin* (1995), 116, 119.

34 "German Claims on Baltic Provinces," *New York Times Current History*, vol. 8 (October, 1918), 93.

35 Document 5, Richard Reusch file (2100-1-13219), ESHA.

36 R. Reusch, "Mein Lebenslauf," 4-5, AELML.

37 Alexander von Bulmerincq, letter recommending Reusch to the director of the Leipzig Mission, 17 December 1920, AELML.

38 Document 33, R. Reusch file (2100-1-13219), ESHA.

39 R. Reusch, sermon manuscript (in German), 3 July 1916, GACA.

40 Emil Reusch file (22415-1-22416), ESHA.

41 R. Reusch, "Mein Lebenslauf," 5.

42 Willam Bell, "Elegy XII," *The Faber Book of Twentieth Century Verse*, edited by John Heath-Stubbs and David Wright (1953), 65.

Betty Anderson

Richard Gustavovich Reusch was ordained on Easter Sunday, April 22, 1917, less than seven months before the Bolsheviks came to power in Russia.

REVOLUTION AND CIVIL WAR
The Baltic Region, 1917-1919

He that loveth not knoweth not God; for God is love.
— I John 4:8

Adjunct Pastor Reusch prepared his ordination sermon, his confession of faith, during the chaotic days of April 1917. Civic institutions had collapsed, the Tsar and his family were under house arrest, the Provisional Government now ruling in Petrograd was unable to bring order, and the desultory war dragged on. His studies of Old Testament prophets, particularly Hosea and Jeremiah, had led him to an analysis of the Gospel of St. John, the Apostle of love. "I gradually gained understanding of the other books of the New Testament," he explained, "and when I had to give a confession in my Ordination Sermon I had only one: 'God is Love.'"[1]

His ordination was scheduled for Easter Sunday, April 22. Wartime conditions did not permit his family, who had moved to Rostov-on-Don, to travel to Dorpat for his special day. The Provisional Government had released Siberian political exiles, and Reusch hoped that Professor von Bulmerincq would return in time.

Among the assembled faithful at St. Johannes that Easter Sunday were the von Lipharts and a handful of clergy and professors scattered through the diminished ranks of the congregation. After he received the laying-on of hands, the twenty-five-year-old pastor climbed the steps into the pulpit. He looked into the vast space of the nave to his left and right, raised his arms, and intoned the comforting and familiar words: "The mercy of Jesus Christ, the love of God, and the unity of the Holy Ghost be with us all. Amen." Then Pastor Reusch proceeded to read the text:

> Let us listen to the Word of God that we find written in John's First Letter, in the 4th chapter, verses 7-12: "Beloved, let us love one another: for love is of God; and everyone that loveth is begotten of God, and knoweth God. He that loveth not knoweth not God; for God is love. . . . Beloved, if God so loved us, we also ought to love one another."

He began his sermon by contrasting the ancient Greek concept of destiny with the God of the New Testament. The Greeks believed in a dark and mysterious power that ruled over the gods in the heavens and humankind on earth; Christians believe that the Ineffable is a "gentle and blissful power, or law, called Love, Eternal Love, the most important feature of our Almighty God." The congregation ought to welcome the message of the Apostle, he said, especially "in this time of poverty, selfishness, strife and discord on earth" when "it is especially important to strengthen our belief that God is love."

Pastor Reusch was certain of his thesis:

> And so today let us consider the following truth, that love is the basic law of the world: first, as it is written in heaven, God is love; second, as it is written on the cross, Christ is love; and third, so should it also be written in our hearts, because to be a Christian is to love.

He developed his three main points by citing only Holy Scripture and restating basic premises of Christian doctrine. He concluded,

> You cannot say that you believe in God, that you know Him, just because you know what He said. That does not make you a Christian. No, if you do not have love, you do not know God. . . .
>
> God lets the sun of his love rise above both good and evil, and lets the rain of his mercy fall upon the just and the unjust. It is written in the sky with starry letters and on earth upon the cross in the blood of the Son: God is love. . . .
>
> And therefore, every Christian shall bow his heart and fold his hands and pray, "Love, who suffered and died for me, Love, who has fought for eternal bliss; Love, I submit to You and want to be Yours forever."
>
> Amen.[2]

After serving one year under the supervision of Head pastor Wittrock at St. Johannes, the Riga Lutheran Konsistorium issued pastoral license No. 1979 (in the Russian language) to Gustav Otto Richard Gustavovich Reusch on April 27, 1917.[3] At various times during the next year he served at all three Lutheran churches in Dorpat. He was especially concerned for the children's welfare and often gave a brief Sunday morning sermon prepared just for them.

The end of time seemed near, and the birth of a child brought both joy and anxiety. But in time of war, famine, pestilence and political upheaval, the ritual of Holy Baptism brought a measure of comfort and hope.

According to parish records, Pastor Reusch officiated at the baptism of a baby boy, Evald Treulob, at St. Johannes on March 18, 1917. (Two years later, on April 16, 1919, little Evald died at Mitau, Latvia, during the last days of the civil war.)[4]

Giesela Margarete Schnakenburg was born at two o'clock on the morning of April 1, 1918. A month later, Pastor Reusch went to the parents' home to baptize little Giesela in the name of the Father, Son and Holy Ghost.

At eleven o'clock on the morning of April 27, 1917, Leo Eugene Rattenberg came into the world, and on May 27 Pastor Reusch baptized him in the sacristy of St. Johannes.[5]

The last recorded baptism that Reusch conducted was for George Lipp, born in the city of Novgorod at eight o'clock in the morning, December 21, 1916. Pastor Reusch baptized the five-month old child on May 31, 1917 in a house in Dorpat where George's refugee parents had found shelter.[6]

REVOLUTION

In April 1917 the Provisional Government in Petrograd appointed a native Balt as commissioner of the new autonomous province of Estonia, and in May the people elected their first National Council. The revolutionaries, however, regarded those developments as a reactionary attempt to preserve the *status quo*.

Just twelve years earlier, during the 1905 Revolution, land-hungry Estonian peasants had plundered a third of the German estates, and some barons and members of their families lost their lives in the uprising. The von Liphart estate remained unscathed even though workers and police clashed in the streets of Dorpat, where a socialist manifesto had been issued: "Down with the government, down with the landlords and their castles! The pastors, into the bag or on the gallows! Away with the present community and school boards! The draftees should stay home! Seize the weapons! Take whatever you can take! Do not stand idle and wait for a favor from the government!"[7]

Imperial Russian army and local police units contained that revolt, and together with some German nobility wreaked vengeance upon the rebelling Estonian workers and peasants.

Those who in 1905 had railed against the powerful Baltic barons now possessed weapons and prepared to take control of Dorpat. The Bolsheviks in Petrograd nearly wrested power from the wobbly Provisional Government in July as fractious political parties fought for power. Reusch was a loyal subject who had sworn to uphold the imperial autocracy. He despised the Bolsheviks, but he also understood the popular appeal for "peace, bread and land."

For his text at University Church on the Fifth Sunday after Trinity, July 15, 1917, Pastor Reusch chose the words of the Old Testament prophet, Amos. A pestilence of locusts swarmed over the land of Israel, "and it came to pass that, when they had made an end of eating the grass of the land, then I said, 'Oh Lord Jehovah, forgive, I beseech Thee: how shall Jacob stand? for he is small.'"[8]

His stories now came from Holy Scripture alone. Pastor Reusch spoke directly and eloquently about the storm that engulfed them all, comparing the Reds with the plague of locusts described by Amos:

> Dear neighbors, we are in a situation not unlike ancient Israel. For three years the terrible war has continued. For three years the eternal God has been ringing the bell of war in nearly all the Christian countries of the world, that bell with its frightful sound. And so the judgment of the living God has come upon us. The shout of the Lord was to be heard far and wide: "Listen! Listen to My words!". . . And now hunger comes. Already with his skinny arms, Death pulls the rope and the bell's sound is heard throughout the country.
>
> My dear, dear parish, the dark and terrible clouds of thunderstorms are rising everywhere. Storm clouds are coming which bring thousands of dangers in them. They come here like terrible clouds of locusts. After they settle on a field and leave, only naked earth remains. We are facing such dangers. Behold! They are coming! They want to destroy the last hope of the human heart. And we are desperate.

He then relieved the dissonance he had just induced by invoking the imagery of Martin Luther's "mighty fortress":

> It is dark around us now, pitch black, but a beam of light still shines. Our text shows us this beam of light because it is a godly word full of comfort. As in the text, the locusts will eat the grass around us. . . . Maybe this is our last chance to think about our faith, our last chance to pray, our last chance to be rescued. . . . Think of our Evangelical church as a mighty fortress of belief, the waterlines around the castle are the tears of the believers, and its walls built by the praying hands of the faithful.[9]

Luther's hymn, *A Mighty Fortress Is Our God*, brought inspiration and hope to suffering Lutherans everywhere in Russia during those days.

The 400th anniversary of the Reformation was celebrated at the end of October 1917, one week before the Bolsheviks came to power. At a service in Moscow, Theophilis Meyer, General Superintendent of the Lutheran Church in Russia, remarked that the civil war has "made us tremble for life and body, soul and property. But has not much of our sacred heritage been born in the sounds of the Reformation? Thanks be to God, the echo of revolution is silenced in our hearts by the echo of the Reformation!"[10] As he left the pulpit the congregation stood and sang the "The Battle Hymn of the Lutheran Church," *Ein Feste Burg*.

> A mighty fortress is our God,
> A mighty shield and weapon;
> Our help amid the flood
> Of mortal ills prevailing.
> And were the world with devils filled,
> All seeking to devour us,
> Our souls to fear we need not yield;
> They cannot overpower us.

One week later, on November 7th, the Provisional Government in Petrograd collapsed. The Battleship Aurora fired the signal shot at the Winter Palace where provisional government officials were huddled, and the Bolsheviks stormed the Winter Palace. They were looking for the head of state, but Alexander Kerenski had made good his escape. However, his entire cabinet was arrested and imprisoned.

CIVIL WAR

The Russian Council of People's Commissars, under the leadership of the Estonian, Jaan Anvett, immediately installed a Bolshevik regime in Reval (Tallinn).[11] Dorpat University was closed. The Reds declared the newly elected Estonian National Assembly to be dissolved, but its defiant members ignored the order and three weeks later voted to declare independence from the emerging Soviet Russia.[12]

On the First Sunday in Advent, December 16, 1917, Pastor Reusch addressed the St. Petri congregation, taking his text from the Prophet Isaiah: "Say ye to the daughter of Zion, Behold thy salvation cometh." First he described the difficulties of Israel that paralleled his congregation's terrifying situation, and then he emphasized the two themes characteristic of his evangelical homilies, repentance and redemption:

> We are in a situation similar to Israel's in the days of the prophet. And we also need the comfort and the help of the Messiah whose advent we celebrate.
>
> Behold! Our inner and outer enemies come toward us. All our hopes vanish. One does not dare to hope because one has so often been deceived. Oh God, will there be any better times? That's the sigh that comes from the people's hearts because of all the hurt and ache in our souls. In these dark times we also hear the call of the prophet: Behold! Your Messiah is coming! Therefore, prepare yourselves! Prepare, congregation, for Him to come! Behold, your Messiah is already here, full of compassion for your misery. . . .
>
> But we all have to do something to prepare. The prophet also calls us to raise hope! Raise hope because I offer you mercy. Take away the rock of doubt, the stone of sin. The King of healing is coming! . . .The Lord will put His hands over you, my neighbor, as a father protects his child. He will take away your sadness and misery. And then when your last hour has come, when your last struggle is at hand, when your heart fails and the light in your eye fades, He will look with His face into yours. His face will be mild and understanding. He will look into your face, and with His hands He will put the crown of life upon your head because you belong to those He has rescued in this world. He will be the One who will stay with you and through His Holy Spirit lead you through the dark gate of death into a land of eternal light. Therefore, wait for His coming, and ask Him to come to you.
>
> Amen.[13]

Two months after seizing power in Petrograd, in January 1918, Red Army troops invaded Estonia and frantic Baltic Germans appealed to Berlin for help.[14] White Russian factions, some seeking to restore the monarchy, quarreled as they tried to organize an army based in Estonia for the purpose of liberating Red-held Petrograd. A breakdown of White Russian military order resulted in competing rogue officers mobilizing their own private armies. Armed criminal gangs roamed the Estonian countryside. By the last year of the First World War, day-to-day life in Estonia had dissolved into complete chaos. Meanwhile, the heroic Major General Johan Laidoner recruited a rag-tag Estonian army composed of males sixteen years of age and older.

As happens always and everywhere in the world during such times, criminals exploited the collapse for personal gain. An enterprising person with enough nerve could get himself a job as a courier, carrying diplomatic mail from one official (or unofficial) government (or faction) to another. Then he packed a suitcase with black market goods or drugs — cocaine, heroin — and upon arrival at his destination sold his products to eager buyers. Then he bought jewels, icons, gold, silver, furs, art or platinum that had leaked out of Russia and resold the loot elsewhere. According to Walter Duranty of the *New York Times*, after several trips some marketeers made enough profit to retire. In such a milieu, even those acting "chiefly or at least nominally for their country's benefit" connived to stash ill-gotten gain in Stockholm and London banks.[15]

Until April 1917, German forces had advanced no further than the Dvina (Daugava) River, and Estonia was spared the destruction of its infrastructure. However, when the Soviets refused to accede to German demands during negotiations for a peace treaty at Brest-Litovsk, the German Army Command ordered an immediate offensive. Troops crossed the Dvina and advanced across Estonia, eventually occupying Dorpat and Reval. The Baltic Germans welcomed their invading cousins because victory for either the Estonian nationalists or the Russian Bolsheviks would bring an end to their power and way of life. The British and French governments advanced their respective objectives by sending material support and advisors to the Estonians, and from Scandinavia came both equipment and volunteers. The American State Department sent an observer.

By February 1918 the Baltic barons' paramount concern was the Bolshevik troops, supported by local sympathizers, who still occupied much of the country. According to international wire service reports, the "Bolshevist element" began arresting the bourgeois German Balts, holding some for ransom and killing others. "All the food in the Dorpat district has been confiscated," it was reported.[16] Dr. Reusch recalled that during the first days of Bolshevik rule "we noticed no change in our lives," but shortly afterwards "members of my congregation whispered to me that all was not right. They asked me if I had heard gun shots and said that persons of the middle class were being killed by Soviet soldiers."[17]

On Sunday, February 17, 1918, Pastor Reusch delivered a sermon at St. Petri. The familiar text came from the Gospel of St. Matthew, chapter 8. The Apostles are about to perish in a storm on the Sea of Galilee while Jesus is asleep. His terrified disciples awaken him and beg him to do something. The Nazarene chides them for their lack of faith, and then rebukes the wind and the waves. According to the Gospel, "There was a great calm."

"With the text before us," said Pastor Reusch, "let us consider today the storm on the sea, the cry of the people, and God's answer." Pastor Reusch did not shrink from addressing the prospect of death; but, like an Old Testament prophet, neither did he hesitate to condemn the enemy who, in his words, "will be ashes and dust before the Almighty."

First, the storm:

A storm is raging in the world, a storm as huge and powerful as ever the world has seen before. A truly dark night surrounds us. More sorrows are heaped upon sorrows, so that one's heart breaks. . .As the storm moves the bushes back and forth, back and forth, so are we thrown back and forth, back and forth. Murder is normal today. Look, one uproar follows the next, so that even those in power do not hear or see because they are so frightened and turn their eyes away. Life and property are in constant danger.

Second, the cry of the people:

And so our belief becomes weak the same way it happened to the disciples in the boat. It seems as if prayer doesn't matter anymore; it seems the Lord has forgotten about us, that He is sleeping, taking a nap.

And third, God's answer:

Oh, my neighbors, can you really seriously believe that the Person who calmed the elements with one word for a few poor disciples cannot bring calm to our situation today? *When their time is finished, then the Lord Almighty will speak His Word, and they will fall to pieces; they will be like fog disappearing because of the hot noonday sun, and you won't find their traces anymore because they will be turned to ashes and dust before the Almighty.* [Emphasis added.]

God does not forsake His people. But should the abyss of death be opening before you, should the waves of death close over your physical body, He will not forsake you. He has triumphed over the threat of death and the night of desperation. And so it will become quiet around you and in your heart.

But even if you have to go through the examination, if doubt tries to overcome you and stop you from going on, if doubt threatens to smash your boat and your soul trembles with fright, have courage! You must not be anxious, because Jesus, your Messiah, lives! Everything He commands will happen!

May the Lord's peace, which is higher than all human reason, may this peace keep your hearts and minds through Jesus Christ unto eternal life.

Amen.[18]

GERMAN TROOPS OCCUPY DORPAT

Under the steady advance of the German army, the Bolsheviks fell back from Reval on February 23, 1918. The next day Estonian nationalists declared an independent and democratic state. On the 25th the German Army entered Reval, the same day that General Hermann von Eichorn's 18th Storming Company and the 1st Squadron of the 16th Hussar Regiment reclaimed Dorpat from the Reds.[19]

Bolshevik leaders in Petrograd issued a proclamation two days later: "Workers and all oppressed men and women, you must swell the ranks of the Red battalions. To arms, all of you, that the struggle may only cease with your last breath!" Despite talk of a treaty, the Germans suddenly pushed further into Russian territory. Their purpose, the Reds urgently warned their cadres, was to restore the monarchy and "the power of the landlords, bankers, and capitalists."[20]

Like their Russian brothers, thousands upon thousands of industrial workers in France, Germany, Russia, Great Britain, Austria, Hungary and the United States saw themselves as raw material manipulated by greedy capitalists and drafted by their lackey politicians to die by the millions in muddy trenches.

The occupying Germans were merciless. In Dorpat, in order to scour the Bolshevik infection from the body politic, they executed eighty Reds charged with attempting to blow up a railroad track. The Committee of the Workers' Council was likewise put to death.[21] A boy of fifteen, it was said, was sentenced to death for merely picking up a copy of a Communist manifesto.[22]

German troops crossed into Soviet Russia and captured Pskov on March 3, 1918. The Soviet Government signed the Treaty of Brest-Litovsk the same day, agreeing to pull their troops out of Estland and Livonia. Civil war had broken out in Russia, and the Allies had intervened from the north, south, east and west in a half-hearted effort to support the Whites. The future of the Bolshevik Revolution seemed bleak. Even Lenin was pessimistic.

In a supplementary agreement signed in late August, the Soviet Government renounced all claims to their former Baltic provinces. "And so," a German historian wrote, "the German Army liberated the whole of the Baltic area from Bolshevik rule."[23]

Civil War in Finland

Russian troops and local Reds in Finland joined forces to keep the former Imperial Grand Duchy a part of Soviet Russia. General Gustaf Mannerheim, an aristocratic Swedish Finn who had recently seen action on the Eastern Front and served as aide-de-camp to Tsar Nicholas II, agreed to organize and lead the Finnish Whites in what turned out to be an appallingly bitter and brutal three-month civil war. General Mannerheim began his offensive against the Finnish Reds in mid-March 1918. A few weeks later Berlin offered assistance to the beleaguered Finnish Whites, and in April General Count Rüdiger von der Goltz led his Baltic Division to Finland. In addition, a brigade of 2,500 Baltic German volunteers, including infantry, cyclists, cavalry and artillery units were assembled at Reval (Tallinn) under the command of Colonel von Brandenstein.[24]

The decisive Finnish battle occurred near Lahti when 25,000 Reds found themselves encircled: Mannerheim's army on the north, von der Goltz's Baltic Division to the south and west, and von Brandenstein's Baltic Germans, the "gallant brigade" as Mannerheim referred to them, barring escape to the east. The Reds surrendered on May 2nd, 1918,[25] and on May 14th Mannerheim led the victory parade to the square in front of the Lutheran Cathedral in Helsinki. Two months later the Whites expelled from the country the entire Jewish population of Helsinki, some 300 families, because the bankers among them were said to have "placed funds at the disposal of the Red Guards."[26] Even White Russian officers who had helped Mannerheim defeat the Reds were ordered out of the country. The Finnish Whites wanted no more Russians meddling in their affairs.

Professor von Bulmerincq, released some months earlier from Siberian exile, now took over as assistant to Rev. Wittrock at St. Johannes Church so that Pastor Reusch could give more of his time to the St. Petri congregation.[27]

Dorpat, which had officially been named Yuriev by the Russians, regained its former name. Local Baltic German civic leaders were eager to serve in the government imposed by the occupying German army.[28] Even Pastor Reusch cooperated with the German administration: "During the time of occupation, I had, as co-director, to establish a German intermediate school."[29] The performance of Estonian music was forbidden. Bread was rationed at a quarter kilogram per day and meat at a quarter kilogram per week.[30] Dorpat University was reopened, and to reassure the barons on that occasion, Kaiser Wilhelm II sent the following telegram:

Among the changing events and impressions of the war which the German Fatherland has been forced to wage in defense of its sacred soil and its Kultur against a world
of enemies, the reliberation of our German brothers in the Baltic lands from foreign
oppression has given me very special joy. My joy is increased by the fact that the vener-
able Alma Mater of Dorpat has so soon been awakened to new activity as the center of
intellectual life, and that a valuable source of strength for prosperity is regained by the
old German *Kulturland.* [31]

Native Balts suffered under the harsh rule of the Germans. In an appeal for Western support,
one of their spokesmen wrote,

The present conditions ruling Estonia are intolerable in the extreme. Arbitrary rule
is the order of the day. The Press of the Estonian Parties has been crushed, political life
is suppressed, and all meetings are forbidden. The Germans and the landowners are
ruling the country.... Many of the politicians and members of the Estonian Government
have been arrested, and the German barons and Pan-Germanists have a free hand. [32]

Meanwhile, Baltic Reds organized the First Reval Communist Regiment in Petrograd. Their
pamphlets appeared everywhere in occupied Estonia, where many of the war-weary German
soldiers already sympathized with the Bolshevik message and their officers could not always
count on the loyalty of their units.

In Siberia and southern Russia the armies of the Russian White forces occasionally advanced — but invariably had to retreat. In the north they were advancing on Yekaterinburg on
July 16, 1918, when nervous Bolsheviks awakened the Romanov family and executed them and
their remaining servants. In the south, the Red Army later encircled the last remaining Terek
Cossack units at Mozdok. After a five-month siege General Mistulov committed suicide rather
than surrender to the Reds. [33]

Allied forces launched an offensive on the Western Front at the Battle on the Marne. Four
days later, on July 20, 1918, the tide turned against Germany. Kaiser Wilhelm II had no choice
but to abdicate, and he slipped across the border into ignominious exile in The Netherlands.
The Baltic barons feared that the generals in Berlin would recall their troops to bolster the home
front that was already awash with red banners. [34] Baroness Meyendorff and her family fled from
Petrograd to their estate in Estland:

[But] once again the shadow of the Red Terror began looming in the distance — from
the West this time. Was it possible that Bolshevism was going to spread all over Europe
as the Communists prophesied? Many people were hurriedly getting visas to Finland so
as not to get caught in Estonia. "There would be no hope for any of us if the Germans
joined the Russian Soviets." [35]

However, the Bolshevik revolution was by no means secure. A Red leader was assassinated
in Petrograd, and at the end of August there was another attempt in which Lenin was severely

wounded and two others killed. The Bolshevik response was quick and violent. On September 4th Comrade Petrovski, Commissar for Internal Affairs, advocated "an immediate end to looseness and tenderness" and called for a campaign of mass terror. The next day the Council of People's Commissars ordered that class enemies of the Soviet State be isolated in concentration camps, and all persons associated with White Guard organizations, plots and rebellions be shot and their names and the reasons for their executions be published. On the 7th of September the names and reasons for execution of 512 persons in Petrograd appeared in the press along with the slogan, "Long Live the Red Terror!"[36] To many Russians, tsar and patriarch were of the same cloth, and because some of the hierarchy and priests of the Russian Orthodox Church strongly opposed the new regime, Orthodox clergy and monastics also became victims of the Red Terror.

RED TERROR IN DORPAT

The Republican German government signed the Armistice on November 11, 1918, the same day that Baltic barons formed a *Landeswehr* Army in a futile attempt to preserve their legacy.[37] One week later the German command turned civilian authority over to the Estonians.[38] Without the German counterforce, however, Estonia could not hold back Bolshevik forces. Less than a month later, on December 2, 1918, the Russians declared Estonia a Soviet Republic.[39] And so the Baltic Germans were left, as the American observer reported, to "fight their own battle and work out their own salvation."[40]

According to the Armistice protocols, German troops were supposed to have packed up and gone home. However, the Allies, unnerved at the prospect of Russia's Soviet revolution spilling into Europe, allowed the Germans to remain. They later changed their minds when it was learned that General von der Goltz intended to turn the Baltics into German territory by awarding land to his *Freikorps* veterans.

What was left of the German army dawdled in its southward retreat, which gave their Baltic cousins time either to fight or flee. The von Lipharts had survived the previous February Bolshevik occupation of Dorpat unscathed, but others were not so fortunate.[41] According to Ernst von Salomon, in the area around Mitau there "was not a single [Baltic German] family from which at least one member had not been carried off or tortured or killed. Often whole families had been exterminated together with their servants."[42] Now that the German troops were about to withdraw from Dorpat, who would save the barons from a second Bolshevik bloodbath? Certainly not the disorganized native Estonians. Even if they succeeded in establishing an independent state, they wanted to be rid of their Baltic German oppressors. The little train depot in Dorpat was swamped with German Balts determined to leave before it was too late.

Soviet Russia's Seventh Army launched an invasion in late November 1918. The Sixth Red Division struck at Narva, and in little more than four weeks had penetrated almost to Reval. Red military units, charged with the seizure of what is today southern Estonia and northern Latvia, attacked on November 25, 1918. The Red 49th Rifle Regiment of the 2nd Novgorod Division, numbering 1500 infantry and 4 cannon, was ordered to take Dorpat.

On December 9th, Baron Eduard von Stackelberg, a friend of the von Lipharts, wrote an urgent letter to the Imperial Office of the Interior in Berlin: "As one who has striven for years to preserve the German community in this country," and on behalf of Germans living abroad, particularly in the Baltic countries, he urged the Government "to guarantee to those who have been expelled from their homes and are trying to return to Germany that they will be allowed to leave with their personal property, . . . that their naturalization in Germany will be expedited, and that they will be made citizens of the Reich."[43]

The prospect of an imminent second Bolshevik occupation left Baron von Liphart with no alternative but to abandon his estate. On December 13th, Reusch grimly helped the household staff load the family's personal possessions into boxcars — sixteen of them — and watched the train leave the Dorpat station for Berlin. Much of the fabled art collection, however, was left behind.[44]

"Then came the terrible breakdown," recounted Pastor Reusch, when the Bolsheviks returned to Dorpat.[45] As German troops had prepared to withdraw from the town, several local Reds had paid Reusch a visit. His anti-Bolshevik stance was no secret, and the wily Reds had come to put him to the test by demanding that he pray for their cause. He, of course, refused.[46] And so, he wrote one year later, "I had to leave Dorpat before the German troops left."[47]

On December 17th, shortly before the Soviet infantry's arrival, Pastor Wittrock and most of the parish staff at St. Johannes joined their panicky neighbors and crowded into the last trains bound for Riga. According to Pastor J. Sedlatschek, who stayed behind to care for the decimated parish, Reusch was already "absent."[48]

The German troops, weary of fighting and influenced by Communist propaganda, refused to fight against the Reds and began to retreat. The Estonian 2nd Regiment, still in the process of organizing its 821 volunteers, had no choice but to abandon Dorpat on December 21st.[49] Moscow radio transmissions monitored by British intelligence reported that "defeated White Guards are retreating from Dorpat to Fellin and the Estonian [Red] troops are pursuing them. At Dorpat an Estonian Communist paper is being published; another Communist paper appeared yesterday."[50]

The Commune of the Working People in Dorpat decreed that all citizens were to register and surrender their personal guns and ammunition by six o'clock on the evening of December 24th; those who failed to comply would be shot.[51] The penalty of execution was invoked that very day when Max von zur Muhler, Director of Fisheries, was executed.

More executions followed on December 26th when Mikkel Kus, Alex Lepp, Alexander Aland, and Karl Soo were taken to the frozen river, shoved through holes in the ice, and drowned.[52] That same day, under penalty of death, the commissar ordered the churches closed and the clergy to leave the city. Pastor Sedlatschek reported that the town's remaining clergy refused to obey the order and went into hiding. However, thanks to the efficient system of denunciation already in place, "most were soon arrested and taken from their homes."[53] By the end of December

1918, Bolshevik troops, including 6,000 Estonian Reds,[54] had taken control of half the country.[55] "It was a time," General J. Laidoner reflected five months later, "when one could say there was no hope left and that all, land as well as people, seemed to be victims of the Bolsheviks."[56]

The Reds had taken Vladikavkaz by the end of 1918, and the cadets and staff who remained loyal to the idea of an Imperial Russia fled the city. The Cadet Corps facility became a school to train Red Army officers.[57]

On January 9, 1919, eleven more hostages were taken to the Embach River in Tartu and shot, their bodies pushed through holes cut in the ice. When sixteen bodies were later pulled from the river it was reported that all had been tortured, arms or legs broken, skulls cracked. Karl Soo's eyes had been gouged out.[58]

On January 11 the Red Guards came for Pastors Sedlatschek and Werner Gruehn. By then the city jail was full, so the two clergymen were taken to the Credit Bank Building on what is now Kompanii Street opposite the park along the river. The clerics were shoved into a room with twenty-six other women and men.[59]

The Bolsheviks were determined to break the power of the church in the city — Lutheran, Russian Orthodox and Roman Catholic. They demanded that the Rev. Dr. Professor Tragott Hahn, one of Reusch's former professors, and the Russian Orthodox hierarch, Archbishop Platon, sign statements renouncing their Christian faith. They, of course, refused. "As can be seen in the documents left behind by the Maximalists [Bolsheviks]," Sedlatschek noted, "the older pastors were sentenced to be shot to death on January 14th and the younger ones on January 15th."[60]

The Estonian Second Division, commanded by Captain Karl Parts, a native of Dorpat, was on its way to the Narva front when the officer learned that his hometown was hemorrhaging. He took it upon himself to bolster his force with an extra battalion of shock troops and raced south by armored train.[61] As they reached the outskirts of Dorpat on the morning of the 14th, Captain Parts ordered that the train's heavy guns be fired to announce their arrival.

LIBERATION

Caught by surprise, one of the Bolshevik commissars ordered the men and women held in the city jail to be herded into Meat Market Square and mowed down in a hail of machine gun fire. However, as a diversion, the town's butchers and market women started a riot in the square. And when Estonian volunteers began advancing from the railroad station toward the town center, the Bolsheviks fell back to the river. Meanwhile, prisoners held at the Credit Bank Building were already being executed. "In the cell next to us," said Sedlatschek, "the last people taken out were the teacher, Treu, and two of his peers."[62]

And then came the rescue. Kuprijanov's Partisan Battalion, a volunteer force of 250 students and older men from Dorpat, advanced toward the scene of carnage on Kompanii Street. The Reds, interrupted in their executions, fled. Before making their escape, however, they tossed hand grenades through the basement windows into the makeshift cells. In all, more than twenty prisoners lost their lives that morning.

"Everyone who remained alive," testified Sedlatschek, "owes thanks to the brave men of Kuperjan's [sic] Freedom Brigade, who saved the lives of those remaining in the Credit Bank cellar, the butchers, who saved those still alive in the City jail, and to a most merciful nurse" who came to the aid of the survivors.[63]

The liberators had stumbled upon a scene of horror. Some of the victims had lain in the cellar since January 11th. There was the body of the beloved Estonian Orthodox Archbishop Platon, stabbed seven times and shot four times, his brains scattered on the wall; Priest Mikhail Bleive of St. George Orthodox Church, killed by an ax blow which took away half of his face; Priest Nicholas Beshanitzki of the Uspenski Orthodox Church, who also was murdered by an ax blow to the face; and the Rev. Dr. Professor Hahn, lying next to Archbishop Platon. Other victims included Baron Konstantin von Knorring, M. Xarner, the editor of the *Postimees* newspaper; the potter, Susman Kaplan; and a military officer, his "epaulettes fastened to his body with nails." Lutheran Pastor Wilhelm Schwartz was found on the floor, his head and arms dismenbered.[64] The *New York Times* reported a total of 305 persons executed in Dorpat, 225 men and 80 women.[65]

The Bolshevik revolution faced fierce resistance from, among others, Imperial Army officers, industrialists, landowners, religious leaders and private farmers. In a letter to American workers, Lenin explained the reason for the Red Terror: "When the workers and the laboring peasants took hold of the powers of state, it became our duty to quell the resistance of the exploiting class. We are proud that we have done it. We only regret that we did not do it at the beginning, with sufficient firmness and [decisiveness]."[66]

August Winnig, the conservative envoy from Berlin who negotiated the withdrawal of the German army from Estonia, expressed a different view: "Bolshevism in practice is not a political system. It is politically organized crime."[67]

Both Reds and Whites committed frightful acts of violence, which, in the words of Sergei Petrovich Melgounov, became "a monotony of horror."[68] It was so brutal a civil war, said one observer, that "one felt as if time had gone back several centuries and we were suddenly traveling the roads of Europe behind the armies of Wallenstein and Tilly" (in the Thirty Years War between Protestants and Roman Catholics 1618-1648).[69]

Burial services for the Orthodox dead began the next day, and the somber rituals for Protestant and Roman Catholic victims went on for two more weeks. On January 19, 1919, the remaining members of the St. Johannes congregation gathered for a service of thanksgiving and mourning. Of 152 parishioners who died that year, the Bolsheviks executed fifteen, six fell in battle, two more died of their wounds, and one was listed as having "died of depression."[70] Most of the others had fallen victim to the world-wide influenza virus that, by the end of 1918, claimed three times as many lives as had the nine million killed in the First World War.

Under the leadership of Major General Laidoner, the Estonian volunteers pushed the Reds back into Russia in only seven weeks.[71] General Rüdiger von der Goltz returned from Berlin on February 2, 1919 to command the German and *Freikorps* recruits. With the help of the Germans, Estonian and Latvian volunteers drove the Reds out of Riga on May 22, 1919. As in Dorpat, the liberators came upon heaps of corpses. Among them were Reusch's acquaintances: August Eckhardt, senior pastor of Riga Cathedral; Theodor Hoffmann of St. Peter's; Erhard Doebler, pastor of St. James parish, and five other clergymen. A monument was later raised in the city over the common grave of forty martyred Lutheran pastors of the Riga Konsistorium.[72]

Some of the Christian inhabitants of Riga visited violence in kind upon the retreating Bolsheviks, especially upon the "gunwomen" who consorted with Bolshevik troops. "It is strange," observed George Popoff, "how quickly human beings become brutalized." He watched "so-called society ladies, who in normal times would have shuddered to see a beetle crushed, take part . . . with obvious zest in the hunt for their former torturers and watch their execution without a sign of emotion."[73] But then the process of brutalization is inherent to war. Said an Imperial German veteran, "As a seventeen-year-old soldier, what had I learned about life? I knew how to kill people, run around with whores, tell dirty jokes, ransack houses, and keep myself free of fleas."[74]

There were some Christians who had come to believe that Marxist and New Testament ideals were similar: "We are the real followers of Christ. We want to follow the example of the first congregation in Jerusalem!"[75] The "Red Cleric of Riga," Lutheran Pastor Edgar Model, was one of those. He declared from his pulpit that "the great Resurrection foretold by Jesus Christ 2,000 years ago is being fulfilled at this moment, and the Kingdom of this world is being erected before the eyes of this generation in such splendor as no one ever dreamed of."[76] Idealistic students also were "captured by [the Bolsheviks'] sweet sounding words and joined them," Reusch admitted. "But when, two to three months later, they saw their bloody deeds, they became cured forever and . . . joined the liberation army and became very efficient fighters."[77]

Reusch disappeared from Dorpat around the middle of December 1918. Several thousand White Russians served with the Estonian volunteers, and Reusch apparently joined them in pursuing the Reds as they retreated from Dorpat. He certainly had a motive, given the slaughter of his friends and acquaintances and concern for his family in Russia. And because of his military training, he was more competent than most to have led a group of volunteers against the Reds.

Reusch's activities between the middle of December 1918 and the end of January 1919 cannot be verified. However, several of his civil war stories, repeated time and again without variation, convey the authentic tone of personal experience. One of his grandsons recalled one of them:

> On a quiet and bitterly cold evening early in 1919, Reusch and several men under his command approached a peasant dwelling in the countryside. The door to the hut was open, but fearing an ambush they took great care in approaching the structure.
>
> Once they were inside he saw the entire family seated at the table, their hands on either side of the plates in front of them. In the dark interior it appeared as if an odd-looking beard hung from the chin of each person. No one at the table said a word.
>
> As he approached the silent figures, Reusch saw that what he had taken for "beards"

were comprised of frozen blood and gore, and the objects on the plates were the victims' tongues. The peasants' hands had been nailed to the table alongside their plates.

Then he heard a moan. The young girl at the far end of the table was still alive, a strand of hair from a horsetail used to excise her tongue still hanging from her mouth. Reusch wrapped her in his greatcoat and tried to give her some water, but she died in his arms.

Said Dr. Reusch's grandson, "After my grandfather made that last statement he stared at the floor for what seemed like an eternity, and finally said in a solemn voice, 'It was easier to shoot the Bolsheviks after that.'"[78]

The Baltic region had been wrested from the control of the Reds, but Reusch now found himself homeless. He had last seen his family in 1913 when everyone had gathered in Saratov for Grandmother Reusch's funeral. But he had lost contact with them and no longer knew whether they were alive or dead.

Many of Reusch's friends were dead, or like the von Lipharts had become refugees, scattered to the four winds. The Lutheran seminary was closed. The former Russian provinces of Livonia and Estland were no more, the borders redrawn for Estonians in the north and Latvians in the south. Nationalistic Estonians hated their former ethnic German overlords. Dorpat University was reopened as an Estonian institution, and the names of the city and its historic university changed to Tartu. Imperial Russia, the world into which he had been born, was no more.

And so at the end of January 1919 the stateless Russian packed his few belongings and melded into the stream of Baltic refugees making their way westward.[79] The suffering he had witnessed during the past five years of war and his own participation in the violence of civil war left him shaken and numb. He now understood the terrible truth: "He that loveth not knoweth not God."

CHAPTER 5

1   R. Reusch, "Mein Lebenslauf," 5, AELML.
2   R. Reusch, sermon manuscript, 22 April 1917, GACA.
3   License No. 1979, 14 April 1917, issued in Russian by the Evangelical Lutheran Konsistorium, Riga, Latvia, GACA.
4   *Dorpater St. Johannes Kirche Abszhriften der Kirchenbücher*, 1917-1920, 130 (1253-2-61), ESHA. Entries were made in the Russian language before the revolution; afterwards, in German.
5   *Dorpater.*
6   *Dorpater*, 134.
7   Emanuel Nodel, *Estonia: Nation on the Anvil* (1963), 143-147, 152-53.
8   Amos 7: 1-3.
9   R. Reusch, sermon manuscript, 2 July 1917, GACA.
10 Theofilis Meyer, Reformation Day sermon, quoted by W.L. Scheding in "Luther's Heritage in Soviet Russia," undated manuscript ca. mid-1920s (PA 142, Papers, W.L. Scheding), AELCA.

Luther's hymn became a symbol of resistance in both the First and Second World Wars. In 1918 Red Guards stormed into Riga Cathedral during a service to arrest the senior pastor, August Eckhardt. As the elderly cleric was escorted from the pulpit, the shocked congregation "suddenly rose like one man and loudly and confidently sang Luther's old hymn of faith and trust." — George Popoff, *The City of the Red Plague* (1932), 273-75.

During the Nazi occupation in 1943, Norwegians sang "A Mighty Fortress Is Our God" so often that the Nazis became suspicious. Two stanzas of the hymn were finally banned, one that contains the phrase, "And were the world with devils filled," and the other, "Their dreaded prince no more can harm us as of yore; his rage we can endure, for lo! his doom is sure; a world shall overthrow him!" — Ingeborg Stolee, *Luther's Life* (1943), 98.

11 Toivo U. Raun, *Estonia and the Estonians* (1987), 107.
12 F. W. Pick, *The Baltic Nations* (1945), 61-63.
13 R. Reusch, sermon manuscript, 3 December 1917, GACA.
14 Sir Stephen Tallents, *Man and Boy* (1943), 278.
15 Walter Duranty, *I Write as I Please* (1935), 15.
16 "Bolsheviki Arrest Germans in Russia by Wholesale; Hold Them as Hostages, Threatening Butchery," *New York Times*, 16 February 1918, I, 2.
17 "Lectures before Kiwanis / Dr. Reusch argues against Communism in East Chicago," *East Chicago Times*, 10 Sept. 1930, clipping, GACA.
18 R. Reusch, sermon manuscript (in German), 5 February 1918, GACA.
19 "Germans Take Reval and City of Pskov," *New York Times*, 26 February 1918, I, 2.
20 "Calls Russians to Fight 'the Imperialistic Assassins' Who Are Invading Country to Restore Monarchy," *New York Times*, 27 February 1918, I, 1.
21 "63,800 Prisoners Taken by Germans," *New York Times*, 4 March 1918, I, 2.
22 "Denounce Terrorism of Baltic Peoples," *New York Times*, 12 July 1918, I, 2.
23 Georg von Rauch, *The Baltic States: The Years of Independence* (trans. from German, University of California Press, 1974), 46.
24 J. O. Hannula, *Finland's War of Independence* (1939), 173.

25 Carl Mannerheim, *The Memoirs of Marshall Mannerheim* (1953), 174.
26 "Exile for Finnish Jews," *New York Times*, 13 July 1918, I, 3.
27 *Dorpater Kirchenbücher,* 134+.
28 Robert A. von Lemm, *Dorpater Ratslinie, 1319-1889 und das Dorpater Stadtamt 1878-1918* (1960), 165.
29 R. Reusch, "Mein Lebenslauf," 4.
30 "Esthonians Feel the Yoke," *New York Times*, 1 September 1918, I, 10.
31 "Kaiser Greets Dorpat," *New York Times*, 21 September 1918, I, 4.
32 A. Piip, "Esthonia: A Second Belgium," *The Contemporary Review*, vol. 114 (September 1918), 294.
33 General Anton Denikine, *The White Army* (1930), 205.
34 "Baltic Barons in Panic," *New York Times*, 20 September 1918, I, 3.
35 Stella Arbinina, *Through Terror to Freedom* (1930), 239.
36 "Intensification of the Red Terror," *The Triumph of Bolshevism*, 1917-1919, vol. 1, "Documents of Soviet History" series, Rex A. Wade, editor (1991), 214-15.
37 John Hinden, *The Baltic States and Weimar Ostpolitik* (1987), 16.
38 Evald Uustalu, *The History of the Estonian People* (1952), 164.
39 Hinden, 17.
40 John Alleyne Gade, "On the Shores of the Baltic," *Atlantic Monthly* (October 1919), 567.
41 Otto Hellich, German major, *Blood on the Snow: Eyewitness Accounts of the Russian Revolution*, Elisabeth Heresch, ed. (1990), 164.
42 Ernst von Salomon, *History of Political Violence: The Outlaws* (1931; 1983 reprint), 60.
43 Eduard von Stackelberg, letter to the Reichsamt des Innern, Berlin, 9 December 1918 (R 1501/8038, Bd 6), BArch.
44 Hubertus Neuschäffer, *Schlösser und Herrenhäuser in Estland* (1993), 187.
45 R. Reusch, "Mein Lebenslauf," 5.
46 R. Reusch, untitled speech notes, GACA.
47 R. Reusch, "Mein Lebenslauf," 4.
48 J. Sedlatschek, "Jahreesbericht des Oberpastors zu St. Johannes-Dorpat für 1919, Vom 1. Dez. 1918 bis zum 1. Dez. 1919," 1-3 (1253-1- 556), ESHA.
49 *Estonian War of Independence, 1918-1920* (Estonian National Historical Committee, 1938-39; reprint, New York, 1968), 17, 19.
50 "Secret Wireless News Report, Dec. 5-31, 1919" (ADM 233-1), PRO.
51 Sedlatschek, 1-3.
52 "Crimes of the Bolsheviki in Esthonia: Official Record of Horrors," translated from *l'Illustration*, Paris, France, March 8, 1919, in *New York Times Current History Magazine*, vol. 10, pt. 1 (June, 1919), 496-97.

The details reported here are corroborated by other sources, including documents of the European Committee of the National Lutheran Council of America (Erich Køher, "Bolshevism in its True Aspects," excerpts trans. by G. T. Rygh, 1-2 [NLC-3, "Relief, European, Poland & Baltics"], AELCA; and the *New York Times*, "Red Victims Hacked and Clubbed to Death" [27 February 1919], I 3).

53 Sedlatschek, 2.
54 Emanuel Nodel, "Strategy and Tactics of the Estonian Communist Party, 1917-1939," *Conference on Baltic Studies* (1971), 63.
55 Uustalu, 167.
56 General Johan Laidoner, Secret Report to the Prime Minister of the Esthonian Republic, 23 May 1919 (WO 157-1216), PRO.
57 *Great Soviet Encyclopedia*, vol. 11, 3d edition (1973), 18.
58 "Crimes of the Bolsheviki."
59 The building was destroyed in 1944, but a plaque on the present structure memorializes the tragic event that took place there.
60 Sedlatschek, 2.
61 Tallents, 294.
62 Sedlatschek, 2.
63 Sedlatschek, 3.
64 Sedlatschek.
65 "Bolshevist Army Retire in Esthonia," *New York Times* (19 January 1919), 8.
66 Jerome Elmer Murphy, "The Crimson Terror," *Catholic World*, vol. 10 (May 1919), 161.
67 August Winnig, "Bolshevik Invasion of Baltic Germany," trans. from *Die Glöcke* in *The Living Age* (29 March 1919), 788.
68 Sergey Petrovich Melgounov, *Red Terror* (1926), 123.
69 Joseph Chappey, "Fighting the Bolsheviki in Kurland," *The Living Age* (24 November 1923), 379.
70 Sedlatschek, 4.
71 Uustalu, 167. General Laidoner was arrested when the Soviet Army invaded Estonia in 1939 and was never seen again.
72 W. L. Scheding, "Final Report, NLC — Luthco: Work in Russia 1922-23 with ARA," 19-20 (PA 142, Papers, W. L. Scheding, 1922-24, 1929), AELCA.
73 Popoff, 329-30.
74 Stenbock-Fermor, *Deutschland von unten*, p. 113, cited by Klaus Theweleit in *Male Fantasies* (1987), 147.
75 R. Reusch, undated sermon, ca. 1960, GACA.
76 George Popoff, *The City of the Red Plague* (1932), 281.
77 R. Reusch, undated sermon, ca. 1960 (same as note 73 above) GACA.
78 Dr. Reusch often referred to this incident in his notes. The narrative presented here is derived from the recollections of several people, including Neil Anderson in an e-mail letter to the author, 9 March 1999.
79 R. Reusch, visa application (copy) presented at the British consulate in Leipzig for entry to Tanganyika Territory, 9 September 1922 (R. Reusch file), AELML.

Survivors of the Russian Civil War in Tartu honor Richard Reusch (first row, center) upon his successful defense of his thesis for the Magister Diploma, November 11, 1921. Marie von Bulmerincq, his mentor's daughter, sits on the arm of his chair; to his right, Mrs. Sedlatschek, a survivor of the cellar massacre of January 14, 1919; and Professor Alexander von Bulmerincq stands behind Reusch.

Chapter Six

STATELESS
Germany and Denmark, 1919-1923

At last, with sweat of horror in his hair,
He climbed through darkness to the twilight air,
Unloading hell behind him step by step.

— Siegfried Sassoon[1]

The devastation of war and revolution in the twentieth century has been documented in thousands of photographs. But it is the faces of First World War soldiers and refugees that drew the attention of one historian because of the "forlorn hopelessness and despair in their eyes," an inner emptiness reflecting "the death of all the ideals and hopes for which they had fought and suffered."[2]

Thousands of homeless nationals, destitute soldiers, veterans and disoriented foreign refugees roamed the pavements of European cities in 1919, many of them, like Reusch, stateless Russians. The Austro-Hungarian, Russian and German empires had vanished. Kaiser Wilhelm II was in exile, and General Ludendorff resigned as chancellor shortly before Reusch arrived in Berlin. Thousands of army deserters roamed the streets. Endemic unemployment led to starvation, and police could not cope with all the incidents of robbery and murder.

Marxists believed that the revolution spawned in Russia would engulf Germany and the industrial world. Spartacists fought pitched battles in the streets in the name of the proletariat. On January 16, 1919, about the time that Reusch arrived in the capital, two leftist leaders, Rosa Luxemberg and Karl Liebnecht, were shot to death by right-wing mobs.

Destitute Lutheran clergymen and their families streamed into Berlin from all regions of Soviet Russia, and the German Church assisted in their resettlement. The senior pastor in Rostock had work for someone with Reusch's credentials, so the refugee from Dorpat, not unhappy to leave Berlin, left for the northern port city on the Baltic Sea.

ROSTOCK, NORTH GERMANY

Reusch made his way to Bei Marienkirche 2, the parsonage across the lane from the great cathedral in the center of the city. Pastor Frahm introduced him to his assistant, Pastor

Kleinminger, the parish city missionary. Together they showed their Russian colleague through the medieval Lutheran Cathedral of St. Mary.[3]

Although he had not yet processed the chaos of the past years, Reusch plunged into volunteer work at St. Mary's and the nearby neighborhood parish of the Holy Ghost as if he were vicar: conducting children's services as he had done in Tartu; working with *Blau-Kreuz Verein*, a support group for alcoholics; taking over Kleinminger's youth group to free him for other work; organizing a young women's guild; and founding a Christian boys' club. The former university professor also lectured and led "the scientific evenings," discussions sponsored by the local theological association. Perhaps he threw himself into extraordinary activity hoping to block out the hellish civil war experiences that scarred his memory. As a refugee who worked for room and board, he was not formally registered with the Mecklenburg Lutheran diocese.[4] However, in May 1919 Kleinminger resigned to take a rural parish, and Frahm offered the city missionary's full-time position to Reusch.

But a letter from Denmark suddenly complicated his decision. It was from Anna von Liphart who was planning to purchase the Søborg-Gaard estate near Copenhagen, and she and her husband invited Reusch to join them.

What should he do? He had been taught from age six to be loyal to his emperor. He had studied theology and been ordained. But his emperor was dead. The Baltic German community had dispersed. Loyalty to his Heavenly King meant taking the position he had been offered. But he was facing a personal crisis: "Lord, I believe; help thou my unbelief."[5]

Germany was tilting on the edge of civil war. Communists won elections in first one city and then another. Conflict between right and left wing groups often turned violent.[6] Reusch had been through all that before in Estonia. His hatred of the Reds remained undiminished, but perhaps he was afraid of being drawn into the violence once again. Whatever his reasons, he declined Frahm's offer and left for Denmark in a state of lingering confusion and depression.

ØLSTYKKE, DENMARK

"After years spent among people incessantly harassed by hunger and uncertainty," wrote Nicholas Wreden, a refugee from Estonia, "the Danes appeared to us like strange beings out of another world." The stateless Russians could not believe their eyes and ears: well-groomed men and smartly dressed women leisurely strolled the sidewalks without a care, the children laughed without restraint. "We had been hounded for so long," said Wreden, that "every stranger was to us a potential enemy, and to be noticed invariably meant to be in danger."[7]

Baron von Liphart had abandoned the historic family estate at Dorpat, which was almost more than he could bear. The family had arrived in Berlin on December 13, 1918. Von Liphart's ancestors had come from Prussia and Scandinavia, so he and his wife went straight to the Danish Embassy where they were immediately granted visas. The next day, December 14th, they left Berlin for Rostock, and with two of their children, eight-year-old Arved and Karl, eighteen, took the ferry to the Danish port of Gedser. From there they continued to the Central Station in Copenhagen and registered at the nearby Hotel Terminis.[8] Friends later invited them to stay in their spacious home at the end of a quiet street in the Charlottenlund suburb. The parents were relieved when their sixteen-year-old son, Gotthard, joined them in March.[9]

It was Anna von Liphart who saw to the purchase of the estate near Ølstykke. After their sixteen boxcars arrived from Berlin and the family was settled, the von Lipharts summoned their dear friend from Rostock.[10] Reusch applied for a visa at the Danish consulate in Hamburg, and on May 26, 1919, crossed from Rostock to Gedser, Denmark.[11] The eldest son, twenty-five-year-old Reinhold, arrived two days later, shortly after the Reds were driven from Latvia. Paul, age twenty, did not appear until October. That was when the Estonian government enacted land reform legislation and officially seized the Baltic Germans' estates.[12]

Reusch and the von Lipharts were not the only Russian émigrés to settle in Denmark. The Danish and Russian royal families were related, and a number of Romanovs found refuge there. King Christian IX's second daughter, Marie, had married Tsar Alexander III and given birth to the last tsar of Russia, the ill-fated Nicholas II. The Dowager Empress had barely escaped with her life from her estate on the Black Sea, and would live out the rest of her life in melancholic isolation in the kingdom of her birth.

Census lists and tax records indicate that Reusch worked for his room and board by tutoring the younger von Liphart boys and doing manual labor on the estate.[13] Reusch had occasional contact with other exiles, all desperate for news from loved ones trapped in Soviet Russia. Clustered mostly in the capitals, as many as 200,000 Russian refugees made it to Poland; 250,000 escaped into Germany, where bad conditions were nonetheless preferable to life in Soviet Russia; as many as 200,000 made their way to France; 100,000 were stranded in China; 100,000 reached the United States; 70,000 settled in Romania, 30,000 in Yugoslavia, 25,000 in Bulgaria, 20,000 in Czechoslovakia, and 4,000 in Great Britain.[14] Every major city in Europe had its Russian colony. A relative of Richard's, Friedrich Reusch and his family, walked across Siberia to Harbin, Manchuria, and ended up in Brazil.[15] A conservative estimate put the number of Russian refugees at one million; other estimates range from two to three million.[16]

The von Lipharts did not worship in the Danish Folkchurch in Ølstykke, but instead took the local train to Copenhagen where they attended St. Peter's German Evangelical Lutheran Church. Reusch still suffered from acute depression, but on Sundays he always accompanied his hosts to church. On one of those occasions, he wandered into the nearby Romanesque Lutheran Cathedral (before the Reformation, the Church of Our Lady). He saw the white marble statue of Christ, arms outstretched, standing above the high altar. The words "Come Unto Me" were inscribed on the pedestal. Forty years later, Dr. Reusch used the third person to describe his state of mind that day:

> A man whom I know came into that cathedral, saw the statue, came closer. Almost audibly he hears "Come unto ME." The guide whispers, "You will not be able to look into HIS face unless you kneel at his feet." The man knelt & could look into HIS face. Again the almost audible whisper: "Come unto ME."

The man looked up & saw HIS eyes full of compassion, but sad, suffering eyes. The man had lost his faith in mankind, was suffering. "Come unto ME! I will give you peace."

The man looked at his hands, hard hands, covered with blood from battles with enemies who had made him lose faith in mankind. — And he went away from the statue.

And he saw the statue of Peter, keys in hand, the unstable man whom CHRIST had made to be a rock. And opposite was Paul, whom CHRIST had snatched as a brand from the blazing fire of earthly emotions and made out of him the greatest missionary.

And he saw Matthew with a tablet and pen writing his Gospel, and opposite was John on his knees, looking up into heaven, hearing the words: "Be you faithful unto death & I will give you the crown of life."

"Faithful, faithful" — But I have no inner peace any more, I am moved by emotions. My relatives murdered, my estates gone, my King dead. Faithfulness requires stability. Where can I get it?[17]

That summer the former professor and pastor worked as a field hand, took responsibility for the poultry flock, established a colony of bees, and laid out a vegetable garden.[18] A previous owner had planted an orchard of 200 fruit trees,[19] and the physical labor required to bring the sixteen-year-old trees to harvest was good medicine for Reusch's body and soul.

A uniform of his former regiment was tailored for him. Perhaps he attended some now-forgotten Russian émigré event in Copenhagen. Or perhaps he was invited to attend some special event with the von Lipharts, or the nearby Frederiksborg Castle, the royal family's summer palace that had become the center of European court life in those days.[20] Years later in Africa Reusch's three daughters used the uniform as a costume in their play until their mother threw the thing away, tattered and dirty.

The idea that Russia could be retaken from the Bolsheviks by military force was still considered credible by some. General Nikolai Nikolaiovich Yudenitch, who had established an office in Helsinki, arrived in Estonia in July 1919 to take command of the White Army of the Northwest.[21] His first attempt that August failed. A group of wealthy Danes and Russian émigrés worked to raise money and recruit volunteer soldiers for Yudenitch, who was planning a second campaign to retake Petrograd from the Soviets.[22] However, Reusch was repelled by the "sweet smiles" of the scheming factions.[23]

The Yudenitch campaign was launched in September 1919. Russian exiles everywhere avidly consumed every headline and story. Indeed, in mid-October the news was so promising that some optimistic Russians began making plans to return to their homes and estates in Russia:

October 15th: *Northwest Army Moving on Gatschina*
October 16th: *Anti-Reds Winning on Three Fronts; Petrograd Doomed*
October 18th: *Anti-Red Forces Now in Petrograd*
October 21st: *News of Fall of City Hourly Expect in London*

But then the good news turned into tragedy for the Whites:

October 22nd: *Yudenitch Army in Hard Fighting Near Petrograd*
October 25th: *Trotzky Mobilizes All Petrograd Men*
October 28th: *Yudenitch Losing Ground to Reds*

On Saturday, November 1st, the press reported Trotski's charge to the victorious Reds: "Onward. Do not give the enemy time to rest. Drive him, strangle him, beat him mercilessly. The hour of rest will come when the offal has been destroyed." Few White émigrés could bear to read the news stories in the following days:

November 5th: *Report Yudenitch Army Surrounded*
November 17th: *Yudenitch Resigns*
November 26th: *Northwest Army Dwindled Away*
December 2nd: *Russian Wounded in Pitiable Plight*[24]

By the turn of the year, the routing of General Yudenitch's troops was complete. Walter Duranty wired the *New York Times* office from Riga:

> Appalling conditions are reported from northwestern Estonia, where typhus and other epidemics among the debris of the Yudenitch army and the Russian refugees have utterly submerged the relief and sanitary workers. . . . Living and dead are huddled pell-mell on the bare floor, without even straw to lie upon, in all the horror and filth of typhus, dysentery, smallpox, wounds, frostbite, pneumonia, and gangrene.[25]

The terrible cost of the failed attempt to free Petrograd had to do with a failure of leadership and corruption. General Yudenitch was arrested by the Estonians and charged with depositing Northwest Army funds in personal foreign bank accounts instead of paying for the care of his sick and dying men,[26] who represented, according to a reporter on the scene, "some of the bluest blood of imperial Russia."[27] The mortality rate among the 12,000 volunteers exceeded 50 percent.[28]

Facing more pressing challenges on other fronts, the Soviets signed a treaty in Tartu on February 2, 1920, guaranteeing Estonian independence.

A CALL TO EAST AFRICA

During one of their visits to the city, Baron von Liphart introduced Reusch to his friend and scholar, Frants Peter Buhl, a professor of Semitic languages at the University of Copenhagen. Reusch had read his books and articles while studying at Dorpat University, including Buhl's most influential work, *Kanon and Text des Alten Testaments* (1891). Von Bulmerincq persuaded Reusch to finish the research for his Magister Diploma. He would be enrolled at Tartu University and advised by von Bulmerincq, but would complete the research for his dissertation under

Buhl's direction in Copenhagen. His topic was the historical context of the Old Testament prophet, Micah.[29]

As Reusch told the story, one day in the autumn of 1920, he received three letters, one from Alexander von Bulmerincq at Tartu, offering him a professorship in Oriental languages. Another informed him that his friends from his Terek Cossack regiment had perished in the war. The third came from the Evangelical Lutheran Mission in Leipzig: Might a stateless Russian Lutheran be interested in applying for missionary work in East Africa?[30]

Reusch grieved for his friends from the Cadet Corps who had lost their lives. He probably also felt some measure of guilt for having escaped their fate. But he was never one to gaze into a rear-view mirror. Two options were now open to him: Return to academia, or set his sights for Africa.

East Africa in the First World War

European colonial governments drafted Africans to fight in their war. British and Belgian troops first engaged German forces in mid-August 1914. The Germans fell back from their East African colony in 1916 and crossed into Mozambique, and then into Northern Rhodesia, where they remained at war's end.[31]

At the Paris Peace Conference on May 6, 1919, the Supreme Council, comprised of the victorious Allied powers of Great Britain, France and America, disposed of Germany's former Pacific, Far Eastern and African colonies. Most of German East Africa was assigned to the British under mandate of the League of Nations.[32] Because of the heavy obligations of its far-flung empire, the British government had no desire to accept the mandate and pressed the United States to take responsibility for Tanganyika. The Americans declined.[33] The Tanganyika Mission Trust was created under Article 438 of the Treaty, which placed the property of the German missions under its jurisdiction.[34] Borders between British territories (Kenya, Uganda, Tanganyika, Rwanda and Burundi) and the Belgian Congo were then drawn on the basis of projected colonial railroad construction rather than existing tribal homelands.[35]

British authorities in East Africa had ordered the detention of all German nationals in 1917, intending to send them to internment camps in Egypt. No German missionaries were exempt, Roman Catholic or Protestant. When the South African Boer Commander, General Smuts, learned of the British plan, he told the Leipzig missionaries in the Kilimanjaro District to remain at their posts.[36] Finally, in the summer of 1920, the British ordered thirty-one of the Leipzig missionaries to leave. Rev. and Mrs. Leonhard Blumer and Alexander Eisenschmidt, Baltic Germans from Estonia, were permitted to remain since they carried Imperial Russian passports. Rev. and Mrs. Henrich Pfitzinger, on furlough in Alsace-Loraine, would be permitted to return.

But what would happen to the African Lutheran communities that had matured since the Germans first sent missionaries to the Kilimanjaro region in 1893? How could two missionary couples provide for the spiritual needs of 5,445 baptized Christians, supervise 87 schools with 111 African teachers and 8,270 students, and provide medical services throughout the region?[37]

That was the issue put to the National Lutheran Council, an organization through which most of the independent American ethnic Lutheran synods addressed global issues.[38] European economies were in shambles, and millions of people faced food, housing and fuel shortages. American synods were the only Lutheran bodies in the world at the time with resources sufficient to respond to the global mission crisis triggered by the First World War.

"I rejected the call at first," Reusch said, "because it [paid] the equivalent of six dollars a month." But his conscience chided him: "You would sell those in Africa who Jesus loves for thirty pieces of silver?"[39] His duty was clear: "I could not betray the motto of my regiment: 'Loyalty for loyalty, blood for blood, life for life.'"[40] And so the letter from Leipzig he took as "a hint from my Saviour to fill the gap and take over the highly endangered mission work."[41] On October 21, 1920 he sent a letter to the Leipzig Missions director offering his services.[42]

With a renewed sense of purpose, the 29-year-old Reusch vowed to serve the Mission with the same loyalty he had pledged to his Tsar and regiment. He concluded his application in characteristic style — assertive, eloquent, colorful, always mindful of his audience, and invoking his Imperial Russian military ethos — while at the same time striking a modest and humble stance:

> As it was once my intention to serve my emperor (the unfortunate Nicholas II, as I am a Russian subject) faithfully unto death in the fight against heathen and Islamic powers, so will I now do it for my heavenly King. Without reservation, I am prepared to commit myself unconditionally to His service in Africa, and to follow Him, my Saviour, anywhere as his faithful officer through thick and thin, through hunger, trouble and all dangers, through life and death. I know that my powers are weak, that my experience is limited, that my knowledge is small, but I know also that He, the infinite Love, is mighty in the weak and that He, the all-merciful, will permit the sincere to succeed in the work of God's Kingdom. To Him be praise forever![43]

The applicant listed the names of several churchmen as references: Professor von Bulmerincq in Tartu; Rev. Wittrock, the former senior pastor at St. Johannes, Tartu, now living in Mecklenburg; Rev. Frahm in Rostock; and Rev. Lampe, pastor of the German Lutheran Church in Copenhagen. The mission director, Dr. Paul, put a series of questions to those men: "Is he a good Lutheran? Is he reliable, conscientious, of humble and tolerant character? Is he physically fit and without ailments?"[44]

Professor von Bulmerincq, who had hoped his former student would accept his invitation to rejoin the faculty at Tartu, was the first to reply:

> I have known Pastor Reusch since 1911, and have seldom seen a student so strongly devoted to his studies. In addition, he finds enough time to support others.

His examination, which he passed in 1915, was simply a feast for the commission [dissertation committee]; equally excellent was his dissertation on David's Testament (II Samuel 23: 1-7), which should have been published. I know that he feels drawn to missionary work, and I believe that because he keeps a regimen of strict physical exercise, and because of his modesty and ability to make his way under difficult circumstances, and especially his devoutness and his passion for God, you will find reasons to choose him to convert pagans.

"In spite of that," von Bulmerincq stubbornly insisted, "academia seems to be his true field of work in which he will do his best as a teacher and researcher."[45]

Pastor Lampe had "no doubt that the man is serious about the task he wants to undertake, and it is very helpful that he comes to you with special language and ethnographic skills." He concluded, "I can only say that the Baron [von Liphart] loves and admires him and especially values his academic qualifications."[46]

Reusch was an ideal candidate to look after Leipzig's interests. He was an ordained pastor of the Lutheran Church in Russia, and as a stateless Russian he would be acceptable to the British. Reusch was elated to learn that his application had been accepted.

Although a mission transfer agreement between the Germans and the Americans had not been concluded, Reusch was invited to Leipzig to begin preparing for his new assignment. The von Lipharts were saddened to think of losing the young man from the Caucasus whom they had come to think of as their adopted son. Even though their resources were now somewhat limited, the Baron and his wife provided for Richard's expenses by sending funds in his name to Leipzig.

In February 1921 the eager and aspiring missionary informed Dr. Paul that he intended to defend his Magister dissertation at Tartu in the middle of March — but not if the door to Africa were to open. "Let me know when to come to Leipzig," he pleaded, "and of my prospects for being sent to Africa because I need to apply for a passport and have it verified." Should he exchange money immediately? Did the mission director recommend that he secure an affidavit from the Imperial Russian consulate in Copenhagen stating that he had no connection with the Bolsheviks?[47]

In the first years of the civil war, Russian embassies and consulates were still staffed by foreign service personnel loyal to the imperial government.[48] Baron E. Schilling, former assistant foreign minister under Sazonov in 1916, was in charge of the Russian embassy in Copenhagen. He dictated and signed the following affidavit, No. 1169, on March 3, 1921:

The Russian Consulate-General in Copenhagen certifies herewith that the Russian citizen, Pastor of the Evangelical-Lutheran church Gustav Otto Richard Reusch, born October 18th 1891, in Samara, Russia, is personally known to this Consulate-General as in every way reliable and trustworthy having never associated with bolsheviks. He left Russia in 1918 owing to the present conditions in that country, fearing bolshevik prosecution.[49]

Reusch was an ideal candidate to represent Leipzig's interests, but the ultimate decision depended on the outcome of negotiations with the Americans. Therefore, early in March 1921, Reusch wrote to the National Lutheran Council to say that he was ready to leave for Africa if they were willing to send him. No, replied Lauritz Larsen, not until Council representatives had visited Africa and secured British approval would it be "possible for us to do anything in the matter of issuing a call to any new workers in the Leipzig field. Until such call has been issued to you, it is useless to apply to the British Government for a permit for you to enter the Tanganyika Territory. It grieves me that it is necessary to send you such discouraging news just at this time."[50]

Upon receiving news of the delay, Reusch took matters into his own hands. On April 14 he reminded the Tartu faculty that he had worked under the direction of Professor von Bulmerincq from 1915 to 1918, continued his studies with Professor Buhl in Copenhagen, completed his dissertation, and was prepared for his oral examinations. A week later Reusch said farewell to the von Lipharts.[51] The baron gave Richard a photograph of himself inscribed with the words, "To his true friend, Richard Gustavovich, with gratitude. R.v. Liphart."[52] The couple, along with their five sons, walked Richard through the orchard to the crest of the hill. Under the last row of trees they said a final farewell, and watched their friend stride down the hillside through the field to the railroad tracks where he waited for the local train to Copenhagen.

Richard Gustavovich and the von Lipharts never saw each other again.

AMERICAN LUTHERANS VISIT AFRICA

David Livingstone's adventures dramatically raised the consciousness of "Darkest Africa" among Christians throughout Europe and North America. With the expansion of colonial empires grew a corresponding urge among British and other Christian university students to evangelize the world — in their generation, as they believed.[53] In the United States, for example, students from Augustana College (Rock Island, Illinois) had petitioned the delegates at the 1917 convention of the Augustana (Swedish) Evangelical Lutheran Synod to begin a mission in Africa. Their elders agreed, and Pastor Ralph Hult and his family were subsequently commissioned for work in Sudan.[54]

The Iowa (German) Synod provided financial assistance to the African Leipzig Mission in the difficult years during and immediately after the First World War, but they did not have the resources to take over the work. Since the Augustana Synod was about to begin mission work in Africa, the National Lutheran Council asked the American Swedes to consider taking responsibility for the abandoned Leipzig fields in Tanganyika Territory.[55]

In 1921 the National Lutheran Council sent two representatives to survey the fourteen Leipzig mission congregations in the Kilimanjaro District. Dr. Clarence L. Brown (United Lutheran Synod) and Rev. A. C. Zeilinger (Iowa Synod) visited Lutheran congregations, some comprising less than 100 congregants and others numbering 1,000. African church leaders, chiefs and congregations welcomed them everywhere they went. Despite the ravages of the World War, the African Lutherans had kept the faith. On their walk from Marangu to Mwika, for example, 700 to 800 Mwika Christians, carrying banners and singing hymns, came to meet and welcome the Americans.[56]

In Mwika, Brown and Zeilinger were presented a petition from the district chief, Noemasi. He was not a Christian, but he had a message for the Americans:

> Sirs:
>
> Many greetings, and again greetings. I have one thing on my mind for which I would like to petition you, and through you the Christian leaders in America, and the cause for which I ask is this. I earnestly ask that you will not forget me. I desire very much to have a teacher in my country. Here in Mwika there are sheep and there are people who would like to have the sheep just as the leopard wants to break in the house where sheep are. I do not like it that my people should be without a teacher for so long a time, as I too appreciate meeting a teacher from time to time. This is my petition. And begging heartily to greet the Christian leaders in America,
>
> Yours with greetings, Chief Noemasi.[57]

Neither of the two Council representatives returned to America. Dr. Brown died in West Africa before he could file his report, and Pastor Zeilinger was so moved by what he saw and heard while visiting the Kilimanjaro District that he asked to remain as a missionary.[58]

As a result of Zeilinger's report, in the autumn of 1921 the Augustana Synod informed the Council that, yes, they would adopt the orphaned Leipzig missions. An Augustana official, Peter Peterson, explained the reason for the Synod's decision: "We are going there to bring the black sons and daughters of Africa to the feet of Jesus that they might be saved."[59]

The Ralph Hult family was in Sudan, charged with the task of selecting an appropriate area in which to begin their work. In October 1921, just before he left for Leipzig to negotiate the terms of transfer, the president of the Augustana Synod, G. A. Brandelle, instructed the Hults to leave for a new assignment in Tanganyika. "I ought to tell you," Brandelle wrote to Hult,

> that on this field there are at present two missionaries from Estonia and also one, Rev. Zeilinger, from the Iowa Synod. The men from Estonia are willing to remain on the field for all time to come. They were not driven out since they were not Germans. There are also two more men to be had from some source in Europe, I think from some one of the Baltic provinces, but whether or not the [Mission] Board would feel like calling them I do not know.[60]

Representatives of the Leipzig Mission demanded that in addition to its Estonian missionaries, Blumer and Eisenschmidt, Augustana must call two more of its personnel from "some one of the Baltic provinces."[61] That the vanquished Germans had the gall to insist on a condition of any kind irked some less forgiving Swedish American church leaders. However, Brandelle readily agreed because of the urgent need for replacements.

There was a second condition: "[W]hen the Leipzig Society will be permitted to take up [future] work in Africa, the field will be divided [between Leipzig and Augustana]."[62] The British Colonial Office sanctioned the transfer with two conditions of its own: That the Missionry Conference of Great Britain give its assent; and that the Augustana Synod invest resources, financial and personnel, sufficient to maintain the level of the former Leipzig Mission educational and medical services. Augustana agreed to send a minimum of six missionary couples.[63]

As his future was being decided elsewhere in the world, an impatient Reusch once again petitioned the Tartu faculty to quickly schedule his examinations so he could proceed with his preparations for Africa. On October 10th he was examined in his knowledge of Holy Scripture, theology, archeology, Aramaic and Gurkic (an obscure Caucasian language).

Diploma No. 9497, dated November 11, 1921, declared *Herr R. Reusch als Magister der Theologie*.[64]

Reusch returned to Leipzig in January 1922 to begin intensive training for Africa. For the next ten months he studied tropical medicine, the Swahili language, and poured over the accumulated ethnographic literature of East Africa published during three decades by scholarly German missionaries. He also began studying the three languages spoken in the Kilimanjaro region of Tanganyika Territory: Ki-Swahili, Ki-Masai and Wa-Chagga.

Leipzig was no sedate university town like Tartu, but a city of elegance and high culture, a banking center that rivaled Berlin. The Egyptian Museum on Schillerstrasse boasted collections of rich resources, splendid artifacts of the ancient world, including African Coptic culture. Reusch sometimes worshipped at St. Thomas Church, where Johann Sebastian Bach had served as director of sacred music for twenty-seven years. In 1509, at the beginning of the Leipzig Dispute between Luther and Johann Eck, the Augustinian reformer preached from the St. Thomas pulpit on at least two occasions. As Reusch sat in a pew facing the pulpit, he gazed at the heroic stained glass windows: King Gustav II Adolph of Sweden; Johann Sebastian Bach; Martin Luther; Elector Friedrick the Wise of Saxony; Melanchton and Kaiser Wilhelm I.

The Lutheran seminary in Leipzig, affiliated with the city's prestigious university, had strongly influenced the Baltic seminary at Tartu. Faculty of both institutions were orthodox in their traditional Lutheran interpretation of Holy Scripture. Like their Lutheran peers in America, they rejected neo-orthodox biblical criticism. However, the German clergy were more formal, sophisticated and intellectual than their more pietistic Swedish American brethren.

The cultural differences between European and American Lutherans were substantial. The more formal European evangelical tradition held greater respect for the weight of history and the context of culture. For example, there was no scholarly Augustana cleric and missionary to equal the credentials of the Rev. Dr. Prof. Bruno Gutmann, the Leipzig scholar and missionary who developed his theory of missiology based upon African cultural traditions.[65] The Augustana Synod in the American Midwest denounced dancing, movie-going, playing cards, the use of tobacco and the consumption of alcohol — including wine and beer. None of those "semblances of evil" had a place in the life of a Christian, a notion dismissed by a philosophy professor at one of the Synod's colleges as "Midwestern corn silk theology."[66]

The Americans were also committed to secular egalitarianism — never mind the many social contradictions, including racial prejudice — while Europeans accepted class distinctions. Moreover, most Swedes were members of a state episcopate, but their American cousins and their descendants wanted nothing to do with an authoritarian church hierarchy. Even the title of "bishop" was abhorred, and so parish delegates elected church "presidents" in the American democratic tradition. That such differences would lead to tensions between Augustana and Leipzig should have come as no surprise. It would undoubtedly be splendid, said an Iowa Synod official, if missions could rise above nationality, but the difficulty is that "missionaries still remain human and are therefore in greater or lesser degree nationalists."[67] Despite those cultural differences, Leipzig and Augustana Lutherans continued to work together to create a successful transfer.

NEWS FROM THE USSR

In March 1922, Richard learned that his father and family had survived the civil war in Taganrog, a city near Rostov-on-Don, which had been caught in a fierce tug-of-war between the Reds and Whites. Over and over again he read the letter from the Passport Office of the Foreign Ministry in Berlin:

> Your father, teacher and church official, Gustav Reusch, living in Taganrog, Russia, asks us to allow him and his entire family to enter Leipzig. However, before we can give permission, according to law we need permission from the Leipzig police and the municipal housing office. In order to proceed, you are requested to secure these documents and send them to the German Embassy in Moscow, which received your father's request.[68]

Richard immediately began the process to secure the necessary permits. The police assented to his request, but the housing authority, due to shortages of food and shelter, refused to accept the refugees. When Soviet authorities later frustrated a second attempt, Gustav Ivanovich accepted his fate. The family remained trapped in Soviet Russia.[69]

Red Army Takes Vladikavkaz

Richard's relatives survived a twelve-day battle as Osetians and a remnant of Terek Cossacks fought to repel the Red army that was closing in on Vladikavkaz. The Reds took the northern suburbs, including Mikhailevskaya, and the Whites fell back to the city center where they fired on the advancing Red troops from the steeple of the Lutheran Church. Rev. Aksim, Richard's confirmation pastor, was called to the side of a dying man to administer Holy Communion and was not present. According to a church report, "After gaining possession of the church, the Reds wanted to burn it and execute the pastor. It was due solely to the courageous interference on the part of the pastor's wife that the church was not destroyed."[70] The Reds controlled the city, and the Imperial Cadet Corps was closed.[71] A few church members lost their lives in the fighting, some were subsequently arrested and sent to forced labor camps, others managed to flee Russia, but most were left to survive as best they could. The loss of members and the effect of Soviet decrees so weakened the congregation that it could no longer support Pastor Aksim. He and his wife returned to their native Estonia.[72]

Soviet agents had fanned out across Europe to lure back to Russia and then arrest émigrés regarded as enemies of the Soviet regime. Others were assassinated — in Paris, London, Stockholm, Berlin and elsewhere. Richard did not want Soviet agents to learn of his whereabouts and therefore never sent letters and food parcels to his parents. In the first two decades after the Revolution, Soviet authorities continued to forward mail addressed to persons living in former Russian provinces, such as Lithuania. Gustav Ivanovich knew that his letters were opened and read by Soviet postal inspectors, but some of them reached his daughter, Olga Hirsch, who lived in Kounau, Lithuania. She forwarded letters intended for Richard to the Leipzig Mission, and Richard sent his letters and food parcels intended for his parents to Olga, who copied his letters, rewrapped his parcels and addressed them in her own hand to their parents in Rostov.

STARVATION

Food and housing in post-war Germany were in short supply, and conditions grew even worse after the Allies refused to reduce the size of war reparations specified in the Treaty of Versailles. In 1922 the exchange rate soared from 162 to 7,000 marks to the dollar, and a year later to 4,200 *billion* marks to the dollar.[73] In America Dr. J. A. Moorhead, president of the National Lutheran Council, tried to rouse member synods to action. There were, reported Augustana's President Brandelle, "thousands upon thousands in Germany today who are freezing and starving. Men, women and children are suffering the pangs of hunger. They grit their teeth and bear it as best as they may."[74]

Soviet Russia, too, was caught in the grip of another terrible famine. Despite food, shelter and clothing shortages in Germany, faithful German Lutherans collected funds to aid their brethren in Russia, as did Sweden and Norway. "But," scolded Brandelle, "the greater number of our own congregations, slick and fat, and with a super-abundance of food and money, appear to be turning more or less a deaf ear to these piteous cries for help."[75]

The 1921 famine in Russia was brought on by a combination of factors — civil war, Soviet policy that forced farmers into collectives, and another drought. The National Lutheran Council sent President Moorhead to Russia where he was to assess conditions and supervise the distribution of church-sponsored relief among the Germans living in the Volga and Caucasus regions.

The American Relief Association (ARA), a government-sponsored program under the direction of Herbert Hoover, coordinated efforts of various secular and religious agencies.[76] "To see Russia makes one wish that he were dead," wrote an ARA official. "If I were condemned to live here always I should prefer death, and yet there are millions of men and women, as good and better than I am, who are condemned to this very thing."[77]

Morehead worked among the starving and sick through the long winter months while at the same time contending with suspicious and uncooperative Soviet authorities. Said the American churchman, "If Dante ever imagined a more horrible scene, he failed to include it in his 'Divine Comedy.'"[78] In the spring of 1922 his body "went Bolshevik," as he put it, and to recover his health and equilibrium he withdrew to a sanitarium in Germany.[79]

American Lutherans finally responded to their synods' appeals. Students at Gustavus Adolphus, a college of the Augustana Synod, sent nine containers of food to their peers at Saratov University. Each container held numerous 150-pound bales, containing flour, rice, lard, sugar, tea and powdered milk. The students' generous gift arrived during the first week of May 1922. Some weeks later the Americans received a carefully hand-painted scroll of gratitude from their Russian peers. "Dear Colleagues, so distant, but akin by spirit," began one of two enclosed letters:

> We beg you to accept our deepest and most sincere gratitude for the attention you have shown to us in these our painful days, when we, students, have to make incredible efforts, on the verge of total exhaustion, in order to force our way and to attain our aim in the dreary surroundings of actual Russian life.
>
> Your help has proved not only a material support for the needy students of a famished country, but also a spiritual one, because it has again kindled in our hearts the almost extinct faith in the best feelings of men. We, the undersigned, students, send you our love and beg you to believe that the memory of your kind deed will forever live in our hearts.[80]

By the spring of 1922, 14 million Russians were receiving one meal a day from ARA kitchens. International aid coordinated by ARA totaled 500,000 tons of food, almost matching the tonnage supplied by the Soviet government.

The National Lutheran Council undertook a campaign in December 1922 to raise another $725,000 for European and Russian relief. Promotional ads asked each member in each Lutheran synod to contribute pocket change to the campaign. "Thirty-three cents for a movie or three dollars and thirty cents for a more elaborate attraction is *just* a minor part of our lives. It is not so in a Russian Lutheran's life. There it is a matter of life and death," admonished the copy.[81]

Despite tremendous international relief efforts, some 2 million Russians had perished by the time the famine dissipated.[82]

AFRICA BECKONS

In the summer of 1922, Missionary Reusch was assigned an extensive speaking tour to promote foreign missions. After Reusch's visit to Landshut that June, Pastor G. Seidel sent a report to Mission Director Paul. When speaking to the children, Seidel noted, Reusch "spoke in very picturesque language." But it was Reusch's Russian manner that consumed the substance of his report:

> That evening, speaking from the pulpit in the church, he spoke about Russia's famine and was very powerful and descriptive as he talked about his family in Russia, indeed, most vivid and lively. He spoke in a friendly yet devout style, not in the routine humble manner of German missionaries but according to the Russian style — admiringly, kissing hands, and using many superlatives. For my family that at first was strange, almost awkward. But through him I was reminded of many similar experiences I had in Russia. As the hours passed, we grew closer to each other because I've seen many places and towns in Russia in which he also walked, especially during the days of our Russian military campaign.

Seidel concluded, "He has clear eyes and seems to be a faithful man and effective despite all his travel and speaking, which is a real physical and mental achievement. May he become a useful instrument."[83]

Augustana officials finally accepted Leipzig's conditions concerning the mission transfer: Reusch and the Pfitzingers would join the Blumers and Eisenschmidts as Leipzig's representatives in Africa, and at such future time when Leipzig might return to their missions, agreed to divide their areas of responsibility. In a letter of July 20, 1922, President Brandelle informed Reusch that the Augustana Board of Foreign Missions had voted unanimously to call him as a missionary. His salary was set at $60 per month plus living and travel expenses.[84]

In September 1922, Reusch filled out and signed an application for a British visa for Tanganyika Territory:

> I hereby undertake to pay all due obedience and respect to the Government of Tanganyika Territory and while carefully abstaining from participation in political affairs, I desire and purpose ex animus to work in friendly cooperation with the said Government in all matters which my influence may properly be exerted; and in particular, I undertake, if engaged in educational work, that my influence shall be exerted to promote loyally the Government of Tanganyika Territory in the minds of my pupils, and to make them good citizens of the British Empire.[85]

It was a promise that in years to come would cause him grief, but he could not have anticipated that in 1922.

Bishop Ihmels commissioned Pastor Reusch in a service at the ornate St. Nicholas Church in

Leipzig on the evening of January 6, 1923. The Mission director, Dr. Paul, read from Isaiah 49: "Sing, O heavens; and be joyful, O earth; and break forth into singing, O mountains: for Jehovah hath comforted his people, and will have compassion upon his afflicted."[86]

Reusch signed a Leipzig Mission contract that specified the terms of his assignment:

> Since the contract between the Augustana Synod and Leipzig Mission says that the part of the missionary area in which you will work will one day again belong to the Leipzig Mission, we therefore expect that you also must follow the orders of the Leipzig Mission. We intend to set up a Lutheran branch church in Africa; therefore, please follow the principles under which the Church functions. Should you be uncertain of how to proceed, please ask your colleagues [Leipzig missionaries from Estonia and France] for further instructions.
>
> One of the rules of Lutheran Missions is that we expect you to learn the language of the country. Therefore, when you first arrive use a great part of your time and energy to study the language that is spoken in your area. After not more than two years you will have to pass a language exam.
>
> We expect you to be obedient to the American missionary office, to us, and to your colleagues. At the same time we promise to care for you.

He was to be neutral in political matters; he would initially live with an established missionary family; and the Mission would determine when he would be allowed to marry. He was to send timely reports to Leipzig for the promotion of mission work among the parishes in Germany, and the Mission director must clear whatever he might wish to publish. Finally,

> [This document] pledges you to formal duty as a missionary for life, even though we cannot guarantee that you will stay a missionary for your entire life. But still we hope that God will give you health, strength and joy as a missionary so that you can do your work faithfully for many years, as God wills, to the end of your days.[87]

In America, meanwhile, the Augustana Synod launched an initial $50,000 campaign to finance its commitments in Tanganyika Territory, and a special collection was set for the Third Sunday after Epiphany.[88] Parishioners were told,

> As a Synod we now face a mighty challenge. We will either succeed in our missionary effort or go down in the annals of missionary undertakings as failing to measure up to the trust placed in us by the Lord Himself. It is up to us as an Augustana people to decide what it shall be.[89]

Reusch received his visa for Tanganyika Territory at the British consulate in Leipzig on January 12, 1923, and on the 29th he left Leipzig for Marseilles where he and the Pfitzingers boarded a ship for Africa. After passing through the Suez Canal, they were scheduled to debark at Mombassa, Kenya, sometime in the middle of February.

"And so I went to the most dangerous spots in the Dark Continent," said Reusch in his characteristic style, and "plunged into dangers, hoping that they would bring an end to [my] sufferings."[90] Once again he faced the challenges of adapting to a new vocation in a foreign land. His childhood fantasies of African adventure were about to come true.

Missionary Reusch (right) and the Henrich Pfitzinger family transit the Suez Canal on their way to Tanganyika Territory in February, 1923.

Betty Anderson

CHAPTER 6

1 Siegfried Sassoon, excerpt from "Dreamers," *Modern British Poetry*, Louis Untermeyer, ed. (1950), 311.
2 Marc Raeff, Russia Abroad: *A cultural History of the Russian Emigration*, 1919-1939 (1990), 118.
3 R. Reusch, "Mein Lebenslauf," 3.
4 Piersig, Landeskirche (Mecklenburg) Archivist, letter to the author, 7 October 1997.
5 Mark 9:24.
6 F. L. Carsten, *Revolution in Central Europe*, 1918-1919 (1972), 149-50.
7 Nicholas Wreden, *The Unmaking of a Russian* (1935), 303.
8 Von Liphart family visa registration documents (Rigsarkivet 1353 Rigspolitichefen/Lb. nr. 631), DNA.
9 Visa registration cards (Rigsarkivet 1353, Rigspolitichefen, Lb. nr. 630), DNA.
10 Census, real estate and tax data for 1919 and 1920, LHAO. Decades later, according to the archivist, one of the estate laborers recalled unloading and hauling the contents of *thirty* boxcars to the von Liphart's manor house.
11 Visa registration card for Richard Reusch (1353 Rigspolitichefen/Lb. nr. 631), DNA.
12 Toivo Raun, *Estonia and the Estonians* (1987), 128.
   The von Liphart residence and its art collection were nationalized.
13 Von Liphart tax records and census data, LHAOR. R. Reusch, "Mein Lebenslauf," 5-6.
14 Martin Gilbert, "The Russian Exodus, 1917-1923," *Atlas of Russian History* (1972), 107.
15 "List of Heads of Families of Harbin Refugees" (LWC 16-11), AELCA.
16 Gilbert, 107; and Raeff, 24 and 202-03.
17 R. Reusch, chapel sermon notes, 26-27 February 1958, GACA.
18 R. Reusch, "Mein Lebenslauf," 3, AELML.
19 J. C. C. LaCours, *Danske Gaarde* (1907). Eighty years later, one apple tree and one pear tree continued to grace the south lawn of the manor house.
20 Palle Lauring, *A History of the Kingdom of Denmark* (1960), 234-35.
   The Royal Lists from 1912 to the present are not open for public inspection; however, the senior assistant archivist at the Danish National Archives conducted a search and reported to the author (letter, 29 June 2000) that Reusch's name does not appear on any of the Royal Lists for 1919-20.
21 Dimitry V. Lehovich, *White Against Red: The Life of General Anton Denikin* (1974), 316.
22 There are various descriptions of Danish efforts to aid the Whites, such as that described in *Interventsiya po Severo-zapade Rossii, 1917-1920* (1995), 210-15.
23 R. Reusch, undated speech notes (ca. 1972), GACA.
24 Headlines are quoted from issues of *The New York Times*.
25 Walter Duranty, "Esthonia's Fearful Toll of Typhus," *New York Times*, 22 January 1920, sec. 1, p. 2.
26 "Yudenitch Arrested by the Esthonians," *New York Times*. 30 January 1919, I, 2.
27 Arthur E. Copping, ""Russian Wounded in Pitiable Plight," *New York Times*, 2 December 1919, I, 17.
28 W. P. Coates, Zelda K. Coates, "The Baltic States, General Yudenitch, and the Soviet," *Armed Intervention in Russia, 1918-1922* (1935), 177-97.

29 Professor Buhl (1850-1932) also taught for eight years at the University of Leipzig and was published in German, Danish and English. His article, "Dichtkunst bei den Israeliten," according to *Encyclopaedia Judaica* (vol. 4 [1974], 1468) anticipated form criticism (the identification of literary types and analysis of associated cultural contexts). His scholarly works included studies in Semitic languages, biblical studies, geography of the Middle East, and Islamic studies. Reusch's work with von Bulmerincq and Buhl determined his own scholarly interests that led to the publication of *Der Islam in Ost-Afrika* (1930) and *A Short History of East Africa* (1954).

30 R. Reusch, various speech notes, GACA.

31 W. E. F. Ward and L. W. White, *East Africa: A Century of Change, 1870-1970* (1972), 80-81.

32 "Fate of the German Colonies, Mandataries Named," *New York Times Current History*, vol. 10, pt. 1 (19 June 1919), 350-51.

33 W. E. F. Ward and L. W. White, *East Africa: A Century of Change: 1870-1970* (1972), 161.

34 Secretary of the Conference of Missionary Societies, letter to the Under-Secretary of State, Colonial Office, London, 21 December 1926 (CO 691-85/2), PRO.

35 "German East Africa Divided Up," *New York Times Current History*, pt. 1 (May 1920), 350-51.

36 George J. Fritschel, "The East Africa Lutheran Mission," pt. 3, *Lutheran Companion*, vol. 30 (29 April 1922), 259. The periodical was the primary means of communication between the Augustana Synod and its members.

37 Fritschel.

38 The National Lutheran Council appropriated $137,007, a substantial sum in 1921 dollars, to aid former German Protestant missions in China, Japan, India, Africa and South America — Minutes, 14 January 1922, 3 (NLC 1/2, box 18-7), AELCA.

39 This quote appears frequently in his sermon notes, including an undated manuscript at Stacey, Minnesota (ca. 1970), GACA.

40 "Professor Recalls Turns on Trail of Adventure," Minneapolis *Star*, 26 April 1961, sec. C, 18.

41 R. Reusch, "Mein Lebenslauf," 4.

42 R. Reusch, Letter to Leipzig Missionswerk, 21 October 1920, AELML.

43 R. Reusch, "Mein Lebenslauf," 4.

44 Mission Director Paul, letter to Rev. Wittrock, St. Paulskirche, Mecklenburg-Schwerin, 3 November 1920, AELML.

45 Alexander von Bulmerincq, letter of recommendation to Mission Director Paul, 17 December 1920, AELML.

46 Head Pastor Lampe, letter of recommendation to Mission Director Paul, 27 January 1921, AELML.

47 R. Reusch, letter to Mission Director Paul, 11 February 1921, AELML.

48 Raeff, 63.

49 Baron E. Schilling, affidavit, 3 March 1921, GACA.

50 Lauritz Larsen, letter to R. Reusch at Søborg-Gaard, 29 March 1921, AELML.

51 R. Reusch's visa registration card (Rigspolitichefen 1353-882), DNA.

52 Photograph of Baron von Liphart, with inscription, 7 March 1921, GACA.

53 George Hall, *The Missionary Spirit in the Augustana Church* (1984), 9.

54 R. Reusch, "East Africa," undated manuscript that outlines the history of Augustana mission work in East Africa, ca. 1954, 1, GACA.

As various ethnic Lutheran European groups settled in the U.S., each organized its own Lutheran Church, or Synod. Many Swedish Americans were members of the Augustana Synod. Germans clustered in communities that affiliated with the Missouri Synod, Iowa Synod, or the Wisconsin Synod (among others). Each synod was independent. After a series of mergers, the largest Lutheran Church body in America is the Evangelical Lutheran Church in America (ELCA).

55 "Proceedings of the Lutheran Foreign Mission Council, 15 September 1919, 3-4; and Iowa Synod official in a letter to Nathan R. Melhorn, National Lutheran Council, 18 May 1921 (NLC 1/2, Box 13-11), AELCA.

56 Peter Peterson, "A Few Facts Concerning Our New Mission Field in East Africa," *Mission Tidings*, vol. 17 (September 1922), 14. The periodical was published by the Augustana Women's Missionary Society. The women raised more money for foreign missions over the years than the Synod allocated to its Board of Foreign Missions (Hall, 16-17).

57 Peterson, "A Few Facts,"14.

58 Ralph D. Hult, "A Greeting from East Africa," *Lutheran Companion,* vol. 31 (12 May 1923), 291.

59 Peter Peterson, "The Object of Our Mission Work in Africa," *Lutheran Companion*, vol. 31 (13 January 1923), 25.

60 G. A. Brandelle, letter to Ralph Hult, 5 October 1921 (WMT 322), AELCA.

61 Peterson.

62 Minutes, NLC, 16 November 1922, 10 (NLC 18-7), AELCA.

63 Minutes, NLC, 14 January 1922, 3 (NLC 18-7), AELCA.

64 Magister Diploma (2100-1-13219), ESHA. In Africa three years later, Reusch received another copy of his diploma — in the Estonian language (GACA).

65 See Paul Fleisch, *Lutheran Beginnings around Mr. Kilimanjaro: The First 40 Years*, trans. from German by Martin and Ernst Jäschke (1996); Ernst Jäschke, *Bruno Gutmann: His Life, His Thoughts and His Work* (Erlangen: 1985).

According to Rev. Donald Flatt, *Gutmann* "took care not to break family ties by hasty baptisms of individual converts," but waited until family elders chose to do so; and the traditional blood-brother oath that bound three or four warriors to each other was incorporated into the Rite of Confirmation. *Gutmann* strove to avoid the destabilization of collective family and tribal social order. — Unpublished memoirs.

66 Oscar Winfield, author's notes of lectures at Gustavus Adolphus College, 1963.

67 Iowa Synod official, letter to Nathan Melhorn, 18 May 1921 (NLC 13-11), AELCA.

68 Passport Office, Foreign Ministry, Berlin, letter to Richard Reusch, 23 March 1922, AELML.

69 Letters from his family grew more guarded in the late 1920s and ceased entirely by 1937. Not until 1963 did Reusch receive another letter from his sister, Aurelia, informing him of the death of their parents, their sister Olga, and brother Erich.

70 "Einige Mitteilungen aus dem Leber der evangelisch-lutherischen Kirche in Sowjet-Russland — Confidenteill," 20 (NLC 2-12), AELCA.

71 *Great Soviet Encyclopedia*, vol. 11, translation of 1973 3d edition (Macmillan, 1976), 18.

72 "Einige Mitteilungen," 20.

73 John Carey, in his introduction to "German Inflation, 19 September 1922," *Eye-Witness to History*, ed. by John Carey (1987), 497.

74 G. A. Brandelle, "Dr. Brandelle on Conditions in Europe," *Lutheran Companion*, vol. 30 (25 March 1922), 185.

75 "Brandelle on Conditions...."

76 See Frank Golder, Lincoln Hutchinson, *On the Trail of the Russian Famine* (1927).

77 *War, Revolution and Peace in Russia: The Passages of Frank Golder, 1914-27*, ed. by Terence Emmons (1992), 92-93.

78 J. A. Morehead, "Fighting the Famine in Russia," pt. 1, *Lutheran Companion*, vol. 30 (8 April 1922), 218.

79 Nathan R. Melhorn, "Commissioner Morehead Talks to the Church," pt. 1, *Lutheran Companion*, vol. 30 (16 December 1922), 801.

80 Marie Rausehenbach and others, letter to students at Gustavus Adolphus College, 7 May 1922 (Saratov file), GACA.

81 "Thirty-three Cents? — For What?" *Lutheran Companion*, vol. 30 (30 December 1922), 833.

82 Golder and Hutchinson, 18.

83 G. Seidel, Pastor, letter to Mission Director Paul, 12 July 1922, AELML.

84 G. A. Brandelle, Rock Island, Illinois, letter to Rev. Richard Reusch, 20 July 1922, AELML.

85 Copy of "Form of Application to be filled out by Persons of Alien Nationality Desiring to Undertake Missionary, Educational or Philanthropic Work in British Territory," signed by R. Reusch, 9 September 1922, AELML.

86 Commissioning Service, outline, 6 January 1923, AELML.

87 "Instruktion für Mag. theol. Richard Reusch," document dated 6 January 1923, AELML.

88 G. A. Brandelle, "Remember Our East African Mission on Sunday, January 21st," *Lutheran Companion*, vol. 31 (6 January 1923), 13.

89 "Our Mission in East Africa," editorial, *Lutheran Companion*, vol. 31 (6 January 1923), 2.

90 R. Reusch, manuscript for daily chapel at Gustavus Adolphus College, 26 & 27 February 1958, GACA.

PART II

Tanganyika Territory, East Africa
(1923-1954)

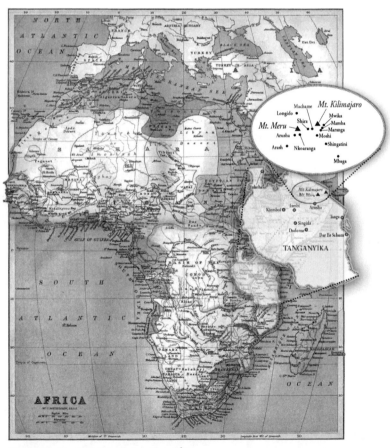

Tanganyika Territory (Tanzania), East Africa

128

Missionary Reusch arrives at Arusha, Tanganyika Territory, March 7, 1923.

Chapter Seven

FIRST TERM, TANGANYIKA TERRITORY
Kilimanjaro District, 1923-29

For he will give his angels charge over thee,
To keep thee in all thy ways.
They shall bear thee up in their hands,
Lest thou dash thy foot against a stone.

— Psalm 91

Missionary Reusch set foot on African soil at Mombassa on February 17, 1923. He was thirty-one years of age and in excellent physical condition because of a program of rigorous physical exercise that had become a daily ritual since his years at the Imperial Cadet Corps. The euphoria that often characterizes the initial stage of cross-cultural adjustment is evident in his first reports and letters, as is his practical nature. After his first eleven exciting days in the Territory, Reusch described all that had happened in a report to Dr. Karl Ihmels in Leipzig.

The veteran Pfitzingers looked for inexpensive lodgings for the night and chose the Imperial, in Reusch's opinion, "quite a shabby hotel owned by a Greek from Rhodesia."[1] Unlike the Pfitzingers, who returned to their mission station at Shigatini, Reusch's first task was to become acquainted with each of the fourteen orphaned Leipzig mission stations. The next day the party packed up their bags and boarded a train to Moshi, where Leipzig's Alexander Eisenschmidt and the Zeilingers from America were waiting to welcome them. "We quickly became friends," Reusch assured his superior in Leipzig.

The stateless Russian joined a diverse team of Lutherans: the Pfitzingers from Alsace-Lorraine, the Blumers and Eisenschmidt from Estonia, the Zeilingers and Hults from America, and the John Steimer family, Swedes who had emigrated to America. The missionaries had come to convert the heathen, but preaching had to wait until they had done what they could for the injured and sick who stood in long lines outside their doors each morning.

The next morning Mrs. Zeilinger opened the small dispensary. Reusch had been trained to administer parasiticides, treat open sores, tend other minor ailments, and dispense quinine to relieve the ravages of malaria fever. He confidently reported, "I was also allowed to help her with suggestions and doing things right away."

The next day, after presenting his documents to the British district officer, Mr. Dunders, Reusch set out on a hike to the next station, located at Masama. The day was beautiful, but by one o'clock that afternoon the temperature reached 50°C (120°F). He arrived at 8 o'clock that evening. Not to worry, he later assured Ihmels, "I can easily cope with the heat."

The next day, Reusch and Bwanna Rehak, a local white man hired by the Mission as a buildings and grounds supervisor, rode mules while two African porters walked to the mission at Machame. That is where Ralph Hult was based, the American cleric who was in charge of the new Augustana mission. "The Hults don't speak much German," Reusch noted, "but since they speak Swedish they were happy when I began speaking Danish to them." When they parted that evening, "Mr. Hult shook my hand and said that he felt as if we had known each other for a long time. I felt the same way. No wonder, since he knows a little Arabic and has an interest in the Orient."

Reusch wanted to visit the mission at Ashira, and perhaps to avoid the heat of mid-day they traveled that night by the light of the moon. Suddenly, on the path ahead they heard shouts and the sound of jingling bells. It was a group of Africans, coming from a circumcision ritual on their way to celebrate. "These dances usually end with many immoral excesses," Reusch wrote. "Just that morning I had the impression of being in a Christian area where I heard the singing of Christians. And now the opposite." He was eager to learn about tribal customs and hurried to observe the celebration. To his regret, his slow-moving party reached the site too late.

The next morning the two white men saddled their mules and for the next five hours slowly made their way through the verdant forest. "It's nothing for someone used to sitting in a saddle," noted the former cavalry officer, "but those donkeys are no horses, and one has to use one's whip quite often."

On their return trip from Ashira to Masama the party decided to take an alternate route through the bush:

> We suddenly came upon a wounded gazelle, which we didn't get because we had only our jackknives and no guns with us. The sunset became darker and darker and the savanna much wilder. Around seven o'clock the donkeys became very agitated . . . Suddenly, right behind us, there was screaming and my donkey got up on his hind legs. The next moment, very close on the right side of us near the river, a distance of perhaps 40 to 50 meters, there was a rumbling roar. The blacks came very close to us. 'Simba!' they cried in frightened whispers.

The men drew close together. "I didn't even notice the danger," Reusch confessed, until he heard Mr. Rehak whisper,

> "The lion is hardly a hundred steps from us, and the other one even closer. Take out your knife. We have to cross the river as fast as possible or we shall be lost. The lions can smell our donkeys."
>
> I took out the knife, but the donkeys did not want to go. Finally, into the water we went, but in the middle of the river the animals stopped, trembling. That's when the

whips helped. When we got to the other side the donkeys moved quickly.

Again another rumbling roar. There was nothing to do but get off the donkey and go ahead with a knife in my hand while Mr. Rehack secured the rear.

That we passed through danger with such luck was God's great mercy. There could have been a huge fight, which we would have lost with our half-meter-long hunting knives. But to have lost in this fight would not have been shameful because they were huge and big and strong opponents.

Back at Masama, Reusch wanted to know how the gazelle had come to be wounded. His host explained that a few cattle had also been killed in the vicinity, and since domestic cattle were easier prey than sprightly gazelles, he guessed that it must have been the King of Beasts who had failed in an attempt to bring down the animal. The explanation fascinated Reusch. Humbled by his first encounter with a lion, he asked a favor of his Leipzig supervisor: "If I do not find a gun in Arusha, then I would like to ask very politely that you send me a good rifle from Germany."

Ever mindful of expenses, he promised to write a longer letter from Arusha, "and will also send you the bills for our trip."

In a postscript he added, "It is wonderful in Africa."

COMPETING INTERESTS OF COLONISTS AND MISSIONARIES

British subjects were barred from participating in the African slave trade in 1807, and in 1815 the European colonial powers declared the slave trade "repugnant to humanity." However, Spanish and Portuguese slave traders, along with Muslim Arabs and Africans, continued to traffic in the capture, transport and sale of human beings well into the next century. In 1888 African leaders rebelled against their German colonial masters, and the unrest spread to the neighboring British East African colony. Missionaries had given refuge to escaped slaves and refused to surrender them to the traders. "Unfortunately," wrote the president of the Royal Geographical Society, "the excessive anti-slavery zeal of the missionaries complicated matters and greatly irritated the Arab population whose friendliness it was desirable to secure."[2] Said British Prime Minister Ramsay MacDonald, "As soon as the missionary appears, slavery is doomed. I think the missionary requires no further justification."[3]

Timeline

1848: May 11, Two German missionary-explorers, Johann Rebmann and Johann Krapf, are the first Europeans to see Mt. Kilima-Njaro, the highest mountain on the African continent. Their report of a snow-capped mountain at the equator is not believed.[4]

1857: The explorer-missionary, Rev. David Livingstone, touches off a fever for foreign missions when he appeals to students at Oxford and Cambridge Universities to join in making Africa "free, civilized and Christian."

1860: The Roman Catholic Black Fathers establish a Christian mission on Zanzibar in 1860;

1868: followed by the British Universities Mission;

1876: the British Church Missionary Society (CMS);

1877: the London Missionary Society;

1878: and the White Fathers.

1885-1890: The European powers scramble to establish colonies and protectorates throughout Africa. Protestant and Roman Catholic missionaries arrive on the heels of the colonial administrations.

1886: Great Britain and Germany divide Kenya and Tanzania between themselves.

1887: The Berlin (Lutheran) Society and the Moravians establish missions in German East Africa;

1888: then the Benedictines of St. Ottilia.

1889: October 3, A Leipzig professor, Hans Meyer, is the first European climber to reach Kilimanjaro's Kibo Peak.

1890: The German Bethel Mission arrives.

1892: The Evangelical Lutheran Leipzig Mission takes over the British CMS missions in the Kilimanjaro District.

1896: The Leipzig Mission begins work among the Chagga on the slopes of Kilimanjaro, and develops stations in the Parre Mountains, among the Meru tribe who live between Mts. Meru and Kilimanjaro, and the Masai near Arusha.

1900: Tribal leaders resist the diffident and high-handed European taskmasters who care little about the cultural and social bases of African life.

1905-06: The Maji Maji Rebellion gets the Germans' attention, but they make few changes. Berlin complains that colonization is costly in the harsh and uncompromising equatorial environment, populated with "primitive and superstitious" natives.

1907: Seven Lutheran and three Roman Catholic missionary organizations are at work in German East Africa. Both provide basic medical care and elementary education, services that win converts. German colonial justice is swiftly administered. Hanging trees are designated in Moshi and Arusha from which those Africans found guilty of serious crimes are hanged.[5]

1911: Britain and France accuse Germany of "cutting in on their monopoly," and everyone knew "there would come a showdown on Africa."[6]

1914-1918: Colonial powers in Africa sign the Congo Agreement, promising not to involve Africans in a European war. Nevertheless, they all draft Africans into their armies. The British drive the German forces out of Tanganyika and Kenya in 1917.[7]

1918: The Treaty of Versailles strips Germany of all its colonies. The United States declines Great Britain's suggestion that it take the former German East African territory under its wing.

1920: Article 22 of the League of Nations treaty states that colonial powers shall govern their territories on the basis of "promoting African interests."[8] The Church of Sweden took over the Leipzig Mission work in India, and the American Augustana (Swedish) Evangelical Lutheran Synod took responsibility for the Leipzig missions in Tanganyika Territory.

1923: Dr. Reusch arrives in East Africa as post-war inflation wipes out export markets, bringing hard times to Tanganyika Territory.

The European colonial powers included Spain, Portugal, Great Britain, France, Germany and Belgium, whose investment companies and colonial administrators had sometimes rounded up Africans against their will and sent them to work in mines and on plantations. When they were not building roads or rail lines, the Africans in German-controlled East Africa had been forced to learn the German language, and recalcitrant students were beaten. Alfred Batson, a German colonist, wrote,

> "This was Kultur, and this cramming down a black's throat of a language and customs is distasteful to him. And it was this that caused me and many another loyal Germans in the colonies to deplore the aggressive way the Germanization of our dependencies was being undertaken by the junkers in Berlin."[9]

But, he added, "There is one group of white men in Africa who seek African redemption, and development, but not by sword or investments or laws."[10] That group was the missionaries. Competing Protestants and Roman Catholics regarded each other with suspicion in those days, but the two denominations were sometimes united in their opposition to colonial policies.

The objectives of church and state in Africa were quite different. Missionaries went to the uttermost ends of the earth to bring the light of the Gospel, and the only return they sought on their sacrificial investment was the redemption of souls, the alleviation of suffering and basic education. Their responsibilities were explicit: feed the hungry, give water to those who thirst, clothe the naked, visit those in prison, heal the sick, and comfort the comfortless.

The objective of colonial government, on the other hand, was primarily to facilitate business development. Funds were allocated for scientific research into the causes and treatment of tropical diseases and maladies — for the purpose of enabling white colonists to prosper in tropical Africa. The colonial powers were nominally responsible for native welfare, but large-scale health care and education programs were expensive, and in the early years colonial administrators were content to leave those responsibilities to the missionaries.[11] As a commission reported to Belgium's King Leopold II, "The missionary becomes for the native of the region the only representative of equity and justice."[12] However, the historian, Ann Beck, assessed the missionary enterprise a bit differently. The missionaries, she wrote, concerned themselves "more deeply with the nature of the African and his ability to accept values which would help western officials to make his protégé accept a new outlook on life."[13] Said an African Lutheran bishop who had been baptized at the age of nine by Dr. Reusch, conversion came as a result of exposure over time to the way of life in Christian communities.[14]

One particularly grim event occurred in the Meru district when missionary and colonial aims were mistakenly seen as one and the same. In 1895 colonial officials ordered the seizure of fertile Meru land on which to establish German-owned plantations. This, naturally, led to deep resentment among the Meru. The following year, two Leipzig Society missionaries, Ewald Ovir and Karl Sagebrock from the Russian provinces of Livonia (Estonia), went to Meru territory to explore the possibility of establishing a mission station there. Assuming they were government officials who had come after their land, on the night of October 20, 1896 Meru and Arusha warriors killed the two missionaries and two of their assistants at their camp near Akeri. A retaliatory German military expedition, including 8,000 warriors loyal to the Germans, killed 600 Meru defenders, drove off their livestock, and took numerous young women captive. Before leaving Akeri, Captain Johannes buried the spear-wounded bodies of the missionaries.[15] Upon the Germans' departure, however, the Meru dug up the bodies and threw them into the Akeri River.[16] The martyrs' bones were later gathered from the river and reburied.

Along with the gospel, missionaries certainly did impose their own cultural values and traditions upon their converts, which no doubt had the effect of helping colonial officials to achieve their purposes. It does seem odd to find German and American church architecture, altars and pulpits in the Kilimanjaro foothills and congregations singing hymns composed by Europeans and Americans. Nevertheless, Africans in large numbers chose to identify with the way of life that fallible missionaries brought to their communities.

One of the Augustana missionaries, Mrs. Annette Anderson, summarized the impact of European colonial policies as she saw it 1928: Portugal still permitted the practice of forced labor, which was a kind of slavery; and like the French, the Germans were intent on imposing their language and culture. It was her impression that only Great Britain "has perhaps been the most faithful to the principle" set forth by the League of Nations. "Although at this stage the native does not openly resent this encroachment upon his right to develop naturally as an African," she warned, "he does so secretly."[17]

INTERCULTURAL ADJUSTMENT

Reusch was first assigned to replace a deported Saxon missionary at Nkoaranga. The Baltic German based in Arusha, Rev. Leonhard Blumer, had told the nearby Nkoaranga congregation that a new missionary from Russia, from the land of Ovir and Sagebrock, would arrive in a few months. Said Reusch, "Apparently this news produced some interest among the people, especially since it had been told to them that I had fought against the Bolsheviks."[18]

At the end of his first month in Africa, an enthusiastic Reusch wrote to a friend in Strasbourg that he could sense a spiritual awakening moving in the land. During a recent three-year period only thirty baptisms had been registered, but in the last 18 months seventy had been baptized, and 150 catechumens were preparing for the Rite of Baptism, including a former sorcerer. It was possible, wrote the ebullient missionary, "that by Christmas 1924, God willing, I shall have the privilege of baptizing something like 300 souls."[19]

The Curious Story of A Ringing Bell

Not long after Reusch's arrival, several parishioners told their new pastor a curious story. A year before, around midnight, believers and unbelievers alike heard a bell ringing somewhere in the direction of Akeri. Thinking that the new missionary had arrived, they rushed to the graves of Ovir and Sagebrock. They were astonished because the eerie sound seemed to come from somewhere in the night sky. Suddenly, they heard the sound of a trumpet from the heavens and a choir singing in Swahili, *"Njooni kwa Mponya, njooni leo,"* "Come to the Savior, make no delay. The mysterious phenomenon had occurred before, and the frightened Christians were certain that it signaled the end of the world. Reusch listened with interest but regarded their story with skepticism, considering it a product of overactive imaginations.

On New Year's Eve, 1923, Dr. Reusch led his first midnight service of Holy Communion at the little church in Nkoaranga. He was removing his black Luther gown in the small house next door when he heard a bell ringing with such force that the windowpanes trembled. He rushed to see if someone was ringing the little bell next to the church but it was making no movement or sound whatsoever. Meanwhile, from some unearthly locus, the great bell continued to peal.

The sound began to move from Nkoaranga in the direction of Akeri, and Reusch looked at his watch: It was twenty minutes past one. The sound grew fainter as it seemed to move southward and out over the Masai Plain, where it died away. "Are my nerves already so weak that I am having a hallucination?" he wondered.

The next morning Reusch learned that others had heard the pealing bell. The chief African evangelist at Nkoaranga, Andrea Balankyo, nodded and said, "It is the same bell about which we have spoken to you so often." Whether the phenomenon was caused by "the night wind blowing into the deep caves of the nearby Meru Crater or something else which produced this sound of a ringing bell, [I am] not able to say," wrote Dr. Reusch. It was simply, he admitted, "beyond my comprehension."

A few days later a delegation of Abyssinians (Ethiopians) arrived from Lekitatu, a settlement south of Nkoaranga on the plains. As Reusch related the episode, one of them said, "We have heard that you are from Moscow." Their ancient Coptic Church in Abyssinia was always closely connected with the Eastern Orthodox Churches.

"We are, herewith, requesting you to come down to teach us and the Masai, and to baptize us."

[Reusch replied,] "But I am a Lutheran, and a staunch one."

"That does not matter; you are from Russia, and that is sufficient. We have heard the voice of the bell before you arrived here, and we heard it again in the New Year's night. So we came to invite you to come down to us in the plains. Please, come!"

After hearing this [I] could not refuse to come down to the hot plains. . . . In less than three years [I had] a small congregation in Lekitatu consisting of Abyssinians, Masai and Wachagga, and the Gospel was preached in seven or eight other neighboring places — the result of the voice of the "ringing bell."[20]

American and European Lutheran missionaries left their stations in August 1923 to gather for their first annual conference at Machame. The veterans — Rev. and Mrs. Ralph Hult and son Paul (Machame), Rev. Alexander Eisenschmidt (Masama), Rev. and Mrs. Henrich Pfitzinger (Shigatini), Rev. Richard Reusch (Nkoaranga), Rev. John Steimer (Mbaga), Rev. and Mrs. A. C. Zeilinger and daughter Sylvia (Moshi), and Rev. and Mrs. Leonard Blumer (Arusha) — were happy to welcome four recently arrived Augustana recruits. Rev. Herbert and Anna Magney and son Herbert Jr. were assigned to Mamba, Rev. N. Ludwig Melander to Gonja, and Nurse Selma Swanson to Mbaga. There were fourteen former Leipzig mission stations to keep in repair, medical supplies to provide for each station, nine missionary families to maintain, the salaries of 136 African Christian teachers to pay, schools to be rebuilt, seventy-five schools to equip (slates, pencils, crayons, books or tablets), "and a multitude of other things that must not be overlooked." After the meeting, Herbert Magney made an urgent request to the Augustana Foreign Mission Board for an additional $7,000 above the $30,000 budget that the Synod had appropriated.[21]

The Anglican bishop of Zanzibar, the Rt. Rev. Frank Weston, believed that all Christian nations were guilty of the sins of pride, cruelty, and a warlike spirit. But there were two reasons why the Germans were especially guilty: Because (1) they had elevated science above God, and (2) their theologians had applied methods of literary criticism to the Bible. Therefore, the deportation of German missionaries from East Africa was justified.[22]

However, any lingering desire to punish the vanquished Germans disappeared among the American missionaries in the face of the challenges they faced. The little band of American and European Lutherans faced an impossible task. The Leipzig missionaries left behind 100 schools with 8,700 enrolled students.[23] Three years later fewer than fifty schools remained open, serving only 2,000 children. The Marangu Training School that had prepared Afrcan teachers was closed during the First World War, and Superintendent Hult was committed to reactivating the institution. Therefore, he requested that the Augustana Syod send a teacher in addition to a physician, three nurses, and a builder.[24]

The Blumers were to leave Arusha for their year-long furlough in March, 1924, and it was decided that Reusch was the best qualified to take responsibility for Arusha, since he was the only one among his remaining peers who could speak the language. At Nkoaranga he was already in charge of seventeen schools and keeping them in repair, and now he would serve another community as both pastor and medical aide.

In the first eighty days at Arusha he saw 5,000 patients, an average of more than sixty cases per day. Mrs. Blumer had previously provided obstetric and pediatric care, and in her absence Reusch begged the Augustana Synod quickly to send a female nurse. "I am neither engaged nor married," he explained, "and therefore would request that you not send a younger nurse, since that would probably start rumors."[25] Neither Reusch nor Melander were married, and that irritated Superintendent Hult. In his letter supporting Reusch's request for a nurse, he grumped, "Africa is no place for unmarried folks, living alone at a station."[26]

The missionaries spent so much of their time providing medical care that there was little time for language study and evangelism, which, as Mrs. Gertrude Hult believed, was a serious handicap to the long-term success of their work.[27] But they could not do otherwise. Herbert Magney agreed:

> Directly after breakfast I went over to the dispensary, as I do each morning, to treat the sick. There were the common cases of malaria, the running sores that often defy treatment, the fevers and obstinate itches, the bruises and the worm cases. But what can a missionary do with such? Turn them away? It is due principally to the fact that we have no nurses, but one, on this entire field of a population exceeding 150,000 people. How long can we bear up under it? Or shall we cease to receive the sick and let them die without compassion? It is in our homeland where this question must be answered.[28]

Do not forget, John Steimer reminded his fellow Swedish Americans, that in addition to preaching the good tidings of the kingdom, Jesus also healed all manner of sickness among the people. "Is there not a doctor in the Augustana Synod today," he pleaded, "who will say: 'Lord, here am I; send me'?"[29]

At its November meeting in 1923, the Africa Committee of the Augustana Foreign Mission Board voted to recruit a physician, three nurses, a builder, and an educator to prepare Africans to become teachers in the Mission's primary schools.[30]

On Safari to Ruruma

In September, Hult, Reusch and thirty-one Masai warriors traveled by foot on a difficult thirteen-day safari to Ruruma, a village on the southern Iramba Plateau more than 300 kilometers southwest of Arusha.[31] Superintendent Hult wanted to determine the feasibility of reopening the former Leipzig station there, abandoned in 1916. [32] The last German missionary to serve at Ruruma had suffered a mental breakdown and had baptized thousands of people without providing them instruction of any kind. When they reached Ruruma they found a ruined mission station, a few loyal teachers, and "about two dozen real Christians."

Hult's presence was required in Dar es Salaam, and so he left by train while Reusch brought the expedition back to Kilimanjaro. Their food supplies ran out toward the end of their journey, and on the last night they made camp and went to sleep hungry. In the middle of the night one of the warriors awakened Reusch.

"Where did you get those potatoes?" asked the startled missionary.

"It is not stealing," replied the Masai warrior. "I did not take them to make a profit or for myself. I took them to help you, for I did not want you, our leader, to be hungry."

Reusch was deeply moved by the Masai's loyalty and distributed the tubers among his men. He later sent money in payment to the man whose crop had been raided.[33]

In contrast to the Kilimanjaro and Meru districts, life was harsh on Iramba Plateau. His Masai companions came home sick with malaria fever, and Reusch contracted tick fever. He lay ill for the next three months.[34]

EUPHORIA TO DEPRESSION

The person who has not experienced the stress of adjusting to a radically foreign culture cannot fully appreciate what those missionary volunteers endured.[35] Dr. Reusch was more adept than most, but he, too, experienced culture shock.

Missionaries worked in isolation at their stations, and only on rare occasions enjoyed the company of other missionaries, European settlers, or British colonial officers. This accounted for Superintendent Hult's concern about the unmarried Reusch and Melander. Reusch was also isolated by language. He had begun studying English only as a part of his preparation for life in a British colony, and in Africa he continued to do so by memorizing words from a dictionary. Therefore, in his first year he had little opportunity to develop the interpersonal relationships that are so necessary for a sense of well-being. He stayed with the Blumers in Arusha, but their personalities were so different that he derived little comfort from their company. He was alone in a foreign land, and it is not surprising that his initial enthusiasm gave way to depression. His experiences in Tartu during the war and the precarious status of his family in Russia probably contributed to a growing sense of malaise.

Neither was his work among the Masai going well. Medicine men resented his medical intervention and tried to poison him on three occasions. The Masai expected one of two reactions: If the white man was a warrior he would retaliate; if not, he would flee. Reusch was a puzzle, for he neither fled nor retaliated. Six Masai came for religious instruction, but after their baptism the medicine men cut off their ears. "Again I did not retaliate," said Reusch. "So they cut off the fingers of five others whom I baptized later. Again I did not retaliate." And then they began to maltreat the children who came to his mission "and continued their attempts to drive me out of their country."[36]

One afternoon he heard a child's cries and was horrified to find a sorcerer tramping with his feet upon a little girl. When he saw it was Lena, a child who had been coming to his station, the missionary "saw red." He grabbed the man by the hair and broke his horsewhip over his back. The shaman ran off yelling, "The European is an *Ol-Bushnot*," a *berserk*, a crazy man. "I am sorry to confess it," admitted Reusch, "but I felt in this moment like a Berserk."

He brought the trembling Lena, blood running from her mouth and nose, to his house and tended her wounds. When she was able to speak, the child explained that she had been beaten for coming to the mission. "Please do not send me away," she begged. He continued to care for her that day, but a broken rib had punctured a lung. She continued to weaken.

A few days later she asked Reusch to baptize her because she felt as if "I must die, and I want to go to my Saviour after my death. He loves me, and I want to be with him."

Little Lena had heard his preaching at the mission, but she had not taken instruction. So he asked her, "What do you believe of God, child?"

"God is love because Christ the Savior is love," she replied. It was the theme of his ordination sermon, one that he continued to preach in Africa. "A better answer she could not have given," said Dr. Reusch, and he baptized her in the name of the Father, Son and Holy Spirit.

Lena died not long afterwards. He grieved her death, but her example, said Reusch, restored his battered faith. His depression lifted.[37]

Ten days after Lena's death Reusch's dogs were poisoned. But his breaking point came a few nights later during a rainstorm when he realized that Masai warriors had come to steal his cows. This time he decided to stand his ground: "'Well,' I thought, 'go on boys, finish your work. Two missionaries you have already murdered; murder the third. But know that he is not as 'good' as the first two. He will take a dozen of you with him into eternity and repay you for what you have done to the Christians.' I loaded my rifle, revolver [and] shotgun [with buckshot], and waited."

It was in the black of night, and he could not see even the outline of the thorn bush corral, but when he heard the warriors pull aside the gate he blasted away with his shotgun. "After six or seven shots they ran away. I thought, well, that's the end of my work, and maybe of myself."

The next day a deputation of Masai arrived, leading six fat cattle. "We know you have killed a lion," they said to the missionary, who had earlier shot a marauding male, "and walloped the sorcerer. You have shot at warriors — and so we know you are a man. We've come to make peace with you as a man."

Reusch first instructed his visitors to give the cattle to those whose ears and fingers they had cut off. Then he declared, "I am ready to make peace with you. But first I want to say the following: If you will kill or poison me, I shall forgive you; but if you touch anyone coming to my God, I shall without mercy shoot you. And now let us make peace."

"From that day on," he mused, "I could put my head in the lap of every person of this part of the tribe and go to sleep without any danger."

Reusch quickly developed an enduring relationship with the Masai, whom he characterized as brave, honest, loyal, reliable, conservative, deeply religious, and superb hunters, scouts and pathfinders. "They are proud, have their own moral code and [live by] their own logic"; and of special importance, they were "free from the worship of the golden calf called money." Unlike some of his peers, who spoke grimly of "heathens living in spiritual darkness," Reusch reveled in those components of Masai culture that were so similar to the values and behaviors he had adopted in the Caucasus. "Words alone mean very little to them," he reminded his fellow-missionaries. "They want to see deeds, strength, heroism. A missionary must remember this!"[38]

ACCULTURATION

As his experience, understanding and appreciation of tribal cultures increased, Dr. Reusch began keeping a record of herbal and other medicines that the shamans used to treat their patients. Stanley Moris, a medical doctor who came to Africa from the Augustana Mission in China, agreed with Reusch that medicine men in Africa, as in China, had learned through the ages of trial and error which roots, bark or seeds were good for curing various diseases.

On one occasion Dr. Reusch was bitten on the arm by a green tree snake and credited a local medicine man for saving his life. On another occasion he and his mule fell from a cliff and he broke some bones in his right foot. He managed to reach a mission hospital, where his foot was immobilized in a cast. The fractures did not mend properly, however, and it was suggested that the bones be broken and reset. Said Reusch, "Remembering some sad experiences from my time in the army, I hesitated." A medicine man heard of his injury and immediately came to examine his foot. He advised that under no circumstances should Reusch agree to any new operation because it would, in his opinion, leave him a cripple. The native healer "promised to send me a certain medicine, 'which would surely cure the evil.' Well, as we say in my homeland: 'If there are no fishes, a crab counts for a fish.' He made me also promise not to show [the medicine] to any European doctor. I gladly promised it."

Late that evening a warrior appeared in Reusch's room bearing a container fashioned from an animal horn. Inside was a clear yellowish liquid, a concoction that included bone marrow from an ostrich. Said Dr. Reusch,

> He told me to rub it on my foot every morning and every evening. I did it, and every time I had the feeling as if liquid fire covered my foot for a minute or so, and afterwards a feeling of warmth spread over my foot. Within a few days the crooked bones softened and straightened out, and so did the tendons. In less than a fortnight I could comfortably walk. Two months later I could climb Mt. Kilimanjaro again.[39]

"Sorcerers," as Reusch referred to them, knew how to treat wounds, broken bones and snakebites, but the causes of disease they attributed to evil spirits and tried to cure them with exorcism. Said Reusch, "I have never in my life seen a tick fever cured by exorcism."[40] However, the chief Masai medicine man, the *Oloiboni Kitok Varit*, developed a vaccination against sheep plague that was later refined and dispensed by government veterinarians.

One day Reusch was firing bricks for a new school when the head Masai medicine man came to visit. Reusch innocently asked the *Varit* if it was true that he could walk through fire. Oh yes, he replied, it was true. And so Reusch invited the man to walk through the blaze he had prepared to fire a pile of raw bricks. Under some pretext or another, a bemused Reusch recounted, the sorcerer refused to do it and "became quite angry with me, and did not visit me after that for a long time."[41]

In addition to native medicine, Dr. Reusch became a student of African history, legends, geography, ethnography, botany and zoology. Everything in Africa attracted his curiosity. He appears to have moved directly from cultural rejection to acculturation.

GERMANS RETURN

At the time Reusch left for Africa in 1923, Mission Director Dr. Paul had begun lobbying the British government for permission to send Leipzig missionaries back to Kilimanjaro. The small band of American missionaries learned at their second annual mission conference in August 1924 that the newly elected British Labour government had agreed to consider German missionary visa applications on a case-by-case basis.[42] The short-handed Americans were initially relieved because, in the words of Melander, "Africa needs the required effort of every faithful mission society, the untiring effort of each single missionary, if this dark continent is to hear the saving gospel of Christ."[43]

But then someone remembered the clause in the agreement signed in 1922: At such future time as the Germans might return, the former Leipzig field would be divided between the Augustana and Leipzig Missions. But how would that be done? The subsequent attempt to reach a consensus blew up into a nasty dispute between the Augustana and Leipzig missions, generated two factions among the Americans, and led to a bitter fight between American missionaries and their own Board of Foreign Missions.

Several factors accounted for the conflict that ensued. Not only did the Germans lose the World War, they also continued to suffer under the vindictive terms of the Versailles Treaty. Therefore, negotiations began under a pall of national inequality — defensiveness on the part of some Germans and an attitude of superiority on the part of some Americans. Cultural differences between the Leipzig and Augustana Lutherans also played a role. But the critical factor lay elsewhere: The Germans had a legitimate claim to the successful work they had initiated and nourished over the years, while the Americans, who had committed themselves body and soul during the Germans' absence, were reluctant to give it up. Dr. Reusch was caught in the middle of a struggle for power. His superior in Leipzig, Dr. Paul, confidentially informed him that he intended to regain the entire Meru area.[44] Two months later he declared, "We shall not give away Kilimanjaro, either."[45]

"Our present position is ticklish," Brandelle wrote to Magney. "As to the Germans, only this will I say: They are not our friends at court."[46] The Germans did not deny that American assistance had been necessary, but Hult was "not at all certain that our aid was altogether welcome."[47] Melander put it this way:

> Our German brothers in the faith have different ideas as to how to carry on mission work. We have much to learn from them. But as American Christians we will always have different ideas as to how to spread the Gospel. I feel it might be difficult for us to be placed in a position where we would need to rub shoulders with our German brethren constantly.[48]

The mission squabble landed in the laps of British authorities. Leipzig's Raum and Gutmann explained to members of the British Tanganyika Mission Trust that "the American and German missionaries are one in doctrine, but as to that which is seen by our natives, as to their practice and their methods, they differ widely from each other."[49] The Trust declined to enter the fray and passed the matter to the British Conference of Missionary Societies for mediation.[50]

Without consulting their missionaries in the field, the Augustana Board of Foreign Missions proposed splitting the Chagga congregations between the Germans and Americans, and uniting both the Meru and Masai tribes into one mission field under its jurisdiction. It was a foolish proposal made by men in far-off America who understood nothing about tribal sensibilities. Reusch was appalled, as were Pfitzinger, Zeilinger, Hult, Melander and Steimer. But most grievous of all, no Africans were included in the debate.[51]

At a conference of Augustana missionaries held in Moshi on October 26, 1924, the Americans voted on not one but four proposals for dividing the field. Magney voted to retain the eastern Kilimanjaro district while Hult, Steimer and Melander voted against.

Reusch, Pfitzinger, and Zeilinger did not participate in the deliberation since they were not Augustana missionaries. However, Herbert Magney believed that Leipzig had been working through Reusch and Pfitzinger to influence Hult, Melander and Steimer. Brandelle was inclined to agree; indeed, the Synod president had come to wonder "whether or not the Germans really learned anything in the late war."[52] Leipzig's Karl Ihmels remarked, "Shall we demand cooperation, or must we ascertain that cooperation is under all events impossible?"[53]

With Brandelle's support, a determined Magney worked behind the scenes to retain possession of the East Kilimanjaro congregations, including his Mamba parish — the largest one and self-supporting. When Steimer learned that Magney had been sending cables to Brandelle for the purpose of subverting the majority will, he went after Magney with a vengeance, questioning the "agitator's" motives. The question ought to be, Steimer wrote in a long letter to Brandelle, "How can those great congregations on the Kilimanjaro Mountains best be served? Who are best qualified, we young and unexperienced [sic] Augustana Missionaries or the former experienced German Missionaries who have spent from 10 to 25 years among these people and know their languages and religions?"[54]

Nevertheless, Brandelle convinced the members of his mission board to accept Magney's proposal — retain eastern Kilimanjaro. Hult and Melander could not understand so foolish a plan that kept for Augustana not only the biggest and self-sustaining German-nurtured parishes but also the mission printing press, teachers college and best agricultural land. To Steimer the proposal constituted outright theft. Even worse, it was absolute lunacy to split and combine tribes. You asked us in the field for our opinion, Steimer wrote in a blistering letter to Brandelle, but as a consequence "we have been accused of being pro-German, disloyal and disobedient." It is the Africans, he asserted, who pose the most important question of all: *"Why don't you ask us in this matter?"*

Reusch had the confidence of Hult, Steimer and Melander; but conscious of his dual loyalties, he wisely maintained a low profile during the dispute.

In the end Steimer's argument prevailed: Augustana would withdraw entirely from the green and comfortable foothills of Kilimanjaro to the hot and sometimes inhospitable Iramba Plateau to the south. Leipzig was relieved, and so the proposal was forwarded to London for consideration. Several months later the plan was accepted.

ANOTHER AMERICAN CONTINGENT

As his colleagues had done before him, Pastor Melander made a point of visiting the gravesite of Ovir and Sagebrock soon after his arrival in Tanganyika Territory. After that visit, Melander wrote to his American Church, "The cruel manner of their death only made me all the more anxious to follow in their steps. Perhaps Ovir and Sagebrock can grip your heart too, causing you to come out here and finish the work they began."[55]

Several Americans responded to the Synod's plea for volunteers, and another contingent of Midwestern Augustana missionaries arrived in 1925: Rev. George and Annette Anderson, Dr. Bertha Anderson, M.D., and a nurse from Kansas, Elveda Bonander.

As a secretary in Chicago, Bonander felt that she had been "living the most useless life that anyone could live." She was aware that the Synod was recruiting missionaries for service in East Africa, and the idea of responding to the call came to her one night in an Ashland Avenue streetcar on her way home from work. Shortly afterwards she quit her desk job and began training to become a nurse, but her motive was to bring justice as well as the Gospel. Before she left for Tanganyika Territory she wrote,

> The African people have suffered untold agonies for many generations. If you read the history of the African people you will read of the cruelty that they have suffered. This is no credit to the Christian people here. Even if we had no gospel to bring them, we would be under obligation to go there just the same to remedy some of the terrible things that have been brought there.[56]

Reusch, who had been asked to go to Moshi and meet the Americans, had gone on safari to a Masai village in the southern plains. When it was time to leave for the rendezvous, he donned a Russian peasant shirt, strapped a revolver to his waist, threw bandoleers over each shoulder and grabbed a rifle for the six-day walk north across the plain.

Nurse Bonander and the other three Swedish Americans now debarking from the train did not know what to make of the strange short white man and several Masai warriors, "dirty and hungry like leopards,"[57] who came to meet them. A chain smoker, Reusch was puffing on a fowl-smelling cigar as he approached the startled Americans and introduced himself. ("A missionary, smoking *tobacco*?") Then he bowed, clicked his heels and kissed the women's hands. ("Who *is* this man?") No one noticed the grin that appeared under his mustache as he watched the addled Americans sort their piles of luggage. Feigning impatience, Reusch curtly warned that the walk through the bush could be dangerous, and unless they left promptly he would not be responsible if some man-eating lion or leopard ravaged them in the dark of night. ("What *next*?") The nervous Americans obediently scurried to organize their baggage and get under way. But Mrs. Anderson could stifle her indignation no longer: How could a missionary set such a poor example for the Africans by smoking tobacco!

"It is, Madame," Reusch explained with a wry twinkle, "the best way of driving away the mosquito which carries the malaria fever."[58]

A few pietistic Americans were offended by Reusch's use of tobacco and were troubled by his respect for non-Christian belief systems and rituals; others, especially British colonial officers, charmed by his stories and courtly bearing, respected his knowledge, courage, stamina; all admired his commitment to sound Lutheran doctrine. "He comes from Russia," George Anderson noted, as if that single fact explained everything.[59]

But Anderson had come to Tanganyika with instructions from an angry Synod president: "Dint it into [Hult's, Melander's and Steimer's] ears that they must work in harmony with the Board, and the Board must be obeyed." Steimer brazenly responded in kind: "Is it necessary to say that we were quite astonished to receive such a message from a newly arrived missionary?"[60]

The issue continued to fester for the next three years until the Board finally took action. O. J. Johnson, Board president, expressed concern for the continuing "lack of brotherly love that seems to exist among the missionaries themselves, and deeply regrets that so much of personal animosity has entered into the prosecution of the missionary work in Africa." Therefore, the Board recommended that Steimer and Hult be transferred to the Sudan, since both men were "still of the conviction that it is the Lord's will that they should bring the Gospel into that region."[61]

Hult and Steimer were due for furloughs in 1928. Hult did not return until 1941, and again in 1943 when he died in Dar es Salam. Steimer never returned to Tanganyika.

Betty Anderson

The Augustana Mission vacates Kilimanjaro district for Irambaland.

AUGUSTANA MOVES SOUTH

A cablegram from the Augustana Mission Board confirmed that the Kilimanjaro and Pare stations were to be returned to Leipzig, and negotiations were underway to find a permanent African field for the Augustana mission, most likely the Iramba District some 320 kilometers southwest of Kilimanjaro.[62] No missionaries from any denomination had settled among the 120,000 persons living there, and the Board hoped to relocate to the new field before the end of 1926.[63]

Reusch was relieved to welcome his Leipzig colleagues and serve full-time under the Mission that had sent him to Africa. In March, 1925, the Americans gathered at Machame to welcome the first two returning Germans, Senior Pastor Johannes Raum and Dr. Bruno Gutmann, and invited them to attend the next Augustana Mission Conference, scheduled for February 1926.

Anderson, Magney and Melander set out that April on a journey to survey the Iramba district. This time they traveled not by foot but in an automobile, a new Model-T Ford. The three men drove from Moshi to Arusha, 80 kilometers distant, where, according to Magney, they hoped "to meet with our good brother missionary Reusch." The party arrived just after dark, but their host did not return until midnight. "All the next day we spent with brother Reusch and truly enjoyed his hospitality and congeniality, a congeniality that is distinctly his own," Magney reported, and watched him "tend the sick in a way in which only brother Reusch can do it." In his report Magney bitterly reminded the folks at home that the Synod had invested 9,000 shillings in Arusha — which now belonged to the Germans.[64]

Downpours, muddy roads and swollen rivers delayed the three Americans as they made their way from Arusha toward Ruruma. In fact, the trip took longer by automobile than by foot. In Ruruma they found Africans afflicted with ulcers, leprosy and other tropical diseases.[65] Indeed, they agreed, there was important work to accomplish on the Iramba Plateau.

When he had visited the graves of Ovir and Sagebrock in 1923, Reusch decided to construct a proper memorial of cement and erect a steel cross. He finally got around to doing that three years later. He later constructed a stone church and school at Akeri, carrying the heaviest stones himself and working with the laborers to cement them in place.[66]

The German-American separation took effect on September 1, 1926,[67] and the last Augustana mission conference in Leipzig territory was held at Marangu four months later. "It is with much pleasure we record the cordial and harmonious relationship with Leipzig *this* year," George Anderson wrote at the end of 1927. "We have seen that Leipzig lacks neither men nor means, and therefore we can leave knowing that our withdrawal works no hardship."[68]

Nurse Bonander went to work in the south, at Ruruma, while Reusch remained with the Leipzig staff at Machame in the north. Melander was relieved, because at Ruruma the Americans would not have to rub shoulders with the Germans.[69]

But there was also dissension among the Germans. Leonhard Blumer, the Estonian missionary, would never have continued to work with Reusch had it been his choice. Upon returning from furlough, he requested that his younger colleague be transferred out of Arusha; or better yet, having heard that von Bulmerincq still hoped that Reusch would return to teach at Tartu, Blumer suggested that Reusch be encouraged to quit Africa entirely.

His superior, Rev. Raum stood firm:

> I believe you, that you don't like his ways, that you and your wife do not like him. But a transfer is very difficult, especially since there is no objective reason. . . . Especially now since the Catholics are in the city, I would think our mission would suffer great harm if Reusch were to be taken away from there. That would be the best thing we could do for the Catholics.[70]

Blumer later complained that during his absence Reusch had apparently "spent only a third of his time in Arusha and two-thirds somewhere else." Reusch's dramatic manner was attractive to Africans, Blumer admitted, and catechumens preferred to take instruction from him. To Blumer that constituted "fishing in other people's ponds," and it galled him that his younger colleague's assistants were known as "Reusch's evangelists." Furthermore, neither Blumer nor his

Evangelisch-Lutherische Missionswerk, Leipzig

Leipzig Mission staff (Reusch, 3d from left) gathers for a photograph on the steps of the Training School at Marangu, Tanganyika.

wife could bear to host Reusch in their home because of his erratic schedule. Blumer had enough: "People are being blinded by a young missionary who accomplishes much with his mouth and devout way and knows how to impress people, and against whom I could prove a high number of exaggerations, overstatements and lies — whereas people distrust an old worker and his arguments."

Reusch had neither the inclination nor the time to defend himself. That he was successful in his work was abundantly clear. Dr. Paul wrote in a letter to Richard's father in Soviet Russia,[71]

> I am very sorry that you have been worrying about your son for such a long time. Mail must have gotten lost here. Your son was sick from malaria, but in the meantime he has fully recuperated. Only yesterday I received very good news about him. Our senior missionary, Raum, reports that he is working untiringly and successfully in his missionary field. The church pews reach far into the grass, and everywhere the gospel is received with pleasure. He travels from place to place, is in Arusha, then Nkoaranga, then in Legitatu, and then down onto the plain. It is also reported that he takes great pleasure in his younger colleagues. I want you to know that so that you can be pleased about that with us.[72]

HEADMASTER

As funding became available, Leipzig missionaries slowly returned, one by one, to Tanganyika. Early in 1926 both missions joined forces to reopen Leipzig's Native Teachers Training School at Marangu, a facility that now would serve African young people from both the Kilimanjaro and Iramba regions.[73] George Anderson initially served as assistant headmaster, but when he left for Irambaland in June 1927, Reusch came in from the Masai plains, sick with malaria fever, to take his place.

By year's end Reusch's students had mastered "the small multiplication tablet" and "in zoology they could beat their teachers."[74] When the British Deputy Director of Education inspected the school eleven months later, he was satisfied that the institution was worthy of government support. After another inspection in March, the inspector wrote that he was "well-satisfied with the progress since my last visit," and noted that the students were "well-disciplined."[75]

Seventy years later a young cleric asked the Bishop of the Northern Diocese if it was true that Reusch actually drilled the boys at Marangu like soldiers. "Oh yes," Bishop Erasto Kweka smiled, "he had them march two-by-two while singing 'Onward, Christian Soldiers!'"[76]

Nathaniel Mrenga took courses in geography, mathematics and science from Reusch. "He did not lecture from a text," he recalled, "but sat on a window sill and talked. He measured each student individually, not by some official and distant standard."

Did Mr. Mrenga think of Reusch as a German or a Russian?

His reply was immediate and emphatic: "A *Russian*, of course! Yes, he told us all about the tsars and the Bolsheviks!"[77]

Betty Anderson

Reusch plants the Christian flag on Kibo Peak of Kilimanjaro, the highest mountain on the African continent.

SON OF KIBO

Mt. Kilimanjaro's blue and purple volcanic form rises in awesome majesty above the plain. Mt. Meru, modest in comparison, shields Kilimanjaro from the Serengeti. The occasional cone-shaped mounds that dot the Serengeti are not unlike those that Reusch had climbed as a boy on the plain south of Pyatigorsk.

The short but strong missionary was too busy to plan a climbing expedition to Kiliman-jaro's Kibo Peak until 1926 when, as he told the story, he overheard two young British officers disparage the soft and meek missionaries and brag about their own failed attempt to reach the summit. Reusch promptly decided to put an end to such talk and prepared to make his first climb. Unlike the young officers, he succeeded in his first attempt and, to put an end to the stereotype of soft and meek missionaries, planted a Christian flag on the summit. Richard Reusch was the seventh person to sign the log that Professor Hans Meyer had left there for that purpose in 1889. As proof of his accomplishment, the missionary returned with a photograph taken at the summit along with Meyer's record book.

Reusch made three more ascents in 1926, and as a result his name and fame spread beyond the mission communities. By the end of 1935 he had reached Kilimanjaro's summits, Kibo and its twin peak, Mawenzie, twenty-five times. The Masai began to refer to him as "Son of Kibo."[78]

Kilimanjaro became Reusch's passion. He subsequently founded the East African Mountain Club and trained the first African mountain guides. He repeatedly climbed to the summits, in part to test his physical strength. But there was another reason. Although he could not account for the effect, he always felt a boost in energy after a climb. A missionary physician decided to test a hunch: Before Reusch's next climb he took a blood sample and found that he had a low red blood cell count, a result of recurring malaria fever; but after the climb his count was normal. Why? Apparently, the doctor concluded, the body more readily replaces red blood cells at high altitudes.

SOLDIERING ON

Nurse Elveda Bonander found a life of greater purpose in Africa than she had imagined. Working with Dr. Bertha Anderson, the two-person medical team served as a mobile clinic, visiting the communities served by the mission. They visited the parish at Lekitatu while making their regular circuit in 1927. "Their pastor, Rev. R. Reusch, can visit them only occasionally," Bonander wrote. "Therefore, the vitality and spirituality of the church depends much upon the faithfulness of the three elders."[79] That was the goal: to develop leaders for an indigenous African Lutheran Church.[80]

In August 1927 the relatives of the American missionaries in Ruruma received heart-breaking news. A mysterious tropical fever had stricken the George Andersons and their son

Mark, the Magneys' son, Edward, and Nurse Bonander. Pastor Magney drove over terrible roads for hours to fetch the nearest British doctor, but they returned too late. Mark had died,[81] and Elveda Bonander was "very, very, very sick" from what had been tentatively diagnosed as "malignant malaria."[82]

Malaria came with the territory, as did the stinging bite of the tsetse fly that carried sleeping sickness. Tick fever, yaws and leprosy, along with poisonous snakes and dangerous wild beasts were other threats to the well-being of everyone.[83] And yet Mark's mother, Annette Anderson, urged her fellow Lutherans to join the missionary enterprise: "Why do you not come, you volunteers?"[84]

In the autumn of 1927 Dr. Ihmels made an inspection tour of Leipzig's African missions. There was a letter from Russia waiting for him when he returned to Leipzig from an impatient Gustav Ivanovich:

> I know that my son did not let you leave Africa without giving you the task of letting his parents know how he is doing. Therefore, I ask you, please write us about everything you know about our son, what you saw and heard while you were with him. This is all very interesting to us. Just to read one of his travel reports would give great pleasure.[85]

Richard suffered from malaria, Ihmels replied, but the mission physician found his health satisfactory. Ihmels wrote,

> You can believe that his judgment is accurate because your son climbed Mt. Kilimanjaro three times in the last months. Nevertheless, I asked him to come to Germany for a vacation because he has spent five years in hard and difficult work — but he himself urgently wishes to stay in Africa, and so I gave in. Right now your son is teaching at a teacher's training institute at Marangu. He is working very hard there, and his students appreciate the lively way in which he deals with them.[86]

A WEDDING AT MARANGU

About a year after Nurse Bonander had first visited Lekitatu, an announcement appeared in *Mission Tidings*, the periodical of the Augustana Women's Missionary Society: "Miss Bonander resigned at the close of the year and moved back to Kilimanjaro and married one of the German missionaries there."[87]

"I do not know if you have received news from your son," Leipzig Director Ihmels wrote to Richard's father in February 1928, "but in general he doesn't write many letters. Only through other people did I learn that his wedding took place on the 3rd Sunday of Advent."[88]

Richard did not write many letters to family, nor did he file timely required reports, nor take the time to keep in touch with friends, even the von Lipharts. At the end of 1927 Reinhold von

Liphart's sister, Helene Wolff, wrote Dr. Ihmels to learn the whereabouts of their dear friend.[89] Contact was re-established, and when asked what gift might ease his burdens Reusch asked for a typewriter. Anna von Liphart promptly sent one to the Mission House in Leipzig. "I ask you," she wrote Director Ihmels, "to send this gift to the enormously good, exceptional and noble Reusch."[90]

The couple had asked George Anderson to officiate at the ceremony scheduled for December 11, 1927. And so the Andersons and their son Paul, Rev. Melander and Dr. Bertha Anderson set out by car on the rugged 470-kilometer journey to Marangu. The party left Ruruma early on the morning of Tuesday, December 6th, and stopped at Singida to pick up Nurse Selma Swanson. On the second day the party had to abandon their car a short distance from their destination because of a rainstorm.[91]

Betty Anderson

Elveda Bonander and Richard Reusch were married on December 11, 1927. Rev. George Anderson, standing next to Reusch, officiated at the ceremony.

The Americans were happy for Elveda, but her departure for the Leipzig field worried Melander because "our present force of missionaries with its few workers is so small that we can ill afford to lose one of our number." The Augustana community admired and respected Elveda's husband, "a gifted preacher" and a born teacher. Said Melander, Reusch "has felt at home among us from the first. And among our number he has found his best human friend." But, like Magney, Melander felt uneasy among some of the Germans who "have been neither kindly nor fair toward us. With Rothers and with brother Reusch this cannot be said. They, as well as a few others, have been charitable toward us at all times and have been enthusiastic about the Augustana Synod's work. We are thankful that we have a few such friends in the Leipzig Society." He reassured Elveda's friends in America that "Mrs. Rother assumed the role of mother to the lonely American girl" and her husband "took a fatherly interest in the young bridegroom."

The return trip took nine days as the Americans made their way south, camping at night along the road and during the day pausing to watch enormous herds of giraffe, zebra and wildebeest.

Dr. Reusch always insisted — with a twinkle in his eye — that he had intended to remain celibate like the Apostle Paul and the medieval Knights of the Sword, but an attack of malaria fever weakened his resistance and he succumbed to the wiles of the nurse who cared for him, his wife, "zee beautiful desert flower."

Elveda's work would leave little time for loneliness, counseled Melander, but "such times will come when you will want to throw in the towel." He admitted that he, too, felt "cut off and alone out here. We have the blessed joy, which only they can enjoy who do the will of God," he wrote in a letter to the Mission Board. "But we need the comfort, the help, the cheer, the encouragement that your prayers give."[92]

A school for girls was about to open in Moshi. Elveda was happy in her role as Richard's wife, but at the same time she envied "these teachers their opportunity. For the last three years that kind of work has been close to my heart — that and teaching of mothers how to care for their infants." She looked forward to the resumption of the 1928 academic term at Marangu because she was to serve as the school nurse, a job she had been unable to perform in recent months because of malaria.[93]

A year later the Reusch's first child, Elveda Louise, was born at Marangu. But happiness turned to grief when the baby died the following day. The heartbroken parents buried her in the cemetery on the grounds of the Marangu Teachers College at the foot of Kilimanjaro.

Elveda was scheduled for a furlough in 1929, a respite that she badly needed. The rigors of life in Africa were hard enough, but she also had to cope with an intercultural marriage to a Russian man while living in an African community where her peers spoke German; that, in addition to suffering the lingering and disturbing effects of malaria and grieving the loss of her baby. But she was determined to leave for home as scheduled because her elderly mother was not well, and Elveda needed to see her one last time.

As was the custom for missionaries at the end of a term, she traveled from Mombassa to Germany where she checked in for a thorough physical examination at the Clinic for Tropcal

Medicine at Tübingen. "She went through a lot out there [in Tanganyika]," Dr. Kippenbauer reported to the Leipzig Mission director, "and right now we are assuming she has malaria." His hunch was confirmed when tests revealed that she had suffered a virulent attack of cerebral malaria. Unfortunately, the extremely high fevers that had nearly taken her life left minor but permanent neurological damage. The examining physician also reported, "She is anemic, and is in the second part of her second pregnancy."[94] That she was again pregnant, and that she was going home, lifted her spirits.

Elveda returned alone to her family in the United States on August 1st, and she was thrilled when a daughter, Betty Ruth, was born a month later.[95]

Reusch had worked with Americans during most of his first term. The Swedish missionary, Gustav Bernander, wrote, "This was a new and foreign atmosphere for a man brought up in the aristocratic tradition of Czarist Russia, trained as a soldier, and a total stranger to the Western democratic ideal." Because he was raised in the patriarchal Caucasus, Dr. Reusch "appeared deeply shocked that there were in his [Augustana] mission more women with a vote than men." Although he married an American, "he was always the typical Russian aristocrat, charming, and gallant, an athlete and open-air man whose passion was mountaineering."[96]

Reusch also had an insatiable passion for knowledge and adventure. Indeed, by the time his wife left Marangu to begin her long homeward journey he had already set out on a ten-month odyssey of his own to learn more about Islam.

And to do that he planned to travel through African and Middle Eastern deserts and mud-walled Arabian cities disguised as a whirling dervish from the Caucasus.

CHAPTER 7

1   The citations in the following paragraphs are from Reusch's first report from Africa to Leipzig Mission Director Ihmels, 28 February 1923, LELMA.

2   J. Scott Keltie, *Africa*, ed. by Albert Galloway Keller, "History of Nations" series, vol. 19 (Philadelphia, 1906), 185.

3   Prime Minister Mac Donald's remarks at the Congo Jubilee Exhibition, quoted in "Ramsay Mac Donald on the Missionary," *Lutheran Companion*, vol. 37 (26 October 1929), 1357.

4   Bringing the light of the Gospel to the heathen who sat in darkness proved to be more complicated than some of the early missionaries expected. It was said that Krapf and Rebmann initially exhorted the Africans to repent of their sins and be saved. Their preaching elicited no response, so they changed their approach by proclaiming God's love for his lost sheep. "Of course God loves us," said an elder, because "he sends us rain, palm wine and clothes." William B. Anderson, *The Church in East Africa*, 1840-1974 (1977), 3.

5   Ann Beck, "Medicine and Society in Tanganyika, 1890-1930," *Transactions of the American Philosophical Society*, pt. 3, vol. 67 (April 1977), 5-13.

6   Alfred Batson, *African Intrigue* (1933), 29.

7   Henry S. Wilson, *The Imperial Experience in Sub-Saharan Africa Since 1870* (1977), 179.

8   Donald Cameron, *My Tanganyika Service and Some Nigeria* (2nd edition, 1982), 84-85.

9   Batson, 33.

10   "Mission Studies — Africa," *Mission Tidings*, vol. 18 (October 1923), 5.

11   For example, in 1923 there were 119,500 Tanganyikan pupils enrolled in 65 government, 1455 Roman Catholic, and 737 Protestant schools — E. R. Danielson, "Tanganyika Territory in the New Africa," *Lutheran Companion*, vol. 37 [12 January 1929], 44.

12   Batson, 33.

13   Beck.

14   Rev. Erasto N. Kwika, Bishop, from the author's notes of an interview, 21 January 1996.

15   Anton Nelson, in *The Freemen of Meru* (1967, 9-10), drew from three sources for his summary account: a 1897 issue of *Leipzig Missionblatt*; the Meru version of events published in *Kitabu cha Isomisa van kya Kirwa* (Leipzig Mission Press, 1931), 77; and *Blutzeugen am Meru* (Leipzig Mission Press, 1936), 14.

16   Gustav Bernander, *Lutheran Wartime Assistance in Tanzanian Churches, 1940-45* (1968), 14.

17   Mrs. George Anderson, "News from Africa," *Lutheran Companion*, vol. 36 (1 December 1928), 1412.

18   These story elements are taken from R. Reusch's unpublished manuscript, "The Masai," 35-38, GACA.

19   R. Reusch, letter published in *Der Friedensbote*, Strasbourg, France, translated and republished as "News from Africa," *Lutheran Companion*, vol. 32 (26 January 1924), 50.

20   R. Reusch, "The Masai," 75.

21   Herbert S. Magney, "The First Annual Conference of the Tanganyika Lutheran Mission, *Lutheran Companion*, vol. 31 (1 December 1923), 754.

22   Cited by William B. Anderson, *The Church in East Africa, 1840-1974* (1977), 79.

23   Anderson, 75.

24 O. J. Johnson, "We Need a Doctor, Three Nurses, a Builder and a Teacher," *Lutheran Companion*, vol. 31 (15 December 1923), 786.
25 R. Reusch, Nkoaranga, letter to Augustana Board of Foreign Missions, 16 August 1923 (WMT-322), AELCA.
26 Ralph Hult, letter to the Augustana Foreign Mission Board, 5 November 1923 (Reusch file), AELCA.
27 Gertrude Hult, "Mashame Station," *Mission Tidings*, vol. 18 (December 1923), 9.
28 Herbert S. Magney, "One Missionary's Experience for a Day at one of Our East African Mission Stations," *Mission Tidings,* vol. 18 (January 1924), 17.
29 John and Edla Steimer, "Our First Month at Mbaga," pt. 2, *Lutheran Companion*, vol. 31 (10 February 1923), 83.
30 O. J. Johnson (Chairman, Augustana Board of Foreign Missions), "Missions," *Lutheran Companion*, vol. 31 (15 December 1923), 786.
31 R. Reusch, "The Masai," 30.
32 Charles L. Brown, "The German Missions in Tanganyika Territory, East Africa" *Mission Tidings*, vol. 16 (January 1922), 18.
33 R. Reusch, "The Masai," 30.
34 R. Reusch, "History of the Mission in East Africa After the First World War," undated manuscript, 1, GACA.
35 A 1984 study reported that one-third of all Americans who had accepted offers to work in foreign countries could not adapt and returned home before finishing their terms. Craig Storti, *The Art of Crossing Cultures* (1990), xiv.
36 R. Reusch, "The Masai," 36.
37 R. Reusch, "The Masai," 39-40.
38 R. Reusch, "The Masai," 27.
39 R. Reusch, "The Masai," 18.
40 R. Reusch, "The Masai," 34.
41 R. Reusch, "The Masai," 34.
42 "Reports, Correspondence, Societies" (WMT-322), AELCA.
43 N. L. Melander, "Annual Conference Tanganyika Missionaries," *Lutheran Companion*, v. 33 (4 July 1925), 419.
44 Dr. Paul, Leipzig, letter to R. Reusch at Nkoaranga, 4 June 1924, ELMLA.
45 Dr. Paul, Leipzig, letter to Reusch at Nkoaranga, 16 August 1924, ELMLA.
46 Brandelle, letter to Herbert Magney, 31 July 1924 (WMT-322), AELCA.
47 Ralph D. Hult, "A Greeting from East Africa," *Lutheran Companion*, vol. 31 (12 May 1923), 291.
48 N. Ludwig Melander, letter to Dr. O. J. Johnson, 25 August 1924 (WMT- 322), AELCA.
49 Herbert Magney, letter to Brandelle, 20 April 1925 (WMT-322), AELCA. The Tanganyika Mission Trust was created under Article 438 of the Treaty of Versailles to administer former German mission property.
50 Conference of Missionary Societies, letter to Under Secretary of State, Colonial Office, 21 December 1926 (CO 691-85/2, file 1642), PRO.

51 George Hall, *The Missionary Spirit in the Augustana Church* (1984), 37-38.

52 Brandelle, letter to O. J. Johnson (WMT-322), AELCA.

53 Carl Ihmels, quoted by Bengt Wadensjö, *Toward a World Lutheran Communion: Developments in Lutheran Cooperation up to 1929* (Uppsala, 1970), 202-203.

54 John Steimer, "Statement," undated, 6 (Box 326, World Missions: Tanganyika, John Steimer file), AELCA.

55 M. L. Melander, "Glimpses from Tanganyika," *Lutheran Companion*, vol. 34 (6 March 1926), 221.

56 Elveda Bonander, "Why I Chose Africa," *Mission Tidings*, vol. 18 (June/July, 1924), 5.

57 R. Reusch, "The Masai," 42-43, GACA. The rest of the story is recalled by family members to whom he confided the details.

58 Donna Kavanaugh, "Novel-like Interview with Church Worker," *Ramsey County Review* (26 May 1965), 6.

59 George N. Anderson, "Interesting Information from Our Field in Africa," *Mission Tidings*, vol. 22 (October 1927), 284.

60 Steimer, "Statement."

61 O. J. Johnson, "Addendum to the Report of the Board of Foreign Missions," *Lutheran Companion* (3 August 1929), 973.

62 Elveda Bonander, "The Annual Conference at Marangu Mission," *Lutheran Companion*, vol. 34 (12 June 1926), 557.

63 Mrs. A. Rehner (Chairwoman, Women's Missionary Society, Lutheran Augustana Synod), "Annual Convention Minutes, 1926," *Mission Tidings*, vol. 21 (August 1926), 57.

64 Herbert S. Magney, "A Visit to Iramba, Our African Mission Field," *Lutheran Companion*, vol. 34, pt. 1 (4 September 1926), 846.

65 R. Reusch, unpublished manuscript, "East Africa," 1.

66 R. Reusch, "The Masai," 35.

67 Bertha Anderson, M.D., "From Our Field in Africa," *Lutheran Companion*, vol. 34 (4 December 1926), 1158.

68 George N. Anderson, "African Mission — Tanganyika," *Lutheran Companion*, vol. 35 (2 September 1927), 902.

69 N. Ludwig Melander, letter to Dr. O. J. Johnson, chairman of the Augustana Foreign Mission Board, 25 August 1924, (WMT-322), AELCA.

70 Raum, letter to Blumer, 5 April 1927, LELMA.

71 Leonard Blumer in Arusha, letter to senior Leipzig Missionary Raum at Machame, 19 April 1927, LELMA.

72 Leipzig Mission Director, letter to Gustav Reusch, 13 October 1925, LELMA.

73 "The Door of Opportunity," *Mission Tidings*, vol. 21 (August 1926), p. 20.

74 R. Reusch, "East Africa," 1.

75 Quotes from the institution's log book, read to the author by a school employee at Marangu, 22 January 1996.

76 From the author's notes of a discussion with clergy at Uhuru Lutheran Hostel, Moshi, 21 January 1996.

77 Nathaniel Mrenga, from author's notes of interview at Marangu, 22 January 1996.

78 Erik W. Modean, "Lutheran Missionary, 61, Climbs Kilimanjaro for the 50th Time and Helps to Measure its Height," National Lutheran Council press release, 23 September 1952, 2, AELCA.

79 Elveda Bonander, "A Trip to the Plains in Tanganyika Territory," *Mission Tidings*, vol. 35 (October 1927), 176.

80 Although Augustana mission superintendents in Africa all had the goal of assisting the development of an indigenous African Church, from their letters and articles it is clear that not all missionaries shared that goal. Missionary thinking, wrote M. Louise Pirouet, "was based on the premise that African Christians, deprived of European leadership (during and immediately after the First World War), would be bound to wander into wrong paths or lapse into heathenism. Being children, they needed paternal guidance." — M. Louise Pirouet, "East African Christians and World War I," *Journal of African History*, XIX, I (1978), 117.

See Bruno Gutmann, "The African Standpoint," *Africa: Journal of the International African Institute*, vol. 8, No. 1 (January 1935), 1-19; Ernst Jaeschke, *Bruno Gutmann: His Life, His Thoughts, His Work — An Early Attempt at a Theology in an African Context* (Erlangen: Verlag der Ev. Luth. Mission, 1985); and J. C. Winter, *Bruno Gutmann: 1876-1966: A German Approach to Social Anthropology* (1979).

81 "News from Africa," *Lutheran Companion*, vol. 35 (24 September 1927), 925.

82 Annette Anderson, "Letter from Africa," *Mission Tidings*, vol. 22 (January 1928), 285.

83 People had to be mindful of wild animals in the Kilimanjaro district as well. One evening at sunset, recalled Stanley Moris, Paul Rother went to visit an African teacher and his family at their home nearby. In the cool of the evening, the mother brought their new baby out onto the verandah as they conversed.

After Rother went home, his friend heard a scraping sound from the verandah but paid no attention because he assumed it was his wife dragging the bassinet back into the house. When he went to help her, to his horror he saw a leopard dragging his wife down the path. He screamed in horror. The animal dropped his prey and ran off. The terrified man ran to his wounded spouse. She was unconscious, so he ran up the path toward Rother's house, yelling hysterically. The two men ran back down the trail. The woman was dead. — Stanley Moris, *Which Doctor: Medical Experience on Three Continents* (privately printed: 1997), 138.

84 Mrs. George (Annette) Anderson, "News from Africa," *Lutheran Companion*, vol. 36 (7 July 1928), 740.

85 Gustav Reusch, Volsk, Russia, letter to Dr. Ihmels, Leipzig, 30 November 1927, ELMLA.

86 Mission Director Ihmels, letter to Gustav Reusch, 29 December 1927, LELMA.

87 "Proceedings of the Annual Meeting of the Women's Missionary Society of the Augustana Synod," *Mission Tidings*, 23 (August 1928), 61.

88 Mission Director Ihmels, letter to Gustav Reusch, 28 February 1928, LELMA.

89 Helene Wolff, letter to Ihmels, Leipzig, 15 December 1927, ELMLA.

90 Anna Mathilde von Liphart, München, Germany, letter to Ihmels, ca. March 1929, ELMLA.

91 N. L. Melander, "An African Journey" (copy prepared for publication), 28 December 1927, GACA.

92 N. Ludwig Melander, "Miss Bonander Married," copy supplied for *Mission Tidings*, dated Iramba, 28 December 1927, 1, GACA.

93 Elveda Bonander Reusch, "Moshi, Tanganyika Territory, East Africa, *Mission Tidings*, vol. 23 (December 1928), 216.
94 D. Kippenbauer, M.D., Tübingen, letter to Leipzig Mission Director, 18 July 1929, ELMLA.
95 From the author's notes of interviews with family members.
96 Bernander, 32.

The city of San'a, Yemen, where in 1929 Reusch saw Imam Jahja, regarded by a sect of Shi'a Moslems as an agent of the Hidden Imam.

Chapter Eight

IN SEARCH OF THE HIDDEN IMAM
The Middle East, 1929

As soon as I reached our caravan-serai, I drank like a thirsty camel, yet could scarcely quench my desert thirst. Afterwards I washed myself and changed my dusty Dervish garment for a fresh one. After a frugal meal consisting of boiled rice and mutton roasted on a stick over the open fire, an inner voice urged: "You are near the shore of the Holy Stream worshipped by the ancient Egyptians as the god Hapi, on whose banks Moses, the great prophet, was born. Go and see it.

— Richard Reusch[1]

While a student at Dorpat University, Reusch had hoped to visit the Middle East, but the First World War cancelled his plan. Fifteen years later he finally set out to see for himself some of the sites of the ancient world. Islam was gaining substantial numbers of converts in sub-Saharan Africa, and for that reason Reusch decided to dedicate his first furlough to learning more about various secret Islamic *tariqas* (societies, brotherhoods). Not unlike the Protestant and Roman Catholic missions that carved out their respective spheres of influence, Muslims had divided East Africa into districts and assigned each district to a specific Islamic brotherhood whose responsibility was to convert the inhabitants to Islam. Each Muslim was expected to contribute at least ten percent of his annual income to the effort, and missionaries were recruited during the *hajj*, the annual pilgrimage to Mecca.[2]

The expectation of a messianic figure is common among many religions, and Reusch was struck by the varieties he found in Africa: The Masai looked for the coming of a warrior who would bring about a new world; the Jewish Falashas in the mountains of Ethiopia hoped for the Messiah promised in the Old Testament; and Coptic believers in Ethiopia and Egypt awaited a powerful messiah. But Reusch was interested in learning more about the Muslims in East Africa, especially those who were devoted to a messianic figure known as the Hidden Imam, *al-Mahdi* (the guided one).

"Shortly before the birth of Mohammed," Reusch explained,

Allah took a beam out of the light from his throne, wove it together, and gave it to the Archangel Gabriel to pour deep into Mohammed's soul. This light of eternity made the Prophet sinless by automatically transforming all his deeds into devout works. The fireball opened his eyes to see the future and gave him prophetic energy. This gift was passed on to his son, the fourth Calif Ali; to his son Hasan; and to his son Husain. Only one carries this light in each generation, and he is known as "the Imam."[3]

Calif Ali was a cousin and son-in-law of the Prophet. His son, Husain, was killed at Karbala. The followers of the Prophet who believed that leadership should fall to the descendants of Calif Ali were known as Shi'a (Shiites). However, those who believed that califs should be elected, and that religious scholars should decide issues of faith and life, were known as Sunnis.

The Twelve-Imam Shia believe that twelve Imams succeeded the Prophet Muhammad. Hasan al-Askari, the Eleventh Imam, died in a Samara prison. His son, Abu al-Qasim Muhammad, the Twelfth Imam, was said to have gone into hiding to save his life. In 934 his agent on earth delivered a message: The Twelfth Imam had gone into "occultation"; that is, Allah had miraculously hidden him from view, hence, the Hidden Imam.

The Ismaili tradition of Islam believes that the Prophet's succession ended with Jafar as-Sadiq's son, Ismail, the designated Seventh Imam. According to the story Reusch was told, Ismail was resting in a cave along the Nile. The cave suddenly collapsed, and his servants and bodyguards dug through the debris but could not find his body. Therefore, it was concluded that the Imam was not dead but had disappeared into the fourth dimension, invisible to human eyes.

Other branches of Islam have defined themselves differently. Although there is disagreement among them as to which descendant of the Prophet is the Hidden Imam, it is believed that he will appear at the end of time and "restore Islam, rebuild all mosques, destroy all pigs and apostates, close all synagogues and churches, and establish a Muhammedan world empire."[4] By means of fire and sword, the Hidden Imam will return as *al-Mahdi* and unify the Schools of Law and all Islamic sects. Thus will the world be brought under Islamic spiritual and temporal rule and righteousness be restored before the second coming of the Prophet Jesus and the Day of Judgment.[5] Believers know that the Hidden Imam hovers in the world, sometimes giving political or religious instructions to a *naqiba*, his deputy on earth. His orders are then put into effect by secret societies (brotherhoods) called *tariqas*.[6]

Mystics, and sometimes a cynical political figure in one or another branch of Islam, have at various times in history claimed to represent *al-Mahdi*. Indeed, in 1885, only six years before Reusch was born, a Sunni mystic, Muhammad Ahmad, claimed to be the Hidden Imam. He and his Dervish followers besieged British headquarters in Khartoum and murdered General Gordon in an attempt to rid Sudan of Anglo-Egyptian control.

Reusch first heard about a Hidden Imam in 1908 while camped with his regiment along the Persian border. According to historians, Persian intellectuals, believing that a secular legal code ought to replace Islamic law, *sharia*, joined with young revolutionaries to demand that the corrupt Shah Ali proclaim a constitution and establish a parliament. They succeeded. But an Anglo-Russian agreement in 1907, followed by Russian support of a counter-coup by the shah, scuttled the constitution. However, in 1908 the revolutionaries succeeded in driving the shah from Persia.

Along the Araxis River that summer, Reusch heard a different story. According to rumor, the Hidden Imam instigated the revolution by issuing an order through his earthly deputy: Shah Ali must grant a constitution and summon a parliament. The corrupt despot complied, but when the parliament refused to ratify his proposed budget Shah Ali dissolved the parliament; and when the MPs hesitated to leave, the Shah seized the parliament building. The Hidden Imam sent a second message: Ali was shah no longer. A revolution broke out, and despite Russian military assistance, the Shah's dynasty came to an end.

Reusch sought to identify the reasons for Islamic success in gaining converts in Africa, but there was another question that motivated his search: Was there a mystic alive in this generation through whom the Hidden Imam worked his will?

Reusch was fluent in Arabic and Ki-Swahili, and could communicate in several other African and Turkic languages. He had studied the history and cultures of the Middle East and had absorbed scholarly articles published by German, French and British archeologists who had recently been digging at sites throughout the Middle East. Undoubtedly he had also read Johann Burckhardt's account of a journey through Syria to Africa in the early 1800s. The Swiss explorer traveled in the disguise of a Muslim trader, and when asked by suspicious Arabs about his accent he claimed to come from India.[7] Reusch decided to dress as a dervish, and to explain his Arabic accent would claim to have come from the Caucasus.

From Marangu, Tanganyika, he traveled north through Kenya to Addis Ababa, Abyssinia (Ethiopia). There he joined a camel caravan and eight days later reached the oasis at Khartoum, Sudan. "It was towards eleven o'clock, and the full moon was almost at the zenith," he wrote in his notebook. "Away from the waves of smoke produced by the camel dung fire, I went in search of the river bank. In less than ten minutes I was standing on a high bank, and below me was the mysterious White Nile, glittering like molten gold between green palms." And then:

> I heard a shrill blare of a trumpet coming from the other side of the river, from Omdur-man, the holy Mohammedan city. And I heard the tom-tom-tom of the Zikr-drums . . . For hours they whirl like human tops with outstretched arms, moving at the same time in a large circle, until foam comes from their mouths and they collapse in their ecstasies . . . [Up] to 110 times in one minute they whirl themselves around continuing for five or six hours without interruption, crying, groaning, moaning, murmuring, yelling the name of their God, Allah.[8]

Reusch learned in Khartoum that one of King Feisal's ministers in Baghdad claimed to be a disciple of *al-Mahdi*. A Turkish governor in Iraq who opposed the Mahdist movement lost his life when a follower of the Mahdi, wearing a poisoned golden ring, shook his hand. Could it be true that the Assassins were once again active in the modern world? In 1094 the Nizari Ismaili began a Persian-based brotherhood known as the Assassins. In the name of the Hidden Imam, they did away with princes, generals and religious leaders who opposed them. Assassins in Syria went after Crusader leaders, and succeeded in murdering Conrad of Monteferrat, King of Jerusalem. Poisoned food and beverages, and flowers dipped in perfumed poison were other means used by the Assassins to implement the will of the Hidden Imam. He also heard rumors that agents had infiltrated several contemporary Arab governments.

Having gained that anecdotal information, Reusch continued his journey into Egypt and the Sinai Peninsula:

> I visited Nabata, the ruined capital of the ancient Kingdom of Cush. In Egypt I spent many weeks visiting the museums of Cairo, the pyramids, the ancient ruins of Memphis, the Great Bitter Lake called the Sea of Reeds, and the land of Goshen where Israel once roamed. Disguised as a Dervish, I went to the Sinai Peninsula, following the way of Israel after its exodus from Egypt, visited Dophkah, the ancient Egyptian mining town, and the oasis of Feiran where Israel once camped. I climbed Mt. Sinai, where Mose[s] received the Ten Commandments, ate the mysterious Manna, and studied the conditions of Kadesh Barnea where Israel camped for many years.[9]

His pilgrim journey effected a kind of ecstasy as his senses confirmed what he had heard in lectures, learned in books, and seen in museums.

The pilgrim made his way to the southern region of the Arabian Peninsula to see the ruins of es-Scheba (Saba), known in biblical times as the land of the Amalekites. While Reusch inspected the ancient ruins of the Queen of Sheeba's palace and the remains of an ingenious nearby irrigation system, he was told by a member of a secret Muslim brotherhood that an agent of *al-Mahdi* lived in San'a, the capital of Yemen, which was said to have been founded by Noah's son, Shem. It was also a walled city in the mountains that was not easy to reach. "So I decided to go there," said Reusch.

On the way to San'a he took a detour south to Sheik Othman, a village overlooking the volcanic crater and the old city of Aden. The area had become a center of Arab resistance directed against the British who had colonized the region in 1839. Indeed, rumors of al-Mahdi's appearance often followed as a response to European colonization.

He had come to visit a nearby mosque, which contained the grave of an Islamic scholar with whose work Reusch was familiar. But the attendant guarding the holy site was suspicious of the stranger who stood before him. "If the greatest sinner makes a pilgrimage to this grave and touches it, all his sins will be removed by its power and he leaves cleansed of all his sins. But an infidel can destroy that power by his touch — and that would eliminate our livelihoods."

"I understood," Reusch explained, "and therefore put a gold coin in his hand." The suspicious Arab considered the pilgrim's accent as he studied his clothing. From what country had the visitor come, he wanted to know.

"Being honest, I told him that I came from the Caucasus and grew up among the brave Circassians, who are known as true Muslims."

"By the beard of the Prophet," said the sheik, "you must be a believer, otherwise you wouldn't be so generous! Come in!" Reusch took off his shoes and entered the mosque.

He was taken to a room not unlike a sacristy, a domed cubical room with narrow slits in the walls for windows. In the center of the room lay a slab of precious green stone with sacred Arabic inscriptions etched in gold, and on the slab stood a wooden structure like a small house. On one side was engraved the name and title of the holy man who was buried there; on the other, the confessions of Islam.

"But this is not the grave," Reusch said.

"No," the guard replied, "it is below."

"I want to see it," said the pilgrim.

The sheik pushed the stone slab aside, and they climbed down into an earthen chamber. But just then a sudden terrible commotion erupted in the square in front of the mosque, and hearing it, they scurried up out of the chamber to look through the narrow windows. "The square was black with people," said Reusch, "swearing and crying and throwing sand into the air. Some tore stones from the ground and threw them at two men dressed in khaki-colored clothes. Both Westerners were pale as chalk. A rock had knocked the tropical helmet off one of them. The other terrified man managed to keep a short pipe firmly clamped between his teeth. The people wanted to stone them to death. Why, I do not know. Somehow the foreigners must have done something to enrage the devout Muslims."

Just in time, several desert policemen on horseback entered the square. They lowered their lances and charged into the crowd, which parted in panic. The policemen put the Westerners onto a camel, and away they went. The stunned crowd was speechless with rage.

Then a man beyond Reusch's line of sight yelled to the crowd, "We've gotten rid of two infidels, but a third one is inside — and he desecrates the holy grave! Down with him!" And the whole crowd stormed inside, shouting, "Where is the infidel? Where is the sheik, the traitor? Down with them both!"

Resistance was useless, so the two shaken men went to meet the angry mob. "Since you claim this pilgrim is an infidel, let us put him to the test," said the sheik. "If he is, then his blood must be poured over the holy grave. If he is not, let him go away in peace."

"Yes, yes!" yelled the crowd, "but if he is an impostor then you, too, will die." The sheik's face went pale because he was not certain of the outcome.

"Bring water!" he ordered. "Do the ritual washing!" he commanded. As if preparing to enter the mosque to pray, Reusch performed the rite flawlessly.

"Bring the Holy Book." The Koran was brought.

"Read!"

As a student of Arabic, Reusch had memorized many of the surahs (chapters). He opened the sacred book and read the Exordium:

IN THE NAME OF GOD

THE COMPASSIONATE

THE MERCIFUL

Praise be to God, Lord of the Universe,
The Compassionate, the Merciful,
Sovereign of the Day of Judgment!
You alone we worship, and to You alone we turn for help.
Guide us to the straight path,
The path of those whom You have favored,
Not of those who have incurred Your wrath,
Nor of those who have gone astray.[10]

The angry crowd remained unconvinced.

"Go on reading," the sheik said quietly. Reusch turned to the last pages and began reading Surah, 112:

In the Name of God, the Compassionate, the Merciful.
SAY: 'God is One, the Eternal God. He begot none, nor was he begotten.
None is equal to Him.'

Closing the sacred book, and mindful to keep it above his waist, he quoted from memory the final Surah, 114:

In the Name of God, the Compassionate, the Merciful.
SAY: 'I seek refuge in the Lord of men, the King of men, the God of men, from
the mischief of the slinking prompter who whispers in the hearts of men;
from jinn and men.'

The hostile crowd remained unconvinced. Reusch looked up at his inquisitor.

The sheik challenged the assembly, "Are any of you able to read the Holy Book as well as this man?" A murmur swelled from the ranks. "Could he be an infidel?" the sheik persisted, gesturing at Reusch. "Why then all this commotion? Let us pass through."

The crowd reluctantly obeyed. After the two men walked through the gate and onto the street, the sheik whispered to Reusch, "Get away from here. Right now they are speechless because they are surprised. But in five minutes you will no longer be safe."

Said Reusch, "I took that to heart and disappeared, thankful that I was saved from the fury of the crowd. From then on I became more careful."

Arriving at San'a, Yemen, Reusch visited the Kalis Mosque in the old part of the city. It was originally a Christian church, built by Abyssinians in 525 A.D. "To this day," Reusch noted, "it is called Kalis, from the Greek, *ekklesia*, meaning 'church.'"

He felt at ease in the marketplace, but when he saw the beautiful palace of Imam Jahja (John) he was filled with excitement. It was Friday, the Muslim holy day, and Reusch watched as the venerated cleric, surrounded by bodyguards, walk slowly through the crowd toward the mosque. The crowd silently parted before the Imam, lowering their eyes. "Al-Mahdi! Allah's blessing is on him!" they chanted. Reusch, too, was caught up in their fervor. "Just for a moment I glimpsed an older man of middle height, broad shoulders, and a short gray beard. At his side he wore a gold sword, a turban with a golden ring on top, and a green coat with a golden buckle."

Reusch concluded,

> So he exists, the Hidden Imam, who possesses incredible power, whose followers use the dagger and poison to prepare the way for a Muslim world empire. The thought haunted me: To build a world of peace by means of a great name and tradition, with fire and sword, with dagger and poison. This is impossible. It is idealism, but it is wrong. My poor Muslim friends. I have seen such attempts [in Russia] and how they failed because they were combined with weapons and threats, with force and much blood. [11]

Reusch left Yemen, his quest fulfilled, and returned to Egypt. From Cairo he traveled north to Leipzig, arriving on April 21, 1930.

It was not uncommon for missionaries to return ill with malaria or other maladies and in great need of rest. But not Reusch. The mission director informed Richard's father in Russia that his son was in good health and looked fit: At the Mission House "he is now writing a book about Islam, and from morning to night has been typing the manuscript."[12]

Only when he had finished did Missionary Reusch leave Leipzig to join his wife in the United States.

CHAPTER 8

1 Richard Reusch, "A Vision of the Holy Stream," *Lutheran Companion*, vol. 47 (18 May 1939), 618.
2 R. Reusch, manuscript, "The Islam in East Africa and its secret religious confraternities," 3, GACA.
3 The details and quotations in the following story are taken from a pamphlet by Richard Reusch, *Ich lebte unter Mohammedanern*, no. 26 in the series, "Auf den Strassen der Welt" (Evangelischer Missionsverlag G.m.b.H., Stuttgart, 1954), GACA.
4 R. Reusch, *World Religions* (privately printed at Gustavus Adolphus College for use in his World Religions course, 1955), 93.
5 The Twelve-Imam Shi'a continue to predominate in Iran, constitute the majority in Iraq, and are found in Syria, Lebanon, Pakistan, some of the Gulf states and eastern Saudi Arabia. See Karen Armstrong's excellent book, *Islam: A Short History* (2002), 149. Armstrong also states that the Israeli victory in the 1967 war so humiliated the Arab world that, given the failure of secular policies, it led to a religious revival — Islamic "fundamentalism" — throughout the Middle East (xxxii).

   John Esposito, Islam: *The Straight Path*, 3d ed. (2005), shows the relationship between the Shi'a belief in the Hidden Imam and the overthrow of Iran's Shah Palavi in the 1950s (181), and the rise of Iranian Ayatollahs (233).
6 R. Reusch, "The Islam in East Africa," undated manuscript, 1. GACA.
7 "Burckhardt, John Lewis," *The Dictionary of National Biography*, III (London, 1917), 292-294: quoted in Joan Mary Braun, "St. Catherines Monastery Church, Mount Sinai: literary sources from the fourth through the nineteenth centuries" (Ph.D. dissertation, University of Michigan, 1973), 90.
8 R. Reusch, "The Islam in East Africa," 3.
9 R. Reusch, foreword to an unpublished manuscript, "Let These Stones Speak," 1, GACA.
10 This and subsequent citations are taken from an English translation of *The Koran*, trans. by N. J. Dawood, 5th revised edition (Penguin, 1990), 9, and 434-35.
11 R. Reusch, *Ich lebte unter Mohammedanern*, 12-13.
12 G. Weishaupt, Leipzig Mission, letter to Gustav Reusch, 28 May 1930, AELML.

Betty Anderson

The Gustav Reusch Family poses for a cyanotype photograph in the early 1930s. Standing second from the left is Emil, a Lutheran pastor. The parents, Ottilia Filipovna and Gustav Ivanovich, sit in the second row.

Chapter Nine

ON FURLOUGH
America and Europe, 1930-1931

*The frontiers of Bolshevism are in the human heart. So be it. A fight is always going on
for the possession of man's soul. Faust is with the Devil; Job is with God —
it has been going on through the ages.*

— John Moorhead[1]

"I am so happy and deeply thankful!" Elveda wrote when she learned that her husband had
returned safely from his Arabian adventure.[2] He passed through U.S. Immigration at New York
City in May 1930 and boarded a train for East Chicago where Elveda's brother, Frank Bonander,
was pastor of St. Paul's Lutheran Church.

Missionaries on furlough always faced a daunting schedule of speaking engagements to
increase the visibility of foreign missions and raise money. Reusch undertook this responsibility
with his usual zeal. But he did not model the stereotype of the pious, self-effacing missionary.
His gift for storytelling mesmerized church audiences as he related his African adventures, and
American women were enchanted by the former Imperial Russian cavalry officer who clicked
his heels as he bowed to kiss their hands. At each of his presentations, Reusch identified two
enemies of the Gospel in Africa. One was Bolshevism, "which comes from the abyss of the
Antichrist," and which he feared had gained a foothold in South Africa. The other was fanatical
Islam, "whose intention it is to convert in the days to come the whole of Africa with fire and
sword." He concluded each speech with a plea for financial support and urged his audience to
volunteer for missionary service. "As the Lord of Hosts once asked the prophet Isaiah 2,600 years
ago: 'Whom shall I send to this people? Who will be My messenger?' So is He asking you today,
'Church of Luther: Whom shall I send to Africa? Who will be My messenger of love and mercy?'
What will you answer? It is up to you."[3]

But America was in turmoil. Eight months earlier the New York Stock Exchange had
collapsed, and now the world economy had fallen into a Great Depression. America seemed to
be falling apart. Unemployed workers attended outdoor rallies that sometimes turned violent.
Organized labor in Chicago struggled "desperately to hold its own against the Capone-Barker
racketeers," reported the *New York Times*, "who are alleged to be turning legitimate unions into
agencies of plunder, profit and power."[4]

Politicians, businessmen and anxious citizens also worried about the active and growing Communist Party USA. Reusch was not familiar with the threat posed by Chicago gangsters, but he was acquainted firsthand with Communist methods of subversion and was horrified to find that Communists posed a threat even in America. Fully one-fourth of the Party's 10,000 dues-paying members lived in the Chicago area.[5] No one but the upper echelon of the Party knew it at the time, but from Moscow had come the order for American Communists to "fight for the streets."[6]

In New York City, the March 6th headlines in the *New York Times* read, "Reds Battle Police in Union Square; Scores Injured, Leaders Are Seized," and "Tear Gas Routs Reds Before White House."[7] Communists in Detroit and elsewhere were said to be infiltrating labor unions. In Chicago, among their other activities, Communists were alleged to be spreading propaganda in the public schools.[8] Walter Steele, one of several self-proclaimed experts on subversion, whipped up the Red Scare frenzy when he estimated that the number of American Communists in 1930 exceeded two million.[9] Senator Hamilton Fish traveled the country, conducting hearings about the growing threat of an organization that owed its allegiance to Moscow. The Fish Committee determined that the number of Communists living in the United States was approximately 51,000. Of these, he was told, 70 percent of American Communists were "aliens" (foreign-born immigrants); 20 percent were African-Americans, among whom Communist agitators were able to take "special advantage of the unemployment situation"; and 10 percent were "native born,"[10] a reference to whites, not Native Americans.

On August 9th, according to the *New York Times*, "all available police squads on Chicago's North Side were rushed to Belmont and Wilton Avenues to break up a demonstration by 3,000 Communists."[11] The former imperial cavalry officer was appalled to learn that Moscow's influence reached even into the heartland where the Communists' anthem, the International, echoed even in the streets of Chicago.

The missionary's fame was spreading quickly among the Augustana Lutherans in northern Illinois, and he was swamped with speaking invitations. However, he also felt compelled to alert Americans to the threat of Bolshevism. To church groups he continued to speak about mission work in Africa, but when interviewed by the press or invited to address civic groups he let loose with a lurid account of the Russian Civil War. The local press avidly reported his speeches. The Moline *Daily Dispatch* identified Reusch as "an Imperial Russian citizen" whose career was "filled with thrills and excitement that is probably unequaled by any other in his line of work."[12] He spoke at the East Chicago Kiwanis luncheon on September 9, 1930. "Horror of Red Rule Revealed by Missionary," blared the headline in the *Calumit News*.[13] The *East Chicago Tribune* reported the story the next day:

> One of the best arguments against communism ever presented before a group of local people was given yesterday before the East Chicago Kiwanis Club by Rev. Dr. Richard Reusch, former pastor and professor at the University of Dorpat in Esthonia who led his people in revolt against the unspeakable cruelties indulged in by Soviet leaders.

"In speaking before you," said Dr. Reusch, "I will say nothing of the arguments for or against the Soviet rule, but I will tell you only of my own experiences during the years 1917, 1918 and 1919 and let you judge for yourself.

"In 1917, the Russian armies were beaten and three quarters of our army threw away their rifles and fled to their homes desiring peace. The emperor became a prisoner in his own home and the government was under the leadership of Kerensky. Then we heard of Lenin and Trotsky," Dr. Reusch continued. "They were able men, and they held forth the promise of peace and bread to the people.

"They gathered about them an army of 40,000 or 50,000 imported Mongol troops and threw open the prisons releasing criminals who would make your Chicago gangsters appear as innocent children.

"At first we noticed no change in our lives in the city of Dorpat, which is a community of 50-60,000 persons. But, in three or four weeks members of my congregation whispered to me that all was not right. They asked me if I had heard gun shots and said that persons of the middle class were being killed by the Soviet soldiers.

"At first I would not believe, until at last they arrested almost every pastor of churches in our city, then they brought in a guillotine which they set up in the main square and they began to offer $10 for the head of every person who was an enemy of the Soviet.

"I was called to Petersburg (Petrograd) by the Finnish government which asked me to distribute money among the prisoners of war held in Russia and who had not received any funds since the break down of organized government.

"While in Petersburg I saw 3,000 persons who had attempted to reach the headquarters of Lenin to beg for food, shot in the main street of the city.

"I went on to Moscow and there waded through the blood of 11,700 former Russian army officers who had been asked to register by the Soviet government. I saw three officers pushed through the ice of the River by Mongol soldiers, and when they tried to crawl out of the water, their arms were cut off by axes.

"I left the city that very night to return to my home, and reached there to find that all of the pastors had been executed and all of the professors of the university.

"I became convinced that it were better to die in battle than give my life away to these barbarians," Rev. Reusch asserted, "and I formed a company of former officers and my students numbering 250 men. The torch of the counter revolution was lighted when the Soviet officials ravished a group of noble ladies and then tortured them to death."

Brutal killings witnessed by Rev. Reusch and an exciting account of fights in the counter warfare which finally freed his country with the help of German soldiers, were graphically sketched by the speaker who declared that a surrender to communism of the Russian type was an exchange of good government for robbers. "Americans," he said, "will never become sovietists because every person in this country has something to lose."[14]

The image of a Lutheran cleric removing his collar and taking up his Cossack sword against aetheistic Bolsheviks certainly made for compelling drama and colorful propaganda.

It is not surprising that Reusch felt compelled to sound an alarm. Shortly after arriving in Africa in 1923, Richard's father wrote that the Communists "have initiated a bitter war against the churches, yes, against all religion. It is as if they have unleashed the devil."[15] That information was especially distressing because his Lutheran family remained trapped in Soviet Russia where his father was a deacon and his brother a pastor.

THE LUTHERAN CHURCH IN SOVIET RUSSIA

After the collapse of the monarchy in 1917, Russian Lutherans were initially optimistic about the future of their Church because the Provisional Government called for the separation of church and state. For minority Christian faith traditions, this raised the hope that they would gain equal footing with the Russian Orthodox Church, which had formerly been linked with the imperial court. In 1918, months after the revolution, the Bolsheviks wrote the first constitution for the Union of Soviet Socialist Republics (USSR). Article 124 seemed to guarantee religious freedom: "In order to ensure to citizens freedom of conscience, the church in the USSR is separated from the state, and the school from the church. Freedom of religious worship and freedom of anti-religious propaganda is recognized for all citizens."[16] However, subsequent Soviet decrees soon made it clear that the state was no friend of organized religion.

In 1918 all personal property and real estate of individuals as well as private and religious institutions were confiscated by the state — church structures, parsonages, rental properties, land, schools, charitable institutions, cash, securities, legacies and donations.[17] Since the state had seized all religious assets, the clergy now depended solely upon the contributions of members, who themselves had been stripped of their property. Farmers were forced into collectives. Agricultural production plummeted. Rail transportation failed, and tons of state requisitioned farm produce rotted in piles alongside railroads and wharves. Food became scarce. Store shelves emptied. And then in 1919 famine and disease brought yet another wave of grief.

The Bolsheviks understood that in order to break the power of reactionary organized religion it was necessary first to isolate and then eliminate the clergy and lay leaders. Parochial schools were closed, and Gustav Ivanovich found himself unemployed. The Lutheran schoolmaster and deacon, who had always depended on income from a secular job as well, now readied himself to find new work. But a new decree terminated that option. The state declared itself the sole employer, and it was not hiring clergymen or deacons for work of any kind. The effect of the new decrees was dramatic. Without a means of earning their daily bread, and their parsonages requisitioned, many clergy and their families were made homeless.[18] In Petrograd, for example, where sixteen Lutheran clergy served in 1917, only four remained in 1921.[19] The Soviet policy of dismantling organized religion was efficient and effective.

Some Lutheran clergy emigrated to Germany, Scandinavia, Switzerland, and the newly independent Baltic republics of Estonia and Latvia. The decimated parish in Taganrog, where Richard's family lived, was unable to support Pastor von Törne, and after his daughter and son-in-law died of spotted typhus he left for Estonia with his orphaned and starving grandchildren.[20] Another clergyman was said to have "deserted" his Crimean congregation in 1920 and "sailed away on an English steamer."[21] Some clerics successfully escaped through Ukraine;

others, like Pastor Keller who baptized Richard, were apprehended at the border and forcibly returned.[22] Those clergy who remained with their congregations, it was reported, "are discharging their duties in the face of inconceivable difficulties." And yet, wrote a clergyman, "One has the feeling that the worst lies not behind us but before us."[23] That grim prediction proved accurate. By 1921, as a result of famine and Soviet policy, one-half of the remaining congregations were without pastors.[24] W. L. Scheding warned the National Lutheran Council that there were few clergy "who are determined to remain at their posts to the last under any and all conditions."[25]

Seizing on the phrases "freedom of conscience" and "freedom of religious worship" in Article 124 of the Soviet constitution, Lutheran Bishop Theophil Meyer of Moscow applied to the Kremlin in 1923 for permission to convene an All-Russian Lutheran Synodical Convention, the first in Russian history. His request was denied,[26] but he applied again the following year and was exuberant when a Kremlin official issued a permit for the meeting to be held in Moscow on June 21-26, 1924.[27] No imperial tsar had ever permitted such a gathering.

After Pastor von Törne left Taganrog, Richard's brother, Emil Gustavovich, moved to his parents' city and tried to hold the congregation together. As Richard undertook his second year of missionary work in Africa, his father and brother Emil somehow raised enough money for the trip to Moscow as delegates to the historic synodical convention.[28] The delegates gathered to reorganize the structure of the Church, and to affirm the articles of the Lutheran faith. The existing Church was but a remnant, but twenty-seven clergy and twenty-nine laymen nevertheless assembled in Moscow from the four corners of Soviet Russia — from Vladivostok to Petrograd and Omsk to the Crimea. The independent synods in Finland, Estonia, Latvia and the Caucasus also sent representatives.

At the opening worship service, the delegates listened as Bishop Meyer, speaking in Russian, welcomed those in attendance, and read letters of greeting from Dr. Morehead of the National Lutheran Council in the United States and Dr. Paul, director of the Leipzig Mission, on behalf of the German Evangelical Church. Then Pastor Hörschelman preached the opening sermon in German, "O Holy Ghost, Abide with Us."[29]

A Notable Church Convention
as reported in The *Lutheran Companion*

On Sunday morning, June 22nd, the opening public divine services of the Synodical Convention were held in the Evangelical Lutheran Church of St. Peter and St. Paul in Moscow. The Church was beautifully decorated with palms, laurels and flowers. A choir of seventy-five voices, trained for months for the occasion, led the congregation in singing the musical portions of the service. The two General Superintendents, the Revs. Theophil Meyer and C. Arthur Malmgren, followed by clerical and lay delegates, entered the church in festal procession. Confessional service was conducted. The musical climax of the service was reached in the use of the Luther Hymn, "A Mighty Fortress is Our God," sung by the entire congregation, accompanied by the pipe organ and a trumpet choir.[30]

The delegates honored Richard's father, Kirchenrat (Church Leader) Gustav Ivanovich, by electing him to serve as a secretary of the convention.[31] In a letter of appreciation to the Soviet government, the emboldened delegates voted to include the following statement, which Secretary Reusch transcribed in his own hand:

> The Synod notes with peculiar joy that *freedom of conscience* has been proclaimed by the constitution of the Union of Socialistic Soviet Republics and that *freedom of faith* is guaranteed by law. The Synod is convinced that the Central Government of the Soviet Union will not swerve from the principle of *liberty of conscience* and will see to it that the local organs of the Soviet will adhere to this principle in order that believers may be able freely to engage in the *exercise of their religion without hindrance.*

After underscoring what they regarded as positive language in Article 124, the Lutherans pledged their loyalty to the government:

> The confession of the Evangelical Lutheran Church places the obligation upon every member in his relationship as a citizen to respect authority and the existing constitution, to fulfill the decrees of the government, and to discharge all the obligations laid upon its citizens, including that of military service. Therefore, the people confessing the teachings of the Evangelical Lutheran Church have always been loyal and always will be.[32]

But survival also depended on the freedom of the Church to offer catechetical instruction to its youth, which the delegates insisted was their right "at any time and at any place."[33]

The convention agenda included the framing of a Church constitution, and Bishop Meyer was chosen to lead the Church.[34] The Tartu seminary had been closed, so the delegates voted to open one in Russia, a necessity since only ninety-five active pastors remained in the country. Rev. Malmgren of Leningrad would represent the Church abroad and take responsibility for the seminary.

Some younger delegates, reflecting the dramatic political and social changes of the previous seven years, argued for more radical organizational changes and an expression of faith along Marxist lines.[35] However, the First Synodical Convention affirmed the traditional standards of the Lutheran faith: Holy Scripture, Luther's Catechism and the Augsburg Confession.[36] On the basis of that declaration, the National Lutheran Council in New York readily promised to raise $35,000 in support of a new seminary.[37] In a politically astute gesture, it was made clear that aid was intended for a *Russian* Lutheran seminary, "whether they speak German, Estonian, Lettish [Latvian], Finnish or Russian."[38]

Before the First Synodical Conference was adjourned, the bishops reassigned remaining clergy to known viable congregations. In September 1924, Pastor Emil Gustavovich and his wife, Helen, moved from Taganrog to the Helenendorf colony in the Trans-caucasus.[39]

Bishop Meyer was surprised to receive permission from the Kremlin a year later to open a new seminary in Leningrad.[40] Thirty students had enrolled, Malmgren reported, "filled with zeal and fervor to receive training and education."[41] On September 15, 1925, twenty-four students gathered to begin their studies in a building attached to Malmgren's parish, the Lutheran Church of St. Anne. "We are greatly encouraged by the fact that the seminary has actually opened," Malmgren confided in a report to Morehead.[42] At the same time, however, it was also apparent to observers in Germany that "a vigorous but comparatively secret [Soviet] undermining activity has begun."[43]

In 1926 Moscow Lutherans planned to mark the 350th anniversary of St. Michael's (1576) and the 300th anniversary of Sts. Peter and Paul Lutheran Church (1626).[44] However, a demolition crew tore down the historic St. Michael's structure shortly before its August anniversary.[45] Across the Soviet Union, two-thirds of all Lutheran parishes were vacant, and only seventy-nine names appeared on the roster of active clergy — one-fourth of whom were over the age of 60.[46] Membership figures were revised downward, from 2,000,000 to 900,000.[47]

Even as the Church suffered, a few Lutherans cooperated with Soviet authorities and denounced their neighbors, some because of genuine conviction while others sought retribution for previous slights and injuries. During the famine a cadre of "red pastors" emerged from the ranks of the poverty-stricken village schoolteachers and deacons. Desperate times gave rise to desperate measures, and some became entrepreneurs who requisitioned famine aid for their parishes and then sold the food staples on the black market and pocketed the proceeds.[48]

Parish contributions to the All-Russian Lutheran Church tallied only 2,400.06 rubles ($1200) in 1926, but the widow's mites were made sufficient by contributions from Lutheran Synods in Austria, Czechoslovakia, Denmark, Finland, France, Germany, Hungary, the Tamil Lutheran Church in India, Latvia, the Netherlands, Norway, Romania, Sweden, the United States, and Yugoslavia. As late as 1927, Bishop Malmgren, clinging to the words of Article 124, expressed the hope that it still might be "possible to rescue some of the valuable aspects of the shattered Czarist Russia, among them the churches, and to preserve them in the new social order." However, prospects for the future appeared so bleak in 1927 that no new students were admitted to the seminary.[49]

Sixteen seminarians graduated in June 1928. Initially, six were assigned to Siberian congregations and ten to parishes in Western Russia,[50] but those assignments were later changed in an attempt to stem the hemorrhaging of the Church in the Volga valley and southern Russia.[51] In September of that year, a dismal Second All-Russian Synodical Conference was held in Leningrad. Neither Kirchenrat Gustav Ivanovich nor Pastor Emil Gustavovich was able to attend.[52]

A struggle for power between the right and left wings of the Communist Party had ensued after the death of Lenin in 1924. Joseph Stalin ruthlessly consolidated his power and ultimately emerged the victor. The Georgian's first five-year plan, implemented in October 1928, called for the elimination of two elements entrenched in Old Russian culture: religion, and the *kulak* class of independent farmers, including the tenacious German Russians — Lutheran, Roman Catholic and Mennonite.

Although expedited unevenly throughout Russia, the state now controlled daily necessities and could withhold access to food, clothing, shelter, jobs and education at will. Most church members were cowed into submission. Sunday was just another day of labor. Few parents in larger towns dared to baptize their children. Young Lutherans no longer came for confirmation instruction. Engaged couples did not marry in church because the state levied a tax on that ritual. People were afraid to be seen in church. Some were so fearful that they crossed the street rather than risk being seen in public greeting their pastor. Funerals were conducted privately in homes. Clergy no longer dared to call on parishioners because of the anxiety their visits caused. Constant harassment and the threat of arrest and exile produced "tremendous suspense and nerve-wrecking tensions," according to one clergyman, and so "the elasticity of the mind dies down, the body becomes worn and weak."[53]

Katerinenstadt (Marx), in the heart of Volga German territory, was selected for special attention in 1929. First, Pastor Arthur Kluck was arrested and sent to a labor camp. Then the authorities seized the Evangelical Lutheran Church, the largest in Russia.

"Out of 6,800 parishioners," the local newspaper reported, "4,184 signed the petition 'for the conversion of our church into a home for culture.'" According to the *New York Times*, "A further 1,000 signatures were wrung from frightened residents so that it could be claimed that five-sixths of the population was in favor of the change."[54] Later, as a crowd watched, a young Communist climbed onto the church roof and shimmied up the spire, loosened the cross and sent it tumbling to the ground — lost his grip, and fell to his death before the stricken onlookers.[55] Soon, however, in the place of the cross "waved triumphant the blood red flag of the Proletarian Revolution." On Christmas Eve 1929, the Evangelical Lutheran Church was reopened as the Karl Marx Palace of Culture, and "Comrade Bartil delivered a magnificent festival oration which was one long attack on religion and the churches."[56]

On the following day the seminary community in Leningrad was thrown into turmoil. Four students were arrested on Christmas Day 1929, and later sent to labor camps. Morehead suggested to Bishop Meyer that perhaps the Lutheran World Convention might send a delegation to survey the situation and appeal to Soviet authorities.[57] No, Meyer advised, that would only draw attention to the Church and hasten its demise.[58]

Two months later the authorities evicted the house parents and remaining seminarians from St. Anne's. Peasants in a Finnish village nearby took them in; however, the seminary was licensed to offer instruction only in the City of Leningrad. Their professors gone, their seminary building off limits, the seminarians had nowhere to go. Thirty pastors were known to be in prison.[59] To no avail, Morehead appealed to President Hoover on behalf of Rev. Koch of Odessa, who was sentenced to a five-year term.[60] The aged Pastor Hörschelmann was released from prison, but he was forbidden to return to his parish in the Crimea.[61]

The end of the Lutheran Church in Russia was at hand.

As Dr. Reusch wound up his American speaking tour, he was unaware that his cousin's family had been walking across Siberia to Manchuria, dodging Red troops and risking their lives to get out of Red Russia. The Kremlin had faced a potentially explosive situation in the autumn of 1929 when approximately 20,000 German Russian farmers and their families, stripped of their property, made their way from Ukraine and Volga colonies to Moscow, demanding permission to emigrate. About 15,000 were given the necessary exit visas.[62] According to the German consul in Washington, D.C., a thousand others crossed into East Prussia. Another contingent escaped across the southern border into Persia.[63] "Some 3,000 wandered eastward towards the Chinese frontier," reported Charles Kastler, the Lutheran pastor in Harbin, Manchuria, "and by crossing the Amur River finally landed in various parts of Manchuria. About half of them came finally to Harbin." The others were driven out of Moscow and "had to go back to their old places or find another way out of the land of sorrow and death."[64]

On Christmas Day, 1930, a distraught Pastor Kastler scrawled an appeal for assistance, which landed on the desk of Dr. Moorhead in New York City. The letter was signed by members of the refugees' own committee. The third signature was that of Friedrich Reusch, born in the Orlovka colony not far from Baratayevka.[65]

Like the German Jews in the 1930s, the German Russian Lutherans from Harbin were denied refuge by one government after another. Canadian provinces declined to accept the refugees. So did Australia. Neither would the United States government accept the Russian farmers. Morehead implored every friend in Washington, D.C., including President Hoover with whom he had worked in the American Relief Administration during the famine of 1921-23. But his efforts were to no avail. Overtures to Mexico and several South American countries failed to produce a welcome. Finally, Brazil agreed to accept the stateless Russians.[66]

Fewer refugees were arriving in April 1931 because, according to Kastler, "the Bolshevist Authorities are shooting them down wholesale when they are caught in their flight. Only a few days ago over 80 were shot down at the frontier." The Soviets were threatening to come across the border and grab the refugees, whom they regarded as counter-revolutionaries. At the same time, Nationalist China was contending with Mao's revolutionary troops and Japanese invaders. Kastler had to promise the Chinese that the Lutheran refugees in Harbin would leave by the end of 1931. "I therefore pray you, dear brethren," he implored Moorhead, "to do all in your power that they can immigrate to some country as speedily as possible."[67]

By the middle of December 1931 there were more than 1700 Russian refugees hunkered in Harbin.[68] The 400 Lutherans continued to wait patiently for word about their future,[69] but their situation flared into a crisis when the Chinese, fearing Russian intervention, threatened to repatriate the hapless *kulaks*. At the last minute the Nansen Refugee Commission of the League of Nations intervened to prevent that from happening — at least until March 1932.[70]

Morehead, faced with the challenge of raising $56,805 to get the refugees from Harbin to Shanghai, chartered a ship to take them to Brazil, and provided for their resettlement. The stress of the years took its toll, and Morehead's health failed. Yet he remained at his desk, cajoling support from the international Lutheran community. He asked each Lutheran Synod in America to contribute its fair share, notifying the Augustana Synod that it was expected to come up with $10,000.[71]

"FINLAND SENDS 330 DOLLARS HARBIN RELIEF," cabled Archbishop Gummerus from Helsinki.

"STILL INSUFFICIENT FOR ACTION STOP FORWARD ALL LUTHERANS TO THE RESCUE," Morehead cabled in reply.[72]

"[O]ptions and contracts, covering transportation and location in Brazil, [are] ready to be signed as soon as funds are available," the pastor of Grace Lutheran Church in New York City wrote in a fundraising letter to his congregation on March 16, 1932. "But the time is short — March 31st."[73]

The Mennonites quietly and quickly removed their Harbin brethren to safety in Paraguay. The international Lutheran response to Morehead's urgent pleas, however, was insufficient. The Nansen Committee granted one final extension that saved the refugees from repatriation while Morehead and others scrambled to raise the necessary funds. Times were tough, and only $31,000 had been collected when time ran out on the last extension. Therefore, a loan was secured for the remaining $25,805.[74]

On May 9, 1932, a ship with 393 Russian Lutherans aboard departed Shanghai harbor.[75] The Friedrich Reusch family was bound for Parana, Brazil.

An estimated 30,000 Russians fled to China after the Revolution. By 1949 approximately 1,000 Russians remained there as Comrade Mao's victorious armies drove the hapless Nationalists onto the island of Taiwan.[76]

THE VOICE OF MOTHER AFRICA

At the end of September 1930, Reusch returned alone to Leipzig. There he corrected proofs for his book, *Der Islam in Ost-Afrika, mit besonderer Berücksichtiggung der Muhammedanischen Geheim-orden*, which was published in 1931 by Adolph Klein Verlag, Leipzig. The eight chapters include:

1. The History and Spread of Islam in East Africa
2. Shi'a Communities in North and East Africa
3. Sunnites
4. Rituals and Worship in African Islam
5. Tariqua Fraternities
6. Islamic Eschatology and Its Effect
7. Reasons for Islam's Influence and Power
8. Strengths and Weaknesses of Islam

In his review, Prof. G. Kampffmeyer, president of the German Society for Islamic Studies, wrote that Reusch's publication deserved to be read not only by those associated with foreign mission work but by anyone with an interest in the unfolding events in Africa.[77] Walther Bjorkman, a prolific scholar and Orientalist, published his review in *Africa: Journal of the International African Institute*. He noted that Reusch had been given access in Khartoum to a secret British Intelligence document, "The Religious Confraternities of the Sudan" (1922), which did, in fact, contain new information. Bjorkman cited numerous factual errors in Reusch's text, but added, "We should be pleased that there is a missionary who has actually tried to understand Islam and describe the reasons for its enormous appeal." Reusch had cited two salient features of Islam that, according to Bjorkman, explained its appeal to Africans: First, the Muslim belief about death, the afterlife, the coming Day of Judgment and the return of the Mahdi (p. 321); and second, the appeal of Islamic values, such as caring for the poor and equality of all Muslims (p. 273).[78]

By Reusch's estimation, Islamic missionaries had succeeded in attracting and converting more than half the East African population. An Anglican, D. Julius Richter, warned, "The deplorable fact is that up to the present Christian missions, Protestant as well as Roman Catholic, seem to ignore the rising tide of Islam even at the risk of their own fields being slowly yet irresistibly swamped by it." He cited Dr. Reusch's work as one of only two such publications to provide context to the issue.[79]

The Leipzig Mission scheduled a series of appearances for Reusch throughout Germany. In January 1931 Professor von Bulmerinq summoned Reusch to Tartu University. Because the faculty regarded the publication of *Der Islam in Ost Africa* as a significant contribution to Oriental scholarly literature, by Tartu University Order No. 7372, Reusch was granted a doctorate degree.[80] Meanwhile, in February, Elveda and Betty left Chicago for New York City on their return journey to Africa.

The newly minted Dr. Reusch left Tartu for Leipzig to resume his speaking tour. After delivering a lecture to a full house at the Great Festival Hall in Hamburg, on April 29, 1931 he was featured on Hamburg Radio, speaking on the subject, "Four Months with the Dervish."[81] Then he was off to visit more churches in southern Germany and Czechoslovakia.

In May the popular speaker finally rejoined his wife and daughter in Tanganyika, already settled at the Marangu Teachers Training School. A month later another daughter, Ingrid Eleanor, was born.

Dr. Reusch had made a name for himself in the American Midwest, and many who heard him speak were interested in following his adventures in Africa. The first of Reusch's articles for Augustana periodicals appeared in *Mission Tidings*, October 1931, edited and given lyrical form by Elveda:

> It was when suffering from a severe attack of malaria that I was sitting at the door of the little chapel of one of my congregations on the hot plains of Africa. . .It was midnight. The moon had begun to disappear behind the rocky peaks of Meru, but still I could see the ice-covered peak of the crown of Africa, Mt. Kilimanjaro. . . The chill of malaria came over me when suddenly a long, painful sound arose from the southern horizon, went higher and higher on the firmament, ascended slowly and died high under the sky. It was a cry resembling the cry of a mother filled with anguish and pain over her children in mortal danger. The natives among whom I was working call this sound the "Voice of Mother Africa."[82]

CHAPTER 9

1 John Morehead, "European Protestantism and Lutheran World Service," *Lutheran Companion*, v. 34 (6 February 1929), 135.

2 Elveda Reusch, East Chicago, Illinois, letter to Dr. Ihmels, Leipzig, 14 May 1930, AELML.

3 R. Reusch, "The Cry of Mother Africa," *Mission Tidings* (October 1931), 164. Reusch often referred to Mohamad Ahmed ibn Abdullah. According to Charles Trench, "In May 1881, at the age of thirty-eight after years of spent in prayer, fasting, Koranic study and contemplation of the decay of Islam, he had proclaimed himself in a triple role: as the Imam, holding temporal authority over all Muslims; the Successor of the Prophet of God, implying that he had spiritual authority and a task similar to that of the Prophet in restoring the purity of Islam; and the Mahdi, the Expected One, the eschatological figure whose advent foreshadowed the end of the world in its present state." With an army of 300,000 devoted Dervish followers, ibn Abdullah launched a rebellion against Egyptian and British rule. The British garrison at Khartoum was taken and General Charles Gordon killed in 1884. — Charles Chenevix Trench, *The Road to Khartoum: A Life of General Charles Gordon* (178), 187.

4 "New Drive to Break Chicago Gang Rule," *New York Times*, 1 September 1930, 2.

5 Harvey Klehr, *The Heyday of American Communism: The Depression Decade* (1984), 164.

6 Klehr, 32.

7 "Reds Battle Police in Union Square," *New York Times*, 7 March 1930, 1.

8 "Say Reds Agitate in Chicago Schools," *New York Times*, 29 July 1930, 12.

9 Klehr, 37.

10 "Puts Communists in Nation at 51,000," *New York Times*, (30 July 1930), 2.

11 "Chicago Police Fight 3,000 Communists," *New York Times*, (10 August 1930), 19.

12 "Missionary Visiting in Moline Tells of Experiences in Russia and Africa," *Moline Daily Dispatch* (7 June 1930), clipping, GACA.

13 "Horror of Red Rule Revealed by Missionary," *Calumet News*, (11 September 1930), clipping, GACA.

14 "Lectures Before Kiwanis, Dr. R. Reusch Argues Against Communism in East Chicago," *East Chicago Times* (10 September 1930), clipping, GACA.

15 R. Reusch, Arusha, letter to Dr. Paul, Leipzig, 12 April 1923, ELMLA.

16 Article 124, Constitution of the USSR, *The Soviet Crucible: The Soviet System in Theory and Practice*, ed. by Samuel Hendel (1959), 322.

17 R. Walter, Moscow, "Conditions in the Lutheran Church of Russia," translated from the German by Pastor Mueller, ca. 1919, 7-8 (NLC-2-12), AELCA.

    For a summary of the impact of Soviet policy on the Russian Orthodox Church, see William B. Husband, *Atheism and Society in Soviet Russia*, 1917-32 (2000).

18 W. L. Scheding, a confidential report, "Einige Mitteilungen aus dem Leben der evangelish-lutherischen Kirche in Soviet-Russland" (5 March 1921), 4 (NLC 12, 2/1), AELCA.

19 Scheding, 9.

20 Scheding, 15.

21 Scheding, 20.

22 Scheding, 15.

23 Scheding, 23.

24 Walter, 4.
25 Scheding, 22.
26 W. L. Scheding, "Very Confidential Supplemental Report" to the president of the National Lutheran Council, ca. December 1923, 3 (PA 142), AELCA.
27 Bishop Theo. Meyer, letter to John Morehead, Executive President of the Lutheran World Convention, 25 August 1923 (LWC 2-11), AELCA.
28 John Morehead, "The First Convention of the Evangelical Lutheran General Synod of Russia, pt. 2, *Lutheran Companion* (20 September 1924), 592, AELCA.
29 "Report of the First General Synod of the Ev. Lutheran Church in Russia," 1 (LWC-6-24), AELCA.
30 Morehead, pt. 1, p. 576.
31 "Report of the First General Synod of the Evangelical Lutheran Church of Russia," Moscow, 21-26 June 1924, 1 (LWC, 1923-47, Correspondence, 6-24), AELCA.
32 Morehead, pt. 2, p. 592.
33 Morehead, pt. 3, pt. 624.
34 Meyer's predecessor, General Superintendent Willelrodt, could not adapt to life under the Bolsheviks and committed suicide in Moscow. — W. L. Scheding, "Luther's Heritage in Soviet Russia," unpublished manuscript, ca. 1929, 33 (PA 142), AELCA.
35 Morehead, "In Memory of Bishop Meyer of Moscow, Russia," file copy, ca. May 1934, 4 (LWC 22-16), AELCA.
36 Dr. John Morehead, letter to the Oberkirchenrat Meyer, 26 November 1924 (LWC 2-36), AELCA.
37 Morehead, letter to Meyer, 2 August 1926 (LWC 4-25), AELCA.
38 Morehead, letter to Meyer, 28 December 1928 (LWC 7-23), AELCA.
39 Report of the First Synodical Convention, Sec. III, "Personalia," 7 (LWC-3-27), AELCA.
40 Morehead, "In Memory," 4.
41 Malmgren, letter to Morehead, 7 September 1925 (LWC 3-27), AELCA.
42 Malmgren, letter to Morehead, 11 November 1925 (LWC 3-27), AELCA.
43 "State and Church in Soviet Russia," trans. from *Kirchenblatt* (chuch publication serving Lutheran congregations in Prussia and Breslau (22 March 1925), 1 (LWC 3-8), AELCA.
44 Morehead, letter to Meyer, 1 April 1926 (LWC 4-24), AELCA.
45 Meyer, "Bericht des evangelisch-lutherischen Oberkirchenrats in Russland ueber das Kirchenwesen von Sommer 1926 bis zum Sommer 1927," 3-4, undated (LWC 6-8), AELCA.
46 Morehead, "European Protestantism and Lutheran World Service," *Lutheran Companion*, vol. 34 (13 February 1926), 158; based on statistics provided by Bishop Meyer in "Bericht des evangelish-lutherischen Oberkirchenrats in Russland," 5.
47 Meyer, "Bericht...," 2.
48 Scheding, "Luther's Heritage" manuscript, 33+ (PA 142), AELCA.
49 Morehead, letter to Malmgren, 2 August 1927 (LWC 6-7), AELCA.
50 Malmgren, letter to Morehead, 18 April 1928 (LWC 7-22), AELCA.
51 Peter Peterson, "An Appeal for Russian Relief and Aid to Orphaned Foreign Missions," *Lutheran Companion*, vol. 36 (28 April 1928), 425.
52 Morehead, letter to Consul Kiep, German Embassy, Washington, D.C., 5 December 1930 (LWC 14-1), AELCA.

53 Otto Seib, Nikolaiev, Russia, letter to "my dear professor" (perhaps Ihmels in Leipzig), translated from the German by C. Gloeckler for the Lutheran World Convention, 29 November 1929, 3-4 (LWC 11-1), AELCA.

54 "Marxists Use Church as 'Palace of Culture,'" *New York Times,* 9 February 1930, III, p. 8 (special correspondence from *Die Reichspost,* Vienna, Austria, which reprinted the story from *Prokovsker Nachrichten,* Marxstadt).

55 Testimony from the video documentary, *A Light in the Darkness.*

56 "Marxists Use Church..."

57 Morehead, letter to Malmgren, 8 April 1930 (LWC 13-8), AELCA.

58 Meyer, letter to Morehead, 24 June 1930 (LWC 13-8), AELCA.

59 Morehead, letter to Thomas Hartig, Manitoba Lutheran Synod, 3 June 1930 (LWC 13-23), AELCA.

60 Morehead, letter to President Hoover, 10 July 1930 (LWC 14-1), AELCA.

61 Morehead, letter to Rev. Ulmer, 15 October 1930 (LWC 13-23), AELCA.

62 Charles W. Kastler, "Who Helped Our Brethren in Need," summary report of the Harbin episode, 23 May 1934, 1 (LWC 22-18), AELCA.

63 O. C. Kiep, Consul, German Embassy, Washington, D.C., letter to John Moorhead, 10 March 1930 (LWC 13/23), AELCA.

64 Kastler, "Who Helped Our Brethren."

65 Kastler, letter to Moorhead (in German), 25 December 1930 (LWC 13/23), AELCA.

66 Moorhead, report to Rev. Ulmer in Germany, 4 June 1930 (LWC 18/19), AELCA.

67 Kastler, letter to Moorhead with attached "List of Heads of Families of Harbin Refugees," 17 April 1931 (LWC 16/11), AELCA.

68 Kastler, "Who Helped our Brethren," 2.

69 Chauncey W. Goodrich, Central Bureau for Relief of Evangelical Churches of Europe, letter to Moorhead, 16 December 1931 (LWC 16/10), AELCA.

70 H. S. Bender, telegram to Moorhead, 29 August 1931 (LWC 16/11), AELCA.

71 Moorhead, letter to Brandelle, 17 February 1932 (LWC 18/19), AELCA.

72 Archbishop Gummerus, cable to Moorhead, and Moorhead's reply, 11 March 1932 (LWC 18/20), AELCA.

73 Pastor, Grace Lutheran Church, New York City, mimeographed letter to parish members, 16 March 1932 (LWC 18/20), AELCA.

74 L. W. Boe, letter to American Lutheran Synod Presidents, 25 June 1932 (LWC 18/19), AELCA.

75 Moorhead, letter to Olaf Moe, 9 May 1932 (LWC 18/19), AELCA.

76 "Admit White Russians?" *Lutheran Companion,* vol. 57 (5 October 1949), 5.

77 G. Kampffmeyer, reproduced in the introductory pages of *Der Islam in Ost Afrika.*

78 Walther Bjorkman, untitled review of *Der Islam in Ost Afrika* in *Africa: Journal of the International African Institute,* vol. 7, No. 2 (July 1934), 238-240.

79 D. Julius Richter, *Tanganyika and Its Future* (1934), 55-56.

80 Diploma, Richard Reusch file (2100-1-13219), ESHA. Also cited by Pent Nurmekunt, "Dr. Reusch: D. Reusch im Archiv der Ev.-Luth. Mission zu Leipzig," item 131, S.1-10, p. 3 (Papers, Professor Pent Nurmekunst, V 30:8) Tartu University Archive (TUA).

81 Nurmekunt, S.245.
82 R. Reusch, "The Cry of Mother Africa," *Mission Tidings*, vol. 26 (October 1931), 164.

Betty Anderson

Six Christian Soldiers

Chapter Ten

RETURN TO EAST AFRICA
Second Term, 1931-38

Kilimanjaro is a snow-capped mountain 19,710 feet high,
and is said to be the highest mountain in Africa. Its western summit is called
by the Masai "Ngàje Ngàje," the House of God. Close to the western summit
there is a dried and frozen carcass of a leopard. No one has explained
what the leopard was seeking at that altitude.

— Ernest Hemingway, *The Snows of Kilimanjaro*[1]

The Leipzig missionaries found life pleasant in the foothills of Mount Kilimanjaro. The Reusch family lived at Marangu where, at an elevation of more than 5,000 feet, the climate was temperate, the water cool, and the foothills green with coffee and banana trees growing from rich volcanic soil.

The parents and their two daughters lived on the grounds of the Teachers Training School in a stone house built years earlier for a German colonial officer. Dr. Reusch resumed his work as assistant headmaster and Elveda served as the school nurse.

More than a hundred students were enrolled at the Teachers' Training School from four Lutheran missions: Augustana and Leipzig, and two other German missions, the Bielefeld and Berlin Missions. Augustana's Iramba Mission sent twenty-one boys to study at Marangu, six of whom were later trained as medical assistants. Justino and Imanuel Kilinga, Samweli Kingu, Nikodemo Daudi, and Melanchton and Filemon Mkumbo went on to work at two of Augustana's new hospitals at Iambi and Kiomboi.[2]

The British colonial administration prescribed the curriculum, but Headmaster Paul Rother and Reusch controlled extra-curricular activities. Rother taught the boys to sing and encouraged them to learn how to play the organ,[3] and Assistant Headmaster Reusch drilled the students, marching them in military formation to the beat and sound of drums and bugles.

Daily life was more formal in the Leipzig north than in the Augustana south. German-born women did not wear slacks, an emerging American fashion that was regarded as improper, not unlike "cinching a beautiful saddle on a work horse." African household servants assisted Mrs. Reusch, who also was responsible for welcoming a continuous stream of visitors, and a German nanny was in charge of the two girls. "Our mother," said Betty, "was always entertaining guests — scholars, mountain climbers, clergy, missionaries, scientists, royalty and British colonial officers. We lived in a German community and played with children from an international community. That is why we girls identified more as Europeans than Americans."[4] The sisters grew up speaking English, German, Ki-Swahili, and Wa-Chagga.

Richard and Elveda welcomed a third daughter, Dagmar Evelyn, at the end of October 1932. When Betty, the eldest, was old enough, Mrs. Reusch conducted home school from 9:00 a.m. until noon each day.[5] In addition to caring for her family, offering hospitality to visitors, and serving as the school nurse, Mrs. Reusch acted as surrogate mother for the Marangu students.

The missionary enterprise sent bearers of the Good News down jungle paths and over hot dusty plains to remote parishes and stations for weeks at a time. In contrast, a teaching assignment was by its nature more sedentary. However, sometimes Reusch disappeared for weeks at a time to pursue his own agenda. The Masai walked in regal grace across the savanna beyond the Christian missions, and he was often among them as he visited congregations and missions at Masama, Machame, Moshi, Kidia, Lekitatu, Chem-Chem, Upper Nduruma and Shaush Agar. During his first term he had walked or ridden a donkey. In his second term he often traveled in a car or truck. But he never learned to drive. Instead, like any ranking military officer, he depended on a driver.

Chief Zambeke once invited Dr. Reusch to observe a Masai male circumcision ritual for 2,000 young men, including some of Zambeke's sons:

> For about three months before the circumcision the boys and girls receive through male and female teachers their initiation instructions in special separate camps far away from any other Masai camp, somewhere in the bush or forest where they are instructed in sexual life, in married life, in the Masai morals and religion. The circumcision times are fixed as to time and place and made known by the *Oloitoni Kitok* [chief medicine man] every seven or eight years.
>
> It is usually performed early in the morning. The boys to be circumcised are by themselves surrounded by a great number of their male and female relatives. Only in exceptional cases it is allowed for men to be present at the circumcision of girls. Medicine men or sorcerers circumcise the boys; women perform this operation on girls.
>
> I shall describe a boys' circumcision as I have seen it myself. Every one to be circumcised had to sit down on the same ox hide. Before the operation the medicine man made a line with a piece of chalk sideways along the whole body, starting at the right ankle. Then he began the operation with a deliberate slowness. He used an old rusty pocketknife (although sometimes they use a piece of tin). The Masai circumcision has no resemblance to that of the Jews or Mohammedans. It is quite different. It is not a circumcision at all, but just a certain operation on the sexual organs. The circumcised had no permission to utter any sound, otherwise they would have been covered with shame for their whole life.
>
> Into the wound the medicine man put some ashes from a nearby pot. Having circumcised ten to twelve boys, he poured their blood away into a hole as a sacrifice for the spirits of fertility. A tiny piece of the foreskin was given to every boy who put it as a protective charm over the door of his hut.
>
> After the circumcision the boys and girls cover themselves with red clay and lime,

put a crown of one hundred small birds on their heads, adorn themselves with ostrich feathers and live for three to six months in special camps, the girls in one camp and the boys in another nearby camp. During those months they have full liberty for sexual intercourse. They use the opportunity, especially the boys, without limit since they are not punished. In later life they live more chaste lives and punish adulterers.

Afterwards they return to their homes and to their customary work. A circumcised boy becomes a warrior and is called *Olmuran*. They wear one or three braids, and as long as they wear their braids they cannot marry although a certain sexual liberty is allowed. The old and senior warriors shave their heads.

The previously circumcised become warriors and receive permission to marry. After the next circumcision they become senior warriors, and enter the class of the older men who are eligible for the Office of Elders.[6]

Betty, Ingrid and Dagmar seldom saw their father. On occasion they met on the road, headed in opposite directions, but they always stopped for a quick conversation and a hug before going their separate ways. Those times were treasured when Daddy gave them his full attention. On one occasion he and daughter Betty were walking home together when they came upon a dead civet cat along the path. The two agreed to tell the same story when they got home: Daddy had grabbed the cat by the neck, and daughter, after getting hold of its tail and twirling it around her head three times, flung it so high into the sky that it died when it hit the ground.

Betty was permitted to sit in the living room as her father entertained guests after dinner, perhaps a European crown prince, an Islamic scholar, a German grand duke, a Swedish archbishop or Jesuit priests. During their erudite conversations, Betty was permitted to ask questions, "but the moment I became silly," she recalled, "I was whisked off to bed."

On his way to the Middle East in 1929, Dr. Reusch had met Alfred Buxton, a missionary

Betty, Richard, Dagmar, Elveda and Ingrid Reusch, Marangu, 1934.

Betty Anderson

serving with the British Church Missionary Society (BCMS) in Abyssinia [Previously established]. Like Reusch, Buxton also believed that "the Bible IS the Word of God." But Reusch admired the Englishman for another reason: He had not hesitated to work among cannibals in the Belgian Congo. The two had become good friends.

In 1932 Buxton confided in a letter to Reusch that Emperor Haile Salassi of Abyssinia (Ethiopia) looked favorably on Buxton's proposal to open a seminary in Addis Ababa. Would Dr. Reusch consider taking the position of seminary president? Reusch replied that he would accept the offer on one condition: Leipzig must grant him a leave of absence.

In a letter to his Leipzig superior, Reusch explained that Abyssinian nationalists desired independence from the Egyptian Coptic Church. Because there was no Abyssinian Coptic seminary, the country was served by Coptic and Orthodox priests from Egypt and Greece, few of whom spoke the Abyssinian language. Although he was a Lutheran, he was acceptable to the Abyssinian Copts, Reusch explained, because the Emperor had come under the influence of a Swiss Protestant missionary. British mission societies and the Abyssinian government would underwrite the cost of the seminary; and, Reusch pointed out to Ihmels, the *Abuna* (the Bishop of the Ethiopian Coptic Church) and the *Negusi-Negaschti* (Emperor Haile Selassi, "The Lion of Judah") both supported his call. In 1929 Reusch had spent time in the company of both the bishop and the emperor, and he believed "this is a call from God which opens a new door to the spirit of the Reformation." Then he not so subtly implied that he was the candidate best suited for the task. If BCMS chose him to work in Abyssinia he would gladly take up the work; however, if Leipzig recommended someone else — with credentials similar to his, of course, someone with his Oriental expertise and language skills — so be it.[7]

Buxton also wrote to Director Ihmels. Dr. Reusch, he argued, "combines the needed qualifications in a remarkable manner": he was familiar with Eastern Orthodox and Coptic faith traditions; his academic background in biblical scholarship, patristics, and knowledge of ancient history and cultures fit the position; he was an effective teacher with experience in Europe and Africa; and he understood and valued the cultures of Africa better than most Europeans.[8]

Ihmels did not reply. Six months later Buxton wrote again,[9] and yet again in another six months.[10] After consulting with the superintendent of the Kilimanjaro district, Dr. Ihmels finally sent his answer: The local committee in Africa simply could not spare Reusch.

Unfazed, in 1934 Buxton proposed that Reusch come to work with him and Abyssinian scholars to produce a translation of the Bible in Amharic, the official Semitic language of the country. Said Mrs. Buxton to her husband, "There seems to be a link between you and Reusch even more than between you and B.C.M.S. workers."

"Well," replied Buxton, "I think it is that Reusch would be willing to take a risk and dare anything."

"And that is really how I feel," Buxton wrote to his friend. "I hope that already you are nationalised British," he added, "so that we are together subjects of two Emperors — the Lord Jesus, and King George; and may the time be short when together we shall be serving a third Emperor, Haile Selassi."[11]

However, international events again intervened to alter Reusch's plans when the Italians invaded Abyssinia in 1936.

GLOBAL ECONOMIC DEPRESSION

Economic hardships of the 1930s affected not only Lutherans in America and Germany but also the missions they supported throughout the world. At the end of the third quarter of 1932 the Augustana Synod had collected only $12,000 for foreign missions compared to $20,000 the year before. Missionaries experienced salary cuts, and for lack of funds ten volunteers who were prepared to serve as missionaries in Africa unpacked their trunks and remained at home.[12] The situation worsened in 1933 when the Synod collected only one-fifth of the amount budgeted for home and foreign missions.[13] Three years later, in 1936, Synod convention delegates, meeting in St. Peter, Minnesota, felt they had no choice but to further reduce the budget. Rev. George Anderson, who had come to Tanganyika in 1924, was home on furlough that summer, and Synod President Brandelle invited him to address the parish representatives.

"May I remind you," Anderson scolded in the Swedish accent shared by nearly everyone attending the convention, "that the other day you voted an annual budget for your Africa Mission of only $35,000, nearly $5,000 less than was actually received in cash last year!" Since the delegates probably did not understand the implications of their vote, Anderson declared, it was his responsibility to enlighten them.

For example, the Mission's old Model T was worn out and had been scrapped; in fact, they now needed two cars to serve their far-flung stations in Irambaland. "Did your vote the other day mean that we may not have these trusty 'assistant missionaries'? Well, we can trudge along on foot under the tropical African sun or follow our lowly Master in riding the lowly *punda* (donkey), but as you whizz along on your paved highways at 70 miles an hour, may the good Lord save you from tire trouble, but may He give you a double dose of conscience trouble."

Then he described a series of urgent projects, each punctuated by a stinging question:

"We had put into that budget a small amount for a beginning of medical work among the lepers. *Must that wait?*

"One of our greatest needs in Irambaland is to get a training school for native workers, for, after all, the evangelization of Africa or any other pagan land must be done mainly by the native Christians. We put a modest request for that in the budget. *Must that wait?*

"Neither the Augustana Synod nor the Lutheran Church in America is fully conscious of its obligation according to God's word, to the non-Christian world," he charged. "This must not continue. The Lutheran Church in America has not contributed one single outstanding missionary-statesman. Why? Where are the Motts and Speers of the Lutheran Church?"

Furthermore, what about Mussolini's invasion of Christian Coptic Abyssinia that pitted Italian machine guns and poison gas against African spears? "Men," Anderson thundered, "that wasn't a war — that was a massacre, a slaughter of the innocents!" In Ruruma a Christian man had asked him, *"Sababu gani, vita hii huko Habwshi, sababu gani wazungu wanatuonea sisi watu weusi?"* (Why this war in Abyssinia, why do the white men treat us blacks this way?)

"What would you have answered?" Anderson asked rhetorically. The delegates sat in stunned silence. As democratically elected representatives from their congregations, they were not used to being chastised as if they were schoolboys. But Anderson was not finished: "Are we Christian? *Are we?* Then let us, by the grace of God, counteract the hate sown by this damaging, despicable, devilish war more or less throughout Africa and among the colored races, by a great flood of Christian love revealed through a renewed, consecrated missionary support of our own missions."

Anderson then took his seat. Some delegates felt a need to loosen their ties. President Brandelle finally broke the silence by deftly setting Anderson's hook. The annual per capita contribution to foreign missions, he said slowly and deliberately, was a mere *twenty cents*. "There is something the matter with the Augustana Synod," he added in an emotional stage whisper, "and it isn't the depression."[14]

The chagrined delegates voted to amend the budget, including funds for a leper clinic — built and fully operational several months later.[15] Between 1927 and 1937, despite the Great Depression, the fledgling Augustana Mission in Irambaland established seven new stations, founded two hospitals, opened a leper clinic and dedicated a boarding school for girls.[16]

Meanwhile, in Irambaland the twelve Augustana missionaries (six clergy, two doctors, two nurses, one school teacher, and one religious instructor) reaffirmed at their 1933 annual conference the primary Mission goal: to hasten the development of an indigenous African Lutheran Church. The number of Christians had grown, from a dozen at Ruruma in 1927 to 3,482 ten years later, among whom were 88 trained evangelists, teachers and medical personnel.[17] Africans were in charge of numerous parishes, some on their way to becoming self-sustaining. For example, under the leadership of Pastor Yesaya Aaron, the congregation of 900 souls at Kiomboi decided on their own to build a new church structure.[18]

A year later, in 1937, members of the Augustana Women's Missionary Society raised $60,000 for the work in Africa, twice the amount of the Synod's appropriation. Not only did they scrape up money in desperately hard times, they also taught their children to support foreign missions. Thank-offering boxes were distributed to Junior Mission Band members of the Sunday schools, and the Sunday following Thanksgiving the children brought their boxes to church, stuffed with pennies and nickels. Those same dedicated Swedish American women, many from Midwestern farms who met in parish halls with names like Bernadotte, Lindstrom, Mora, Norseland, Scandia and Vasa tore up their old bed sheets and rolled the strips into bandages for use in the leper colony and hospitals in Irambaland.

But it was a precarious year-to-year struggle. In 1938, only one-half of the Synod's missions budget was forthcoming. Once again the Augustana Women's Missionary Society helped to make up the shortfall, as did the British colonial administration. After their annual conference that November, the missionaries returned to their respective stations "to carry on our work with practically no money for salaries of assistants or to keep up the general work."

They met again early in 1939 to decide what programs to cut. Eleanor Lindbeck's plea was published in the Synod's periodical: "These teachers, hospital-helpers, and preachers of the Word are our *friends*, our co-workers in Christ out here, and we cannot desert them." Therefore, the Synod must "bend all our efforts toward keeping the hospital doors open to the sick hundreds who come daily, and to maintain our schools, thus seeking to keep up the work of laying the foundations of an intelligent Christian life."[19] Some Lutheran missionaries may have embarked for Africa with the goal of converting pagans. But it did not take long for most of them to join in "laying the foundations of an intelligent Christian life." That commitment to provide for the needs of the whole person set Lutherans apart from some fundamentalist evangelical Protestant groups who were primarily interested in converting the heathen.

NAZI EDICTS

Augustana's Board of Foreign Missions and its missionaries survived despite grim economic times, but the Leipzig Mission contended with a crisis that was both economic and political in nature. Unable to secure the usual bank loan in Germany to cover expenses during the summer of 1931, Dr. Karl Ihmels turned to the Lutheran World Convention for emergency assistance. But the worldwide depression had left that organization's coffers empty.[20] By 1932 the German Evangelical Church was bankrupt.[21]

Bad turned to worse in 1933 when Adolph Hitler became chancellor. The Evangelical Church had been responsible for administering public human services in Germany, but Nazi decrees put an end to that. In 1934 the Church was forbidden to send Reich marks out of the Third Reich. German missionaries everywhere were effectively cut off from any external support whatsoever and were compelled to invent various schemes to support themselves. Dr. Reusch contributed to the general operating fund the income he earned from guiding mountain climbers and selling butterfly collections.

1934: A Year of Scarcity

In Tanga and Northern Provinces the Lutheran Evangelical Leipzig Mission (LELM) ministers in the languages of three tribes: the Chagga on Mt. Kilimanjaro, the Pare people in the Pare Mountains, and the Masai in Arusha District and Masailand.

It operates 17 mission stations with 26,664 Lutheran members and 2,525 Catechumens; 11,576 children are enrolled in our schools.

The European staff consists of 16 ordained missionaries, 7 laymen and 6 Deaconesses; the African staff, 10 pastors and 254 teachers.

L.E.L.M. runs 6 dispensaries and hospitals, staffed by 1 European doctor and 7 European male and female medical helpers, and assisted by a number of Natives.

Since October 1934 our treasurer could not pay our missionaries their salaries any longer. Most of our native pastors, teachers and evangelists are working for very low wages. The statistics given here are those available at the end of the year 1934.

— J. Raum, Senior of the L.E.L.M. in Tanganyika Territory[22]

In Europe and elsewhere, whenever mountain climbers talked about Kilimanjaro, Reusch's name and fame often was part of the conversation. As a result, the missionary and his wife welcomed a stream of unusual guests who appeared at their doorstep. Sometimes expedition leaders arranged for Reusch to serve as their guide before they arrived at Marangu; other visitors, after spreading their maps on his dining room table and listening to his stories, requested his services on the spot.

Thomas Kloss, a German who owned the Kibo Hotel at Marangu, became a victim of the worldwide economic depression as fewer tourists and climbers contracted for his hotel and guide services. Kloss was irked, therefore, when the occasional visitors who did come to the area passed the turnoff to his hotel and continued the short distance up the road to the Leipzig Mission. Finally, he could stand it no longer. In March 1933 he raised a ruckus with the British District Officer and the Mission. Kloss wanted it known that Reusch had accepted 190 shillings for guiding Herr Dr. Prof. Fritz Wettstein, a biologist from Göttingen, up Kilimanjaro; furthermore, Reusch had acted as host and guide for the Grand Duke of Mecklenberg and, among others, a Swiss geographer. "Since I know that missionaries are not allowed to make any money on the side or have any businesses on the side," Kloss tattled in a letter to the Mission director, "I have to tell you that Dr. Reusch is dealing in butterflies. Once he sold a collection for 300 dollars."[23]

Reusch was irritated for having to defend himself against such trivial accusations at a time when the Mission and its resources were stretched beyond their limits. Nevertheless, he felt compelled to respond to Kloss's charges, and even placed the issue on the agenda for discussion at the next mission conference. In a letter to Dr. Ihmels two months later, Reusch explained that, yes, Dr. Prof. Flückiger, a Swiss geographer and member of the Swiss Alpine Club, had stayed with him for a month because the two of them were collaborating on a book about Mt. Kilimanjaro. However, Reusch declared, whether he sold chickens or furniture or books — or butterfly collections — it was none of the hotelier's or anyone else's concern.[24] That broadside put an end to the matter.

By the mid-1930s agents of the Third Reich were working to develop pro-Nazi sentiment among Afrikaners, South Africans of European descent, who owned plantations in Tanganyika. As well, some of the German settlers and missionaries who were allowed to return to Tanganyika believed that the British protectorate rightfully belonged to Germany. As the Nazis blustered and tested their growing power in Europe, disturbing intelligence reports began accumulating in Dar es Salaam and London.

The British Colonial Office grew increasingly wary of the Germans and Afrikaners living in East Africa. Letters from Germany sometimes bore, as part of the address, *"ehemaliges Deutsch Ostafrika"* (former German East Africa), a phrase that connoted a threat to the British. In April 1937 the British military attaché in Paris passed along secret information to MI3 in London:

French intelligence reports confirmed that the Germans were indeed "infiltrating into British African Colonies and mandated territories under the guise of colonists."[25]

Concerns over the possibility of war were increasingly difficult to ignore. "No one," said George Anderson, "can predict in the welter of world politics what may happen."[26]

Already the Native Church held its own annual meetings to decide matters of church discipline and responsibility.[27] At their annual 1937 conference, Augustana missionaries recognized the necessity of "taking native Christian leadership into confidence on committees which are working out the foundations of the Native Church." Thereafter, representatives from each congregation sat on the Committee on Native Church Polity and shared the same rights as the white members. Native churchmen were also seated as equals on the Committee of Devolution and the Translation Committee.[28]

But none of the Missions, European or American, had gotten around to opening a seminary to prepare African clergy — without whom there would be no indigenous Church. The German Bethel Mission proposed the idea of opening a joint Protestant seminary to speed the preparation of African clergy.[29] But Augustana was considering three proposals for Irambaland: open a teachers training school, a Bible school to prepare evangelists, or a seminary.

THE DEMISE OF THE LUTHERAN CHURCH IN SOVIET RUSSIA

In September 1931 Richard received a letter from Lithuania. It was from his sister, Olga. She had received the money he sent, purchased food staples, and sent them to their parents in Taganrog. Knowing his father would have to pay a duty on the packages, Richard provided for that expense as well. But when Gustav Ivanovich went to collect the parcels Soviet customs agents insisted the duty had not been paid. The old man had no money to pay the bribe and therefore went home empty-handed. Do not worry about us, Papa Reusch wrote to Olga in his next letter, because the family had sufficient food and there was no need of further shipments. As for the family, "poor Aurelia" was quite thin; Marie was in Kratuk working as a factory physician; and Emma had been sent to Vologda to teach German. Albert and Erich, "thank God, are all settled and do not complain and want our parents to move to Rostov with them."[30]

The persecution of the Lutheran Church in Russia continued with renewed vigor as Dr. Reusch returned to Africa in 1931. Leningrad police arrested the two remaining seminary professors. One was beaten until he agreed to resign and leave the country, and the other, a Russian, was internally exiled. In the spring of 1931, Bishop Malmgren ordained seven men.[31] Half of the remaining seminarians were homeless that summer because their parents' farms had been seized, and the young men did not know if their parents were still among the living. And if they were alive, where were they? To which Karelian or Siberian gulag had they been sent?[32] By 1932 three-fourths of the Lutheran parishes in the USSR were without clergy due to emigration, natural death, internal exile, imprisonment, and execution. Of the remaining 53 active clergy, the roster counted forty-six Germans, four Finns, two Latvians and one Estonian.

In 1932 Gustav Reusch made a final attempt to apply for an emigration visa. The following year Soviet officials told him his papers and fees had been lost and he would have to begin the process all over again. Despite encouragement from the Leipzig Mission, he realized his cause was hopeless. He and his family would have to live their lives in Soviet Russia.[33]

The third and final synodical meeting of the Evangelical Lutheran Church in Russia took place in the fall of 1933.[34] Neither Gustav Ivanovich nor Emil Gustavovich attended. Only a handful of delegates appeared, and several of them were arrested as they left the closing session. A year later, in 1934, Bishop Meyer's son was arrested and charged with espionage. He was shot in the NKVD's notorious Lubyanka Prison on April 19, a bullet to the back of his head. Nine days later, Bishop Meyer died of heart failure, and Mrs. Meyer was left destitute. Her daughter was arrested shortly after her husband's funeral. Fortunately, the German Evangelical Church, through the offices of the German embassy in Moscow, saw to it that Mrs. Eugenie Meyer did not starve.[35] By mid-1934, Bishop Malmgren presided over a Church that existed only in memory. With the exception of Bishop Jürgens in the North Caucasus, Malmgren was the only remaining church leader who was not in prison or serving a sentence in a northern gulag.[36] A single church remained in the Crimea, and another at Vladivostok. Malmgren asked rhetorically, "Whereto shall I send the [last seven] graduates of the seminary?" Drained of energy and spirit but without self-pity, he confessed to Moorhead,

> In the struggles and worries of the past 20 years I have become a lonely man, who in these days will complete his 74th year. Up to now God has kept me well in body and spirit, but in view of the daily increasing need and the apparently hopeless future of the Lutheran Church in Russia I have become weary and I long for the time that God takes me to His rest.[37]

Morehead replied to his dear friend, with whom he had worked so closely since 1921:

> In all your heavy labor under existing hard conditions in Russia for the Church, I am not surprised that you have grown very tired and long for rest. But my prayer is, because as it seems to us the Lord and His Church greatly need you and your service, that He by His unfailing grace cause your strength to be renewed like the eagles and give you abundant daily grace and strength of body and mind for the meeting of every opportunity and responsibility of service, that the true witness of our Lord and Savior in your country may be continued.[38]

Bishop Malmgren was not uplifted by his American friend's optimism. Just before Christmas, 1934, he replied to Moorhead in direct and unambiguous language:

> Even an organized church has no guarantee of perpetual existence on earth but is subject to the same law of change and decay which governs nature and history. The Gospel will remain, of course; it will not perish, even the gates of hell shall not prevail against it. But the Lutheran Church of Russia will not continue much longer; the hour of death is nigh at hand. Let there be no illusion on this point.[39]

Two years later, in 1936, of the Lutheran clergy still alive in the USSR, forty-seven were serving sentences in Karelian or Siberian forced labor camps. Of the remaining thirty-six pastors, Malmgren could confirm the whereabouts of only fourteen.[40] Pastor Arthur Kluck from Saratov was sentenced to ten years at forced labor, which was tantamount to a death sentence. Waldemar Jürgen in Pyatigorsk and Ossip Thorosjan in Vladikavkaz were forbidden to perform pastoral duties.[41] Later that year Soviet authorities granted Bishop Malmgren permission to attend a meeting in Europe. However, he was subsequently refused permission to re-enter the USSR.[42]

By 1938 all Protestant churches in Leningrad had been demolished or put to other uses. These included the Lutheran churches of St. Catherine (1768), St. Anne (1775), and St. Michael (1874), and the Reformed churches of St. Mary's (Finnish, 1803), the Dutch (1833), German (1863), and St. Catherine's (Swedish, 1863). The last to close was the Lutheran Church of Sts. Peter and Paul (1832) on the Nevskii Prospect. These eight church properties had been seized by the state more than a decade earlier, and the congregations had been compelled to lease their former structures from the Soviet government. Like a vise, the rents were gradually increased until the hard-pressed parishioners had no choice but to vacate the premises. Through the same process the Lutheran Church of Sts. Peter and Paul in Moscow was closed a few months later.[43]

A swimming pool was installed in the sanctuary of Leningrad's Sts. Peter and Paul. The Evangelical Lutheran Church in Marx (formerly Katherinenstadt), which had been converted into a Palace of Culture, was later put to more popular use as a dance hall and bar. In Tashkent, Uzbekistan, the German Evangelical Lutheran Church was burned and the ruin left to stand as proof to schoolchildren that there was no God. The destruction of the Lutheran Church in Russia was complete. Not even a list of former parishes survived.[44]

The Russian Lutheran Church in the Post-Soviet Era

In 1996 German engineers began dismantling the swimming pool in St. Petersburg's Sts. Peter and Paul; a remnant of the former congregation in Marx once again met for Sunday services in a corner of their former church; and in Tashkent, twenty-three-year-old Pastor Dmitri Schweitz preached to a standing-room-only congregation in his native Russian language. According to the Reverend Georg Kretschmar, Bishop of the Lutheran Church in Russia and Independent States, forgotten parishes were popping up at a rate of one per month.

The last letter Richard received from his father was dated November 27, 1937. He heard nothing more from his family in the Soviet Union until 1963. "What has happened to our beloved parents, brothers and sisters, that only God knows," Olga wrote in 1938. "I have written them but without an answer, and now I am afraid to write so as not to make any harm come to them."[45]

Richard knew that NKVD agents occasionally questioned members of his family, intent on discovering his whereabouts. And he knew that his brother, Emil, had taken the parish in the Caucasus at Annenfeld, a colony near Helenendorf. But he did not know that late on the night of Christmas Eve in 1936, two strangers, a man and a woman, had begged his brother to come and baptize a baby. It was a trap, and the clergyman was imprisoned. After his release in 1937, Emil took his ten-year old son with him by train to Baku, the oil town on the Caspian Sea. NKVD agents were waiting at the station. Emil was arrested. His son was sent back to Annenfeld alone. The next day Pastor Emil Gustavovich Reusch was executed.

Nor did Richard Gustavovich know that in Rostov there had come a knock at the door, Number 310 Transportnaya Street. The security police had come for Kirchenrat Gustav Ivanovich. A terrified Aurelia explained that her father was not at home. When the elderly man returned a little later, the four of them — Gustav Ivanovich, his wife, Ottilia Filipovna, and daughters Aurelia and Marie — waited in agony for the agents' return.

The knock came early that evening. The 75-year old man was arrested. Among the papers confiscated by the agents was a photograph of the Kirchenrat with several other German Russian teachers. "You see," commented the agent in charge, "he conspires with the foreigners."

One of the security agents stood at the window, impatiently watching for the black van to arrive as Marie clung to her father, weeping and begging that her father be spared. The tearful fuss became too much for the agents, who escorted their prisoner out of the small noisy house to wait in the street. The elderly man stood quietly, but Marie and Aurelia emerged to continue their wailing outside. The arrest had now become a public spectacle that embarrassed the agents. Where was that prison van? Wishing to end it, the arresting officer abruptly told the Reusches to return to their apartment. He advised them to lock the door and pretend they were not at home.

The family sat together through the night, waiting for the officers' inevitable return. But the expected knock at the door never came. As Aurelia said, whenever something terrible was happening to a family member, someone kind was always nearby. In this instance it was an NKVD officer who apparently decided to "lose" the arrest order.

When Aurelia reported to her classroom the next morning the principal said kindly, "I can see that something happened during the night. You should not work with the children today. Please go home and try to rest." At the hospital where Marie worked as a physician, her supervisor also surmised what had happened and urged her to go home.

The thought of being sent to a gulag terrified and haunted Gustav Ivanovich. The strain of the years, his near arrest, and the constant nagging fear that the NKVD might return was too much for him to endure. He was stricken with a heart attack or stroke and died not long afterwards.[46]

The capricious Stalin purges of 1937 and 1938 claimed the lives of as many as 2,000 people in one day.[47] In the same two-year period, according to figures released by the Russian Government Commission on Rehabilitation of Victims of Political Oppression, 168,200 Russian Orthodox priests were arrested, 106,800 of whom were executed. The Soviets martyred as many

Christians in the first two decades of their rule, said Victoria Morozova, as the Roman emperors dispatched in 300 years.[48]

WAR CLOUDS OVER AFRICA

Nazi Germany repudiated the Versailles Treaty in 1935, introduced compulsory military service, and in 1936 occupied the Rhineland. Italy invaded Ethiopia. Japan invaded China. Civil war raged in Spain. Then Hitler signed a pact with Mussolini. In 1937 President Roosevelt signed the U.S. Neutrality Act, and in Tanganyika the Augustana Mission began making contingency plans in case the German missions might have to quit Africa a second time.

It was doubtful that the poverty-stricken Leipzig Mission could much longer carry on its work. Even Reusch admitted that the work in Marangu was quite "rundown," and rumors circulated among the Americans that, if war came again, Dr. Reusch would likely be put in charge of the German missions.[49]

Instead of a seminary, the Americans opted to open a training school for teachers and evangelists at Kinampanda, and they asked the most capable and effective leader they knew to launch the new institution. Dr. Reusch's academic credentials, experience and reputation for getting things done made him the most desirable candidate. During his term at Marangu he had authored an array of materials in Swahili: a series of textbooks (arithmetic, geography and physical education), an introduction to the Old Testament, a revision of an earlier edition of his introduction to the New Testament, and had begun working on a history of East Africa.[50] As well, he had earned an impeccable reputation among British district and provincial officers and in Dar es Salaam. A formal call for Reusch to head up an Augustana training center was issued in February 1937.

Herbert Magney and Anton Lundeen, Augustana's field secretary for Foreign Missions, drove to Marangu to persuade their prime candidate to accept their offer.[51] Reusch said he was not in a position to give an answer until he and his family returned from their upcoming furlough. This was a matter he needed to discuss in person with his colleagues, and with the Mission Board in Leipzig — without whose blessing he could not accept Augustana's bid.[52]

Because the viability of the Leipzig Mission was doubtful, and because of an unstoppable downward spiral into another world war, Reusch's superiors agreed that he ought to accept Augustana's call. From his beloved Leipzig Mission he had received "a life call," but once again fate intervened. Reusch wrote to the president of the Augustana Foreign Mission Board, "I look forward to finding in the fellowship of your missionaries and under the guidance of the Board a real home in the work on the Iramba field."[53]

The Reusch family's second furlough was scheduled for September 1937, but Richard postponed his leave due to the intensifying international crisis. Elveda, however, was determined to be home by Christmas, so she and her three daughters left at the end of September as scheduled. In Tübingen, Germany, the examining physician noted that the missionary complained of backaches and a rash on her hands — which mysteriously disappeared whenever she left Marangu. "She looks pale and tired, but in general she is healthy. So are her daughters."[54]

TANGANYIKA COFFEE RIOTS

One of the issues in Tanganyika during the summer of 1937 was a growing resentment among Chagga coffee growers. The Coffee Trust, which was controlled by white plantation owners and the British government, set coffee bean prices, and its policies drew the ire of native Chagga coffee growers. Sir D. M. Kennedy, Acting Governor of Tanganyika, described the situation in a letter to the Secretary of State for the Colonies in London. To Kennedy, the astute Chagga businessmen were, in his words, "a curious people easily swayed by oratory and moved to mass hysteria." He warned that "the possibility of an outbreak of lawlessness cannot be disregarded . . . From the political as well as the economic viewpoint, matters cannot be allowed to remain as they are."[55]

Chagga resentment boiled over on September 18th when rioters destroyed coffee storage sheds owned by the Trust. A Reuter wire service story filed from Mombassa attributed the cause of the rioting to "dissatisfaction among the natives with prices received for their coffee, but it is also ascribed in some quarters [e.g., Reusch] to an infiltration of 'Bolshevist propaganda' from South Africa."[56]

The riots took place in Leipzig Mission territory, and that posed serious political implications. British Intelligence monitored the activities of several German colonists in the Moshi area who were active members of the Nazi Party, as well as German missionaries.[57] Reusch believed that the Communist Party in South Africa was involved in subversive activities throughout the continent, but casting blame on the "Bolshevists" in this instance may also have been intended to shield German missionaries who opposed Nazi policies.

The coffee riots became a lightning rod for international censure when BBC radio broadcast an erroneous story, claiming that British troops were bombing Chagga villages and firing on the people. The German press cited the BBC report as justification for reclaiming their former East African colony, and the Japanese, internationally criticized for having attacked the Chinese, now accused the British of doing that very thing in Tanganyika.

Other disturbances occurred as well, including a demonstration on September 27th during a conference in Moshi called by the British government to consider Chagga claims.[58] By the end of October, however, Governor Kennedy reported that "order now prevails on Kilimanjaro and I hope that the incident may be regarded as closed." He invoked the Deportation Ordinance against thirteen Chagga ringleaders and initiated proceedings against 120 others.[59]

Reusch's second term in Africa was not, however, entirely filled with stressful issues and challenges.

A LETTER FROM THE KAISER

When the Germans controlled that part of East Africa, they had named a point on Mt. Kilimanjaro's Mawenzi Peak in honor of Kaiser Wilhelm I. When the British decided to rename it, Dr. Reusch, President of the East African Mountain Club, successfully appealed the decision. Reusch had never met Wilhelm II, but he knew the emperor was interested in archeology, especially that which illuminated biblical history, and they both believed that religion was an antidote to socialism. Wilhelm believed that "only a good Christian can be a good soldier."[60] Reusch, however, believed that only a good soldier could be a good Christian.

While at the Imperial Cadet Corps, Richard Gustavovich and his platoon had saved the Kaiser's nephew from Caucasian bandits, and Wilhelm II had sent him a pearl and gold tie tack in appreciation — which Reusch later lost in Africa when he rushed off to fight a forest fire without removing his tie.[61]

Some twenty years later, after guiding Professor Flückiger around the Kilimanjaro area, Dr. Reusch asked the Swiss geographer to deliver a gift to the former emperor, a stone from the Kaiser Spitze mounted on a silver and ruby base. Flückiger agreed. From Basel, the professor sent a report of his African journey and Reusch's gift to Wilhelm, living in exile at Haus Doorn in the Netherlands. Not long thereafter a lettergram arrived in Marangu from *Seiner Majeſtät des Kaiſers und Königs*, dated 23 March 1933. A photograph was enclosed, signed "Wilhelm J.R." The message read,

> I thank you very much for the piece of rock from Mawenzi Peak that you collected at the risk of your life. . . .[It] will always be to me a treasure, a memorial to the German colony, which started to bloom under my government, and will always be meaningful proof of the thankful affection, which dwells in a true heart.[62]

THE HEMINGWAY RIDDLE

Ernest Hemingway made his first East African safari in 1933. In 1936 Esquire magazine published Hemingway's short story, "The Snows of Kilimanjaro." It begins with an epigraph:

> Kilimanjaro is a snow-capped mountain 19,710 feet high, and is said to be the highest mountain in Africa. Its western summit is called by the Masai "Ngàje Ngàje," the House of God. Close to the western summit there is a dried and frozen carcass of a leopard. No one has explained what the leopard was seeking at that altitude.[63]

John Gunther, in his 1955 volume, *Inside Africa*, described his own Kibo ascent and noted, "Dr. R. R. [*sic*] Reusch, a local African missionary of Russian origin, who has a passionate interest in the mountain, has climbed it no fewer than sixty-five times." Gunther also claimed that the "leopard made renown by Ernest Hemingway in 'The Snows of Kilimanjaro' still lies frozen near the summit."[64] Neither of Gunther's statements was accurate. Reusch made fifty successful ascents, the last in 1952 when nothing remained of the leopard carcass. However, there is a connection between Hemingway, the fabled leopard and Dr. Reusch.

Hans Meyer was the first European white man to climb Kilimanjaro. In his book published in 1891, *Across East Africa Glaciers: An Account of the First Ascent of Kilimanjaro*, he reported "as wonderful a discovery as any we made," the remains of an *antelope* on the summit. "How the animal came there is impossible to say," wrote Meyer.[65]

Hemingway's epigraph caused literary scholars to ask the question, What was a *leopard* doing at the summit of Kibo Peak? Someone suggested that maybe Hemingway had read H. W. Tilman's account in *Snows on the Equator*, published in 1937. But that source was ruled out because it was published a year after Hemingway's story appeared. Perhaps the famous big game hunter, Philip Percival, had told Hemingway about the mysterious leopard carcass. But no documentation could be found.

In 1968 a Hemingway scholar, John M. Howell, came across an article written by Dr. Reusch forty years earlier in the *Tanganyikan Times*. The missionary described his first three ascents in 1926, but it was the second climb that drew Howell's attention: "I found the frozen leopard which on the former trip my guide and I had replaced on top of a rock situated on the rim of the crater."[66]

Reusch's story was republished in the Mountain Club's newsletter, *Ice Cap*, in 1932, and again by the Tanzania Society with this addendum: "The Rev. Dr. R. Reusch, D.D., was for many years a missionary in the Kilimanjaro area, and is Hon. Life President of the Mountain Club of East Africa. No account of the mountain would be complete without mention of him." It was this reference that prompted two other literary scholars, R. O. Bevis and A. J. Smith, to report in 1968, "A published account predating Tilman and Percival, may, however, be the ultimate source of [Hemingway's] epigraph. Rev. Dr. R. Reusch climbed Kilimanjaro three times, between September 1926 and October 1927, and on each trip observed the frozen leopard."[67]

Howell subsequently traced Dr. Reusch to Gustavus Adolphus College in St. Peter, Minnesota, and wrote for clarification. Reusch replied that yes, he had seen the remains of a leopard *and* an antelope. The latter was seeking salt deposits that are found at upper altitudes, he explained, and the leopard was no doubt stalking the antelope.

> [However, both animals] were surprised by a snowstorm and died there. I found the body of the frozen antelope on the tongues of the Ratzel Glacier and the body of the frozen leopard in the middle notch. I put the latter on a piece of rock so that he looked into the crater. A number of climbers saw it there, brought down parts of his body, and the place was called "Leopard Point." Both bodies disappeared in the mean time except for a few bones.[68]

"You have answered the riddle!" exclaimed Howell.[69]

THE "ADVENTUROUS FIVE"

A year later, near the Marangu post office, Dr. Reusch happened to overhear five American college boys discussing a vexing problem. They had just learned it was necessary to be outfitted and hire a guide to climb Mt. Kilimanjaro. That was an expense they had not anticipated and could not afford.

Intrigued by their *savoir-vivre*, Dr. Reusch introduced himself. How had they had gotten to Marangu? The leader, Jack Dozier, explained that he had taken a train from California to New York where he set sail for Europe to witness the 1936 Olympiad in Berlin. He found living expenses comparatively cheap in Europe, so he cabled four buddies with a proposal: Join him in France, and together they would circumnavigate the globe.

His friends thought it a keen idea, and some weeks later the five boys cycled through France, sailed from Marseilles for Egypt, made their way by boat up the Nile River and hitch-hiked across Ethiopia and Kenya to Mt. Kilimanjaro, just across the border in Tanganyika.

A climb to the summit of Mount Kilimanjaro always restored his health and set his spirit free as he gazed upon creation from the eternal snows of Mount Kilimanjaro. These were kindred souls, Americans no less, and so Reusch volunteered to guide them to the summit.

"We are all back at the university now, after a summer of fleeting fame as 'The Adventurous Five,'" Dozier wrote. From Africa they had made their way across India to Rangoon, traveled with a mule caravan into China, then to Hanoi, Shanghai, and Yokohama. Having run out of funds, the boys returned home as stowaways aboard a ship.

"Most important of all, Dr. Reusch, if you are in the U.S.," wrote the ebullient Dozier, "it is absolutely a command that you come to see wonderful California and visit us. You <u>must</u> come, and <u>must</u> stay for at least a month." The boys "told all and sundry" about "the good doctor." Their college professors wanted to meet Dr. Reusch. So did Jack's parents, who marveled "that anyone such as you is still alive in this world. Our parents wish to see you, we have to see you, please write *toute suite* [sic] and say 'Yes.'"[70]

"All of us," Jack wrote in a second letter, "consider you as the greatest friend of our circum-navigation."[71]

A BRUSH WITH DEATH ON MARGHERITA PEAK

Before he left for Europe and America, Reusch honored a commitment he had made to guide a mountain climbing expedition. "Dr. R. Reusch," said the document issued by the Commissioner of the Northern Province, "is proceeding to Uganda to take charge of the Italian expedition sponsored by *Gazetta del Populo*," a newspaper in Torino, Italy.[72]

Early in January 1938, according to the *Uganda Herald*, the Rev. R. Reusch, D.D. along with Rev. Borello, Rev. Besoni and Fugemeur P. Ghiglione climbed the northeastern wall of Margherita Peak of the Ruwenzori Range, "which has never been climbed before."[73] But the party nearly lost their lives.

"Courage and strength of a veteran East African mountaineer — Dr. Reusch — saved the lives of his party when climbing the difficult peak of Margherita," reported the *East African Standard*.

The party left Fort Portal for Bugoye, and after six days reached Stuhlmann's Pass. From there the team successfully climbed the 4,955-meter northeastern wall. The story continued,

> On the return journey the Rev. Borello slipped and fell over the side of a steep mountain wall which descends 1,400 feet.
>
> It was without doubt the instinct and skill of Dr. Reusch which saved the party from being dragged down to certain death.
>
> With great fortitude he managed to secure a hold, and stopped the falling man. As he did so, however, the rope almost strangled Dr. Reusch.
>
> The hurt he suffered was so great that he started to vomit blood. Losing a very large quantity, he developed a high fever during the night.[74]

The *Uganda Herald* also applauded this display of heroism. "Dr. Reusch and his party are to be congratulated on this feat, as well as on their miraculous excape [sic]."

After Reusch's expedition in Uganda, the president of the Mountain Club sent a note bidding bon voyage: "As a mountaineer, your climbs of Mounts Kibo and Mawenzi are not likely to be surpassed and indeed you have made history in your climbing exploits."[75]

PREPARING FOR THE INEVITABLE

In 1938 the Nazis marched their swastikas into Austria, and that autumn occupied the Sudetenland. There was no longer any doubt that the British would soon terminate German mission activity in the Territory. The coffee riots had been brought to a peaceful conclusion, and having recovered from his climbing injuries, Dr. Reusch felt ready to pack for the long journey to Leipzig and Minneapolis, where he was to negotiate the transfer of the Leipzig Mission to Augustana's jurisdiction. Without financial support from the Evangelical Lutheran Church in Germany, and because of the growing Nazi menace, he would return to Africa as a member of the Augustana ministerium.

But his students at Marangu and local British officials were reluctant for him to leave because they feared they might not see him again. "I do not have anything but thanksgiving for your love," one of his students wrote in his farewell letter. "God give you peace wherever you go. Remember Africa. Your student, Andrea Moshi." Forty-two of his students signed another letter that stated, "You did not do anything, not even one thing, that ever made us angry." The writer vowed, "We will remember you forever."

African teachers also signed their own letter of farewell: "Today we are saying goodbye to you our teacher and pastor, Dr. Richard Reusch. We want to convey our many thanksgivings for your love and perseverance, that you did not give up under hard work. You did not show favoritism to the big or the small." The missionary must have been especially pleased with the last line: "Dr. Richard Reusch: He who was not conquered."[76]

Betty Anderson

Cut off by the Nazis from financial support, the Leipzig Mission was hard pressed to continue its work in Tanganyika. This photograph of Dr. Reusch was taken in 1938.

CHAPTER 10

1 Ernest Hemingway, "The Snows of Kilimanjaro," *The Complete Short Stories of Ernest Hemingway*, Finca Vigia, ed. (1987), 39.

2 Filemon Mkumbo, "Letter from Africa, *Mission Tidings*, vol. 32 (July 1937), 42.

3 Edna Miller, "Africa Letter," *Mission Tidings*, vol. 26 (April 1932), 363.

4 Betty Anderson, from the author's notes of an interview, 6 June 1995.

5 Elveda Reusch, letter to Mrs. Ihmels, Leipzig, 31 January 1936, AELML.

6 R. Reusch, "The Masai," unpublished manuscript ca. 1954, 33, 21-23, GACA.

7 R. Reusch, letter to Leipzig Missions Director Weishaupt, 21 May 1933, AELML.

8 Alfred Buxton, letter to Leipzig Missions Director, 12 December 1932, AELML.

9 A. Buxton, letter to Leipzig Missions Director, 15 June 1933, AELML.

10 A. Buxton, letter to Leipzig Missions Director, 25 January 1934, AELML.

11 A. Buxton, letter to R. Reusch, 2 January 1934, GACA.

12 Fred W. Wyman, "An S. O. S. Call on Behalf of Our Foreign Missions," *Lutheran Companion*, vol. 40 (3 December 1932), 1548.

13 G. A. Brandelle, President, Augustana Synod, "To the Members of the Augustana Synod," *Lutheran Companion*, vol. 42 (13 January 1934), 2.

14 George N. Anderson, "What About Foreign Missions?" *Lutheran Companion*, vol. 44 (8 August 1936), 998-99.

15 N. L. Melander, "God's Grace in Africa," *Mission Tidings*, vol. 31 (December 1936), 147.

16 Mrs. Wm. A. Peterson, "Africa," Annual Report, *Mission Tidings*, vol. 32 (July 1937), 17.

17 Elmer L. Danielson, "Winning Souls in Africa," *Lutheran Companion*, vol. 43 (12 January 1935), 39.

18 Mrs. Peter Peterson, "From the President's Pen," *Mission Tidings*, vol. 33 (November 1938), 150.

19 Eleanor Lindbeck, "Africa Mission News," *Lutheran Companion*, vol. 47 (3 August 1939), 975. Lindbeck had been a missionary in China until civil war and invading Japanese troops forced the Americans to flee. She and several others, including Dr. Stanley Moris, chose to transfer to Africa.

20 John A. Morehead, "Salient Facts," *Lutheran Companion*, vol. 40 (2 July 1932), 845.

21 "To Aid German Protestants," *Lutheran Companion*, vol. 40 (17 December 1932), 1613.

22 Johannes Raum, "A Short Report on the Present Situation of the Leipzig Ev. Lutheran Mission in Tanganyika Territory, East Africa," in English, 1934 (LWC 24-9), AELCA.

23 Thomas Kloss, letter to Leipzig Mission director, 5 March 1933, AELML.

24 R. Reusch, letter to Mission Director Weishaupt, 21 May 1933, AELML.

25 F. Beaumont-Nesbitt, Colonel, British military attaché in Paris, Secret Report No. 242 (copy), to MI3, (CO 822-91), PRO.

26 George N. Anderson, "Homeward Bound," *Lutheran Companion*, vol. 44 (1 August 1936), 971.

27 Mrs. William A. Peterson, "Africa," *Mission Tidings*, vol. 32 (July 1937), 17.

28 Elmer R. Danielson, "Ten Years in Africa," *Lutheran Companion*, vol. 45 (3 June 1937), 717.

29 V. Eugene Johnson, "African Church Meets," *Lutheran Companion*, vol. 44 (4 April 1936), 429.

30 Olga Gustavovna, letter to the R. Reusch family, 18 October 1933, GACA.

31 Malmgren, letter to Morehead, 3 July 1934 (LWC 22-15), AELCA.

32 Morehead, "The Situation of the Evangelical Church in Soviet Russia," *Lutheran Companion*, vol. 40 (30 January 1932), 143.

33 Leipzig Mission Director Weishaupt, letters to Gustav Reusch, Rostov on Don, 23 December 1932 and 13 January 1933, AELCA.
34 Ingeborg Fleischhauer, Benjamin Pinkus, *The Soviet Germans: Past and Present* (1986), 50.
35 Malmgren, letter to Morehead, 3 July 1934 (LWC 22-15), AELCA.
36 Malmgren, 3 July 1934.
36 Malmgren, 3 July 1934.
38 Morehead, letter to Malmgren, 22 August 1934 (LWC 18-19), AELCA.
39 Malmgren, letter to Morehead, 20 December 1934 (LWC 22-15), AELCA.
40 "The Martyrs of Today in Russia," *Lutheran Companion*, vol. 44 (28 March 1936), 386.
41 Report, Martin Luther-Bund, Erlangen, 1 April 1936, AELCA.
42 Fleischhauer and Pinkus.
43 "Religious Persecution in Russia," *Lutheran Companion*, vol. 46 (10 November 1938), 1415.
44 Georg Kretschmar, Bishop of the Lutheran Church in Russia, from the author's notes of an interview in St. Petersburg, 15 November, 1996.
45 Olga (Reusch) Hirsch, letter to R. Reusch, ca. 1938, GACA.
46 This narrative is synthesized from interviews with family members, including Aurelia Reusch.
47 Andrea Graziosi, "Re: Terminology of Terror," 2 (H-RUSSIA LIST), 7 November 1997.
48 Victoria Morozova, 'New Matters of the 20th Century,' *Smena*, 13 September 2000, 6.
49 R. Reusch, letter to Ihmels, 16 February 1937, AELML.
50 "D. Reusch im Archiv der Ev.-Luth. Mission zu Leipzig," AELML. Reusch produced a flurry of articles in the 1930s that appeared in Leipzig's *Missions Blatt* and elsewhere. An ethnographer educated at Oxford University (Mrs. Shaw, whose husband was a Supreme Court judge in Tanganyika) translated his history of East Africa manuscript from German into English, and Professors Strothmann (Hamburg) and von Bulmerincq (Tartu) critiqued the work. — R. Reusch, letter to Ihmels, 3 May 1936, AELML.
51 R. Reusch, letter to O. J. Johnson, President of the Augustana Board of Foreign Missions, 20 March 1938, AELCA.
52 R. Reusch, letter to Ihmels, 21 August 1937, AELML.
53 R. Reusch, letter to O. J. Johnson, 20 February 1938 (Foreign Missions — Africa, Personnel File, Richard Reusch), AELCA.
54 Dr. O. Fischer, Tropical Medicine Clinic, Medical Evaluation, 18 October 1937, AELML.
55 Sir D. M. Kennedy, Acting Governor of Tanganyika, letter to Ormsby-Gore, Secretary of State for the Colonies, 1 July 1937 (CO 691-159-8), PRO.
56 Clipping, Reuter news story, 21 September 1937 (CO 746-42254-1), PRO.
57 *History of East Africa*, Vincent Harlow, editor (1965), 606-07.
58 Colonial Office notes (CO 746-42254-2), PRO.
59 Sir D. M. Kennedy, Acting Governor, confidential letter to Ormsby-Gore, 27 October 1937 (CO 691-159-9), PRO.
60 Lamar Cecil, *Wilhelm II: Emperor in Exile, 1900-1941*, vol. 2 (1996), 52-53.
61 Betty Anderson recalled her father's story about receiving the tie tack. Reusch explained its loss in 1925. He had been asked by the Provincial Commissioner to take charge of 2,000 Masai warriors and fight a forest fire on Mt. Meru. "During this fire fighting I lost my neck-tie with an expensive

golden pin. This pin with a wonderful pearl was a present from a high personality, given to me many years ago." — "The Masai," 25.

62 Wilhelm J.R., letter to R. Reusch, 23 March 1933, GACA.

63 Ernest Hemingway, "The Snows of Kilimanjaro," *The Complete Short Stories of Ernest Hemingway*, Finca Vigia, ed. (1987), 39.

64 John Gunther, *Inside Africa* (1955), 397-98.

65 Hans Meyer, *Across East Africa Glaciers: An Account of the First Ascent of Kilimanjaro* (1891), 183-84.

66 R. Reusch, "Mt. Kilimanjaro and Its Ascent," *Tanganyikan Times* (10 February 1928), clipping, GACA.

67 R. W. Bevis, M. A. J. Smith, Jr., "Leopard Tracks in 'The Snows...'," *American Notes and Queries*, vol. 6, no. 8 (April 1968), 115.

68 R. Reusch, "Some Kilimanjaro Legends," unpublished manuscript, GACA.

69 John M. Howell, letter to R. Reusch, 14 July 1968, GACA.

70 Jack Dozier, undated letter (ca. 1938) to R. Reusch, GACA.

71 Jack Dozier, letter to Reusch, 12 March 1938, GACA.

72 Commissioner, Northern Province, Arusha, Tanganyika, document, "To Whom It May Concern," 7 December 1937, GACA.

73 "Climbing Expeditions on Ruwenzori. Well-known Mountaineer has Narrow Escape," *Uganda Herald*, 2 February 1938, clipping, GACA.

74 "Veteran Climber's Feat," *East African Standard*, 4 February 1938, clipping, GACA.

75 President of the Mountain Club of East Africa, letter to R. Reusch, 22 May 1938, GACA.

76 Letters dated 21 May 1938, GACA.

Betty Anderson

Superintendent Reusch arrives to conduct the Rite of Baptism at a congregation in the foothills of Mt. Kilimanjaro. The Lutheran Church in Tanganyika experienced unparalleled growth under Reusch's leadership during the war years.

Chapter Eleven

A HEROIC THIRD TERM
The War Years, 1939-1947

The Lutheran Church in America has not contributed one single outstanding missionary-statesman. Where are the Motts and Speers of the Lutheran Church?

— George Anderson (1936)[1]

A miracle has taken place during these war years, much of it due to Dr. Richard Reusch, one of God's missionary-statesmen.

— Elmer L. Danielson (1947)[2]

Dr. Reusch began his brief furlough in June 1938 by stopping for his usual physical at Tübingen, in what was now Nazi Germany. Seven months after Reusch's accident on Margherita Peak, the examining physician found him in excellent health — pulse 72, and blood pressure 125 over 65.[3] He arrived in New York on August 21, 1938, stayed overnight at the Mission Home operated by the Augustana Women's Missionary Society, and left the next morning on a nineteen-hour train trip for Chicago and reunion with his wife and daughters.

On one of his forays into the Windy City, Reusch happened to come upon a policeman beset by three thugs. Applying his martial arts skills, the former Cossack "turned the table on them," and the grateful cop presented the missionary with his blackjack, a "lethal-looking weapon of plaited leather loaded with lead" that could fracture a skull without leaving a bruise. Thereafter, Reusch claimed, he carried it on his person "when traveling in dangerous territory."[4]

In September Dr. Reusch addressed the Synod convention in Rock Island, Illinois, and in October met with the Augustana Board of Foreign Missions in Minneapolis. Given the deteriorating international situation and conditions in Germany, the Leipzig Mission had no choice but prepare for suspension of its work a second time. Reusch discussed with the Mission Board his transfer from the Leipzig Mission. But he also used the opportunity to urge the development of a plan to reorganize the entire mission school system in Tanganyika

Territory.[5] Three months later, on January 3, 1939, Dr. Reusch was declared a member of the ministerium of the Evangelical Lutheran Augustana Synod of North America.[6] Six weeks later he and his family sailed for Hamburg aboard the *S.S. Hansa*, landing on March 3, 1939.

In Leipzig Dr. Reusch briefed Mission Director Ihmels about his meetings with Augustana officials. He confirmed that, should it become necessary, the Americans had agreed to take responsibility for the Leipzig missions in the Kilimanjaro region. That done, from March 10th to the 24th he went on tour, speaking to church groups about African missions. Each day took him to a different city: Bautzen, Dresden, and Chemnitz; back to Leipzig for a visit with his old friend, Bruno Gutmann; to Kouradsreuth, Rehau, Sparneck, and Oberkotzau; to St. Mary's Cathedral in Rostock, where Pastor Frahm still served as senior pastor, and to the Holy Ghost and St. Nikolai parishes where he had served as a refugee twenty years earlier; and finally to Güstraw and Neustrelitz.[7]

It was decided that Elveda and the girls would remain in Leipzig until Reusch had seen to their new living arrangements in Irambaland. From the Scharwächter & Steinbach catalogue he ordered a bathtub, washing machine and kitchen equipment for delivery in Tanganyika.[8] Gestapo agents had followed him from church to church, and then watched as he crossed the border into France.[9]

The Augustana Mission had been at work in Irambaland for twelve years, during which time the number of Lutherans increased from a dozen in 1927 to more than 5,000 members in 1939, with an additional 1,600 catechumens. Reusch had agreed to supervise the construction and serve as headmaster of the new training school at Kinampanda. Anton Lundeen happily reported to the Mission Board. "Not only the African missionaries, but also representatives of the government consider us extremely fortunate in being able to secure Dr. Reusch."[10]

So urgent was the Kinampanda Training School project that the Augustana Mission had decided to launch the facility even before Dr. Reusch returned from furlough. Edith Kjellin and Nderasio Simeoni were assigned the task "without an adequate budget and at a new location where there wasn't a tool available or an extra book to borrow or a chair to sit on."[11]

Dr. Reusch arrived at Kinampanda in April 1939. According to the Mission president, Reusch "began his task without delay." It was the kind of challenge for which Reusch seemed particularly suited. At the Native Christians Conference held at the new church in Kiomboi in July 1939, Dr. Reusch "explained in thorough fashion the meaning and purpose of the new Training School, how it would not only prepare teachers, but craftsmen in masonry, carpentry and other lines."[12] Seventy boys had already been accepted for the fall term, but there was still much work to be done before classes were scheduled to begin.

The curriculum was designed according to British specifications. Most of the school's teachers were Africans: Filipo Shalua taught Standard V; Yobu Nikodemu, Standard VI; and Nderasio Simeon, Standards VII and VIII. Methusala Noe taught carpentry, and Eleanor Lindbeck taught courses in several grade levels. Headmaster Reusch led by example — as a teacher, carpenter and mason. To the students in all standards, he taught Bible, dogmatics, church history, history of Islam, education methods, arithmetic, drawing, and geography. To students in Standards VI to VIII he taught gymnastics. In the carpentry class he taught arithmetic, geography and drawing. Because of his versatility, Reusch also taught masonry, and was put in charge of all the mission's bush schools.[13]

Kinampanda Teachers' Training School

Excerpts from Dr. Reusch's First Annual Report, September 1940

Upon my arrival in April 1939 I found a completed school building with one very big and two smaller classrooms. The two smaller rooms are very fine and fulfill all requirements as regarding light, space, desks, and blackboards.

The school has some seventy students. Of these 32 were left in Standard V, 15 in Standard VI and 19 in Standard VII. Seven of the boys were put into a carpentry class in care of Methusala Noe, the instructor in carpentry. Astonishing progress has been made by the carpentry class. With the help of some private money the necessary tools were obtained.

[When I arrived,] the boys were sleeping in two Iramba huts and cooking outside. The teachers and the carpenter were living in one classroom and all supplies and tools were stored in the other. The first thing to do was to get people and stores out of classrooms. Teachers and boys began to make mud bricks, break stone and collect building material. At the end of the month the first house was ready. This first building proved to me that the native teachers were of the opinion that manual work was beneath their dignity and the boys had somewhat the same feeling. To overcome this attitude there was only one psychological way to do it, namely, roll up the shirtsleeves and work with the boys. Seeing that the white man is not ashamed to do manual work but honors it, they started very slowly to come, take an interest and take part in it. The more the work progressed the more their interest grew.

The boys did not have any spirit of unity and no pride in their school. Those qualities had to be developed. Through class instruction and during devotions those ideas were repeatedly brought to their attention and always kept before their minds as a genuine, Christian, Lutheran ideal. Words like the words of God to Adam, "In the sweat of thy face shalt thou eat bread," and words like those of Paul to the Thessalonians, "that he who will not work, neither should he eat," and others were used to show them the dignity of manual labor. Slowly the best among the boys adopted these ideas and began to influence the others. The visible progress of the building filled them with pride. Up to now they have built two dormitories, one assembly hall, a kitchen, one teacher's house, a second teacher's house, and a few smaller buildings.

The examinations take place in the first week of December, after which the boys will be given a two-month vacation. During July-August a refresher course for village teachers will be held at Kinampanda.

May the students of this school always remember and follow the Word — that our work must be a part of our worship![14]

Stanley Moris, a newly arrived medical missionary, reported that by the end of the first school term, "The Kinampanda Training School has already begun to fill a tremendous need in supplying trained evangelists, teachers, carpenters and candidates for hospital dressers' training." He also noted that the person responsible for the instant success of the school "quotes the Koran about as readily from memory as most of us can our few memorized Bible passages. Exceedingly versatile, [Reusch] makes an excellent teacher."[15]

In the front yard of the Reusch home lay a section of a thick log so heavy that, despite numerous attempts, no one could lift it. However, anyone walking by at 6:30 in the morning could watch Dr. Reusch hoist the beam into the air as he performed his daily weight-lifting exercises.[16]

THE SECOND WORLD WAR

The Leipzigers invited the Augustana missionaries to join them at Marangu for their annual meeting in the spring of 1939. The Americans were surprised to meet some forty Germans, "many more than we expected." Anton Lundeen exclaimed, "How the Germans do this in spite of financial difficulties is a marvel!"[17]

August 31, 1939, was a beautiful day, and Elveda and her daughters enjoyed a picnic with friends near Potsdam. Only hours later, in the early morning of September 1st, the German war machine invaded Poland and began its sweep toward Warsaw. Elveda and the girls returned to Leipzig at once and hurriedly prepared to leave Germany. Everyone had sensed that a second world war was certain; nevertheless, like the final breath of a loved one after a long illness, the inevitable moment came as a shock.

"When one listens to the news there is no question about whether or not we are at war," an Augustana missionary, Ruth Safemaster, wrote to friends in the United States in the spring of 1940. "A British passenger ship was sunk at a point not far below Dar es Salaam a few days ago. When our Post arrives and most of the letters have been opened and censored we also realize that times are not normal. Prices are going up — up — up." The mood in East Africa was tense, Safemaster noted, but the British officials were so well organized "that they feel they are able to meet any emergency which may arise."[18] The American consul in Dar es Salaam advised Americans to "keep on as if nothing had happened." Said Stanley Moris, "We are thankful to God that the European war has had little effect upon our work."[19]

The Augustana leadership in the United States took a strong stance against American involvement in the European conflict, and so did their missionaries in Africa. Missionary Elmer Danielson spoke for many when he wrote,

> [W]hen a white man, a member of the Christian Church, hates and fights and takes prisoner his fellow white man, also a member of the Christian Church, it is a refutation of the Gospel and factual evidence that Christianity is not a good religion, for its brotherhood does not work. . . . The war will give Islam the opportunity again

to remind the African that Islam is the religion for Africa, and that Islam is a brotherhood that works.

"How can Christianity ever hope to win Africa for Christ when Christian nations fight and destroy one another?" editorialized a synod periodical.[20]

The German missionaries posed a dilemma for the British Colonial Office. As enemy aliens, they ought to be deported as in the First World War. However, the British now relied on German and other missions to provide essential education and medical services.[21] The American missionaries proposed that their German peers be "paroled" under their supervision, but that suggestion was rejected because several German missionaries were thought to be Nazi sympathizers. However, the British authorities did agree to offer parole on a case-by-case basis, provided that the German missionaries agree to sign the following statement:

> 1) I declare on my word of honour that I am not in possession of any arms, 2) that I will take no part whatsoever in operations, 3) that I will refrain from subversive propaganda and 4) that I will immediately obey directions of [the British] Government given from time to time in regard to my conduct and movement.[22]

Thirty of the forty-five Leipzig missionaries signed the pledge. For a variety of reasons, fifteen others refused, and were promptly interned and deported. To those who had pledged their word of honor, however, the British provided a small monthly stipend. That gesture, said Herbert Magney, demonstrated a "great magnanimity on the part of British rule. . . practically unheard of in war history."[23] The Nazi press in Germany, learning of the arrangement, condemned both the British Government and the Germans who had signed the parole statement, including Rev. Paul Rother, superintendent of the Leipzig Mission. Magney wrote,

> There is no question as to what will happen to these German missionaries in case the war should be won by Germany and this territory again come under German rule. The radical Nazi sympathizers of Tanganyika who were interned and repatriated have accused those who signed the parole statements of treason. The penalty of treason may be expected in case of victory by the Nazis.

The Augustana Mission offered to act as intermediary between the British authorities and the remaining Leipzig missionaries, and on their behalf to receive and disburse funds. Both parties accepted the offer. "In all our negotiations with the Tanganyika Government regarding the care of these mission fields," reported Magney, "we have received the most friendly co-operation."[24]

British officials hoped that the Augustana Mission might not only supply replacement personnel for the interned and deported Leipzig missionaries but also support those missions financially.[25] Funds could be raised, the Americans believed, but how would American personnel get to Africa? Passenger travel on the high seas was almost impossible because ships were subject to German submarine attack and travel restrictions had been imposed. German, Danish, Norwegian, Swedish, Finnish and American foreign missions throughout the world were suddenly isolated. Like the German mission societies, the Danes and Norwegians were precluded from sending missionaries and providing financial support to overseas missions because of the Nazi occupation, and the Finns were fending off a Russian invasion in the Winter War of 1939-40. Therefore, the Augustana Synod explained to its members, "the Lutheran Church in America is the only section of the Lutheran Church in the world that is left to help."[26]

The Lutheran World Convention was the international Lutheran agency through which humanitarian aid was funneled to the destitute of the world. However, its leadership and offices were located in Berlin, and its activities had been suspended. Therefore, the American National Lutheran Council formed Lutheran World Action as a substitute body and pledged to raise $700,000 to save the orphaned German missions of Africa, India, China and Borneo. The Augustana Synod volunteered to raise $500,000, or 71 percent of the total amount.[27]

NAZI INFLUENCE IN TANGANYIKA

No sooner had Reusch's September 1940 report of the first school year at Kinampanda reached the Board of Foreign Missions in Minneapolis than a cablegram arrived with the news that nearly all German missionaries in Tanganyika Territory had been interned, including those who had signed the parole pledge. With the coming of the war, all the Protestant German missions were thrown into a state of crisis. All the Neukirchen missionaries were interned or repatriated to Germany, only three Berlin Mission deaconesses remained at their stations, and the Bethel Mission lost most of its staff. The Danes hoped to take up the work of the German Moravian Mission, although no one knew by what means, since the Germans now occupied Denmark.

George Anderson explained the reasons for the sudden British action: Because a few of the German missionaries had placed "nationalism above the Kingdom of God," the innocent had to suffer with the guilty; Afrikaners and Germans living in East Africa constituted an internal danger, a potential "fifth column"; and finally, "[British] military operations are already beginning in East Africa, which will be intensified as time goes on."[28]

By April 1941 only 868 enemy aliens remained in the whole of Tanganyika, of whom 570 were German and Italian missionaries (mostly Roman Catholic), and European Jewish and other refugees.[29] A total of 424 German missionaries were eventually paroled, 19 kept in detention, and 51 repatriated to Germany.

In 1944 the Assistant Custodian of Enemy Property in Moshi asked Dr. Reusch to examine seized German records "with a view to collecting evidence of the organisation of the Nazi Party in Tanganyika."[30] The Deputy Governor of Tanganyika later issued a summary report, "Nazi Propaganda in Tanganyika."[31]

According to the report, white South Afrikaners already owned and operated plantations in Tanganyika, and had welcomed the influx of German immigrants who had poured into the Territory after 1925. Both the Afrikaners and German immigrants posed an internal threat, the "troops" upon which the German policy of "peaceful penetration" depended.

By 1932, "the German Government ceased to pretend that they had no designs upon this territory," the report stated. Scores of German immigrants arrived on every German cargo ship. A German Bund was organized in the city of Dodoma, and pro-German propaganda was successful in inciting insubordination among Africans working on European plantations. In October 1933, not long after Hitler was named chancellor, the first Nazi agents arrived in Tanganyika.[32]

British intelligence suspected that German land acquisition was a Nazi project funded by Berlin. Indeed, it was discovered that one of the "immigrants," Prince Gustav von Schoen-auth Carolath, drew on the resources of the German industrialist, Hugo Stinnes, and with the support of Dr. Hjalmar Schacht, Minister of Finance, and Herr von Schubert of the Foreign Office in Berlin, he formed the Chartered Company for African Colonial Development.[33] By 1939, one-third of all alienated land in Tanganyika was held by German nationals, "all of whom looked forward to coming again under the rule of their own country."[34]

The leader of the National Socialist German Labor Party in Tanganyika, Herr Troost, fresh from the Nazi Training School at Altona (near Hamburg), initiated a propaganda campaign to achieve three objectives:

(1) unite the German community in East Africa under Nazi discipline;

(2) consistent with Nazi racial policies, present a glowing picture of the new Germany to the white population; and

(3) prepare East Africans for a return to German colonial rule.

Troost's message was communicated through print, film, and radio media distributed by the German Consulate, the German press and travel bureaus, businessmen, and even some German missionaries.

By 1936 uniformed members of the Hitler Youth were visible in the streets of urban centers, provoking street brawls in Mwanza and Moshi. Some pro-German estate managers marched African workers off to work in the morning with the Nazi salute and "Heil Hitler."[35]

The growing influence of pro-Nazi sentiment was observed in some Protestant communities. In 1934 the German community in Bokaba gathered to celebrate the fiftieth anniversary of German colonization. The British believed that "a very high percentage of the men that now came out to German Missions — men who would have daily contact with literate natives — were youths who had just completed the requisite period of military training at home." Five years later, agents in Bukoba reported that some Greeks, Arabs and Africans were attending Nazi party meetings. "Swastika emblems were distributed and inflammatory speeches were made. German missionaries were, of course, present — male and female."[36]

The report outlined the case against the German missionaries:

> At the German missions in Dar es Salaam, Songea, Lushto, etc., photographs of Hitler and other Nazi insignia began to be placed in prominent places where they would be seen by visiting natives.
>
> The German missionaries in Songea and Bukoba were guilty of many indiscretions and indeed if there remains any doubt in the reader's mind as to the share of German missionaries in Nazi propaganda, he may be convinced by this excerpt from

the Schwartze Korps, the S.S. Nazi Black Guards' Magazine of January 1940: "It is the German Missionary's primary duty to harm the enemies of the Reich. His personal welfare is immaterial, his mission work more so and his religious faith quite beside the point. A Christian's first duty is to overthrow the enemy rather than to help him keep peace and good order by means of mission work among the natives."

The evidence was deeply worrisome to the British. By 1944, the year that the "Nazi Propaganda" report was issued, no German missionaries remained in Tanganyika Territory. The colonial administration reported the presence of 136 foreign missionaries: 93 Americans, 26 Swedes, 16 Danes and 1 "stateless" person (Reusch).[37]

Lieutenant Colonel Kuentzel, Director of Foreign Service in Berlin, had ordered all Germans in Tanganyika to report on "labour conditions, economics, commercial relations, export and import (especially textiles), native unrest and Communist propaganda, the movement of aircraft and technical development," information that was of "immense importance to the Fatherland." Nazi agents then passed the reports on to captains of German merchant vessels calling on East African ports.[38]

In January 1939 Berlin ordered its foreign consuls in East Africa to distribute a leaflet ordering all German Jews to bring their passports to their respective consulates. Those who complied received new documents, but were horrified to find that their names had been changed: all males received the name, "Israel," and all females, "Sarah."[39] When later that year a Nazi official was assassinated in Paris, Berlin levied a punitive tax of 20 percent on the value of all German Jewish property, even sending a bill to a German Jew living in Nairobi, Kenya. The outraged man immediately brought the letter to a British official, who was scandalized by the last line of the address, "Deutsche Ost Afrika" (German East Africa). To the British colonial civil servant, the implication that "Kenya was already incorporated in the Reich" amounted to "gross impertinence."[40]

The Germans also brazenly gathered intelligence information by sending expeditions to East Africa. In 1937, the Nazi foreign minister, Joachim von Ribbentrop, wrote to British Prime Minister Anthony Eden asking permission for the Stuttgart Alpinists to climb Mt. Kilimanjaro. The suspicious British granted permission under two conditions: British officials must accompany the group, and expedition members must refrain from fomenting discontent among the Chagga tribe.[41]

From June 28 until July 30, 1939, a month before the Nazi invasion of Poland, the Hartlmaier Expedition from Bavaria visited the Leipzig Missions at Moshi, Mwika and Sanya, and filmed the Masai at Longido, Ngorongoro, and the Serengetti. The police superintendent of Arusha who accompanied the "expedition" reported that Paul Nuber, a mountaineer and personal servant to Hartlmaier, bluntly told him that the Third Reich would in future demand that Tanganyika Territory be returned to Germany. If not, the Nazis would launch an invasion from Abyssinia, march through Kenya, and reclaim it. Adding insult to injury, "Hartlmaier asked me to order all the [Masai] women to strip to the waist as he said their photographs would then have a higher selling value in Germany." The disgusted police officer noted, "This request was denied by me."[42]

As the Nazi dragnets tightened, European Jews frantically sought sanctuary elsewhere in the world, including Africa. Other countries, including the United States, were reluctant to accept them unless they had a sponsor, the promise of employment and a certain amount of cash. As a result, many European Jews lost their lives in the holocaust.

H. L. Cohen applied for permission to leave Germany in 1938. He was issued an emigrant passport; however, when he applied at the British consulate for a Northern Rhodesian visa he was told a regular passport was required. "Unfortunately," noted the British consulate official, "the only passports issued to Jews in Germany are to enable them to leave for good." Cohen pleaded that "in view of the fact that my sister is guarantee for me and that I have a safe situation to go to," he would be "most grateful" if the rule could be waived. He was granted a life-saving visa.

Like thousands of others, Robert Schlesinger was not so fortunate. He fled Austria for Paris, where his application to the British embassy for a Kenya visa was refused because he had only 400 pounds to his name, no one in Kenya to sponsor him, and no promise of employment.[43]

RETURN TO KILIMANJARO

The nature of the mission crisis in 1939 is apparent from the statistics: the work of 172 interned Leipzig, Bethel and Berlin missionaries was left in the hands of 30 Americans who were themselves short-handed in Irambaland.[44] Eventually more than a dozen Swedish and European Lutheran missionaries relocated to Tanganyika from other African countries, but even with reinforcements the former Leipzig Missions faced a staff reduction of 74 percent.[45] And that worried the British administration, which counted on the educational and medical services provided by the missionaries.

In the interest of continuing to provide medical and educational services, the British first asked the Anglicans to assume responsibility. Ultimately, the Anglicans had to decline because of insufficient personnel and financial resources. But the British Church Missionary Society agreed to send Rev. N. Langford-Smith to serve as headmaster at the Marangu Training School, and the Church of Sweden transferred Rev. Gustav Bernander to work in the Southern Highlands.[46]

In 1940, it was decided that Reusch should go back to Kilimanjaro ("his beloved mountain!") to replace his friend, Rev. Paul Rother, the former superintendent of the Leipzig Mission at Machame. Italian troops had invaded Kenya, so Mrs. Reusch and the three girls remained at Kinampanda instead of going with Reusch to Kilimanjaro. Elveda was separated from her husband "only by some two hundred and fifty miles, but others," she added empathetically, "are separated by oceans."[47] In time, British troops forced the Italians back into Abyssinia, and the immediate threat was averted.

Because of the crisis, the Augustana Mission convened its annual conference earlier than scheduled, in part so that Reusch and Missionary Martin Nordfeldt (transferred to Tanganyika by the Swedish Free Mission) could leave for the Kilimanjaro district as soon as possible. In his report of the October 1940 Mission Conference, George Anderson praised Headmaster Reusch and the six Kinampanda teachers for their progress in setting and achieving high scholastic standards. After citing Reusch's contributions, he added, "It was not easy for Dr. Reusch to give up his work, where he had given himself so unstintingly and for which he had cherished such great hopes, but the call to a larger, more important and more difficult task, he felt, had to be accepted. His interest and counsel in educational missions will continue."[48]

Nordfeldt would supervise the Berlin Missions at Bukoba and the Southern Highlands. Reusch would become the superintendent not only for the entire Leipzig field but also for the Bethel Usambara Mission and the Berlin Mission in the Usaramo District, which included Dar es Salaam — an area four times the size of Minnesota. Said Anderson, "They will truly be bishops-at-large."[49] Reusch whimsically confided to Nathaniel Mrenga, a graduate of the Marangu Teachers College, "I am more than a bishop. I am the archbishop — but no one knows that I am!"[50]

The territorial imperatives and mistrust that drove nations to make war also afflicted the Christian missions in the Territory. The Augustana Lutherans worried that Seventh Day Adventists, Presbyterians, Roman Catholics and Muslims might take advantage of the situation and try to move in on former German mission territory; the German missions were suspicious of Augustana's motives; and the Americans and the Swedes were leery of the British Anglicans. In fact, Augustana's fear of an Anglican takeover had hastened Reusch's departure for the Kilimanjaro district. More than five decades later, the retired American missionary, David Simonson, remarked with a grin, "Unless it were for Reusch, we'd all be Anglicans in these parts!"[51]

The threat of Anglican conquest became moot in 1941. According to the official statement, "Government recognizes the Augustana Lutheran Mission as the sole intermediary between self and the German Lutheran Missions [and] has no intention of recognising any other channel of communication with the former German Lutheran Missions."[52]

Upon reaching the Kilimanjaro district, Reusch first met with African leaders and parish members to figure out ways to preserve and strengthen congregations.[53] The pastors, Christian chiefs and teachers — many who were Reusch's former students — addressed two immediate problems. First, they had to win the loyalty of congregations who identified with their parent Leipzig Mission. That could be done, said Reusch, by making each parish feel "a part of the Lutheran Church based on the same Bible and Catechism, by the same baptism and communion with bread and wine." Second, income had to be generated with which to pay the (albeit small) salaries of the clergy, teachers and evangelists.[54] But through what slight of hand could Superintendent Reusch cause money to appear?

With the help of the school children, Reusch testified, "tens of thousands" of coffee and papaw trees were planted on two Mission plantations, and congregations were encouraged to do the same. Sap from the papaw trees was collected and processed to make pepsin, a stomach medicine that had become especially valuable during wartime. Eight months later the first proceeds from sales to British and American pharmaceutical companies were added to the meager budget.[55] Rev. H. Wynne Jones, an Anglican missionary, reported that Reusch "has put new life and hope in the congregations, and they have responded wonderfully to his call for continued faithfulness."[56]

THE ZAMZAM INCIDENT

The *S.S. Zamzam*, a former British ship sailing under Egyptian registration, left Hoboken, New Jersey, on March 20, 1941, for Mombassa by way of Trinidad and Capetown. German submarines did not often prowl that route, and so eight Augustana missionaries and eleven of their children booked passage for their return to Africa. On April 14th, the *Zamzam* abruptly reversed direction and headed in a zigzag course for South America, trailed by a German raider, the *Tamesis*. However, at 5:30 in the morning on April 17th, nine shells disabled the aged *Zamzam*, and it began to sink.

Rev. Elmer Danielson was looking forward to the arrival of his wife and six children when he learned by shortwave radio that the *Zamzam* had been sunk somewhere between South America and Africa. Ruth Safemaster immediately drove Danielson to the Reusch home in Kiomboi, where Elveda tried to console the shaken husband and father. That was the moment, said the bereft Danielson, when "on my knees the soul's storm broke."[57]

The lifeboat to which Lillian Danielson and her six children were assigned had been damaged during the attack, and it sank, leaving mother and children floating in the cold Atlantic. "With a 'Thy will be done,'" she wrote afterwards, "I clasped Lois Christine, our baby, more firmly in my left arm, grabbed Wilfred's hand with my right, called to Laurence to try to watch Luella, and [told them,] 'Keep praying in your hearts, my little ones, Jesus loves you all. We're safe in Him whatever happens.'"[58]

They and all the other passengers were rescued by the crew of the *Tamesis* and later transferred to a prison ship. On May 20th the missionaries and their children debarked at St. Jean de Luz in occupied France. From there the good news of their survival was flashed around the globe. *Life* magazine featured the story in a photo essay on June 23, 1941 just as the missionaries returned to America aboard vessels filled to over-flowing, including Jewish refugees who were fortunate not only to escape the Nazi dragnets but had sponsors, personal funds and the promise of employment in America.[59]

Lois Danielson, a toddler at the time, had been "happy to board the decrepit *Zamzam* because it was the means of going back home to Africa." In a photograph taken aboard the *S.S. Exeter* upon their safe return from France, all six children, including little Lois, are scowling. Only Mrs. Danielson looks relieved. Missionary kids raised in Africa seldom felt at home in America, and "only later as a student at Gustavus Adolphus College did I feel a sense of belonging," said Lois Danielson Carlson. "As a result, maybe [as adults] we're still all a little different, maybe more independent and better able to cope with loneliness."[60]

For the Danielsons, their return to Africa was delayed until after the war.[61]

LOYALTY TO THE BRITISH

Rev. Langford-Smith, headmaster at Marangu, reported to British authorities in 1942 that Leipzig Mission "furniture and effects not marked as Mission property was removed from

Mission houses under the orders of the Custodian of Enemy Property, including in some cases even crosses and Church vestments, and sold at auction."[62] As a result of his letter, Chief Custodian of Enemy Property MacDonald asked Dr. Reusch to make an inventory of all German Mission property in the Northern Provinces and dispose of it, much of which Reusch succeeded in redirecting to the Augustana Mission. In one of several letters to MacDonald, Reusch asked permission to use an interned missionary's bank account of 100 shillings to pay pastors' and teachers' salaries. Unless the men were paid, he warned,

> I am afraid that such [economic] conditions will make the pastors and teachers open to any kind of bitter feelings and for bolshevistic propaganda . . . If there should be any other accounts of the same kind belonging to the Usambara Bethel Mission, then I am pleading and begging that they may be released, if possible, for the sake of these teachers. Please, Sir, believe me that only the desperate need of these teachers and native pastors forces me to beg for your kind assistance and help [since] I have more than 220 native schools to supervise at Arusha, Meru, Kilimanjaro, Pare, Usambara, Tanga and Usaramo.[63]

MacDonald's replies were always the same, as in this memorandum of 1942: "I confirm that there is no objection to your making arrangements to transport such of the mission property as you may need for mission purposes in other parts of the Northern Provinces."[64]

The Chief Custodian promised to pay 500 shillings per month from the sale of the Leipzig Mission plantation at Makumira, but "if Dr. Reusch thinks that insufficient funds are being released for present-day mission work he should take the matter up directly with the Custodian." By such means Reusch managed to pay all over-due salaries and debts incurred since the departure of the Leipzig missionaries, "partly thanks to the support of the Custodian and partly thanks to the generous gifts of Machame, Shira and some other congregations who sold their coffee for this purpose." He was able to report in 1941, "All congregations are now well organized, provided with native pastors, evangelists and teachers. Generally speaking, their number is sufficient and their qualities are, with a few exceptions, good." Mission work among the Masai, however, required continuing support "because there is only a handful of Christians." And yet, "during my recent inspection of the Masai plains I paid all the over-due taxes for the plots until the end of this year, baptized some Masai, and straightened out everything."[65]

His work for the Custodian of Enemy Property was not pleasant. The job consumed valuable time and energy during those early war years when Reusch faced so many other pressing responsibilities. He had to file frequent reports, an onerous component of his work whether for Mission or Government, a task that he usually put off as long as possible. MacDonald had to press him more than once for tardy paperwork.

Reusch felt bad enough about liquidating his German friends' material possessions, but his confidential work for the Chief Custodian of Enemy Property also aroused suspicion among some Chagga and Meru people who nurtured grievances with the British administration. A teacher, who also served as Reusch's secretary and clerk at the time, recalled that some were "very suspicious of what he was doing. He had a big truck with a closed box, and he and the driver went from place to place. But the driver never knew what Reusch loaded at one stop and unloaded at another." There was even a rumor that Reusch split proceeds with British officials.[66]

Great Britain doubted Swedish neutrality, and therefore district officers kept an eye on the Swedish missionaries. "Paradoxically," Gustav Bernander wrote, "the best protection against the zeal of lower officials was to have good relations with the higher ones. Here Reusch could serve as a splendid introducer," because as president of the Mountain Club "he was known and appreciated by many members of the higher administration." Nevertheless, according to Bernander, Reusch "had to be very careful to follow all regulations which applied to foreigners in wartime Tanganyika."[67] George Hall also believed that Reusch's persona, that of a Russian Czarist military officer, helped him to establish and maintain contacts with the European community and British officials.[68] His Russian character and behaviors also distanced him from German taint.

The colonial administration loaded Reusch with yet another grievous assignment. His work for the Mission and Chief Custodian took him throughout the Northern Province, and he knew most of the Afrikaners and other foreigners living in the region, some of whom were sympathetic to the Nazi cause. He was in an ideal position to note pro-Axis sentiment and activities and was therefore asked to spy for British Intelligence. Reusch agreed, although it was another loathsome job he detested even more than working for the Chief Custodian. Yet, given his code of honor, he had no choice but to accept. He was at heart a loyal and unabashed monarchist, and in 1923 had given his word to work faithfully on behalf of His Majesty's Colonial Government. And so Reusch reported to Major Neil Stewart at the British Intelligence and Security Bureau in Dar es Salaam.[69]

Under the Defence (Alien Restriction) Order of 1940, the Provincial Office in Dodoma issued a permit granting Dr. Reusch, "a stateless person residing at Kinampanda (Augustana) Lutheran Mission," permission to "travel freely throughout Tanganyika Territory."[70] And in 1941 the District Office in Moshi issued a document that declared, "To all whom it may concern. Dr. R. Reusch is travelling on urgent government duty."[71] Reusch never wrote or spoke about his activities on behalf of the Bureau, and documents that might reveal the nature of his work have either been destroyed or remain classified.

As Reusch was dashing about Northern Tanganyika on behalf of the Chief Custodian and British Intelligence, he supervised a vigorous building campaign for the Augustana Mission, reactivating abandoned stations and constructing new schools, chapels and dispensaries. Despite the energy expended in difficult travel to distant congregations, he believed it was his duty to preside when large numbers were baptized and confirmed. According to Bernander, "Reusch possessed a vast capacity for hard work. He could work night and day without showing the least sign of fatigue, and this perhaps led him to take upon himself a burden far in excess of what is normal for one person — incidentally a fairly common phenomenon among the earlier missionaries."[72]

AN INDIGENOUS AFRICAN CHURCH

"Christianity in Africa naturally bears the marks of those who introduced it into Africa," wrote Henry Okullu. "By overstaying their mission and sitting on the infant Church, [the missionaries] eventually became more preoccupied with teaching the doctrines and establishing the traditions than with a witness to the worship of Christ."[73] And, wrote William B. Anderson, "For full indigenization, Christians needed not only to translate their faith but to listen to what African societies were saying." According to Anderson, "In East Africa only a few real attempts were made to listen."[74] The Augustana Mission was one of the few, and under the leadership of Rev. Elmer R. Danielson contributed a unique chapter in the history of foreign missions.

The clear-cut objective "toward which every co-ordinated effort of the Mission and home board should be directed," Danielson wrote at the end of 1939, "is the establishment of a self-propagating, self-governing, self-supporting African Church." The method of achieving that goal, he asserted, may be expressed in these words:

> The objective of every missionary to work himself out of his job as soon as possible by training African Christian leaders to take over his job. Africa will be evangelized by Africans, Africa will be educated by Africans, and eventually Africa will be taken care of medically by Africans. Africa will never be evangelized, or educated, or adequately cared for medically, by white pastors, teachers and doctors.

Danielson warned, "[W]e may not all agree on the method, and how to attain this in the shortest possible time. Events are moving fast, however, and it behooves us to plan even now for the day when we shall no longer be needed."[75]

As for the white colonists, Danielson believed that "race superiority, exploitation, crude domination, immorality, and the inhumanity of white people toward black people has put the Gospel under suspicion among African people, and this on the part of those who claim to have no other religion but Christianity." The American Midwestern populist blamed "our enslaving system of industrial exploitation," those who managed it and worked for it.[76] Five years later Danielson put the issue even more strongly:

> The greatest danger lies in a situation in parts of Africa which is somewhat similar to that in Russia before revolution. The millions of common Russian people were exploited by the privilege classes, and the Church was involved. Today perhaps 125 million African people are being exploited by foreign governments and by the economic control of foreign companies, dominated by profit-making for foreign shareholders. . . . We are not to wonder that some African leaders, raised and trained by the Church, are reluctantly turning away from the Church to social and economic Communism as the only hope for a strangled Africa.[77]

In 1943, a bleak period of the war when an Allied victory was anything but certain, Danielson told the Mission Board he needed at least thirty more volunteers: "If you intend to win the battle, you've got to send soldiers — picked, trained, filled with overpowering love for Christ and the African. We await — action!"[78] But, he cautioned, unless every missionary candidate shares "a high regard for the Negro as a human being in the States, and a sympathetic, helpful attitude toward Negro problems in the States, he can not be born into that regard and attitude by being sent to Africa."[79]

Decades later, one of his fellow-missionaries remarked, "At the time some of us disagreed with Danielson's views, but time has validated his vision."[80]

Meanwhile, in America —

"A Joe Louis Fund for the Race Relations Department of the Federal Council of Churches of Christ in America, to be used 'to better the conditions of my people and create better human relations in America,' has been launched by the world's heavyweight champion. Declaring that he would make the initial contribution to the fund himself, Louis stated that the hardest fight he ever had was against prejudice and intolerance. 'My people know what I mean,' he added. 'They are fighting their way up, and I want to open the door of opportunity a little wider for them.'"

— *The Lutheran Companion*, October 30, 1941

Augustana missionaries received no substantive training to prepare them for the cultural differences they would experience in foreign countries. One of those was Martin Olson, who arrived in 1938. One day as he listened to African teachers and evangelists discuss and debate the issues at a Native Christians' Conference he "realized how many times [African leaders] reasoned out things entirely different from our conceptions of logic, in fact in many cases directly opposite from our way of thinking. To 'think Black' is difficult for us," he admitted:

> Their thought life is not ours and perhaps will never be. But underneath it all we recognize humanity and that these Blacks have hearts and souls like our own. They are moved by the same instincts, torn by the same emotions, and governed by the same physical and psychical laws. And they have the same great need for the Saviour that all men have, the Saviour of the world so long denied them by those who should have known better. Here then is the common ground.[81]

In 1929, at the initiative of German bishops, representatives of the Bethel, Berlin, Leipzig, Neukirchen, Moravian and Augustana Missions had discussed forming a federation of African Mission Churches. But some of the Reformed representatives feared a Lutheran takeover, while the Americans suspected the same intention on the part of the Germans. Therefore, nothing came of the initiative.[82] Although the Lutheran missionaries harbored inter-synodical, denominational and cultural prejudices, they did not intend to replicate their respective national and ethnic synods in Tanganyika.

In the mid-1930s the various missions revived the idea of federation, motivated in part because the British administration was considering a plan to impose its own educational system on the Mission schools, as Reusch warned, *"without religious instruction"* [emphasis his]. In Reusch's view, this would have produced "devastating results for the Mission work because the majority of teachers were Muhammedans, trained in the coastal Government schools where Islam was the dominating religion." And a Muslim, Reusch cautioned, "whether teacher or merchant, is more or less a Missionary of his faith." Reusch reasoned that the British Government would not respond to objections from a lone missionary representing 6,000 or 10,000 church members, but would have to pay attention to a voice representing 100,000 Africans.[83]

The objectives of a Mission Churches Federation (MCF) were defined at a meeting in 1935. In 1937 Leipzig's Paul Rother was elected the first president and a small executive committee consisting almost entirely of European missionaries was also elected.

Two years later, in the absence of the interned President Paul Rother, the MCF General Assembly — with British Government officials in attendance — met in November 1940 at Agustana's Kiomboi mission. Delegates elected Dr. Reusch to serve as acting president, Martin Olson as vice-president, and an executive committee, half indigenous and half white, from the Augustana, Berlin, Bethel, Moravian and Leipzig Missions.

The colonial administration was wary of any developments that might have political implications. They were relieved that Reusch, whom they trusted, had been elected president rather than Elmer Danielson, an outspoken advocate on behalf of an independent African Church.

Apologizing for his tardiness in filing a report of that meeting with Provincial Commissioner Maguire, Dr. Reusch, as he was wont to do, cast the proceedings as well as his role in it in a positive light:

> I hope that the study of this detailed report will reveal to you the spirit of the convention and also give you an insight into the problem we are facing now. I am very glad that I could obtain control and turn their [the indigenous believers'] hearts a bit towards the side of loyalty and thankfulness to the Government . . .
>
> With best wishes for a blessed Christmas and a happy New Year and a handkiss to Mrs. Maguire I remain, Dear Mr. Maguire, Most sincerely and always thankful, yours, (Signature).

Some regarded Reusch as an obsequious British lackey; but the British knew that the little man from the Caucasus could drive a hard bargain on behalf of his Mission. At the same time, they trusted his judgment and his word.

The men elected to MCF leadership, said Reusch, "had the necessary authority and influence because they were *men in whom the natives had confidence*."[84] Or, as Pastor Solomon Kibange of Usambara put it, "One thing is clear: the pastoral care of the congregations has now passed [from the missionaries] into the hands of the African ministry, once and for all."[85] At the end of 1940 the Swedish Fosterland Mission and the former German Neukirchen Mission also joined the MCF.

Chiefs Abdiel Shangali and Petro Marealle helped Reusch draw up a constitution,[86] and "with the knowledge and support of the Governor [of Tanganyika]," noted the loyal missionary, "there was established in June 1942 the Lutheran Church of Northern Tanganyika." However, according to Bernander, a weakness of the Church constitution "was that it tied down the leadership of the church to one person — Dr. Reusch." Nevertheless, the Swedish missionary admitted, the constitution approved by the members of MCF was "eloquent testimony to [Reusch's] position on the Leipzig field."

Reusch's prediction was accurate: British Government listened attentively to the Federation's views and proposals. The new MCF president left immediately for Dar es Salaam to warn officials that their plan to take over the mission schools was a grave mistake. The religious component of the curriculum, he asserted, must be preserved as a means of nourishing the Christian communities — which in turn nourished a civil society. His argument was so persuasively made that colonial education officials shelved their reorganization plan.

The Mission Churches Federation also engendered another important benefit. African Christians reflected the synodical and denominational biases of their parent missions; by contrast, MCF affiliation led to a new sense of common purpose and identity. In Elveda Reusch's words, "Because of common needs and problems arising not only between congregation and congregation of the same mission, but also between mission and mission, the indigenous Lutheran Church is being drawn closer and closer together."[87] Said an African Lutheran, "A bundle of arrows is stronger than a single arrow."[88]

Under Dr. Reusch's leadership, 1940-1948, the MCF introduced a common liturgy with a common Swahili hymnal and translation of the Bible, accepted a common church discipline, operated its own press, and produced its own newspaper. The MCF became, in President Reusch's words, "the most powerful religious organization in Tanganyika" with more than 300,000 baptized members.[89] Martin Olson doubted "if Dr. Reusch ever gets more than four or five hours of sleep in a night due to the tremendous load of work he carries."[90]

Evangelists were sometimes ordained after working closely with a missionary cleric. There were sixteen such clergy on the Leipzig field, and without them, Reusch admitted, his efforts would have come to nothing. He specifically mentioned chiefs such as Petro of Marangu, Henri Abdieli of Machame and others, and African pastors Solomon and Timotheo of Machame, Lazaros of Arusha, Sakaria of Nkoaranga, and Pastor Yobu Andrea of Usambara and Usaramo.[91]

A Report from the Field

Elveda Reusch's letter to Sr. Jenny in Leipzig, May 31, 1943 [92]

On this field we can only be encouraged by the way the native church leaders and church members are and have taken ahold of the work. The native pastors have heavy work but none think of complaining or shirking [and] are a great help to my husband — eager, concerned, faithful, shepherding to the best of their ability the souls of their individual flocks and carrying by necessity far more responsibility than formerly in local church 'showries.'

My husband spent last week in North Pare, is in South Pare this week and then he goes on to Usambara. Every six months a special petrol allowance is given to visit the Masai stations at Kibaya, Naverera and Engaruka. Last August a few Masai were baptized at Engaruka.

My husband keeps well as a rule. Pray much for him. Many heavy burdens rest upon him. The children are well and growing fast. All attend school. I have been ill for several months. During November and December I was in the Moshi hospital [gravely ill with malaria], returned to Machame for a month to get stronger, went to Nairobi where I underwent a goiter operation. . . . May the Lord in His Mercy soon stop the war!

Reusch's first initiative, voted at the 1940 General Assembly of the MCF, was to establish a seminary at Machame. Dr. Reusch was chosen to head the institution, and because of his academic credentials he was also chosen to instruct the first class of twenty-four seminarians.

Dr. Reusch ordained the seminarians at the end of 1943. The positive out-come, in the words of Gustav Bernander, "was that it was the first joint course organized by Lutheran Churches in Tanganyika, and must thus be regarded as an important step forward in the cause of ecumenicity." However, it was Bernander's opinion that, unfortunately, "Reusch could not devote sufficient time to this work, involved as he was with so many other duties." Because of some "partly negative experiences of this first course," no further courses were offered the following year.[93]

Nevertheless, a new spirit of cooperation emerged because of the MCF: the Marangu Teachers' Training School opened its doors to students from other missions; Ubena-Konde sent students to the Kinampanda Training School; Usambara and Usaramo sent students to Marangu; the Bokoba school at Kigaramo hired teachers from Usambara, and Bukoba received two pastors from Usambara. Ubena-Konde hired several teachers from Marangu, and that freed Rev. Nordfeldt to open a primary school, which later evolved into a teachers' training school.[94]

The decisions reached at the 1940 General Assembly were proof that Reusch aimed "to take advantage of the emergency to create a united Church," although Bernander thought it unlikely that all the delegates fully understood the ultimate consequences of the various decisions made at this meeting. "Rather, they may be regarded as an expression of confidence in a man who at the time was strongly engaged in the work of helping orphaned Lutheran missions in Tanganyika."[95]

In addition to his educational, pastoral and administrative responsibilities, Reusch was constantly on the move building churches, schools and dispensaries far from his home base. His heart belonged to the Masai, and he was frequently among them.

Statistics of the Lutheran Church of Northern Tanganyika (1943)[96]					
Mission District	African Clergy	Evangelists	Teachers	Lutherans	Catechumens
North Masailand				40	8
South Masailand			3	52	9
Arusha*	1	4	26	2,800	150
Nkoaranga-Meru*	1	3	32	3,800	190
Ashira*	1	2	10	800	80
Masama*	2	4	28	6,500	250
Machame*	2	6	40	12,000	700
Moshi-Mbokomu*	2	8	40	11,000	300
New Moshi	1	6	9	1,200	70
Marangu*	1	2	48	5,000	135
Mamba*	1	3	16	5,000	?
Mwika*		3	16	5,200	200
Sigatini-Kifula	1	4	30	2,700	40
Usangi	1	2	28	1,000	100
Gonja	1	3	27	1,500	200
Vduee	1	6	19	500	45
Mbaga	1	2	16	800	35
TOTAL	17	58	388	59,892	2,512
*Self-supporting					
Totals in 1945:				68,110	3,919 [97]

THE PRICE OF SUCCESS

Their human natures did not spare the missionaries from cultural and national biases or from jealousy, selfishness and small-mindedness, and Reusch was sometimes on the receiving end. Only a rooted and disciplined individual could maintain his balance and keep long-range goals clearly in mind while wading through one niggling discouragement after another.

One of his early tasks was to remove an African pastor who ran amuck by charting his own course, ordaining unprepared men, and mismanaging funds.[98] On another occasion the *East African Standard* published a letter from the African secretary to Rev. Langford-Smith, the

Anglican headmaster at Marangu, accusing some indigenous Christians of being pro-German. This was by implication especially damaging to Reusch. But that wasn't all. The letter also recommended that the former Leipzig and Augustana mission schools be turned over to the Anglicans — which embarrassed Langford-Smith. The innocent priest was subsequently accused of planting the letter. From the time he arrived at Marangu he had sensed that some Lutherans, whites and blacks, were suspicious of him and of Anglican motives in the Territory. Superintendent Reusch regretfully accepted Rev. Langford-Smith's resignation.[99]

Not everyone liked Reusch, and despite the many benefits derived from his previous association with the Leipzig Mission, his German connection also left him vulnerable. His successful strategy to preserve the Lutheran heritage in the Kilimanjaro region angered a British missionary, who, in a four-page letter to Governor Twining, charged that Reusch was a Nazi spy who had encouraged the Chagga to be disloyal.[100] That accusation cut the former imperial cavalry officer to the quick, but he never avoided a conflict. In this case he went directly to the provincial commissioner in Moshi, Bruce Hutt, to confront the libelous charge. In his Christmas greeting in 1943, Hutt put the missionary's mind at ease:

> With reference to our recent conversation I am writing to confirm that as far as I know you have done everything possible to foster the loyalty of the Chagga to the British Government since you returned to the district in 1940. Having regard [for] the magnificent way in which they have helped the Government since the war started, it is difficult to understand how anyone can accuse them of being disloyal. This is most unjust and it is equally cruel and unfair to suggest that you have [been] doing pro-Nazi propaganda amongst them. Neither allegation has any foundation in fact.[101]

As for Governor Twining, said Reusch in characteristic style, His Excellency "tore the accusation into pieces."

The British Colonial Office began planning post-war policies in 1943, including a policy on the return to Tanganyika of enemy aliens. Sir William Jackson, an official in Dar es Salaam, cabled his objection to London. The very presence of German missionaries and residents would undoubtedly cause "uneasiness" among European residents as well as Africans; moreover, he warned, the British Government would then have to deal with applications from German Lutheran missionaries who "were in many cases strongly politically minded. I trust they will not be allowed to return."[102] Governor Edward Twining, in secret correspondence, also opposed yet another "generation of German pastors."[103] Secretary of State for the Colonies, Oliver Stanley, concurred.[104]

The enemy alien issue was still under discussion in the autumn of 1945. The policy that was finally adopted derived in part from an analysis authored by J. S. Bennett of the Colonial Office:

> There are two categories, Lutheran and Catholic. First, the Lutherans: (a.) Should the German missionaries be allowed to return? In view of the data from 1925, the answer is clearly "no." (b.) If they do not return should the missions be given over to a suitable

British Protestant body? No, because (i) there are no British Lutherans, (ii) we already have an offer in hand from the American Lutherans, (iii) British missions have no pre-emptive rights in a British mandated territory, and (iv) any further discussions with the Germans "might in the end involve us in having to let in the *Swedish* Lutherans [emphasis his], who are undesirable because of their German connexions."[105]

But American Lutherans demanded to know why the German Lutheran missionaries had been removed from their missions and their property liquidated whereas most of the German Roman Catholic missionaries were left undisturbed. Roman Catholic missions, it was explained, were under the supervision of the Vatican, and before the war Rome had transferred their missions under German and Italian religious orders to non-Axis jurisdictions; therefore, none of their properties was seized. Furthermore, the Colonial Office believed that Roman Catholic German missionaries were less likely to sympathize with Hitler than Lutherans; nevertheless, neither Roman Catholic nor Lutheran Germans would be welcome at war's end. The reason was not rooted in vindictiveness or fear of subversion, but because, in the words of a colonial official, they "lacked respect for British culture and traditions."[106]

During the summer of 1945 the Colonial Office received a letter from a Mr. Tyndale Biscoe of Tanganyika criticizing the Augustana Mission. The quality of education provided in its mission schools was poor, he asserted, and he urged that Church of Scotland personnel replace the Augustana Americans. It was a loony suggestion, the Colonial Office realized, particularly because the Africans would greet such a proposal with hostility.

However, any such criticism, whether from a Member of Parliament or a colonial planter, set off a round of inquiry in London. When asked for her reaction, the Assistant Secretary of the British International Missionary Council replied that she was not surprised "to hear of the low educational level of the Augustana Lutherans," and expressed the hope that Canadian Lutherans might take over. The Colonial Office ignored her suggestion. In an internal memorandum, Mr. Cox recommended that, should Augustana be unable to manage Leipzig's territory, American administration, such as the National Lutheran Council, was preferable to the Lutheran World Convention.[107]

At the end of 1947 Rev. George Anderson requested that, if the German missionaries were not allowed to return, their missions "be turned over for permanent care and ownership by us and other Lutherans whose nationality is acceptable to Government."[108] In 1949 Sir Edward Twining signed into law Ordinance No. 68, which assigned the Leipzig Missions to the Americans. Said A. B. Cohen of the Colonial Office in London, "I am very glad to learn that these properties are to be handed over to the Augustana Mission. It is also interesting to hear that Schiotz [president of the National Lutheran Council] has not yet raised the question of allowing German missionaries to return to the Territory. It is to be hoped that he will continue to leave that question alone."[109]

ELEPHANTS, LIONS AND GUINEA FOWL

Dr. Reusch continued to visit Masailand and write extensively about his experiences and the animal life he observed. The elephant was to him a noble, huge, clever and good-natured animal. He admired the ways in which they protected their young while bathing in a river. "Sometimes one can see a dead crocodile in the fork of a tree," he wrote. "The elephant has killed it because it attacked a baby."

In 1936 he had accompanied a British official, Mr. Duncan, and 600 Africans, who planned to use fire to clear an area of brush in which tsetse flies multiplied, insects whose bites transmitted sleeping sickness. They had set the fire on all sides of the zone when:

> Suddenly the crying of an elephant calf and the voice of a troubled cow was heard from the inside of the fire-encircled bush. Mr. Duncan offered a great reward to the natives if they could save the cow and the calf. But nobody dared to do it. Suddenly, from the forest opposite emerged a female elephant. She gave the peculiar elephant sound, forced her way through the fire-ring, lifted the calf high up and brought it out to a safe place. Then she went back and rescued the mother cow. The people were speechless. Mr. Duncan immediately made a report about it to the Government and showed this report to me. At the end of it he added these words: "After this my rifle will never again aim at an elephant, for this mother-elephant has put me to shame with her magnanimous deed." And I must say the same.[110]

Missionaries were often called upon to destroy marauding wild animals who stalked both cattle and people. Reusch told stories about successful lion hunts, but his daughter, Betty, described one in which Reusch and his companions encountered an astonishing animal:

> Some time ago Ingrid went with Daddy on safari to Engaruka, in the Masai Plains. Near Engaruka there are some ancient city ruins near a thorn forest. At Engaruka Daddy went to hunt a huge lion, who seemed to be so fierce that even the other lions would not live with him. That lion has killed several people and lots of cattle and sheep belonging to the natives. They did not get the lion, however.[111]

As Reusch explained the event, he and a large number of Masai warriors, including a young man who had killed eighteen lions, tracked the animal to a stand of trees where they found him asleep after feasting on a warrior's leg and part of a cow. Said Reusch, "I took position at one end of the forest, and the two dozen warriors put a grass fire in a horseshoe shape to drive the lion towards me. But when he awoke and stretched himself, he cleared the waves of fire with one leap, and we saw only the dust behind him when we rushed to the place."[112]

The guinea fowl was Reusch's favorite meat, and whenever he saw some of the birds along the trail he always stopped to bag a few. Losinyari Netili, a retired teacher, recalled an occasion during one such hunt on the Serengeti:

[The birds] flew up and away into some trees. We went in their direction but before he could shoot they flew off again to another tree even farther away. As we followed some yards behind, Dr. Reusch, as he came over a rise, saw a lioness with two cubs. He stood very still and in a soft voice asked the lioness to take her cubs and go home. She was nervous, and the cubs, of course, they were curious and began to move towards the strange creature they had not seen before.

Dr. Reusch still didn't move, not even to take the gun from his shoulder. He only said in a soft voice, "No — no, mama lion, please take your children and go home, mama lion." Then she crouched to leap on him! But he does not move and only repeats his request.

And she did! She pushed her cubs away, pushed them with her paw, and they all three disappeared.

As we ran up to him I asked, "Why did you stand there and joke with the lion? Why did you not shoot when she prepared to spring?"

He answered, "Because she has two cubs. If I kill the mama the babies will die."[113]

Those who met the stateless Russian in Africa eagerly contributed to the stories that made the colorful figure a legend in his own time. Paul Hamilton White, an Australian physician who worked at a government hospital in southern Tanganyika, made a trip north to see Mt. Kilimanjaro. "Many have climbed the nineteen thousand foot peak, and several have lost their lives in the blizzards that sweep the glacier, but none," he declared, "has a mountaineering record to equal that of the amazing little man I met that evening." Over cups of tea in Moshi, Reusch dismissed the praise by replying, "It is so easy with the sardine and the prune for the diet."

The missionary hitched a ride with White to Marangu, but "half-way up the steep, winding road, cut from the hillside, the car sputtered and stopped. I tinkered with the carburetor, but the only way we could get up was to drive backwards up the narrow pass. The mountain was on one side, and a five hundred foot drop on the other. I chose to keep near to the hillside, but, in turning a sharp bend, a rear wheel went into the ditch. My heart sank. I got out the jack, but it would not go under the axle. I tried chocking timber under the wheel, but made no headway."

"Could I not lift the wheel again back upon the road?" Reusch asked his driver.

White looked at Reusch's five feet four-inch frame, and smiled. "She weighs thirty hundred pounds," he cautioned.

"You will permit me to try, perhaps?" Reusch countered.

"Imagine my feelings," said the Australian, "when this amazing little man not only lifted the wheel out of the ditch, but pushed the car back on to the road! Later that day, I saw him bend a copper cent piece in two with his bare hands."[114]

UNFINISHED BUSINESS

The war had come to its hideous end in Europe and Asia when the International Red Cross notified Dr. Reusch that his sister Olga and her daughter had perished in the Allied fire-bombing of German cities in the last days of the war. Olga and her family had fled to Germany in 1944, just before the Red Army drove the Germans out of Lithuania. In 1946 Reusch received a letter from his uncle in Arnstadt, Germany. Feodor Ivanovich, who fled Vladikavkaz after the Bolshevik revolution, wrote that his only son had been killed at Westfalia on April 1, 1945. *"Somit haben wir alles verlosen!"* wrote the broken-hearted 73-year-old man — "And so we have lost everything!"[115]

Even as Reusch received personal sad news, the Lutheran Church in Tanganyika was experiencing unparalleled growth. Reusch cited the highlights in his report of September 1945: "The Arusha and Nkoaranga congregations have awakened to their evangelistic responsibilities to an extent never before seen"; in the western Chagga district "Shira has a fine coffee plantation, Masama a good carpentry shop and Machame a splendid carpentry school from which our local government is ordering its furniture"; "the middle part of the Chagga district has been pressing forward as never before"; "in the eastern part the Mamba-Marangu differences have been settled, thanks to Dr. S. H. Swanson and Dr. G. N. Anderson's visit"; and in the North Pare district, "Gonja has increased by over 500 souls, has surpassed its annual building program, built a water mill, opened a good carpentry school, planted a number of congregational fields and cut some 500 planks for the use and benefit of the Church."[116]

Parish life among the established African congregations reflected New Testament models more faithfully than the parishes in the United States. For example, the church at Machame, serving a congregation of 11,000, conducted community life according to the discipline of the Early Church: Elders heard disputes between parishioners, and if their mediation failed to bring reconciliation, the matter was taken to the pastor; parishioners met in small groups every morning and evening for prayer; and once a month each member met in the home of an elder for advice in spiritual matters. Those straying from the straight and narrow were admonished, and every Saturday elders inspected homes and farms and reminded the families of Sunday services.[117]

The subject of an independent African Church was discussed so often in the Augustana community that it prompted British Government scrutiny. Press clippings of articles and letters authored by the Americans were collected in files for future reference. For example, Danielson's letter to the editor of the *Tanganyika Standard* in 1943 went into his file:

> African Christianity as expressed by the emerging Indigenous Church has to learn to stand solidly on its own feet, devoid of foreign mission domination, if it is to be true and genuine Christianity. The war, by the internment of the German missionaries, has abruptly accelerated the devolving of responsibility upon the Indigenous Church. A word of profound gratitude is expressed to that African Christian leadership, which has shouldered its responsibilities in the humble spirit of our common Saviour Jesus Christ.[118]

MCF delegates voted in 1946 to call Dr. Daniel Friberg to supervise a new seminary they planned to open at Lwandai in Usambara. They also voted to open a secondary school to serve all members of the MCF at Arusha — which Reusch built and opened the same year — and urged the opening of both an agricultural and an industrial training school. They demonstrated their confidence and trust in Dr. Reusch by nominating him to continue for an other term as president of the MCF.[119]

Despite his ability to get things done, no aspect of his work was immune to criticism. Superintendents of other missions were miffed because Reusch had ordained the seminarians in 1943; in the past they had always ordained African pastors in their own jurisdictions. Some suspected that he inflated the numbers of people he claimed to have baptized and confirmed, and pietists criticized him for not enforcing Church discipline more severely. Others accused him of trying to turn the MCF into a "state church" by stacking the MCF Board with Africans sympathetic to his goals.

When an issue mattered to him, Reusch could use direct and blunt language. Martin Olson was elected to replace Herbert Magney as president of the Augustana Mission in 1944, and the Mission Board in Minneapolis, without having communicated with Reusch beforehand, assigned Magney to take over part of Reusch's extensive territory. Although they were not at odds publicly, Magney and Reusch were not friends, especially after the rancorous debate in 1924 over the division of the Mission between Leipzig and Augustana. Soon after the reassignments, Olson received a bristling letter from an outraged Reusch.

"I am glad you were chosen," Reusch wrote to Olson, "because now there is a President to whom I can talk absolutely frank and open without having to fear that my words will be twisted and wrongly interpreted." Then followed his strenuous objection to Magney's appointment: "Not one of us on these fields was asked or even notified [of the Board's decision]. As far as I remember I am still a member of our Augustana Mission. Therefore, I protest against this decision." After defending his performance as superintendent, Reusch concluded, "If the Conference is of the opinion that Rev. H. Magney or anyone else will be the more suitable one, then I am ready for the sake of the work to hand the *whole* field over to him immediately and go to any other place assigned to me or drop out entirely."[120]

The matter was discussed at a subsequent rowdy Mission conference. Fifty years later, Oscar Rolander vividly recalled that such meetings "were always tense, and much more so during the war that I wondered what it was that I had become a part of."[121] President Brandelle dispatched the president of the Board of Foreign Missions to Africa to make amends.

According to Bernander, "Miscalculations, misunderstandings and some measure of human frailty and error" characterized the missions crisis during the Second World War.

RESPITE

The summits of Mount Kilimanjaro always restored Reusch's spirit, but during the war years he was too busy to seek respite on his mountain. After the war he and a missionary friend, George Hall, made an ascent together. In silence they looked down from Kibo Peak on the flat plain below. Suddenly, Hall said, Reusch seemed to fall into some kind of trance, and Hall became concerned. But after a moment Reusch returned to the physical world and explained to

Hall, "I looked in the distance and saw how much work there was to do, and like Moses I know I shall not see it accomplished."[122]

In an article published in Germany in the early 1950s, Reusch expressed the same patriarchal intuition:

> Some day, when the time is right the right person will lead them. Just as the Masai took over Kenya and Tanganyika in a few short years and brought all others to submission, so will they take over Central Africa and bring all to submission before the Lord of the World. I shall not experience that because I must say goodbye to them on the border of the Holy Land. But at the door of Paradise I will greet them and count them, one by one, my Masai. I shall not count dozens or hundreds, but thousands.[123]

In 1946, in a speech at the Mission conference, his last before leaving on a well-earned furlough, Reusch predicted that Elmer Danielson would be the Joshua to lead the Church and its members into the Canaan of independence.[124] "Looking back at the six years of work here," Reusch wrote in his 1946 MCF report, "I must state that this young Church, in a state of growth and transition still, has worked very hard, and the Lord has blessed it. The only explanation I can see is this: HE told HIS church to throw out its net in spite of all problems, difficulties, war and famine. The church did it and its net became filled with thousands." [125]

Although the remarks did not appear in the minutes of the conference, Reusch also directly confronted those who doubted his statistical accounting. "Just recently I heard that it is impossible to have an annual increase of 10,000 members. It is possible, and the numbers will increase still more if the LORD will continue to bless our work in HIS great and undeserved mercy." Furthermore, "men like Rev. Danielson, Rev. Nordfeldt, Rev. M. Olson and Dr. G. N. Anderson, who know the fields, will endorse what I say."

The challenge before them, in Reusch's opinion, was to bridge the geographic separation of the MCF fields. But that problem could "be overcome by winning for CHRIST the powerful and tremendously influential Masai tribe," thus making the entire northern region of Tananyika "a predominantly Lutheran country." He concluded his report by emphasizing these words: *The great future aim is to make the federated Churches to become Conferences of One Indigenous Lutheran African Church, organized not on American or German, but on traditional African lines.*" [126]

And so Dr. Reusch prepared to turn his attention more fully to the Masai. He was already working with a committee of mission representatives and with the Provincial Education Officer, J. W. Smethurst, to produce a Masai dictionary, grammar and instructional materials, including the Bible and a hymnal.[127] Reusch's fourth and last term would be dedicated to working exclusively among his beloved Masai.

"After eight strenuous years — seven of which were spent in the Northern Area — Dr. and Mrs. Reusch and daughters Betty, Ingrid and Dagmar went on leave in April," Danielson reported in the Mission minutes for 1947.[128] "His feats are legendary," Oscar Rolander wrote in his own letter to the congregations in America. "His present term in Africa has now rounded the corner of the seventh year, so he will be coming to America on furlough as soon as possible. Don't miss seeing and hearing him!"[129]

"During Dr. Reusch's past seven years, the Church has had phenomenal growth," Danielson testified. However, the populist mission president was determined to eliminate Reusch's plantations because they exploited African labor. "Missions," Danielson said, "which are among the foremost critics of exploitation, must put their house in order."[130] That criticism did not disturb Reusch because the produce from those plantations had served its purpose, to alleviate a financial crisis. Reusch's attention and energy were now directed elsewhere.

Dr. Bengt Sundkler said that when he left his parish in South Africa for the orphaned missions in Tanganyika there was no European to replace him, and so the Swedish Mission put an African pastor in charge of the congregation. "That," he said regretfully, "was a 'first' after 200 years of mission work in South Africa." Said Stanley Moris, "One good result of the war was that indigenous leadership was greatly hastened by the shortage of missionaries from overseas. Helped by the necessities of war, our Augustana Mission reached the goal of indigenous leadership in 20 years."[131]

The Leipzig Mission had laid the foundation for an independent African Lutheran Church. Augustana's Danielson made it Mission policy, and Dr. Reusch's leadership of the MCF set it in motion. More important, however, it was African pastors, chiefs and congregations who prepared their people for the day when they would hire and direct the work of foreign missionaries.

According to Elmer Danielson,

> A miracle has taken place during these war years in the Lutheran Church of the northern area of Tanganyika, much of it is due to the way God has used His servant, Dr. Richard Reusch, superintendent of the Northern Area, and one of God's missionary-statesmen. Twenty-nine new stone churches have been built during the war years. The people themselves have built these churches. Eighty-six new stone schools have been built. Innumerable chapels and schools of less permanent materials have also been built. Nothing like it happened during all the years of peace.[132]

Archives of the Evangelical Lutheran Church of America

African clergy gather at Machame. Superintendent Reusch stands in the center; Rev. Stephano Moshi, who was elected the first bishop of the Lutheran Church in Tanganyika, is seated in front of Reusch.

CHAPTER 11

1 George N. Anderson, "What About Foreign Missions?" *Lutheran Companion*, vol. 44 (8 August 1936), 998-99.
2 Elmer L. Danielson, "A Miracle Has Taken Place," *Lutheran Companion*, vol. 55 (4 June 1947), 7
3 O. Fischer, medical report ("Ärztliches Zeugnis"), 28 June 1938, AELML.
4 Paul Hamilton White, *Doctor of Tanganyika* (1955), 232.
5 R. Reusch, letter to Leipzig Mission Director, 21 August 1938, AELML.
6 P. O. Bersell, president of the Augustana Synod, letter and certificate dated 3 January 1939, GACA.
7 R. Reusch, itinerary, 20 February 1939, AELML.
8 R. Reusch, catalogue order, AELML.
9 R. Reusch, undated sermon notes, GACA.
10 Anton Lundeen, "Our Africa Field," *Lutheran Companion*, vol. 47 (2 March 1939), 269.
11 Eddythe Kjellin, "Greetings from Africa," *Mission Tidings*, vol. 34 (September 1939), 108.
12 Martin C. Olson, "No Disarmament for Us!" *Lutheran Companion*, vol. 47 (12 October 1939), 1292.
13 "Minutes of the Eighteenth Annual Conference of the Augustana Lutheran Mission in Tanganyika Territory, East Africa," 31 October-7 November, 1940, 13 (Box 326, World Missions/Tanganyika/Augustana Minutes), AELCA.
14 R. Reusch, edited excerpts from "Kinampanda Teachers' Training School, Annual Report," *Mission Tidings*, vol. 35 (September 1940), 100.
15 Stanley W. Moris, "Healing and Helping in Africa," *Lutheran Companion*, vol. 47 (16 November 1939), 1450.
16 Douglas Augustine, from the author's notes of an interview at Gustavus Adolphus College, 27 June 1997.
17 Anton Lundeen, "Our African Field," *Lutheran Companion*, vol. 47 (2 March 1939), 269.
18 Ruth E. Safemaster, "Kiomboi, Mission Station," *Mission Tidings*, vol. 34 (May 1940), 366.
19 Stanely W. Moris, "Gospel Victories in Africa," *Lutheran Companion*, vol. 48 (7 March 1940), 297.
20 "What War Does to God's Cause," *Lutheran Companion*, vol. 47 (2 November 1939), 1379.
21 In fact, only 15 percent of the children attending school were enrolled in government sponsored educational facilities; 85 percent were enrolled in mission schools. Government willingly provided up to 95 percent of the operating budget for the mission schools because they succeeded in meeting education standards at less cost per pupil. — Paul C. Empie, Director of Lutheran World Action, "God's Work in Tanganyika," *Lutheran Companion*, vol. 53 (17 January 1945), 7.
22 Cited by Gustav Bernander in *Lutheran Wartime Assistance to Tanzanian Churches*, 1940-45 (Uppsala: Almquist & Wiksells, 1968), 19. Parole is also described by S. Hjalmar Swanson, "Missionary Notes," *The Lutheran Companion*, vol. 47 (23 November 1939), 1485.
23 Herbert S. Magney, "The War and Tanganyika Missions," *Lutheran Companion*, vol. 48 (9 May 1940), 587-88.
24 Herbert S. Magney, "Relieving German Missions," *Lutheran Companion*, vol. 48 (8 August 1940), 1005-06.
25 "Relieving the German Missions," 1006.
26 "Crisis in Lutheran Foreign Missions," *Lutheran Companion*, vol. 48 (19 September 1940), 1187.
27 "Crisis in Lutheran Foreign Missions."

28 George N. Anderson, "Meeting the Crisis in Africa," pt 2, *Lutheran Companion*, vol. 49 (6 February 1941), 173.
29 Colonial Office notes (CO 822-112-7), PRO.
30 T. M. Revington, District Commissioner, Moshi, letter to R. Reusch, 4 February 1944, GACA.
31 Deputy Governor, Tanganyika Territory, "Nazi Propaganda in Tanganyika," Part IV; cover letter to Oliver Stanley, Secretary of State for the Colonies, London, 20 January 1944, 11 pages (CO 537-2111), PRO.
32 "Nazi Propaganda," 1-2.
33 "Nazi Propaganda," 1.
34 W. E. F. Ward, L. W. White, *East Africa: A Century of Change*, 1870-1970 (1972), 167.

Of 7,259 British and German colonists who operated businesses and plantations in Tanganyika on the eve of the Second World War, 42 percent were German; 3,205 Germans occupied 32.8 percent of the holdings whereas 4,054 British subjects held 26 percent. — *History of East Africa*, ed. by Vincent Harlow (1965), 606-07.

35 "Nazi Propaganda," 4-8.
36 "Nazi Propaganda," 10-11.
37 Notes, Table A, "Return of Enemy Alien and Non-Enemy Alien Missionaries, Germans, in Tanganyika" (CO 537-2111), PRO.
38 "Nazi Propaganda," 10.
39 "Nazi Propaganda," 11.
40 Colonial Office notes, 1939 (CO 822-101-7), PRO.
41 Foreign Office, London, letter to the German Ambassador, 10 December 1937 (CO 822-78), PRO.
42 Assistant District Officer, Moshi, Secret Report to the Provincial Commissioner, Northern Province, Arusha, 2 August 1939, 5 (CO 822-78), PRO.
43 Internal notes and review, Jewish Immigration, Colonial Office, London, 1938 (CO 872-87-13), PRO.
44 R. Reusch, "East Africa" manuscript, 1, GACA.
45 S. Hjalmar Swanson, "Missionary Missive," *Lutheran Companion*, vol. 49 (30 January 1941), 145.
46 "Minutes of the Nineteenth Annual Conference of the Augustana Lutheran Mission," October 22-30, 1941, 23-24 (Box 326, World Missions/Tanganyika/ Augustana), AELCA.
47 Elveda Reusch, "A Thank You," *Mission Tidings*, vol. 36 (September 1941), 77.
48 Anderson, "Meeting the Crisis, Part I," *Lutheran Companion*, vol. 49 (6 February 1941), 173.
49 Anderson, "Meeting the Crisis."
50 Nathaniel Mrenga, from the author's notes of an interview at Marangu, Tanzania, 22 January 1996.
51 David Simonson, from author's notes of an interview in Arusha, Tanzania, 10 January 1996.
52 G. K. Whitlamsmith, for acting Chief Secretary to the Government, letter to Rev. G. N. Anderson, 8 September 1941, reproduced in Minutes of 1941, 26 (Box 326 World Missions/Tanganyika/ Augustana Minutes), AELCA.
53 R. Reusch, "Was there a sudden change in the Church as the German Missionaries left?" a 2-page draft, part of an untitled and undated manuscript, GACA.
54 R. Reusch, MCF Memorandum, 3, GACA.
55 R. Reusch, "Was there a sudden change . . ."

56 H. Wynne Jones, Report, "The Leipzig Mission in the Northern Province, Tanganyika," 1 January 1941 (R. Reusch personnel file), AELCA.

57 E. R. Danielson, "Out of the Depths," *Zamzam, The Story of a Strange Missionary Odyssey*, S. Hjalmar Swanson, ed. (1941), 139.

58 Mrs. Elmer Danielson, "The Rainbow Dawn," *Zamzam*, 56.

59 "The Rainbow Dawn," 16-19, 105-113.

60 Lois Danielson Carlson, "Mission Kids and Culture Shock," a panel discussion at the 1997 East African Lutheran Missionaries Reunion at Gustavus Adolphus College, 28 June 1997.

61 Bernander, 22-27.

62 N. Langford-Smith, Report, January 1942, pt. 1 (R. Reusch file), AELCA.

63 R. Reusch, letter to Chief Custodian MacDonald, 12 March 1941 (Custodian of Enemy Property Box, file for 1940-41), Archives, Northern Diocese of the Tanzanian Lutheran Church, Moshi (ANDTLC).

64 Chief Custodian MacDonald, letter to R. Reusch, 7 February 1942, ANDTLC.

65 R. Reusch, "Report Concerning the Leipzig Field," ca. 1942, GACA.

66 Israel Lema, from the author's notes of an interview at Moshi, Tanzania, 23 January 1996.

67 Bernander, 64.

68 Hall, *Missionary Spirit*, 50.

69 Several documents in Reusch's personal papers dating from 1940-43 include petrol allocations and travel permits (GACA).

70 Travel Permit B, issued by the Provincial Office at Dodoma to R. Reusch, 23 October 1940, GACA.

71 Moshi District Office memo, 28 May 1941, GACA.

72 Bernander, 32-33.

73 Henry Okullu, *Church and Politics in East Africa* (1974), 53, 58.

74 William B. Anderson, *The Church in East Africa*, 1840-1977 (1977), 97.

75 E. R. Danielson, Committee Report on Devolution, "Minutes of the 1939 Annual Conference of the Augustana Mission," 39 (Box 326, World Missions/ Tanganyika/Augustana Minutes), AELCA.

76 E. R. Danielson, "The Challenge of Our Africa Mission," pt. 3, *Lutheran Companion*, vol. 48 (19 December 1940), 1644.

77 E. R. Danielson, "God's 'Operation Africa,'" *Lutheran Companion*, vol. 54 (24 July 1946), 6.

78 E. R. Danielson, letter, "The Day before Good Friday," to Synod headquarters, 23 April 1943 (E. R. Danielson file), AELCA.

79 Elmer R. Danielson, "The Challenge of Our Africa Mission," pt. 2, *Lutheran Companion*, vol. 48 (12 December 1940), 1576.

80 Oscar Rolander, "Old Timers Reminisce," from the author's notes of a panel presentation at the 1997 East African Missionaries Reunion, Gustavus Adolphus College, 29 June 1997.

81 Rolander.

82 R. Reusch, "Memorandum Concerning the Mission Churches Federation," August 1948, 1-2, GACA.

83 R. Reusch, "Memorandum."

84 R. Reusch, "Memorandum," 4.

85 Bernander, note 4, 160.
86 George Hall, *The Missionary Spirit in the Augustana Church* (1984), 51.
87 Elveda Reusch, "A Thank You," *Mission Tidings*, vol. 36 (September 1941), 77.
88 Hall, 2.
89 R. Reusch, "East Africa" manuscript, GACA.
90 Martin C. Olson, "Glimpses of Africa," *Lutheran Companion*, vol. 51 (10 March 1943), 297.
91 R. Reusch, MCF Memorandum, 3.
92 Elveda Reusch, letter to Sr. Jenny in Leipzig, 31 May 1943, AELML.
93 Bernander, 46-47.
94 Bernander.
95 Bernander, 33-34.
96 R. Reusch, "The Annual Report 1943 of the Former Leipzig Mission Field," "Minutes of the 21st Annual Conference of the American Lutheran Mission," October 11-18, 1943 (Box 326 World Missions/Tanganyika/Augustana Minutes), AELCA.
97 "Minutes of the 23d Annual Conference of the Augustana Lutheran Mission, November 19-22, 1945," 52 (Box 326 World Missions/Augustana Minutes), AELCA.
98 R. Reusch, "MCF Memorandum," 2, GACA.
99 Bernander, 77.
100 R. Reusch, "History of the mission in East Africa after the First World War," notes for an unpublished manuscript, 2, GACA.
101 Bruce Hutt, District Commissioner, letter to Reusch, 24 December 1943, GACA.
102 William Jackson, Government, Tanganyika Territory, cable to the Colonial Office, 13 August 1943 (CO 822-112), PRO.
103 Sir Edward Twining, secret letter to Oliver Stanley, Secretary of State for the Colonies, 7 September 1944 (CO 537-211), PRO.
104 Secretary of State for the Colonies, cable to Sir. William Jackson, Tanganyika Territory, 19 August 1943 (CO 822-112), PRO.
105 J. S. Bennett, memorandum, internal review of German and Italian missionary post-war policy, 15 September 1945 (CO 537-2111), PRO.
106 Undated memorandum, "German and Italian Missionary Activities, 1944-47" (CO 537-2111), PRO.
107 Tyndale Briscoe's letter, and internal memoranda in reaction to a Colonial Office draft of "German Mission Disposal," circulated for comment in September 1945 (CO 537-2111), PRO.
108 G. N. Anderson, letter to the Chief Secretary of the Tanganyika Government, 20 December 1947, (CO 537-4685), PRO.
109 A. B. Cohen, Colonial Office, London, letter to E.R.E. Surridge, 22 June 1949 (CO 537-4685), PRO.
110 R. Reusch, "The Masai," unpublished manuscript, 9, GACA.
111 Betty Reusch [Anderson], "Letter from a Junior in Africa," *Mission Tidings*, vol. 37 (April 1943), 309-10.
112 R. Reusch, "The Masai," 8-9, GACA.

113 Losinyari Netili, from author's notes of interview at Ilboro, Tanzania, 20 January 1944.
114 Paul Hamilton White, *Doctor in Tanganyika* (1955), 230-32.
115 Theodore Reusch, letter to R. Reusch, 24 February 1946 (R. Reusch file), AELCA.
116 R. Reusch, "Annual Report of the Northern Area Mission Field," *Annual Conference*, 50-51 (Box 326), AELCA.
117 W. B. Anderson, *The Church in East Africa*, 115.
118 E. R. Danielson, "Former German Missions," *East African Standard* (2 July 1943), clipping (CO 822-112-7), PRO.
119 R. Reusch, "MCF Memorandum," 6.
120 R. Reusch, letter to Martin Olson, President of the Augustana Mission, 5 July 1944, AELCA.
121 Oscar Rolander, panel presentation.
122 George Hall, a story told to him by "a mutual friend," from the author's notes of an interview 17 July 1998.
123 R. Reusch, "Euere Wege sind nicht meine Wege," proof sheets, ca. 1953, GACA.
124 Bernander, 145.
125 R. Reusch, "Northern Area Annual Report of the Former Leipzig Mission Field for the Year," *Minutes of the 24h Annual Conference of the Augustana Lutheran Mission*, 45 (Box 326), AELCA.
126 R. Reusch, "Northern Area Annual Report," 9.
127 Minutes, "Conference on Literature for Masai," 21 June 1946, Nairobi, GACA.
128 E. R. Danielson, "Minutes of the 25h Annual Conference of the Augustana Lutheran Mission, 1947, 70 (Box 326), AELCA.
129 Oscar Rolander, "A Bright Spot in Darkest Africa," *Lutheran Companion*, vol. 55 (2 April 1947), 16-17.
130 Danielson, "Minutes of the 25th Annual Conference, 74.
131 Stanley W. Moris, M.D., *Which Doctor: Medical Experience on Three Continents* (privately printed, 1977), 89.
132 Elmer R. Danielson, "A Miracle Has Taken Place," *Lutheran Companion*, vol. 55 (4 June 1947), 7-

The First Lutheran congregation in Worthington, Minnesota, presented Dr. Reusch with a shotgun for his use in Tanganyika. First Lutheran later raised funds to purchase a jeep for the mission.

Chapter Twelve

VISITING PROFESSOR
St. Peter, Minnesota, 1947-48

*He is a very small man in stature, but when Dr. Reusch stood up
to give an informal greeting to the synodical convention in Kansas City,
it was not long before the delegates realized that they were listening
to a spiritual and intellectual giant.*

— E. E. Ryden[1]

On his third trip to the United States, the Masai Missionary addressed the June 1947 convention of the Augustana Synod in Kansas City. His remarks electrified the delegates. "The fight is on," he warned, "and there are many adversaries. Islam, paganism, and atheistic communism are trying to win Africa." *The Lutheran Companion* reported his speech in the next issue. "Dr. Reusch's achievements have been amazing," wrote the dazzled editor E. E. Ryden. "Just returned from Gospel triumphs in northern Tanganyika, British East Africa, his English was not altogether perfect, but his spiritual fervor was unmistakable." Reusch had explained that the first flag planted atop Kilimanjaro was a German banner, carried by a German officer. When the British took over, they claimed the territory with the Union Jack. "Finally, a Christian flag, with a red cross on a white field, was carried to the highest peak of all, 19,765 feet above sea level. That flag," cried Dr. Reusch, "is a token that Christ's Kingdom is above all earthly kingdoms, and that Africa shall be won for Christ."

"We were curious about that flag," the editor confessed, "and afterwards we took the little missionary aside for a brief interview. It was then that we learned that he himself had carried it to the summit of mighty Kilimanjaro, and with it a copy of the Scriptures enclosed in an iron box."

Under Reusch's leadership from 1940 to 1947, African church membership doubled, more young men studied at the new seminary than were previously ordained in the history of the mission, and 21,000 students were enrolled in mission schools. "Most significant of all," the editor emphasized, "the congregations have been organized into an indigenous Church which has become largely self-supporting, self-governing and self-propagating."[2] Dr. Reusch left Kansas City with a bundle of requests for personal appearances throughout America's Lutherland.

A few days later in Minneapolis, Reusch lobbied the Augustana Board of Foreign Missions for a special mission to the Masai. The board had, he argued, ignored the Masai by concentrating its work among people who, while beloved of God, were at times egotistical, irresponsible, violent and fanatically pagan. For example, the Pare people were "too soft," he claimed, and the Chagga "too concerned about money."

The Masai, on the other hand, were heroic, fierce, honorable warriors who, if converted, would "charge wave after wave in spite of all" as warriors of Christ. He laced his presentation with personal experiences — about being poisoned three times, killing man-eating lions, and witnessing the heroic deeds of the Masai who stood alongside him through good times and bad. "Gold and diamonds we do not have," he said, counting himself as one of them. But in the language of a regimental officer, he added, "With our blood we are ready to serve HIM, our KING and SAVIOUR." He reminded the astonished board members that Elmer Danielson and George Anderson had already endorsed his proposal; two chiefs and a few small Masai congregations shared his vision; four Masai pastors were in training along with evangelists, dressers, carpenters and masons. He concluded his pitch with a flourish of enthusiastic imagery:

> Instead of the green flag of Islam with its crescent, the flag of fire and sword, instead of the red bloody flag of bolshevism with hammer and sickle there will flutter over Africa the White flag with the red Cross, the flag of the SAVIOUR. And peace and love will rule. [The Masai] will not falter and surrender like Napoleon's guards. They will die, for they are warriors of CHRIST. The time is short. Make true the flag and the Gospel on top of the highest point of Africa. "What you have done to them you have done to ME, your KING and SAVIOUR.[3]

After that rhetorical fusillade the stunned Swedish Americans voted to substantially expand the work among the Masai — and put Dr. Reusch in charge.

THE LAND OF LAKES

The Reusches had always spent part of their furloughs with Elveda's brother and his family, but this time they did not entrain for Chicago. Rev. Frank Bonander had taken a rural parish in Minnesota, "Land of 10,000 Lakes," where the kindly members of the Braham Evangelical Lutheran Church warmly welcomed Dr. Reusch and his family. Although they were curious to meet the "Masai Missionary," the parishioners did not intrude upon their guests' privacy.

The Sunday bulletin for August 10, 1947, announced that Dr. Reusch would be in charge of morning worship the following week. In his announcement, Pastor Bonander reproduced information about his guest from a backgrounder he had prepared after meeting Reusch for the first time in 1930: "Dr. Reusch should be invited to every college campus. The seminarians should be given the opportunity of hearing him and counseling with him often. The [Lutheran]

Brotherhood would do well to sponsor missionary rallies with Dr. Reusch as the speaker. He is a man's man. And the youth of the church must hear him!"[4]

In the heartland of 10,000 lakes, the famous missionary stood in the pulpit the next Sunday, and with his opening sentence arrested the attention of each member of the congregation. "Imagine," he began, "that you had been fishing all day and caught nothing." How would Americans react if, toward the end of that luckless day, someone promised that if that they would only fish from the left side of the boat instead of the right their nets would be filled? "It is against sound reasoning," Reusch admitted, "against science and experience. It will be in vain to do it." Nonetheless, that's what the Apostles did — and their nets *were* filled because they were obedient. He went on to argue that when Christians disobey and pursue material wealth, worshipping the Golden Calf like the Israelites of the Old Testament, their spiritual life stagnates like the Church of St. Cyprian, St. Augustine, the Roman Catholic Church of the Middle Ages, and the Russian Orthodox Church. They become self-centered and ignore the command to spread the Gospel. And when that happens the very existence of the Church is in danger.[5]

During his brief visit to Braham, Dr. Reusch also presented a series of Bible studies on the prophets of the Old Testament, about whom he had written extensively at Tartu University. Reusch felt a bond with King David, Amos and Micah, and especially with the prophet Daniel, who was trained from the age of fourteen for imperial service as an officer and page in the Babylonian palace of King Nebuchadnezzar, or "Nebu-kuduru-ussar" as Reusch more accurately pronounced the exotic name. Like Joseph in Egypt, he told them, Daniel was given "exceptional wisdom, the gift to explain dreams, and the spirit of a prophet." Reusch knew that the ancient world of dreams and prophecies was foreign to his practical and sober audience, but his gift for storytelling made the ancient Babylonian Kingdom rise up in central Minnesota.[6]

On his second Sunday at Braham, Reusch charged that many "so-called Christians," relentless in their pursuit of wealth, have turned their hearts away from God.[7] On another Sunday he lambasted those who reject orthodox faith for scholarly reinterpretations of Holy Scripture:

> Modern scientific man declares that Jesus died, that HE is dead — HE who touched the blind eyes of an old man and this man began to see, HE touched the shoulder of a Publican and the Publican became a Matthew; HE touched the soul of his arch-enemy, Saul, and Saul became a Paul; HE touched the withered arm and this arm was restored; HE touched the ears of the deaf and they began to hear; HE touched the heart of a traitor — and he became a Peter, brave unto death.
>
> And HE did and does these things through the centuries of History. He touched the conscience of a sinner, a great scoundrel, and the young Augustine became one of the greatest Fathers of the Church; HE touched the heart of a young warrior-King and there appeared one of the greatest war-lords in history, Gustavus Adolphus II, who saved the Church of the Reformation and sealed his faith with his death; HE touched the soul of a poor monk, and the greatest Reformer appeared, Martin Luther, who brought back to the world the words of the Eternal Gospel.

Here we have a Savior, whose power and mercy extends into eternity. Accept HIM now. HE will accompany you, protect and bless you through this life. And when the last hour will come and you must depart, give your soul into HIS loving hands. HE will bend HIS head with the crown of thorns and will bring you into HIS eternal Kingdom of love and light.

To bring and make HIM known to the children of Africa we Missionaries are called, for it is worthwhile to live, to work, to fight and die for HIM.

Amen.[8]

In his final sermon at Braham, Dr. Reusch described the battle for the soul of Africa by appealing to imagery that resonated with his Swedish American audience:

> The goal is the greatest the Church ever had, a special honour for our Lutheran Church of the Reformation: a Church born on the battlefield, a heroic Church, a picked army of the Lord of hosts. It will fight the decisive battle. And for our Augustana Church there is a special place in this battle, like Gustavus Adolphus at Lutzen and the [Swedish] Stenboch regiment of Småland cavalry. Let us be this regiment in the last battle for the soul of Africa![9]

Never before had anyone like Reusch appeared in the village of Braham. After the service, he was presented with an envelope that contained a spontaneously collected sum of money, offered "as a small token of remembrance and appreciation of your fine services to this congregation." Each member of the parish present that morning, children and adults, had signed the letter.[10]

ACADEMIC ROBES

In 1862, twenty-nine years before Richard Gustavovich Reusch was born, Swedish Lutheran immigrants founded Gustavus Adolphus College in Minnesota. The nation was engaged in a civil war when the largest Indian uprising in the United States set the Minnesota River valley aflame. Established to educate future schoolteachers and pastors, Gustavus Adolphus was one of several liberal arts colleges established by the fledgling Augustana Synod. A number of Gustavus administrators and faculty members were active in promoting foreign missions, including Dr. O. J. Johnson, professor of Christianity (Religion), who had served as chairman of Augustana's Board of Foreign Missions for twenty-nine years. In September 1947, President Edgar M. Carlson welcomed the famous Dr. Reusch to campus as a visiting professor in the Christianity department.

Ruth Tolman, a third year student, worked as Dr. Reusch's part-time student secretary. He called her his "Daughter of the Sun," and always kept a supply of Peppermint Patties on hand for her refreshment. Although she felt no call to be a missionary, her boss was relentless in his attempt to recruit her for service in Africa.

Ruth enrolled in Reusch's course in World Religions. On one occasion that spring when Dr. Reusch was scheduled for one of his many off-campus speaking engagements, he asked Ruth to read to the class his lecture for April 22nd. The subject was ancient Judaism, and the topic of the day was the prophet Amos. She dreaded the assignment, but the blue-eyed blonde did as she was told.

"Around 814-15 B.C.," Ruth read aloud to her classmates,

> Assyria became the predominant Empire of the East under a dynasty of powerful Emperors, founded by Tiglat-Filleser I. This dynasty was later succeeded by the dynasty of Sargon II, whose successors were such Emperors as Sennacherib, Esarhaddon and Assurbanipal, who established an ancient world-Empire . . .

The names meant nothing to the students, but to Professor Reusch the ancient emperors and empires were part of his marrow. Despite merciless heckling from her peers, Ruth continued reading the lecture of the day:

> Amos sums this punishment in the following way in chapters 9, 6 and 4: Luxuriousness and hypocrisy everywhere . . . *On beds of ivory sleep the rich while the poor are starving and dying . . . . They trust in their arms, chariots and horses; but the Assyrian enemy will destroy them and drag the people into captivity (Am. 6). Oppression of the poor and needy everywhere; idolatry in Bethel, Dan and Beersheba; pagan gods are adored, festivals consisting of orgies are held, but the LORD is forgotten and HIS commandments are neglected . . . (compare with Amos 4.)* [Emphasis his.]

Professor Reusch dictated his lectures, even including punctuation: "And ze Israelites vandered for forty years, comma, and ate ze manna from heaven, full-stop."[11] But Reusch's lectures were more than a stale recitation of arcane data. Writing in the present tense, he infused his lectures with adjectives and metaphors to make the prophet Amos of the Old Testament accessible to his students:

> During the festival in Bethel, Amos preaches what he has seen. Like strokes of a heavy hammer his words were falling into the ears of his listeners. Bewildered, speechless, they listen. . . . Like blows of a heavy hammer on an anvil sound his words. Rhythmical are his sentences and highly poetical visions, rendered under the impulse of Divine inspiration. Between 810 and 795 B.C. Amos wrote down his prophecies. Where he died, we do not know; neither do we know whether he died a natural death or was killed. Dead is his body, but even today his book preaches a powerful sermon about the righteousness of the Eternal GOD.[12]

Although by the second semester the word was out that Professor Reusch was an easy grader, his teaching style was undeniably effective. Fifty years later some of his students could recall bits and pieces of his lectures with remarkable clarity. One of those was David Hilding, one of Ruth's classmates:

[Reusch] described how someone was able to outrun a horde of mounted troops to set up the display of God's power, to light his pile of wood while the priests of Baal exhausted themselves in vain prayer. He told about David's supernatural military achievements and mighty physical abilities. At first I thought that this line was what made his class so popular with the college athletes. Later I learned that President Carlson called him into his office to bawl him out for giving only 'A's to his students. Reusch's famous reply was, "I can't help it if you give me nothing but 'A' students!"

According to Hilding, Reusch was late for his first appearance as the speaker for required daily chapel because the former military officer stood at the entrance, holding the door for female students "who dribbled in slowly and late (as usual). He was a chain-smoker, like all the old soldiers I ever knew," Hilding recalled, "a short stocky man who did a lot of weight-lifting." In the company of a group of college football players, Reusch once paused in front of an automobile, gripped the bumper and straightened his knees. With the wheels off the ground, the professor of Christianity challenged the young men to do the same. Not one of the brawny young men could do it.[13]

CASTING A WIDER NET

Although furloughs were intended to provide rest from the rigors of the mission field, Dr. Reusch plunged into a whirlwind year of teaching, speaking and fund-raising throughout the American Midwest and Canada. The fall semester was barely underway when Reusch received a letter from the secretary at the Board of Foreign Missions, who scheduled his appearances. "Requests for you continue to 'storm' into our office," she wrote. He was to cancel a Denver speech until spring, but instead was to address a District Luther League Reformation Rally in the afternoon of October 26th, and a Lutheran Brotherhood Rally that evening.[14] So it went throughout the academic year.

He left a memorable impression wherever he went, and even Lutherans who had no prior interest in Africa enlisted in his cause. "I do not ask for the food from your table," he would conclude his epic narratives in a dramatic whisper, "but like Lazarus, for the sake of those whom Jesus loves, I ask only for a few of the *crumbs*."[15]

Those who heard him speak at Sunday morning worship services, special evening meetings, Women's Missionary Society rallies, Sunday schools, Luther League rallies, and convocations at colleges, universities and seminaries put more than crumbs in the offering plates. His effectiveness was such that the Church fathers considered keeping him in the United States longer than scheduled because no one had ever before generated such enthusiasm for missions. Seminarians and college students were caught by Dr. Reusch's vision, and some later followed him to Africa.[16] As a result of his visit to the East Coast in the autumn of 1947, Virginia Peterson of Middletown, Connecticut, felt called to foreign missions and was commissioned to serve as a nurse in Tanganyika. She left for Africa in September 1948.[17]

In the course of his travels Reusch perceived a tacit suspicion of missions and missionaries. As was his custom, he directly addressed the issue: "Is [foreign missions] really only a hobby in some pious circles?" His apologia for Christian missions comprised five reasons:

I. When governments become corrupt, patriots take action. "Christ saw all the immorality, corruptness and inequities" of his time, and took action to awaken the collective conscience of his people. Before returning "to HIS Heavenly Kingdom HE gave his disciples a Mission Commandment in Mt. 28: 19-20 (Mr. 16: 15; Lk. 24: 46-47; Acts 1: 8). This order was HIS last will and testament to HIS followers."

II. "Many say: 'Let us first clean our own house and then go to other countries.'" The first Christian congregation in Jerusalem opted for that course, "and they became weak and disappeared. Antioch followed the order of the LORD, and Europe became Christian! 'First our own home' brings riches, develops selfishness, self-centeredness, egotism and laziness . . . but brings no blessings, health or strength."

III. Foreign mission work is obedience to HIS last will and testament, and that is to bring the "supreme and eternal law of LOVE" to the world.

IV. As Tanganyika was a British Crown Colony, so "the Christian Church is a crown-colony of the eternal heavenly kingdom of CHRIST here on earth. Foreign mission work means to establish and enlarge this crown-colony of CHRIST in foreign countries because of the universal need of all mankind for salvation — for all have sinned and are under the suspended judgment of GOD (Rom. 3: 9-20).

V. Therefore, our endeavor comprises three parts: (1) preach and evangelize, (2) educate, and (3) heal. Whether preacher, teacher or nurse and physician, the missionary's task is "to preach HIM by one's life. That means to every worker: 'Your daily work must be a part of your daily worship!'"[18]

Dr. Reusch had become a minister of the Augustana Synod in 1938, and in the autumn of 1947 he was sworn as a citizen of the United States. After the ceremony the elderly federal judge asked Citizen Reusch about his life in Russia. At the end of the abbreviated tale that followed, the judge said to him, "May you be as loyal [to the United States] as you have been to your Emperor!"[19]

St. Paul's Evangelical Lutheran Church, St. Paul, Minnesota, celebrated its successful campaign to pay off its construction debt on the second Sunday of October 1947. Dr. Reusch was invited to give the sermon, and as might be expected he challenged the congregation to a greater commitment to foreign missions. It was, said a parishioner, "a gripping message."

During the potluck dinner that followed the service, Reusch happened to mention to Pastor Sunwall his need for a small tractor in Masailand. A few days later an anonymous check for $50 seeded the project as the St. Paul's Women's Missionary Society launched a fundraising campaign. Less than a month later Dr. Reusch was invited to return to St. Paul's, where he was presented with a Farmall tractor, the largest model made by the International Harvester Company at the time.[20]

In 1946 the Augustana Synod had issued a call for 150 new missionaries to be sent to foreign fields by the end of the decade. In response, student members of the campus Missionary Society at Augustana College in Rock Island, Illinois, convened a World Missions Institute intended to encourage students to volunteer. A second World Missions Institute was convened at Gustavus Adolphus College in February 1948. High school and college students from nineteen states and Canadian provinces jammed the St. Peter campus to meet and listen to veteran missionaries from Africa, India and China. Dr. and Mrs. Reusch, Dorothy Eckstrand, Rev. and Mrs. Melander, Dr. Bertil Friberg, Eleanor Lindbeck and Rev. Magney represented Africa.[21] Many of the college students and seminarians who later responded affirmatively to the Synod's call mention Dr. Reusch as an influence for decisions that changed their lives.

Elder Jackson was a seminarian in 1947 when Reusch came to speak at the Augustana Theological Seminary at Rock Island. After his ordination in 1948, Pastor and Mrs. Jackson left for Africa. Six years later, they would be assigned to Nkoaranga, the post that Dr. and Mrs. Reusch would have just vacated.[22] After a lifetime of service in East Africa, the Jacksons retired in 1984.

Eunice Nordby was about ten years old when she first met Dr. Reusch at a family wedding. "He was so dramatic, and so were his stories!" she recalled. "Even to me, a child, he clicked his heels and kissed my hand. Of all the children, he singled me out to come and see his African artifacts. I will never forget his intense dark eyes as he said, 'You, my child, will go to my Masai.'" She later married David Simonson, and when her husband encountered Reusch for the first time at Luther Seminary in St. Paul, the Masai Missionary gazed intently at the young man and declared, "You will be my replacement in Masailand."[23] Simonson said that he was already pointed in the direction of Tanganyika, but, he added, "I think the final lift came from Reusch. He just seemed consumed by his African experience. He certainly energized me in my goal to go to Africa as a missionary, and he did it in a way that no one else had. He was such an extraordinary guy. He made you feel you were there, or that you should be there. I thought of no place else after that."[24]

Stan Benson and Clarence Budke were students at Gustavus in 1947-48. Benson was a preacher's kid, related by marriage to Elveda Reusch; therefore, the subject of foreign missions was not unfamiliar. However, he was planning to become an educator, perhaps to do graduate work in soil science. Recalled Benson, "One day George Hall came up to Clarence and me and said, 'I want you to give two years of your lives to the Lord — we need volunteer missionaries in Tanganyika.'" After briefly considering the idea, Benson, Clarence and Ruth Budke and another Gustavus student, Adeline Lindquist, applied to the Board of Foreign Missions.

"Have you heard of Borneo?" they were asked at the interview. Influenced by Dr. and Mrs. Reusch, Benson had thought only of Tanganyika and the Masai.

"Borneo!" they exclaimed in surprise, and went directly to Dayton's Department Store in downtown Minneapolis to buy an atlas and learn where in the world they were going. All four were commissioned for service on the East Malaysian island. However, Benson and the Budkes were promised that when replacements became available they would be transferred to Tanganyika. Lindquist remained in Borneo, but in 1953 the other three were sent on to Tanganyika. Rev. Stan and Marie Benson lived among the Masai until their retirement in 1992.

FURLOUGH'S END

Each year one of the daily chapel services was dedicated to the memory of Sweden's King Gustav Adolph II. Asked to perform the annual ritual, Dr. Reusch exhorted the students to be proud of attending a college named in honor of such a great military leader and tactician. He described how the great king disappeared into a fog at Poltava "while wearing his gleaming steel armor — never to be seen again. But his troops had made the difference, and the Protestants were victorious. The truce line after that battle persists to this day, separating Catholics to the south and Protestants to the north."[25]

At the end of the spring semester, Dr. Reusch received an honorary Doctor of Divinity degree from Augustana Theological Seminary.[26] The president of the seminary and college at Rock Island, Dr. Conrad Bergendoff, was not about to miss an opportunity for his entire student body to hear Reusch, and invited the Masai Missionary to speak at a college-wide convocation prior to graduation.[27] In his letter of acceptance, Reusch added this curious final paragraph:

> I have some matters to discuss with you, because I feel that I might not see you again. This time it will become dangerous in Africa among the fierce Masai, and I have a feeling that I shall not get out of it [alive]. I would like you and friend [Rev.] Oscar [V. Anderson] to keep an eye on those who are preparing to continue my work and to direct their training.

Despite his disturbing (or calculated) intuition, Reusch was impatient to return to Masailand; but he remained in the United States longer than planned in order to fulfill the speaking schedule arranged for him by the Board of Foreign Missions.

At the end of August 1948, Reusch spoke at Grosvenor Dale, Connecticut. According to the church bulletin, Dr. Reusch "will return to Africa next month to the most dangerous tribe, the Masai. He is one of the best known missionaries in America."[28]

Reusch's new work would embrace 40,000 Masai who occupied 23,000 square miles of Tanganyika Territory. The Augustana Mission had been invited by Masai chiefs to establish evangelistic, educational and medical centers at Lendenai, Olkesement and Ruvu Remiti in the south, and Arash in the northwest. Pastor Lazarus Laiser, Evangelist Petro and missionaries Danielson and Bengtson visited Monduli, Oldeani, Mbulu, and Loliondo to plan for permanent stations in advance of Reusch's return.

Declared Elmer Danielson at the 1948 Mission Conference in Africa, "The development of these opportunities eagerly awaits the coming of Dr. Reusch."[29]

After their yearlong furlough in St. Peter, Elveda and Richard Reusch appear rested and ready to return to Africa by the summer of 1948.

CHAPTER 12

1   E. E. Ryden, "From Cossack to Missionary: A Story That Is Stranger Than Fiction," *Lutheran Companion*, vol. 55 (9 July 1947), 14.
2   "From Cossack to Missionary."
3   R. Reusch notes for his presentation to the Augustana Board of Foreign Missions, 9 July 1947, GACA.
4   The Braham [Minnesota] Evangelical Lutheran Church Sunday bulletin, 10 August 1947, GACA.
5   R. Reusch, sermon notes, Braham, Minnesota, 27 July 1947, GACA.
6   R. Reusch, "The young hostage who became the great Prophet Daniel," manuscript, undated (ca. 1947), GACA.
7   R. Reusch, sermon notes, Braham, 24 August 1947, GACA.
8   R. Reusch, "To find a Saviour," manuscript, undated (ca. 1947), GACA.
9   R. Reusch, sermon notes, undated (ca. August 1947), GACA.
10 Parishioners' letter, Lutheran Church, Braham, Minnesota, GACA.
11 Dale Bosch, "Richard Reusch Tales," 23 May 1995, GACA.
12 Ruth (Tolman) Helland, from the author's notes of an interview, 16 June 1999, and text of Reusch's lecture, which she saved along with her class notes.
13 David A. Hilding, letter forwarded to the author, 6 October 1997.
14 Helen, secretary, Augustana Board of Foreign Missions, letter to R. Reusch, 16 September 1947, GACA.
15 R. Reusch, various speech outlines and manuscripts, GACA.
16 Dennis Johnson, "Gustavus and Tanzania: A Tradition of Service and Love," *Gustavus Quarterly*, vol. 53, no. 4 (Summer, 1997), 12-13.
17 Fritz Soderberg, "The Lutheran Center at Webster, Mass.," clipping from the New England Conference newsletter, undated (ca. September 1948), GACA.
18 R. Reusch, "What is foreign mission work and why is it done?" undated manuscript (ca. 1947), GACA.
19 R. Reusch, undated sermon on Mark 7:31-37, describing his swearing in as an American citizen, and citizenship document, GACA.
20 S. Hjalmer Swanson, "A Tractor for the Masai," *Lutheran Companion*, vol. 56 (1 December 1948), 12-13.
21 "Challenged by Missionary Call: Youth of Synod Meet For Second Missions Conference, *Lutheran Companion*, vol. 56 (10 March 1948), 12-13.
22 Elder Jackson, from the author's notes of an interview, 16 February 1997.
23 Eunice Simonson, from the author's notes of an interview at Ilboro, Tanzania, 10 January 1996.
24 Simonson, quoted by Jim Klobuchar in *The Cross under the Acacia Tree* (Minneapolis: Kirk House Publishers, 1998), 22.
25 Hilding.
26 Hjalmar W. Johnson, Augustana College and Theological Seminary, letter to R. Reusch, 4 May 1948, GACA.
27 Conrad Bergendoff, President of Augustana College, letter to R. Reusch, 15 April 1948, GACA.
28 Church bulletin, Grosvenor Dale, Connecticut, 29 August 1948, GACA.

29 E. R. Danielson, "The Unevangelized Masai," 1948 *Minutes of the 26th Annual Conference, Augustana Lutheran Mission*, 72 (Box 324, World Missions/Tanzania/Augustana Minutes), AELC

Betty Anderson

The Son of Kibo outfitted himself when he climbed Kilimanjaro. In 1953, after his fiftieth ascent of Kibo Peak, British authorities named the crater for Reusch.

Chapter Thirteen

FOURTH AND FINAL TERM
Masailand, 1949-54

Now his stories are part of our country.
— Simon Palajo, Meru Elder[1]

"I hear that you are now back from America and that you are in the process of starting your work in Masailand," Acting Governor Bruce Hutt wrote from Government House in Dar es Salaam. "Please accept my best wishes for its success."[2] The Masai Missionary was gratified to have the confidence of Church officials and was honored when British authorities appointed him to the Masai Administrative Council.[3] He was so eager to begin his work that he moved only a few necessary household items from storage at Machame to his home at Nkoaranga. Then he left on one safari after another to the southern and northwestern regions of Masailand. Meanwhile, Elveda and their three daughters remained in the United States.

The National Lutheran Council's Commission on Younger Churches and Orphaned Missions (CYCOM), based in New York City, took over as the agency responsible for the Lutheran Mission in Northern Tanganyika in June 1949. Native church leaders requested that an international Lutheran missionary staff be recruited to serve the African Church,[4] and therefore Danes, Finns and Norwegians joined the Augustana and Swedish missionaries along with four Germans who were permitted to return in 1953. An international missionary staff was most agreeable to Reusch; but his time and energy were now devoted to the Masai.

The Leipzig missiologist, Bruno Gutmann, believed that people derive their identify from two sources: their nationality or ethnic group and religious affiliation. As Richard Pierard defined Gutmann's approach,

> The messenger must carefully ascertain the structural peculiarities of the ethnic group, penetrate the heathen order of life with the Christian ethos, and adapt the functional forms of the Christian congregation to the social situation. . . Thus, missionaries must orient their efforts toward establishing a peoples' church (*Volkskirche*) that is rooted within the nationality or folk character (*Volkstum*) and the cultural situation there.[5]

Applying the Gutmann model, Reusch searched for ways to adapt the language and context of the Gospel to the Masai worldview. He made his case in the 1946 annual report of the

Augustana Lutheran Mission: The Masai are proud of their language and customs, and they despise the Swahili language, *Enguduc olashumba*, the language of slaveholders and slaves. They are a tribe of born leaders who do not bow to other tribes; therefore, the way to bring the Son of God to them is to present a heroic Christ —

> HE, who could heal every sickness, who could quiet the raging sea and the storm, who could feed thousands with a few loaves and whose orders were obeyed by the evil spirits, HE who could have smashed the Roman troops with one word; but HE chose with HIS free will the way of suffering and death without being forced by anyone! — This heroic side they understand. Free will, self-sacrifice are something in their life and agree with their warrior-ideals.

Loyalty was ingrained in Reusch as an imperial cadet in his regiment, and that same sense of loyalty among the Masai is what attracted him to the tribe. For the Masai warriors, everything else was secondary, including money. Reusch recalled an incident at Engaruka in 1944 to illustrate his point:

> After hunting man-eating lions for two days and nights until we were completely exhausted, I asked Loikwasa, a young warrior who had killed 17 lions with his spear within 4 years: "Loikwasa, what do I owe you for your splendid work during these 2 days and nights?" He answered proudly: "Why do you speak of money? It was done out of friendship to you."

Reusch declared, "The whole Masai-speaking block must in the future be a unity of its own under *one* experienced leader. It should be a Church province by itself." Furthermore, the superintendent of the Masai field must have access to a discretionary budget so he could "act immediately according to the urgency of the situation."[6]

His proposal drew the ire of some of his fellow-missionaries because to them it was patently obvious that he was up to his old tricks: First, he had shamelessly inflated his credibility and applied his rhetorical skill to convince the Board of Foreign Missions to assign him to Masailand; second, as Mission Superintendent Danielson had reminded everyone, "The Northern Area is in a transitional period from a Mission-controlled work to a Native Church-directed work."[7] Despite the changing nature of foreign missions in the post-war period, the Imperial Cossack was proposing that he be put in charge of an independent mission with a discretionary budget. That threatened the development of an indigenous Church, since any discretionary funds would necessarily be siphoned from its meager resources.

Nevertheless, the Masai Missionary began his work at Arash in the northwestern Masai region. A medical missionary, Arthur Anderson, was stationed at Naverera in southern Masai country. Both stations had been closed during the mission crisis at the beginning of the Second World War. By August 1949 Reusch had revitalized the small congregation at Arash and had established a dispensary and a school.

Excerpts edited from
Arash, the Youngest Masai Station
By Dr. Richard Reusch

Arash is a hilly country 5 to 7,000 feet above sea level. It is partly covered by forest, but mostly by dense jungle inhabited by rhinos, lions, leopards, buffaloes, will pigs, baboons and many kinds of antelope and zebras. During the daytime it is very hot because Arash is only 100 miles south of the equator. From December until May it may rain at any time in heavy downpours. During the other six months there is no rain at all. Arash and the surrounding plains are inhabited mainly by the Masai, but there are also a few Wandorobo and Sonjo people.

In 1937 I obtained in Arash a plot of 15 acres, but since I joined the Augustana Mission in 1938 nothing was done at this isolated place 300 miles from Arusha, the nearest town.

The first question was, where to get drinking water. The springs were full of leeches. They stick in your throat and suck your blood. Well, the trousers were turned up, legs and arms rubbed with kerosene which protects against leeches, and into the water we went. Within 2 hours the rushes were cut down and a basin cleaned around the largest spring. We surrounded the basin by a stone wall and built a second basin a little lower for bathing purposes. Next morning both basins were full of pure clear water, and good water it was.

We made hot tea, but when my driver lifted his cup to his mouth a thunderous roar filled the air. He dropped his cup. *"Olng'atuny!"* A lion. I ran back to the truck for my rifle. Again a roar, this time closer to our new well. After 50 minutes or so he decided to go to hunt and left us in peace for the rest of the night. We began feverishly to build a thorn-enclosure. It was not easy in the pitch-dark night, a lion still roaring in the neighborhood. The enclosure was not yet ready when a snorting sound announced that a rhino was close. Those rhinos with their thick skin are dangerous fellows. They are not afraid even of fire. Only 3-4 days earlier when I visited with a Masai Chief a rhino almost turned over our truck. The remainder of the night was quiet, except for the angry spitting of some leopards. The skin of one of them, which I brought home, was 8 feet long.

I decided to build our Arash hospital of stones. From a nearby rocky hill we started to break stones. During the following days arrived by foot 10 Sonjo men sent to help us.

Seeing that nothing helped to make them work quickly, I promised everybody 2 yards of cloth and as much tobacco as they could consume. That worked wonders! Every Sonjo man smokes, snuffs and chews tobacco since time immemorial. To come back to Sonjoland with cloth, which only the Chiefs have, and tobacco! They worked like troopers. I went to Loliondo to obtain the cloth and the tobacco — and it was some tobacco, dear friends! I tried it in my pipe, but in no time my head and stomach became bedeviled for 16 hours!

The chief sorcerer of Arash, afraid to lose his influence, was very hostile. To every one of my proposals, i.e., to build a school, a hospital, to plant fields, to build a dam for artificial irrigation, he replied, "*Mayeu!* " (I do not want it!) But after he saw our new well from which the Masai were welcome to take as much water as they needed, and after I treated his leg, he brought a sheep and made a friendship pact with me. For a number of days I was afraid that he might poison me or my men as his colleagues had poisoned me 3 times in 1923. They are masters in poisoning, those "Medicine-men"!

The work was not only heavy, but it was dangerous. Often, turning over a stone one found under it an angry snake or scorpions up to 8 inches long. When the buildings were ready, we planted a field of corn, beans, onions and potatoes, surrounding it with a high thorn-enclosure. I left a caretaker in Arash and went to Loliondo to build a house for my evangelist there.

Today it looks like a dream to me. In less than two months, 2 houses of tree trunks for the natives and a large stone hospital were finished. Now the Masai want a school, and to make cornfields. For over two months I did not see a crust of bread. In April when I returned to Arusha, I weighed only 108 pounds. But the work was done, and that's the main thing. At the beginning of July I hope to be back there to build a stone school and to place there a good dresser.[8]

In September 1949 a typhoid epidemic broke out in the region, and Reusch rushed to Loliondo to notify the District Officer. A plea for typhoid vaccine was sent by radio to Nairobi, and a week later a truck arrived with the medicine. Twenty days later the epidemic subsided. However, according to Reusch:

> Due to the lack of rain there was no grass in the plains and the Masai drove thousands of their cattle to the Arash River. Dozens of lions, leopards and hundreds of hyenas followed them. From the middle of August on, every day cattle or donkeys were killed and every week some men wounded or killed by lions. The wounded men were brought to our hospital with ghastly wounds. Some died and some recovered as cripples.
>
> But the lions continued their bloody work. The number of wounded increased. Therefore Mr. Stephenson [the British District Officer] gave me a special permit to kill the man-eaters, for it is a "closed area" or game reserve. Handing the permit over to me, my friend said, "Do not count every killed lion. Count only as many as are on the permit, namely four!" Therefore, I counted only four officially, but eleven man-eaters are dead. Hyenas, which attack the children, I killed by the dozens. When my Mauser bullets were finished, I used the splendid shotgun given to me by First Lutheran Church at Worthington, Minnesota. It killed three lions and many hyenas. I do not have sufficient words to thank this congregation for its present. It was a useful present for a Masai missionary.
>
> There was once a cavalry regiment about which it was said that it took its booty from between the horns of satan [sic]. Should the last of this regiment not take the booty of his Lord from between the same horns?[9]

When he went to retrieve two wounded lion-fighting warriors from Olgeju ol-Duka, one with a broken back, Dr. Reusch found starving Masai eating bark from trees. He again called upon District Officer Stephenson for assistance, and as a result 30 tons of corn flour was dispatched from Nairobi.[10] The dry season of 1949 was the worst that Missionary V. Eugene Johnson had witnessed since he had come to Africa in 1928. People coming for treatment at the mission hospitals were so under-nourished that he found it "exceedingly difficult if not impossible to give them any real help." The local chief at Iambi reported that more than 300 people had starved to death. As if to make up for the drought, the December rains came in torrents.[11]

JOURNEY TO EAST AFRICA

In 1949 there were no economical transatlantic flights from New York to Kilimanjaro via Europe. Instead, having reached London by ship after a week or more, a missionary could be stranded for weeks waiting for a cargo vessel bound for Africa. In Capetown, one had to look for a local freighter and then slowly sail around the Cape of Good Hope and up the east coast of the continent. One such outbound journey in the 1920s consumed six months of the missionary's first term.

In September 1949 Elveda Reusch booked passage on the *S. S. African Star*, a cargo ship bound from New York to Durban, South Africa. Her daughters were settled for the school year — Dagmar enrolled at St. Peter High School, Betty at Gustavus Adolphus College, and Ingrid in nurses training at Lutheran Hospital in Moline, Illinois.[12] Elveda was reluctant to leave her daughters, but on Tuesday, September 27, the Missionary Mom left Mankato, Minnesota by train for New York City.

The ship sailed at 11:00 a.m. on Sunday, October 1st. Mrs. Reusch was pleased to meet her cabin mate, Catherine Steed, an opera singer who was a frequent guest on network radio programs. The women became good friends during the voyage. But late on her first night at sea, Elveda wrote in her diary, the *African Star* ran into heavy seas, and the passengers and crew experienced "terrible rolling, pitching, howling of wind." Elveda couldn't sleep. On the third day the ship rolled sharply, and she was thrown from her chair, injuring her left knee.

On Sunday, the 9th of October, she wrote in her diary, "Missed the family terribly today. Felt very lonely." She wrote the same words again the following day.

On October 18th, on the eve of their arrival in Capetown, Captain Wainewright hosted a cocktail party for the passengers. Elveda noted with some embarrassment, "Each received a gift — a pack of playing cards!" The *African Star* reached Capetown the next day, and Mrs. Reusch and Mrs. Steed had lunch on shore. The ship departed for Port Elizabeth late the next afternoon, but a gale overtook them that evening and the captain had to drop anchor in heavy seas outside the harbor. The anchor would not hold, and "by 8:00 p.m. the wind had pulled us out to sea, and for the next three hours the crew worked to secure the anchor firmly enough to keep us in place." She did not fall asleep until morning.

They passed around the Horn of Africa, and at Port Elizabeth the ship had to wait for railroad cars to arrive before workers unloaded unassembled American automobiles Ford, General Motors and Studebaker. On the evening of the 24th the second mate invited Elveda and Catherine ashore to the Officers Club. Elveda declined "with thanks," and after hearing Mrs. Steed's account of the affair was "thankful I did not go." The next day Elveda did go with Mrs. Steed into town to see a movie at the Embassy Theatre that starred Rosalind Russell. "You can get away with anything," said the advertisements, "if you've got *The Velvet Touch*." The next afternoon she and her cabin mate went to visit a snake farm and insect museum.

Storms followed their route and prevented a scheduled landing at East London. Five weeks after leaving New York the ship finally docked at Durban, South Africa. After bidding farewell to Mrs. Steed, Elveda bought a ticket from Durban to Mombassa on the *S.S. Karanja*. The vessel was scheduled to sail two days later, and so Elveda decided to visit a nearby Zulu reserve. She was appalled to see that the Zulu had "certainly been given the poorest land."

The *Karanja* did not sail until noon on November 5th. Mahatma Gandhi's son was aboard, but Mrs. Reusch did not meet him since he traveled first class. The ship stopped at Mozambique to take on gravel, nuts and maize.

After seven weeks at sea, and with Tanganyika Territory close at hand, Elveda declared that she was "really tired of the ocean voyage." On Wednesday, November 16, 1949, at 9:15 in the morning, the *Karanja* docked at Mombassa. Her safari of forty-nine days was not over, however.

Richard had come by truck to Mombassa, but he sent an Indian driver to fetch his wife from the harbor while he loaded building materials. Two days later the truck rolled into Nkoaranga. "Happy to be at journey's end," Elveda wrote, "but oh, what must be done before this house is clean!"

A few days later she was off to Machame to collect more of the stored household items. "Blue, sad and heavy-hearted," she unloaded the truck and "chucked everything in the centerbackroom — a mess." On Thanksgiving Day she "rearranged the bedroom, moved in the wardrobe so I could hang up a few dresses," and plastered the pantry.[13]

Through the months of November and December 1949, Elveda accompanied her husband on journeys to Masailand whenever possible. Like him, she was a good traveler and was happiest when on safari. She was disappointed when she had to stay home and bake communion wafers, do the monthly accounts, or entertain visitors. In her husband's absence, she took out her knitting materials each evening after supper to work on a sweater, her Christmas present for him.

Elveda looked forward to the occasional mail deliveries in hope of a letter from any one of her daughters. Without the company of their children, the joyous season did not seem like Christmas. "Our thoughts are mostly across the waters," the mother lamented. "May God bless the children."

After the forlorn couple opened their few presents on Christmas Eve, Elveda wrote in her diary, "R[ichard] not pleased with sweater. Wants bullets."

ADVENTURES IN MASAILAND

Losinyari Metili had just graduated from Marangu Teachers College when in 1950 Reusch tapped him for a teaching job at Arash. "I have a house and a school for you," Reusch told him. Said Metili,

> On Monday morning he came to pick me up in his Bedford lorry, loaded with concrete and iron. When we arrived there [Arash], Reusch pointed to a tree and said, "Begin your classes over there, in the shade." There was no house. There was no school. But there was a house and a school when he left a few days later. He never rested. He was a good contractor, and kept the builders busy, I can tell you!

The retired teacher also confirmed the nature of the relationship between Reusch and the Masai:

> Sometimes if he was in Arusha for a few days the Masai would send warriors to see if he was all right. He didn't bring a tent to sleep by himself in Masai country, but slept in a boma hut. He lived with them, eating roast meat, drinking milk, even fresh blood from the neck of a cow. When he was thirsty he drank at the potholes where the people, animals and birds also came. No other white man lived this way.[14]

Metili and the Masai did not know that when Reusch returned from those safaris he was often sick for days, even months.[15]

Under the headline, "I Loaded My Shotgun," *Time* magazine profiled the Masai Missionary in its October 2, 1950 issue as a man who had chosen "to work among one of the fiercest tribes in Africa — the blood-drinking, spear-wielding Masai." Reusch was quoted as saying,

> I had come to Longido in the Masai Plains to baptize some adults. The chapel was small and the Christians, the baptismal candidates and many others gathered under the trees. Suddenly during the sermon the Masai chief and his warriors began to come in groups. Within ten minutes our assembly was surrounded by a ring of fully armed warriors looking irritated and with a strange light in their eyes. It seemed apparent that they had come to make trouble. But we were allowed to finish our service unmolested.
>
> Then a few minutes later there was a roar. One of the warriors wanted to spear a father whose son was enrolled at our school. In a few moments the spear was wrested out of the hands of the attacker. Again everything became quiet and everyone, including the attacker, went to eat and drink tea. Until late in the night Christians and pagans ate, drank tea and sang.
>
> Expecting trouble during the night, I loaded my shotgun with small shot. But nothing happened. Only the hyenas roared and the jackals barked hoarsely over the remnant of the festive meal.
>
> Early next morning I heard a knock at my door. I opened, and there was the chief with his elders and a number of warriors. We exchanged greetings and I invited them to

sit down. The weather conditions, the health of the cattle, the condition of the pastures were talked over. The chief was visibly uneasy. The others were also. Quite suddenly, almost abruptly, the following conversation took place.

"Did you know that we speared a government official two years ago at Narok?"

"Yes, I know it."

"Are you aware that we could spear your people even today?"

"Yes, I know it and I expected a spear between my ribs yesterday, especially when I was baptizing your young men."

"What would you have done in such a case?"

"During the service I would have done nothing and would have forgiven those who had speared me."

"Hm,hm, but afterwards?"

"To be frank, chief, if you had speared one of those whom I had baptized, I would have taken this gun and would have fired without mercy all the cartridges of this belt into your crowd."

"Hm, hm, are there bullets in your gun?"

"No, chief, only buckshot and small shot, the kind I use on hyenas."

"The kind you use on hyenas! Why?"

"Because I would have enjoyed letting the aggressors suffer as the hyenas whom I kill to protect your children and goats."[16]

Stanley Benson

Missionaries Clarence Budke, Stan Benson, Richard Reusch, Loikwasa, a Masai tribesman, and one of eleven marauding lions that Reusch shot during his last term in Tanganyika.

Reusch's armaments included three rifles, two shotguns, and two revolvers, a Mauser and Colt.[17] The 16-gauge shotgun that Reusch threatened to use at Longido was a gift from First Lutheran Church at Worthington, Minnesota. After reading about Reusch's appreciation for the gift, First Lutheran's young people set about raising $2,200 to purchase a Jeep station wagon.[18] In St. Peter, students at Gustavus Adolphus College, motivated by "the impact of that powerful missionary to the Masai in Africa," raised $1,500 to support missionary Daniel Friberg, a Gustavus alumnus. They also met to pray for foreign missionaries and visited congregations throughout the Midwest to increase support for global missions.[19]

The tractor provided by St. Paul's Lutheran Church was used at the Makumira coffee plantation for the first year, at the end of which Reusch sent the congregation six 2 lb. bags of roasted coffee beans. The enthusiastic parish then decided to raise money for a needed structure at the Singida mission in southern Tanganyika.[20]

In the words of George Hall, Dr. Reusch had "saved the whole work of the mission during World War II and laid the foundations for the Lutheran Church of Northern Tanganyika in its Constitution, Charter and education of clergy."[21] In 1951 Dr. Reusch was asked again to take over as superintendent of the Northern Area — in addition to his work in Masailand. He did so with characteristic vision and vigor.

Donald C. Flatt, an Oxford University graduate and cousin of Governor Twining, came to Tanganyika as a colonial education specialist. While there, however, he came to doubt that the British Government's secular education system could bring about the desired civil outcomes, so he left the colonial service to become an Augustana missionary. At Superintendent Reusch's request, Flatt outlined the staffing needs for the Marangu Teachers College and the Ashira Girls School. As requested, he also estimated both the cost of operating a primary school system that served 15,000 pupils and for opening and operating four new middle schools. But funds with which to maintain the present system were not forthcoming, much less Reusch's ambitious plan for expansion. The Englishman wrote an impassioned letter to his boss:

> We, under the care of the Lutheran Churches of the great U.S.A., deputized by the whole Lutheran world, live from hand to mouth, beg from pillar to post, and create wonder and amazement in the hearts of those who, not unnaturally, regard the U.S.A. as the greatest nation on earth and capable of working miracles if it sets its heart on any job. . . May we expect to have the policy problems solved and get help this year, or do we start lightening the ship to avoid sinking?[22]

Reusch immediately fired off a letter to the chairman of CYCOM:

> I am left single-handed to be the Superintendent of the Masai work and the manager of three coffee estates. Our youth work must be built up and the bush school system with their 15,000 students must be organized to become a feeder for our advanced schools. How can I do it with only one young and inexperienced Mission-Pastor is a puzzle to me. Be assured that every one of us here on the field will do his duty to the last, but there is a limit to human endurance and strength. If the handful of workers on this field

will eventually break down under the strain of the work, I am asking that I may not be blamed for it.[23]

Stan Benson and Clarence Budke had been influenced by Dr. Reusch while students at Gustavus in 1947-48 to serve in Tanganyika in July 1951, but the Board of Foreign Missions diverted them to Borneo instead. Reusch raised such a ruckus that the missionaries were quickly transferred to Africa.[24] "May I say," marveled Arthur Anderson, "that God is using [Dr. Reusch] in a wonderful way."[25]

Meanwhile, Mrs. Reusch was on call day and night as the obstetrics nurse at Nkoaranga hospital and was summoned to deal with medical emergencies of all kinds.

'Unto the Least of These'
By Elveda Reusch

On March 13th a bit of barely living humanity was prematurely born into this world in the Nkoaranga Maternity room. For a while it seemed doubtful that it would live, but by God's grace it did. Its mother was lying nearby, unconscious and in almost continuous convulsions due to Cerebral Malaria. There was no recourse than to take the little one into our home for there are here as yet no hospital facilities for the care of such little ones.

Ngatareto, the younger sister of the baby's father and its future foster-mother, has come into our home to learn how to give the little one proper care. She loves the little one dearly and is proud of her share in its care as he makes progress.[26]

While Reusch worked to reform the mission's educational system and cajole increased support from CYCOM, the established African congregations did their part by sending volunteers to Masailand, including the villages of Lendenai and Engasumet. They also established new Lutheran missions, schools and dispensaries throughout the Northern Area. The Chagga sent evangelists to the Sonjo tribe, and Iramba evangelists worked among the Turu.[27] An indigenous African Church had taken root.

"PAPAL HORDES"

Interdenominational rivalry characterized mission work in East Africa from the beginning. The various Christian missions jealously guarded their territories and were alarmed when another denomination dared to intrude. At the same time, when missionaries of any denomination experienced trouble on a safari they could always count on assistance and hospitality from missionaries of other denominations. Although Reusch on occasion publicly raged against Roman Catholics, he relished spending an evening discussing ancient history and philosophy with visiting Jesuits or White Fathers. But Lutherans in Tanganyika remained on guard against their historical nemesis, and the rhetoric on both sides could be vicious. "The abysmal depths of proselytizing to which the papal horde has fallen is appalling," one missionary wrote in 1947:

> On the former German mission fields the Catholics are capitalizing on the marriage problem. Due to a disproportion of more [African] women than men, many young women can find no husbands. The Catholics promise to give husbands to our Christian girls if they will join the Roman fold. It has proven an irresistible inducement to many, much to the loss of the Church and the individuals concerned.[28]

Chief Davidi, who had been restored to health at a Lutheran medical clinic and converted to the Protestant faith, built a Lutheran church and promised to build a school and dispensary. However, reported a Lutheran missionary in 1948, one of his sons who had attended a Catholic school met two Lutheran missionaries one day and insisted that they were not saved because they were Lutherans. "Let us pray for this son," the missionary urged, "that the Lord may open his eyes to see that Jesus is the Way, the Truth and the Life and that through faith in Him alone we are saved and not through the Catholic Church."[29]

Fifty years later, however, there was a consensus among the Lutherans in Tanzania, black and white, that the Vatican Councils of Pope John XXIII had radically changed the adversarial relationship of former years. "It was like a window had opened and all the bad air inside a closed room suddenly vanished," said Rev. Stan Benson. "In fact," he added, "afterwards there was a better relationship between us and the Catholics than between us and some Protestants. We work together now through the Tanzanian Christian Medical Association, and even train our Catechists together."[30]

An African evangelist at Mwika understood the issue from a different point of view: "Why should the religious wars of Europe be fought also in Africa?" However, the African quickly posed a direct question to his American visitor: "You *are* a Lutheran, aren't you?"[31] Some measure of the legacy inherited from the European Reformation was, apparently, transferred to Africa.

CULTURAL BARRIERS

Foreign missionaries were bearers not only of the Gospel but also of their distinctive ethnic, denominational and national cultures. So potent are some of those subtle cultural differences that even Lutherans of differing ethnic and national identities could not work harmoniously together. The majority of Americans volunteered because of a complex set of motives, most often explained publicly as obedience to Christ's command "to bring the Gospel to the uttermost parts of the earth." Only in some cases did a hunger to bring social justice figure as a substantial part of their call.

Missionaries survived on a pittance, but they dressed and ate better than their African neighbors. Although their habits of hygiene, food handling, and health care improved the quality of life, the missionaries' culture nevertheless separated them not only from their German peers but also from the people they had come to serve.

John E. Hult, M.D., the son of the first Augustana missionaries to arrive in 1921, practiced as a medical doctor in Tanganyika from 1954 to 1961. For him, even a four-year term was too short a time to become familiar with the complexities of a culture so different from his:

> "Our veteran missionaries told us that even after twenty or thirty years they were just beginning to be sensitive to subtle cultural differences. I was able to speak some Swahili, but not the various tribal languages. For these reasons, many of the things I write in my accounts are subject to cross-cultural misinterpretations."[32]

New recruits suffered from culture shock in the months following their arrival in Africa, but their letters and articles published in church publications seldom reflected the disorientation and loneliness they suffered. The Augustana missionaries were steadfast, however. Only 13 percent of 119 Augustana missionaries who came to Tanganyika between 1923 and 1954 went home before the end of their first term; 31 percent served from five to ten years; 28 percent, eleven to twenty years; and 28 percent, almost a third, invested the greater part of their careers in Tanganyika — from twenty-one to forty-five years in mission service.[33] They were a most hardy, adventurous and adaptable group of Americans.

If they recognized their cultural biases that affected their relationships with Africans, it is not apparent in their letters home until the years just prior to the Second World War when the Africans' desire for freedom — political and religious — became a force that could be ignored no longer. According to a radical African, "When we picture the devil, we want to paint him white, for all whites are devils."[34] The vice-president of the Lutheran Foreign Missions Conference warned in 1935,

> One cannot but notice the radical, even revolutionary changes that have taken place in the foreign field and at the home base in the past two decades. The tremendous changes in the Orient and Africa politically and socially, have been matched by a corresponding change in the attitude of the Occident toward Christian missions. . . . The change is observed also in the attitude of the non-Christian to the missionary message, and in the attitude of the native Christian to the missionary himself. The rising tide of nationalism makes it very difficult for Asia and Africa to accept any advice or help of any kind from the missionary, no matter how desperately they may need him.[35]

Mission Superintendent Elmer Danielson served in Africa from 1928 until 1969. Over the decades he championed the development of an indigenous African Church, challenged the racial attitudes of his Augustana Synod in America, and reminded its missionaries that they must work themselves out of their jobs. Because of Danielson's vision and leadership, the Augustana

Mission and its American Synod stood shoulder to shoulder with Africans who fought for equality, justice and Tanganyikan independence. That story is a remarkable and unusual chapter in mission history.

"To be 'sent' by Jesus Christ thousands of miles from home to a people who are different from ourselves is a very rare privilege which Jesus has not granted to very many," Danielson reminded his constituencies in his 1952 annual report. "While in Africa we are propelled in our lives and work by this consciousness, that Jesus has 'sent' us. We have no other right to be here."

However, he cautioned,

> The missionary has to be a prophet today in that he seeks to understand the present situation of the African in order to relate God's Word to the people's needs and hopes. The Africans, including the African Christians, are in a melting-pot of revolutionary forces which have been pressing upon him from all sides without his invitation. . . . Foreign education, commerce, government, literature, money, industry, travel, European population, Indian population, land problems and other forces penetrating from other parts of the world of which the African is more and more conscious has thrown the African mind and soul into a state of uncertainty, insecurity, restlessness and also growing dissatisfaction.

Rev. C. Walden Hedman, who arrived at the Bumbuli station in 1946, was quick to sense the race factor. He had ordered two books for one of the African teachers, one entitled *The Color Bar in South Africa*. The title shocked him. As he pondered the words, he was reminded of the biblical promise that one day "every tribe and tongue and people and nation would one day gather at the great banquet of the Lamb." Hedman had to admit that the same racism that tortured America — that "wedge of Satan" — was also present in Tanganyika:

> I was aware of it last week as I sat for tea and our noon meal in the home of one of the native evangelists. There in the mud hut we had a delicious meal of rice and broth. But the host realized as well as I that there were barriers between us. He did his best to serve well and to serve the best. Yet, were it not for the grace of God, our mutual joy and fellowship would have been marred.[36]

In 1952, Danielson warned that changing times made it all the more necessary for the missionaries to search their own hearts. He urged them to root out any lingering attitudes of racial superiority:

> There is one danger we confront in our inner life. It is perhaps easier for the missionary to see the sins of the African Christians, particularly such as drinking, stealing, adultery, lying and other grosser sins. And it is easier perhaps for the African to see the sins of the missionary such as racial pride and superiority, unholy anger and impatience, lack of courtesy and understanding, love of self and things and a kind of legalistic Europeanism to which we are accustomed and which we are apt to blindly mistake for New Testament Christianity.[37]

Reusch did not think that the African Church was quite ready for independence, an organic process of evolution that could not be hurried. At the Mission's annual meeting in 1952, Northern Area Superintendent Reusch outlined four stages in the development of the indigenous African Church, and a fifth yet to be realized:

Patriarchal, 1893-1913: the missionary is builder, teacher, evangelist, pastor, and medical aide;

Pastoral, 1913-1927: the missionaries shepherd congregations and train native teachers, evangelists and medical assistants;

Parish, 1927-1942: native pastors, under the direction of missionaries, take over as shepherds of the congregations; hospitals are built, and the educational system is expanded to include schools for girls;

Emerging Church, 1942-1952: African leadership increases, and self-governance develops under a Church constitution; secondary schools and a seminary are established;

Independence, "not yet reached:" when the African Church is fully self-supporting and self-governing.[38]

But as the African Church moves toward independence, "Let us not mix these two [Masai and non-Masai] fields, both of them in a different stage of development," Reusch pleaded. "What is good for stage four may even become dangerous for the development of the new field during its transition from stage one to stage two." But the superintendent was maneuvering for political advantage, believing that the Masai work would suffer under the control of an independent African Church dominated by the powerful and sophisticated Chagga leadership. The Masai field had from the very beginning "subsisted on what was left over on the old field," and as "a mere appendage, we [the Masai missions] shall always be outvoted when staffing questions will come up."[39] Politics played as fundamental a role in church affairs as in matters of state.

Reusch confidently advocated separation of the Masai field from the established African Church because of his previous success in recruiting missionaries and raising funds in the United States. "As an independent unit our position will be different," he explained, because the Masai Mission would then recruit its own volunteers. Therefore, "[I]t must become administratively and financially an independent unit."[40] However, Reusch failed to gain the support of either Danielson in Africa or the Board of Foreign Missions in Minneapolis.

At the same time, the development of an independent African Church was important to Reusch. In a confidential memorandum to Dr. Arvid Bäfverfeldt, the Church of Sweden's Mission director, Reusch argued for tribal Lutheran synods united under a common constitution. The effect, he claimed, would awaken "the interest of native Christians for 'their Church'" because "for the African 'our Church' is little different from 'our Mission.'"[41]

The evolutionary process leading to religious independence was one familiar to most Augustana missionaries because it was similar to the experience of their immigrant forebears in America, who were initially nurtured in mission congregations, became self-supporting and later built educational institutions, hospitals and seminaries. Reusch, however, was far more cautious. "It is of no use and even dangerous" to artificially accelerate the process of making the African Church independent. "Until the right time has come, there will always be needed a white superintendent, education secretary, heads of institutions and heads of the different branches of the rapidly growing work."[42]

But who would determine when the right time had come? That was the question that troubled Tanganyikan church leaders. Some Africans and missionaries interpreted Reusch's statement as paternalistic, others as self-serving, intended to protect his own role as head of an independent Masai mission.

GOVERNMENT'S RESPONSE TO SOCIAL CHANGE

Racism was inherent to the colonial system and had always been apparent to Africans, if not to missionaries. But in the post-war years it became an issue with which the Colonial Office in London was also forced to contend. To that end, a special conference was convened at Cambridge University during the summer of 1947. Subsequently, in a confidential letter to the governors of all the British African territories (Nigeria, Gold Coast, Sierra Leone, The Gambia, Kenya, Uganda, Tanganyika, Northern Rhodesia, Nyasaland and Zanzibar), Colonial Secretary A. Creech Jones directed that the conference summary report "be adopted as a general basis of policy on this difficult subject."[43]

"Ultimately government depends on the consent and goodwill of the governed," said the report.[44] "The best possible personal relationships will not be enough to hold together men of different races if a serious political division draws them apart." The report noted that it is easier to describe the problem than to suggest solutions because the only real answer to the problem "is a growth in human wisdom."

There were, however, initiatives that the Government must pursue: the adjustment of civil service salary inequities between Europeans and Africans; active recruitment, training and promotion of Africans; and to allow and encourage the governed to participate in public affairs. It was also necessary to examine statute books and amend laws that discriminate between the races; address racial discrimination in clubs, hotels and railways, "particularly as we believe that events in India can teach us lessons about the danger of ignoring it"; ameliorate poverty, which breeds discontent; and persuade "public opinion to necessary reforms."

The report encouraged each colonial administrator to meet the rising force of nationalism "not with hostility, but with understanding . . . and by showing sympathetic understanding of the [younger and educated] peoples' political aspirations." The report concluded,

> It is this politically minded class who will take the lead in the movement known as African Nationalism, a most powerful force which cannot be ignored, and which cannot be met simply by defensive measures or by an attempt to "put on the brake." If it is allowed to become embittered it could easily be fanned by politicians into a violent racial antagonism which will upset all our efforts in local government and in every other field.[45]

The colonial secretary requested that each governor present "a review of the situation as regards race relations in the territory under your administration and of the action being taken" by the end of the following year.

Despite the insight contained in the report, the mills of social change ground slowly — so slowly and blindly, in fact, that the bloody Mau Mau rebellion and tragic Meru Land Case would speed the lowering of the Union Jack over East Africa. Both the British Colonial Government and the Lutheran Mission had stated from the beginning that their objectives were to prepare Africans for independence.[46] The British administration in Tanganyika Territory was far more progressive than some other European colonial governments, including the British administration of Kenya. However, their response to independence-minded young Africans exposed the taproot of imperial tradition that remained embedded in colonial tradition. Because of Danielson's wisdom and leadership, the Lutheran Church became a champion of African independence.

MISSION POLITICS

In 1948 Dr. S. Hjalmer Swanson, executive secretary of the Augustana Board of Foreign Missions, had asked the National Lutheran Council to guarantee sponsorship of the former German fields "for an extended period with a budget which will meet the natural development and growth." It was doubtful that the British would allow the German missionaries to return to Tanganyika, Swanson reasoned, and he knew that the Augustana Synod could not provide enough recruits to properly staff the fields.[47]

In January 1952 a Colonial Office despatch ordered "a relaxation of the present policy governing the admission of Germans into the overseas territories" — with the exception of the German missionaries.[48] Ten months later, after a flurry of exchanges between London and the National Lutheran Council in New York, the German exclusion was modified: "In view of the conduct of the German Lutheran Mission in the years immediately preceding the last war, none of the persons now to be admitted should have formerly lived or worked in Tanganyika."[49]

When nine German Roman Catholic nuns were permitted to return, the Lutherans were quick to complain of unfair treatment. And because of their personnel shortage, the Americans pleaded with the Colonial Office to consider twelve German visa applications.[50] In the case of Johannes Buchta, M.D., Schiotz explained that the physician's return was requested by the vice-president of the African Lutheran Church, Rev. Lazarus Laiser, and African leaders. "I know that Dr. Reusch has a high regard for Dr. Buchta," Schiotz added, "and would gladly endorse an application to have him admitted for work in Tanganyika."[51] In January 1953 four German Lutheran missionaries were allowed to return: a farm manager, two physicians and one deaconess. "So far as Dr. Buchta is concerned," the Colonial Office declared, "his membership of the Nazi Party completely ruled him out."[52]

Harried civil servants at the Colonial Office found consensus difficult to achieve on the German issue, in part because of the pall cast by the Depersdorf case, the most odious case of German Lutheran complicity on behalf of the Nazi cause in Tanganyika. Rev. Depersdorf served the Berlin Mission's parish at Dar es Salaam in the 1930s. The African Secretary of the Berlin Mission visited Dar es Salaam in 1937 "and by personal instruction forbad all [its] missionaries to become [Nazi] Party members or to accept any office." Depersdorf gave up his party membership. However, in 1939 agents of the British Intelligence and Security Bureau found a picture frame on church premises containing a representation of Jesus on one side and a photograph of Adolph Hitler on the other. Depersdorf was immediately interned and in 1940 returned to Germany. To its credit, the Berlin Mission Society promptly struck his name from their roster.[53]

Depersdorf was an abomination. However, the Colonial Office recognized that not all German Lutheran missionaries had been Nazis. "Go slowly," Mr. Page-Jones wrote in his notes. After those who have returned prove themselves others may be admitted. The German Missions file was stamped, "Closed. No further action to be taken."[54]

East African Images on the Big Screen

Hollywood came to East Africa in the early 1950s to make several major motion pictures. Katherine Hepburn and Humphrey Bogart, directed by John Huston, tramped through Kenya, the Belgian Congo and Tanganyika to make *The African Queen* (1951). Gregory Peck, Ava Gardner and Susan Hayward made *The Snows of Kilimanjaro* (1952) in Tanganyika. Ava Gardner's second shoot in East Africa paired her with Grace Kelly, and their two characters vied for the favor of a big game hunter played by Clark Gable in John Ford's *Mogambo* (1953). "This lousy place, this Dark Continent," she grumbled.

Sidney Poitier starred in *Cry, the Beloved Country* (1952), based on Alan Paton's novel about apartheid in South Africa. Of the lot, it was the only motion picture to deal seriously with contemporary Africa.

Metro-Goldwyn-Mayer shot *King Solomon's Mines* (1950) in Uganda, Kenya, Tanganyika, and the Belgian Congo, starring Deborah Kerr, Stuart Granger and Richard Carlson. The production staff also located a village near Arusha inhabited by relatives of the Masai that suited their imagination. Several hundred warriors were hired to charge past the cameras in pursuit of the white heroes, Carlson noted, "just as Hollywood Indians have chased good cowboys in numberless Westerns." While the company was encamped near Arusha, the *East African Standard* published a story about a streetcar conductor in the American South who had shot a black man for refusing to abide by Jim Crow laws. Said Carlson, "We were acutely embarrassed and hard put to convince our African friends that this was not a daily occurrence in America."[55]

The moviemakers monopolized the gossip of the entire Kilimanjaro area, and crowds gathered to watch them work. On Friday morning, January 6, 1949, Richard was off to Longido before the morning Epiphany service at Nkoaranga, but that afternoon Elveda and another missionary couple walked the four miles to the location shoot and joined the hangers-on.[56] Almost two years later she saw the Technicolor production on the screen in Arusha. She mentioned nothing about the movie, however. All she noted in her diary was that she "had a bad time getting into town because of mud." [57]

HONORS

The colonial administration in Tanganyika trusted and valued Dr. Reusch's loyalty and expertise. Not only did he serve on the government's Masai Advisory Council, but he was also named to serve on the committee charged with the task of describing Masai grammar. The East African Literature Bureau coordinated the translation of educational materials into the Masai language (Reusch was in charge of producing the Ki-Masai Primer), and an interdenominational committee was at work translating the Bible into Ki-Masai (he was responsible for the Book of Romans).

Reusch had meanwhile come to be regarded as Tanganyika's premier resident historian. At Governor Twining's request, J. P. Moffet wrote to Reusch from Government House to ask if in ancient times Kuwaiti sailors from the Persian Gulf had visited East Africa. "From your knowledge of the history of the region," Moffet inquired, "can you say whether the port existed in, say, biblical times and thus is it probable that there have been connections between it and East Africa for a very long time? I should be very grateful for your comments."[58]

Dr. Reusch was invited to address the Royal African Society, and was requested by the Tanganyikan press to provide feature articles about the history of East Africa.[59] A lengthy memorandum on the future of the Masai brought this response from the British Education Secretary in Dar es Salaam: "You will not need me to tell you how very much I value your advice, based as it is on such a long and close connection with the Masai tribe and on such an expert and profound study of their history, customs and legends."[60] When Sir Christopher Cox visited Tanganyika in January 1952, Reusch was invited to Government House to discuss the memorandum with the British Colonial official.

A world-famous celebrity and Islamic leader, Prince Ali Khan, spiritual leader of the Nizari sect of Ismaili Muslims, also sought Dr. Reusch's expertise. In 1949 the playboy prince and religious leader had married the Hollywood starlet, Rita Hayworth. Two years later, their marriage in trouble, the famous pair went on a second honeymoon, a safari through East Africa. Film footage shot by an amateur was later edited into a travelogue aptly titled, "Rita Hayworth's Champagne Safari."[61] Prince Ali had heard of Dr. Reusch's scholarship and interest in Islam, and wanted to learn more about his own lineage, which originated with the Prophet Mohammed's brother. Therefore, he invited Dr. and Mrs. Reusch to join him and Miss Hayworth for luncheon in Arusha. On Friday, January 19, 1951, Elveda Reusch drove to Arusha and splurged on a new wardrobe for the occasion.[62]

The next day the prince and princess left their elaborate and luxurious camp in the Kenya bush and flew to Arusha to meet the Reusches. The modest Lutheran woman wrote in her diary that night, "Again to Arusha to attend buffet lunch in honor of Prince Aly & Princess RITA HAYWORTH!"[63] The topics of their conversation are unknown.

In March 1952, Paramount Chief Petro and the British governor, Sir Edward Twining, were scheduled to bestow a decoration for meritorious service upon Dr. Reusch. The missionary couple was to be feted at a luncheon in Marangu, and so on Monday, March 17, Elveda left early for Moshi to buy a new hat before joining her husband for the official ceremony. She was astonished to find herself in the company of His Excellency, Sir Edward Twining and Lady Twining, and in her excitement invited them to her home in Nkoaranga for tea the next day. Chagrined at what she had done, right after the ceremony Elveda rushed to Machame to borrow a silver coffee service and raced home to bake two kinds of cookies and prepare lemon-pineapple sherbet. Her feverish preparations were joyful, however, because that afternoon a letter arrived, announcing the birth of her first grandchild.

The next morning she cleaned and polished everything outside and in, and then decided to add puffballs to the menu before going to inspect the hospital. All was ready by two o'clock. The Governor's party of three arrived an hour and a half later, and Elveda presided over the tea on the front porch of her home that nestled against the verdant forest, from which the guests looked out over a pastoral and lovely green Eden. A profusion of flowering bushes dotted the lush pasture below where a cow grazed in the late afternoon sun; halfway down to the right, the hospital; and the Nkoaranga church farther down to the left. The hostess and her husband took their guests on a tour of the medical facility before the dignitaries departed at six o'clock. "Very charming people, easy to entertain," Elveda wrote in her diary that night.[64]

While Governor Twining was on leave that summer, Acting Governor Bruce Hutt invited Dr. Reusch to hobnob with the elite at a "sundowner," as British colonials across the globe referred to the ritual cocktail hour. From Government House in Dar es Salaam came the formal invitation:

His Excellency
Acting Governor and Mrs. Hutt
request the pleasure of the company of
the Rev. Dr. REUSCH
at a sundowner on Friday July 11, 1952
at 6:30 p.m.

The invitation ranked as a Royal Command.[65] Although there is no confirmation that he attended, it is impossible to imagine Dr. Reusch being anywhere but Dar es Salaam that Friday evening, where his courtly Imperial Russian behavior and stories undoubtedly made him a center of attention. "Drama is part of his makeup," wrote a friend:

> When Reusch is in the midst of a social gathering it is not long before other voices go down one by one and those on the periphery move closer to catch the low-pitched recounting of high adventure — stories of the hunt wherein he was the hunter and others in which he was the hunted, accounts of weird rites among primitive people, of the intrigues and destruction of war, and of escapades in the Caucasus.[66]

It was the Masai, however, who conferred his greatest honor. They made him an honorary warrior. The initiation was a simple ceremony: The *Il'muran* (warriors) sat on stones in a wide circle on the ground. One place was vacant. In the middle of the circle several other warriors roasted beef ribs on old spears. The two famous lion hunters, Loikwasa and Lais, escorted Reusch to the edge of the circle, and then one of the senior warriors stood up and asked, pointing at Reusch, "Is he a warrior? *Lemuran*, has he the strength, endurance and valor of a real *Ol'muran*?"

"Yes, many times he has done these things!" chorused the assembled warriors. And so Loikwasa and Lais escorted Reusch to the empty stone seat and one of the others brought him a double portion of roasted meat. Each of the others received one rib. Said Reusch, "Loikwasa and Lais patted me on the back with the words: "Now you belong to us, for you are a Masai warrior. Do not forget it!"[67]

A DEFINING MOMENT: THE MERU LAND CASE

Northern Tanganyika Territory was tense when Reusch returned in 1949. Nomadic Masai warriors had recently killed a British officer, and the Meru were at a serious impasse with the British administration. Reusch's earlier presentiment of danger was justified, since he worked in Masailand and lived in Meru territory.

In 1946, British administration of Tanganyika Territory came under the supervision of the Trusteeship Council at the United Nations Organization.[68] In contrast to the League of Nations, which had given the British authority over the Tanganyika, Third World members of the UN participated in decision-making.

At the same time there was a shift in the focus of British policy in Tanganyika, from regulating tribal interests to encouraging more efficient use of land, as it was put, "for the good of all." On one hand, native populations had substantially increased, and fixed tribal territories no longer met their needs; on the other, the growing cattle herds were tended on land regarded by whites as best suited for producing coffee beans. The post-war shift in British policy favored white plantation owners, and that was the nexus of the problem.

The final white paper issued by the British Lands Commission recommended the creation of a contiguous zone of white-owned plantations. To that end, the Meru were to be removed from Engare Nanyuki and Leguruki and resettled at Kingori and land to the south, which was an arid region, infested with tsetse flies and malarial mosquitoes. The plan, noxious to the Meru and regarded by African nationalists as a racist plot, was a significant event that galvanized the movement for independence.

The eviction was announced at a *baraza* (general meeting) in the heart of Lutheran Meru territory in July 1951. Tribal opposition was fierce. When a UN Visiting Mission arrived in Arusha to review British stewardship of the territory in September 1951, Meru representatives petitioned the delegation to intervene — which caused the British to redouble their effort to implement the redistribution of Meru land. "In an attempt to preclude UN action," wrote historian Thomas Spear, "the administration rushed through an ordinance allowing them to evict Meru forcibly from Engare Nanyuki."[69]

The Soviet UN representative, Aleksander A. Soldatov, returned from Tanganyika with seven recommendations for the British: take measures to ensure native participation in democratic self-government; end racial discrimination; return all land taken from the indigenous population; prohibit future land alienation; replace the poll tax with a progressive taxation system; and increase the budgets for health services and education.[70] The British dismissed Soldatov's proposal as a communist propaganda ploy. It is noteworthy that Soldatov's recommendations reflected the same hopes for Tanganyika expressed by Augustana's Elmer Danielson.

On November 17, 1951, the British commenced "Operation Exodus," as the eviction was called. Seven British officers, 66 armed African police, and about 100 laborers from Kenya began burning houses and driving off the livestock as the majority of Meru watched from a distance.[71] The Lutheran dispensary, school, and the church building at Poli were destroyed. According to the Meru, almost 3,000 persons were evicted. Some of the livestock perished in the bush as they were herded toward Kingori — cattle, sheep, goats, donkeys, and chickens.[72] Eight Meru women suffered miscarriages in the commotion, and an elderly man died. On November 19, a distraught Elveda Reusch noted in her diary, "Engare N[anyuki] people really moved — by force."[73] The world press reported the non-violent Meru struggle the next day.

A few days later Mrs. Reusch noted, "R[ichard] is very tired & resentful & discouraged."[74] District Officer Stubbings wrote in his report of the operation, "It is clear that an opportunity has been given to mal-contents to make considerable political capital out of this operation for many years to come, . . . a happy hunting ground for political agitators."[75] His forecast turned out to be an understatement.

Superintendent Danielson opened a new dispensary at Kingori to serve the needs of the Meru people, but he strongly opposed the British action. The soft-spoken missionary did not issue public declarations in the matter because he knew that government agents were watching him, monitoring his correspondence, and could revoke his visa at will.[76] Privately, however, he was direct in his communication with officials. In a memorandum to Provincial Commissioner Page-Jones, Danielson wrote, "As a Church, we are concerned that this major problem . . . may be settled in a way which [the Meru] consider just."[77] The British administration later offered compensation for the church structure that had been destroyed, but Danielson refused to accept the money because to do so "would be to acknowledge to Government that its action was condoned."[78]

The Meru decided to take their cause to the Trusteeship Council of the United Nations in New York City. Earle Seaton, a Bahamian lawyer practicing in Arusha, presented the Meru case to the Trusteeship Council on June 30, 1952. The other representative chosen to address the Council was Kirilo Japhet, son of a Lutheran evangelist in Nkoaranga. Despite British attempts to stall and prevent him from leaving the country, Japhet finally arrived at UN headquarters on July 17th.[79] Four days later Seaton again made a careful legal presentation, followed by Japhet's impassioned plea for justice in which he described the eviction and charged that Meru land had been seized in order to allow a few wealthy white Afrikaners to purchase it. Japhet concluded by pleading,

Crush the head of the serpent of racial segregation, or apartheid, which has dared show itself in a United Nations Trust Territory. Save the peoples placed in your trust from the misery, frustration and bitterness which such policies have produced in Kenya and South Africa and, inevitably will produce. Restore to us our lands for the resettlement of our three thousand homeless tribespeople. Revive in us our confidence and our faith in the United Nations.[80]

The Pakistani delegate was astounded that 3,000 Africans had been evicted to make way for thirteen white farmers. Sir Alan Burns, United Kingdom representative, tried to refute Japhet's testimony, but the Meru tribesman produced documents and notes of meetings with British authorities as evidence in support of his charges. Sir Alan unwittingly revealed the colonial state of mind when he replied, "It is most unlikely that a tribe would take written records of a meeting between the District Commissioner and themselves. I have never heard of such a thing happening."[81]

Great Britain and its allies constituted a majority on the Trusteeship Council and adopted a resolution offered by the New Zealand delegate that expressed regret over past events but called for no corrective action. Both the Meru petition and Trusteeship Council resolution were forwarded to the General Assembly's Fourth Committee.

When the Committee met in November 1952, the Indonesian representative and eight other members from Asian, African and Latin American countries moved a second resolution that not only condemned the British action but also ordered the land be returned and compensation paid. The Canadian delegate offered a third resolution that condemned the action but accepted the eviction as a *fait accompli*. The Indonesian resolution was voted and sent to the General Assembly.

During Assembly debate the British ambassador brazenly declared, "It is not very dignified for this Assembly to pass resolutions which the Administering Authority has no intention of carrying out."[82] The Canadian ambassador introduced a resolution similar to the one he had moved during earlier Committee debate, but neither the Indonesian nor Canadian resolutions garnered the required two-thirds majority. The Meru appeal for justice at the UN failed. The British action was condemned in the court of world opinion, but the eviction remained in force.

AMERICAN LUTHERANS TAKE ACTION

In 1953 the American Lutheran National Council president, Dr. Fredrik Schiotz, hastened to London where he appealed directly to officials at the Colonial Office. He told Mr. E. B. David that the Lutherans in America felt strongly about the treatment of the Meru, and that unless something were done to rectify the situation, the Protestant churches in the USA would probably initiate another appeal to the UN. Schiotz's words infuriated the Colonial official. In a personal note to Bruce Hutt in Dar es Salaam, David reported that he "made it clear in reply that this appeared to be in the nature of a threat." The droll colonial officer then described the naive American's solution to the problem: Gather all the parties concerned at a round table at "which he seemed to imagine that, in accordance with true Christian principles, the truth would emerge and everyone would disperse happily."[83]

Hutt replied that Danielson had met with the Deputy Provincial Commissioner in July:

> [Danielson] came, so he said, to give us his point of view on the trend of Meru feeling and to state the Mission's position. He anticipated that the question of the eviction from Ngare Nanyuki would again be taken to the United Nations and stated that if the Mission were called upon to comment on the matter, it would be bound to be critical both of the principle and method of eviction. . . . He told us in some detail of the visit of Kirilo Japhet to the United States and that the parent Mission body in that country had taken him under their wing.

Then followed a statement indicating a sharp change in British attitude toward the Americans:

> It is my belief that the influence of the American Lutheran Mission has not always, indeed not very often, been a beneficial one on the general political scene in the Arusha District. There has been a gradual slackening of control by the American and European Missionaries and a consequent fostering of a sense of independence amongst the African Pastors and School Committees. I do not say that their general attitude is responsible for the political turmoil in the District, particularly amongst the Meru, but it is certainly a contributory factor in the situation.[84]

Governor Twining shared Hutt's opinion: "Perhaps because [the Augustana Mission] think it is democratic, they have organized their Church Councils in such a way that the Meru run their own church affairs to a very large extent and, for that matter, their schools, and it is believed that these may well become political associations." Danielson's intransigence so irritated the Governor that he urged London to permit German missionaries to return since "they are likely to have a more disciplined outlook."[85] That was to some African Lutherans an undesirable prospect, since Americans seemed easier to get along with, were less formal, and were perceived to practice a greater measure of equality and respect in their relationships with Africans.

Japhet returned to Nkoaranga where his activities were closely monitored. For example, according to the British Political Intelligence Summary of August 1953, Japhet had urged that every Meru "should seek to have land returned to them, including that now occupied by Europeans," but only through constitutional means.[86]

The American Augustana Synod convened its annual meeting during the summer of 1953 and voiced its support of the Meru congregations by passing a resolution, urging American Ambassador Henry Cabot Lodge to persuade the UN to order the return of Meru land. However, Schiotz asked the Synod president to hold the resolution until he had a chance to pursue the issue further with the British on behalf of the National Lutheran Council. He doggedly explained to Bruce Hutt that November,

We do not in any way want to add to the difficulties of Government. However, when our representatives on the field sense a deep, bitter, and burning resentment on the part of the Meru people over this eviction, our job of proclaiming the Gospel falls on fallow ground. For us this condition seems in part unnecessary, in that our Superintendent Danielson warned the District Commissioner nine months before the eviction of what would happen if it were carried out.[87]

Danielson believed that the Meru had suffered a gross injustice. However, according to Anton Nelson, the son of Quaker missionaries, "One missionary, from a particularly paternalistic background, had advised the Meru to accept Government's action and trust British officials to know what was best for them."[88] That missionary was Dr. Reusch.

Dr. George Hall, a professor at Gustavus Adolphus College, was at the time serving a short term with the Augustana Mission in Tanganyika as an education specialist. While on safari with Danielson and Reusch, he recalled that the two men — who agreed on just about every other issue — agreed to disagree about the Meru land issue and did not discuss it during the journey.[89]

Reusch probably did urge the Meru to accept eviction. However, there is no evidence that he personally agreed with the ill-advised British policy. Quite to the contrary, the prospect of eviction and destruction of the church, dispensary and school — which he had helped to build and nourish — depressed and discouraged him. But his response had been imprinted as an imperial subject and military cadet. And he had signed an oath in 1923 when applying for a British visa for Tanganyika Territory that gave the former cavalry officer no choice but to support Government's policy:

> I hereby undertake to pay all due obedience and respect to the Government of Tanganyika Territory and while carefully abstaining from participation in political affairs, I desire and purpose *ex animus* to work in friendly cooperation with the said Government in all matters which my influence may properly be exerted; and in particular, I undertake, if engaged in educational work, that my influence shall be exerted to promote loyally the Government of Tanganyika Territory in the minds of my pupils, and to make them good citizens of the British Empire.[90]

Reusch was therefore compelled by his conscience to stand against the Meru, among whom he lived; the African Lutheran Church he had championed; the Augustana Mission he served; his friend, Superintendent Danielson — and his wife, Elveda.

Mrs. Reusch labored under fewer constraints than her husband. Not only had Kirilo Japhet studied English in a class she taught,[91] but she also delivered the Japhet's first baby.[92] Elveda especially treasured Kirilo's and his wife Enoki's friendship and was actively involved on behalf of the Meru. She worried when the British intercepted letters sent to New York, and helped to translate those documents and correspondence that did arrive from New York.[93]

Rafaeli Mbise, a member of the Meru Committee of Four that had led the protest against the British action, was arrested and exiled to Nkoaranga, where the Japhets and Reusches lived. "Rafaeli came with letters from UNO to translate," Elveda wrote on February 11, 1953. "He realized that Engare Nanyuki is not to be returned. It is heart-rending."[94]

The Meru Land Case is an important chapter in East African history because it was the first time that an indigenous people had appealed for justice directly to an international body. It is also an important chapter in the history of the Lutheran Church in America. In the preface of their summary account of events, Japhet and Seaton paid tribute to the persons and organizations who had lent moral and material support. First on the list of eight was Elmer Danielson and the Lutheran Church of Tanganyika, followed by the Poli parish in Engare Nanyuki and the Lutheran Churches of America.[95]

THE MAU MAU REBELLION

The Mau Mau rebellion broke out in Kenya at the same time as the Meru Land Case was being argued at the UN. Richard P. Gale, a Minnesotan who was in Kenya at the time, wrote that the brutal cult was born of frustration, hunger and hatred of whites for taking native lands. According to one estimate, 800,000 men, women and children of the Kikuyu tribe in Kenya took the bloody Mau Mau oath — some against their will — to kill enough of the hated white oppressors until the remainder fled the country.

Some, including Reusch, blamed Soviet Russia for instigating the guerrilla war. Not so, said Gale. "This is a native job. All the Mau Mau gets from Russia is sympathy." British intelligence had come to the same conclusion: there was no evidence of a direct link between the Mau Mau and Moscow.[96] Neither, according to Gale, did the violence have anything to do with "a great world uprising, white against black. It's a mean, vicious local revolt, the kind that has often failed in the past — not as bad as the Sepoy mutiny in India [1857], nor as bad as the [1862] Sioux uprising in Minnesota."[97]

By October 1952, violence in Kenya posed a threat serious enough for Government to declare a state of emergency. Governor Twining reported that Mau Mau incursions from Kenya into Tanganyika had not won support among the Chagga, "although they are probably watching the situation very closely." The Meru were "still uncooperative and, in their present state would be particularly susceptible to Mau Mau influence." There had been, the governor reported to London, "an attempted intimidation of one of our Masai."[98]

The story was first reported by the *East African Standard* late in 1952: "A report of a sidelight on Kikuyu infiltration across the border into Tanganyika's Northern Province comes from Dr. R. Reusch, the well-known Lutheran missionary," after Mau Mau "thugs" had come to foment trouble near Loliondo.[99] The story was picked up by the wire services, and in London the *Daily Telegraph* reported,

> Dr. R. Reusch, "Missionary to the Masai," related that a few of the tribesmen approached him with some trepidation to confess that they had thrashed, and threatened with a second thrashing, some proselytizers from the Mau Mau movement.

He adds that for once "I was able to assure my violent parishioners that they had acted rightly."

The Masai tribe became deeply antagonistic to the Mau Mau movement after it had taken to hamstringing cattle. This is a deeply immoral act in Masai eyes.[100]

However, Mau Mau guerrillas had infiltrated Tanganyika's Northern Province by the end of 1953 in numbers sufficient to cause Governor Twining to take decisive action. At the end of September, thirty-three Kikuyu were detained in the Moshi District and forty-nine in Arusha. His objective, Governor Twining reported to the Colonial Office, was to expel all Kikuyu from Tanganyika.[101] A raid on December 22 netted more than 475 persons, and a similar operation was planned for Loliondo. Twining reported to his counterpart in Kenya that the Mau Mau had ordered their Tanganyika brethren to kill all Kikuyu in the Northern Province who were loyal to Government, "and murder ten Europeans (to start with)."[102]

Donald Flatt asked Pastor Stephano Moshi why the Mau Mau especially hated the Christian missionaries. The African cleric and future bishop replied,

> When the people see the missionary passive and non-committal about matters of race discrimination, and trying to soothe them and teach them to be patient, they consider that he is, in effect, merely supporting the conduct of his white brethren. They think his heart is not with his African flock, and that he is, at best, a stooge; at worst, an enemy, too.[103]

During the night of December 24, 1953, a Kikuyu informer, his wife and children were slashed to death in their home three miles from Arusha, and two others were hamstrung. Twining was determined to prevent a second Mau Mau front from opening on the Tanganyika-Kenya border, and in February 1954, invoking the newly enacted Restricted Residence Ordinance, expelled all ethnic Kikuyu living in the Northern Province.[104] The last action in Tanganyika against the Mau Mau occurred in 1956, but guerrilla activities in Kenya persisted until 1960.

When it was over, thousands of Kikuyu were dead and 80,000 imprisoned. Nevertheless, according to Henry S. Wilson, the Mau Mau rebellion exploded "the presumptuous notion that Kenya was a 'white man's country'" and hastened the de-colonization of British East Africa. Jomo Kenyatta, president of the Kenya African National Union, was detained on charges of helping to found the Mau Mau movement. He was released in 1961. In 1963 Kenyatta was elected Prime Minister of an independent Kenya.[105]

REUSCH RESIGNS

In August 1952 Bruce Hutt asked Dr. Reusch to lead an expedition of government surveyors to the top of Kilimanjaro to determine the precise height of the mountain. The sixty-one-year-old did not want to do it, but at Hutt's urging he left his work and on August 28th caught up with the expedition. Only three members of the team, including Reusch, reached Kibo's summit where the temperature plunged from a daytime reading of 40°F to -46°F at night. They remained camped on the glacier for three days, where they calculated the height of the mountain, conducted studies on the effects of altitude on pulse and blood pressure, and took blood samples for later analysis. They began their descent on September 1st.[106] It was Dr. Reusch's fiftieth ascent over a period of thirty years.

Reusch returned to his work in Masailand and did not return to Nkoaranga until October 18th. He was exhausted when at last he walked up the slope to his house. The Masai Missionary was not feeling well, and two days later took to his bed. Other than to attend an executive committee meeting at Marangu on the 28th, he did not get out of bed until October 31st. It was his birthday, but according to Elveda, there "wasn't much celebrating."

Dr. and Mrs. Reusch were due for a furlough in 1953. Mission Superintendent Danielson cited the couple's thirty years of service and expressed his gratitude "for the additional task as superintendent which Dr. Reusch carried last year, and also Mrs. Reusch for the extra duties she has carried."[107]

Despite his many achievements over three decades and his unfinished work in Masailand, Reusch decided that he would not return to Africa after his scheduled furlough. He had lost the respect of the Meru and some Chagga because of his stance on the land issue; his plan for separating the Masai mission from the Northern Church was rejected by his friend, Elmer Danielson; he was not convinced that the African Church or the country was ready for independence and saw a tinge of "red" in African independence movements; his wife was exhausted and wanted to return to the United States to be near her daughters and grand-child; and because of his strenuous work and recurrent malaria, his vaunted energy was at a low ebb. It was time to move on — as he had done when he left the military, Estonia, and the Leipzig Mission.

"He was the dominant force during those years," said David Simonson, an Augustana missionary who was similar to Reusch in temperament and also a man of action. "He was a one-man show, going it alone as he pursued his own agenda. But then most missionaries are a strange breed, individualists who often don't work all that effectively in a group. 'Success,' as we use that word, often eluded him. But for sure, Reusch was faithful to the end."[108]

After talking with Reusch about his decision to resign, Michel Ralinafere, the British Commissioner of the Central Province, wrote to his friend:

> May I say to you that your departure from the Northern Province will be keenly felt in the Provincial Administration? Those of us who have had the privilege of knowing you well enough to call you friend (as I have) esteem you highly as an administrator with the interests of the natives at heart, and we shall be sorry, indeed, to lose you. Your decision to go is deplored by me, but from what you told me in our private talk, I don't see what other course you could have adopted.[109]

Missionaries with academic qualifications could be appointed to the faculty at one of the Church's colleges, and Dr. George Hall inquired if Reusch might return to teach at Gustavus

Adolphus College. The reply was affirmative, and the president, Dr. Edgar Carlson, immediately appointed the Masai Missionary to the Christianity faculty.[110]

Mrs. Reusch marked the passing years of her fourth term in anticipation of the furlough that would bring her home. But in January 1953 she stoically wrote in her diary, "Am beginning to believe from R[ichard]'s words that we will not get home this year."[111] Her husband had agreed to extend his term in order to supervise the construction of new buildings for the Lutheran Theological School of Tanganyika at Makumira.[112]

On Friday afternoon, April 24, 1953, Richard went to meet three newly arrived recruits, Stan Benson and Clarence and Ruth Budke, who had finally reached Tanganyika via Borneo. Their arrival meant that the Masai fields would not be abandoned. "The great day has arrived!" exclaimed Elveda.

Early in August 1953 the Chief Game Warden issued a permit that read, "Dr. Reusch has my approval to shoot leopards and lions that are destroying stock. Skins should be handed in to the nearest boma or Game Department office."[113] Reusch described the ensuing adventure, a story he later often told to audiences in North America:

> It was in September 1953. My wife was preparing to leave Tanganyika for the USA. Before bringing her to Mombassa on the coast of the Indian Ocean I went to South Masailand to bring supplies to my schools, baptize a number of catechumens and finish the building of one of my bush schools. It was a journey, a safari as we say, of about one month.
>
> I was passing through Naverera when a native came panting and very excited to me with the words: "*He* has just taken my best goat!" Now, *he* is the leopard, and the natives are afraid to mention his name because it will definitely cause him to come back during the night.
>
> It was about 5:30 p.m. The sun sets in Masailand at 6 p.m. the year around. I left my old truck, took my Sauer shotgun, bore 16, put in two buckshot cartridges, and went with the native after the leopard. As soon as I started my search an inner voice asked, "Are you a coward that you take *two* cartridges for *one* leopard? What will your friends say if they hear about it?"
>
> But there was no time to remove the second cartridge — it was God's mercy — because the native already beckoned, "Here he is."
>
> "Where?"
>
> "In the bush there. Don't you see him?"
>
> All I saw was the moving of some branches in the dense jungle.
>
> There the leopard was with his kill, probably sucking blood. The sun was setting. I strained my eyes and suddenly saw a small yellow spot between the branches. The leopard was working on his prey like a cat on a killed rat. I went down on one knee and began carefully to aim. The leopard was not more than 40 yards away. To wound him lightly meant serious danger, because 40 yards are nothing for a charging enraged leopard. If the first shot did not stop him it was probably the end of me. I aimed, therefore, as carefully as I could in the beginning twilight.

But before I could shoot there was an angry hiss behind me. I glanced back and saw some 25 yards behind me a female leopard, coming out of the bush and preparing to charge me. The lady leopard apparently had made a round to see if there were enemies who could disturb her and her husband during their meal.

The male leopard, aroused by the hiss of his better-half, came out of the bush. Apparently thinking that I wanted to take his prey away from him, he charged wildly. At the same moment the female also prepared to jump. I fired at the charging male. It must have been God's undeserved mercy which guided the shot, for it caught him in the middle of the face and a pellet or two penetrated his brains. Down he went with an angry roar.

I turned hastily back to see the female in the air leaping towards me. I fired blindly. How it happened I do not know, but the shot caught her at a close distance also between the eyes and in the open mouth. With an angry sigh she went down just a couple of feet from me.

There I stood, drying with my sleeve the sweat on my face. I was still alive but the two leopards were dead! I thought it for a moment to be a dream. My first conscious thought was, "It was God's mercy that induced me to take two cartridges instead of one." I was profoundly thankful.

In the darkness we brought the two leopards to the Mission Station and skinned them. The male was a magnificent specimen, probably over 300 pounds heavy. His skin with the tail was over nine feet long.

The next morning Dr. Reusch shot a third cat — three leopards in twenty-four hours:

> The skins were in excess of my license and I was somewhat afraid that Game Warden Swynerton would take them away from me as it is usually done in such a case. But after he had heard my story he shook his head and said, "You are going home in a few months, maybe forever. Well, the Tanganyika Government gives these skins to you as a farewell present, my dear friend."
>
> I arrived home still prouder and still more self-satisfied and gave the skins to my wife. She asked me how I had obtained them, and I told her the whole story, expecting at least a compliment. But, mind you, she shook her finger angrily before my face and said, "Richard Reusch, never again expose your stupid self to such unnecessary danger! Do you hear me?" And she walked out of the room.
>
> I scratched my bald head, filled my pipe and thought to myself, "A just man has to suffer much."[114]

ELVEDA GOES HOME

She had come to Africa in 1925. Alone, Mrs. Reusch left Mombassa by ship on September 24, 1953. Unlike her outward voyage, however, she experienced no loneliness because she was homeward bound. She landed at Brindisi, Italy, and wended her way overland to Venice where she visited St. Mark's Cathedral and strolled along the Grand Canal. "The Italian people love music, dance, and enjoy life," she remarked, but at the same time she wondered how they got any work done, spending so much time sitting around in outdoor cafes.

Mrs. Reusch took in everything on the bus trip to Milan, including the Olympic Theater at Vicenza, and Juliet's tomb at Verona. She debated whether to spend 1300 lira for a city tour of Milan, but her curiosity won over frugality. She was delighted by the city's architecture and the chance to visit the Church of Maria della Gracia to see Leonardo da Vinci's *The Last Supper*. That evening, at a hostel run by the Roman Catholic Grey Sisters, Mrs. Reusch caught up on her reading about the Mau Mau.

In Zurich she was greeted by friends, and that night slept in a luxurious featherbed; in Bielefeld she attended a prayer service for prisoners of war and the many others sentenced to prisons in East Germany; in Nuremberg she was met by Pastor Ernst and Mrs. Jäschke and the next day spoke at their church; and in Leipzig she visited friends and made presentations to church groups about the African Mission. After spending a day with Bruno and Mrs. Gutmann, she left for Amsterdam, took a tour of the canals and visited the Rijksmuseum. In Rotterdam she checked in with the Holland-American Line and on November 11th sailed for America.

Elveda Reusch arrived in New York on November 18th and was greeted by her son-in-law and a representative of the Foreign Mission Board, who presented her with a dozen roses. That evening she was taken to see the Broadway musical, *The King and I*,[115] a fitting homecoming for a woman whose accomplishments were not as dramatic but no less remarkable than her husband's.

In addition to mothering three daughters, she had worked as an obstetrics nurse, kept the parish books throughout the district, paid the teachers, and taught English, health, and home economics; she repaired water systems, baked communion wafers, built retaining walls, laid linoleum, repaired roofs, and took in and cared for abandoned babies; she poured concrete floors, and plastered and white-washed walls, preserved fruits and vegetables, skinned game and feathered guinea hens brought home by her husband; she repaired appliances, managed the household on a minuscule budget, and when time permitted joyfully accompanied her husband on extended trips into Masailand; she edited her husband's manuscripts, including his history of East Africa, and found time to become proficient in Ki-Swahili and had begun learning Ki-Masai. She cooked and cleaned for a constant stream of British colonial officers and dignitaries, American and European missionaries and visiting church officials, African parishioners and clergy, mountain climbers, scholars, authors, European royalty on grand tours of Africa, and big game hunters. It was not uncommon for her to prepare Sunday dinner for twenty guests. And she did all that despite the lingering effects of her bout with cerebral malaria in 1929.

"REUSCH CRATER" AND "ELVEDA POINT"

The vexing issue of German missionaries and American involvement in the Meru Land Case caused problems for the British colonial administration. But Reusch was always loyal. In February 1953 he received a note from the Lands and Mines Department of the Territory. Its contents nearly bowled him over:

> I am directed to inform you that His Excellency [Sir Edward Twining, Governor] has decided that it would be appropriate that some part of Kilimanjaro should be named after you in view of your long and distinguished association with the mountain. After consideration it has been proposed that what is at present known as the "inner" or "ash" crater should now be renamed the "Reusch" crater and I am to inquire whether you would agree to this nomenclature being adopted. If so, the necessary steps will be taken and information would be released to the press.[116]

The letter arrived at Nkoaranga while Reusch was on safari. Having received no reply, the civil servant wrote a second letter: "I am to enquire whether you are yet in a position to reply."[117] To express his gratitude the overwhelmed Son of Kibo sent Governor Twining a dagger from Borneo. At the end of April came a letter from the Governor, thanking Reusch for the gift. Sir Edward added, "I of course am delighted that you have accepted the proposal that a feature of the great mountain should be named after you, and this will perpetuate your association with Kilimanjaro, which has been one which is never likely to be bettered."[118]

Andrew Wielochowski, Map and Guide to Kilimanjaro (1990), Executive Wilderness Programmes, Nirobi, Kenya.

Reusch Crater and Elveda Point (to the right of Uhuru Peak) are features of Kibo Peak that memorialize the missionary couple, the only Americans for whom features of Kilimanjaro are named.

According to the official press release, the Governor's order directed that "the most out-standing point of Kilimanjaro be named after Dr. Richard Reusch and be officially entered into all maps henceforth."[119] An unnamed point nearby was named for Elveda Reusch.

From Leopard's Point, on Sunday, July 26, 1953, Peter Wilkinson, a geologist from the University of Sheffield who was working with two members of the Geological Survey of Tanganyika, penned a letter to Dr. Reusch:

> As the discoverer of the Inner Crater of Kibo and the person after whom the Colonial Survey have named the innermost crater or "Ash Pit", we thought you would appreciate being the first person to learn of the first descent of the "Reusch Crater". As members of a Geological Expedition which is spending 2-3 months on the mountain, on Friday, 24th July, two of us descended on the NE corner of the crater to the bottom. . . . The descent is by no means difficult, but considerable care must be taken.[120]

The following year Governor Twining prepared the foreword for Dr. Reusch's *A Short History of East Africa*. The imperial words came as a benediction on Reusch's years in Africa:

> In the thirty years or so that Dr. Reusch has been in Tanganyika he has gained for himself the position of being one of the outstanding personalities of the territory. He still has the élan of a former Cavalry Officer of the Russian Imperial Cossacks, but underneath is the Lutheran Missionary with a blend of sincerity and robust common sense which has been such a good influence on tens of thousands of Africans in the Northern Province of Tanganyika. But above all he has retained a youthful spirit of adventure and has had the unique experience of ascending Mt. Kilimanjaro no less than fifty times which has given him the well deserved distinction of having one of its features — which I believe is very dear to him — named after him.[121]

Members of the Kilimanjaro Section of the Mountain Club of East Africa gathered in Moshi at the home of Captain R. H. R. Clifford to honor Reusch before he left for America. The club had presented him a gold medal after his twenty-fifth ascent, and during the business meeting voted to strike a medal with diamonds "to commemorate his 50 climbs and long service to the club." The *Tanganyika Standard* reported, "In a moving farewell speech, Dr. Reusch told of his love for kilimangaro, the 'glittering mountain' which has inspired folk tales as far back as the ancient Egyptians."[122] Said the Son of Kibo,

> "It is time for me to take my leave of 'my mountain.'. . . Good has been Kibo to me, a constant source of vigor and health, a place where I forgot my sorrows and troubles, where I was nearer to my God. I have lost my Emperor in 1917 and my country in 1920. As a stateless stranger I was living in countries foreign to me. On the slopes of Kibo I found a new home. The Masai . . . call me 'Son of Kibo.'"
>
> "One last wish I have: that Father Kibo may give to his son a small place somewhere on his broad top for my last rest. There, on the broad chest of Father Kibo I would like to wait for the last call of my Heavenly King, whose throne is higher still than Kibo!"[123]

Reusch may have drawn from an ancient tale in declaring his wish to be buried on Kibo. Menelik I, son of Solomon and the Queen of Sheba, conquered much of East Africa. As he lay dying, the warrior-king ordered his entourage to carry him to the saddle between Kibo and Mawenzi. There, according to the legend, he died and was buried. "Even today," according to a German and Austrian Mountain Club's publication, "natives still ask climbers of Kibo if they saw Menelik's grave and his royal treasures. They cannot believe that anyone would expend the effort [of making the climb] if not in the hope of seeing something."[124]

"I was very sad to see in one of the East African papers that you are leaving Africa and going to America," wrote his friend, John Millard. "Somehow I cannot picture the Northern Province and Masailand without you. How I wish that we could climb again together before you leave."[125]

FAREWELL

In February 1954 Dr. Reusch left Nkoaranga for the last time. He was sixty-two years of age, and had served his King of Kings through thirty-one tumultuous years. Although invited, he never returned to East Africa. It is not uncommon to find yellowing photographs of pioneering German missionaries hanging on Meru and Chagga church office walls. But Reusch's photograph is not among them.

Ten missionaries were assigned to Masailand after Reusch's departure. Stan Benson, who lived with the Reusches at Nkoaranga while he studied the Swahili language, was posted to northern Masailand. Rev. Bill and DeLois Jacobson, in Tanganyika since 1949, were transferred to the Masai mission. Rev. Don and Jean Johnson went to Naberere in south Masailand, and when Johnson became ill, Rev. David and Eunice Simonson took their place; Rev. Elder and Renee Jackson served at Karatu and Oliondi among other places; and Sister Liddy Doer, whom Reusch recruited from Germany, brought her nursing skills to northern Masailand.[126]

Dr. Reusch understood that the era of the foreign missionary and colonial administrator had ended. Once again he turned the page to begin the next chapter of his life in another country. As usual, he never looked back.

One year later the Lutheran Church of Northern Tanganyika became autonomous, and four years later, in 1958, the presidency of the Church passed from a white missionary to a Tanganyikan, Rev. Stefano Moshi. A peaceful transfer of national power took place in 1960 when members of the Tanganyika African National Union were elected to a majority on the Government's Legislative Council, and in 1961 Julius Nyerere was elected the first president of an independent Tanganyika. In 1964 the island of Zanzibar merged with Tanganyika, and the East African nation became known as Tanzania.

The Son of Kibo did not leave by ship from Mombassa, but instead caught a ride from Nkoaranga to Nairobi. From there he flew to Addis Ababa to visit friends. Retracing his earlier journey, he flew on to Cairo and from there traveled eastward to visit Bedouin tribesmen who had guided him through the Middle East in 1929. However, he had to cut short his trip when his lungs began to bleed from a viral infection contracted on the Masai Plains. From Beirut he flew to Tubingen for treatment at the Tropical Medicine Clinic.[127]

The thin and wan veteran visited old friends from the Leipzig Mission living in West Germany, and despite his condition undertook a heavy speaking schedule. The press, secular and religious, covered his appearances. "Theology Professor Was Cossack Officer, Speaks 24 Languages, Rides like the Devil and Bears the Kilimanjaro Medal-with-Diamonds," proclaimed the headline in Nuremberg's morning newspaper. In the opinion of the enthusiastic reporter, "His tales sound like stories out of *One Thousand and One Nights*." Men like Reusch, he added, are as rare these days "as water on the Steppes of Africa."[128]

The headline in *Nürnberg Zeitung* proclaimed his "65 Times on Kilimanjaro [Kibo and Mawenzi Peaks]."[129] When Reusch pulled out his handkerchief during an interview with a reporter from the *Nürnberg Stadtspiegel*, an empty brass cartridge case fell on the floor. "You'll always find this stuff with me," Reusch explained.[130] A reporter for a mission periodical was amazed that Reusch, only two or three inches more than five feet in height and thin, worn and unpretentious, "could be the greatest missionary in Africa."

"It is difficult for him as a man to get close to the female youth," the reporter explained. "That is why he needs a missionary sister who with her magnetic power can draw the attention of the warriors' future wives so that real Christian families can be founded." Said Reusch in an appeal to German pride, "In the U.S. I've been asking for such a Sister, but no one dares to send me one. They are too comfortable, too lazy. Maybe in Germany." And with that, "our guest buttoned his coat against the cold to which he is not accustomed and disappeared into the night."[131]

Sister Liddy Doer regarded Reusch's plea as a call, and prepared to leave for Masailand.

Dr. Reusch had finished his manuscript for a history of East Africa in 1939, and his friend at Government House, Bruce Hutt, had tried to interest the London International Institute in publishing the work. "The manuscript as a whole impresses me as a thorough compilation of literary documents and oral local traditions which have been carefully edited and interpreted," said one reviewer; but, said another, it emphasized Arab and foreign invasions without presenting enough material about the indigenous tribes. Because of the manuscript's scholarly detail, the Institute decided that the market was too narrow.[132] Then came the Second World War, and Reusch was unable to pursue the project. Prior to leaving for the United States, someone suggested that Reusch approach Evangelischer Missionsverlag in Stuttgart. Reusch was pleased when his manuscript was accepted for publication in 1954.

African Studies departments in European and Soviet universities used the book for more than a decade. "But," exclaimed a Russian scholar at a Moscow conference in 1994, "we are surprised to learn that its author was a Son of the Volga!"

Betty Anderson

The stress of Reusch's fourth term in Tanganyika and the effects of a viral lung infection are evident in this photograph taken in Nuremberg, Germany, in the spring of 1954.

CHAPTER 13

1   Simon Palajo, from author's notes of an interview at his farm in the Mt. Meru foothills, 20 January 1996.

2   Bruce Hutt, letter to R. Reusch, 13 January 1949, GACA.

3   R. Reusch's "Biographical Data" form, Augustana Synod, 1949 and 1960, GACA.

4   George Hall, *The Missionary Spirit in the Augustana Church* (1984), 113-14.

5   Richard V. Pierard, "Julius Richter and the Scientific Study of Christian Missions in Germany," *Missiology: An International Review*, vol. VI, No. 4 (October 1978), 496.

6   R. Reusch, "Memorandum Concerning the Mission Work in the Masai-speaking Area," *Minutes of the 24th Annual Conference of the Augustana Lutheran Mission* (1946), 45-49.

7   Elmer Danielson, "Report of the Northern Area," *Minutes of the Twenty-sixth Annual Conference of the Augustana Lutheran Mission* (1948), 71.

8   R. Reusch, "Arash, the Youngest Masai Station," paragraphs edited from a draft of a letter to American pastors and congregations, ca. 1950, GACA.

9   R. Reusch, "With Sweat and Blood They Wrote The 'Song of Arash,'" *Ansgar Lutheran* (5 December 1949), 8-9.

10   "With Sweat and Blood..."

11   V. Eugene Johnson, "Famine Stalks in Africa," *Lutheran Companion*, vol. 95 (22 March 1950), 2.

12   "Missionary Missive," *Lutheran Companion*, vol. 95 (25 January 1950), 16.

13   Elveda Reusch, diary entries, 27 September to 19 November, 1949, GACA.

14   Losinyari Lotalakwaki Metili, from the author's notes of an interview at Ilboro, Tanzania, 20 January 1996.

15   Elveda Reusch noted in her diary numerous times when her husband was ill, in most instances from malaria.

16   "I Loaded My Shotgun," *Time*, vol. 56 (2 October 1950), 50. Reusch was often asked by church officials to supply stories about his work. In this instance his original copy was retyped to form by Eric Modean, a public relations specialist at the National Lutheran Council. *Time* published the NLC release as it was received.

17   Tanganyika Arms License, No. 22210, issued to R. Reusch, 4 April 1953, GACA.

18   Mary Sandberg, "A Dream Come True," *Lutheran Companion*, vol. 95 (29 March 1950), 17.

19   Allen Kroehler, "Zeal Flames on Campus," *Lutheran Companion*, vol. 95 (15 March 1950), 14.

20   Irene Callander, "Harvest in Africa," *Lutheran Companion*, vol. 95 (9 August 1950), 12-13.

21   Hall, *The Missionary Spirit of the Agustana Church*, 113.

22   Donald C. Flatt, letter to R. Reusch, 8 August 1951 (R. Reusch file), AELCA.

23   R. Reusch, letter to Fredrik Schiotz, 23 August 1951 (R. Reusch file), AELCA.

24   R. Reusch, letter to Fredrik Schiotz, 23 August 1951; letter to Foreign Mission Board, 1 September 1951 (R. Reusch file), AELCA.

25   Arthur H. Anderson, "Spiritual, Educational and Medical Work in Southern Masailand," *Mission Tidings*, vol. 46 (October 1951), 13.

26   Elveda Reusch, "Unto the Least of These," *Mission Tidings*, vol. 46 (September 1951), 3.

27   "The Evangelistic Work in East Africa," *Mission Tidings*, vol. 47 (June 1952), editorial.

28   Howard S. Olson, "Roman Menace in Africa," *Lutheran Companion*, vol. 55 (31 December 1947), 13.

29   Amy E. Alden, "The Chief Becomes a Christian," *Mission Tidings* (April 1948), 14.
30   Stanley Benson, from author's transcript of recorded interview, 23 May 1995.
31   From the author's notes of a discussion with church leaders at Mwika, Tanzania, 19 January 1996.
32   John E. Hult, Daktari Yohana: *An American Pediatrician in East Africa* (Springfield, MO: Quiet Waters Publications, 1977), 7.
33   Statistics derived from "American Lutheran Missionaries in Tanganyika/Tanzania," rosters produced by the Mission History and Research Project, Division of Global Mission, ELCA.
34   "An African Viewpoint," quoted from *Algemeine Missions-Nachrichten in Lutheran Companion*, vol. 12 (23 March 1935), 367.
35   Rev. Stolee, vice president of the Lutheran Foreign Missions Conference of America, transcript of a speech delivered at the 16th Annual Meeting, 1935 (Proceedings of the LFMCA, 1935-1944), AELCA.
36   C. Walden Hedman, "The Color Barrier in Africa," *Lutheran Companion*, vol. 56 (23 June 1948), 21.
37   E. R. Danielson, "1952 Report of the Superintendent of the Lutheran Church of Northern Tanganyika," typed copy sent to Dr. and Mrs. Reusch, GACA.
38   R. Reusch, "A Survey," manuscript of his speech at the Regional Conference of the Northern Area Church, Marangu, Tanganyika, 24 April 1952, 1, GACA.
39   "A Survey."
40   "A Survey," 4.
41   R. Reusch, confidential memorandum to Dr. Arvid Bäfverfeldt, director of the Church of Sweden Mission, 19 April 1951, GACA.
42   "A Survey."
43   A. Creech Jones, confidential letter to the British governors of African territories, 29 December 1947 (CO 822-139), PRO.
44   "Race Relations," Summer School on African Administration, Report of Group IV, Cambridge, 1947, 1-8 (CO 822-139), PRO.
45   "Race Relations," 4.
46   In 1938 British Colonial Secretary Malcolm MacDonald declared, "The great purpose of the British Empire is the gradual spread of freedom among all His Majesty's subjects in whatever part of the world they live." — Quoted by Henry S. Wilson in *The Imperial Experience in Sub-Saharan Africa Since 1870* (1977), 304.
47   Albert Anderson, "Would Merge Foreign Missions," *Lutheran Companion*, vol. 56 (25 February 1948), 7-8.
48   Colonial Office, London, Despatch, Circular 4/52, 4 January 1952 (CO 822-517), PRO.
49   P. Rogers, Colonial Office, secret letter to S. A. S. Leslie (CO 822-517), PRO.
50   Freda M. Dearing, International Missionary Council, London, letter to P. Rogers, Colonial Office, 13 March 1953 (CO 822-516), PRO.
51   Fredrik Schiotz, Lutheran World Federation, letter to P. Rogers, Colonial Office, 10 October 1952 (CO 822-517), PRO.
52   P. Rogers, Colonial Office, letter to Fredrik Schiotz, 20 January 1953

(CO 822/517), PRO. Buchta had briefly joined the Nazi Party in Tanganyika, but shortly afterwards renounced his membership.

53 Freda M. Dearing, International Missionary Council, in a letter reviewing the Depersdorf Case to P. Rogers, Colonial Office, 26 March 1953 (CO 822-516), PRO.

54 Page-Jones, Colonial Office, notes, 19 March 1953 (CO 822-516), PRO.

55 Richard Carlson, "Diary of a Hollywood Safari," *Collier's*, 8 July 1950, 22-24, 47-48; 22 July 1950, 20-21, 66-67.

56 Elveda Reusch, diary entry, 6 January 1950.

57 E. Reusch, diary, 24 November 1951.

58 J. P. Moffet, letter to R. Reusch, 8 September 1952, GACA.

59 R. Reusch, "Sultan Yusuf, the Lion of Mombasa," manuscript, and clipping from the *Tanganyika Standard*, 27 December 1952, GACA.

60 Secretary of Education, Dar es Salaam, letter to R. Reusch, 28 May 1953, GACA.

61 *Rita Hayworth's Champagne Safari*, a Jackson Leighter Associates Production (1952), 60 min. The original 35mm color negative faded over the years, but a black and white print was transferred to videotape and released in 1998 by Kino Video. The film's narrator notes that, unfortunately, the photographer was not allowed to accompany Prince Aly and Rita Hayworth to Arusha.

62 E. Reusch, diary, 19 January 1951.

63 E. Reusch, diary, 20 January 1951.

64 E. Reusch, diary, 18 March 1952.

65 Dr. Paul Hamilton White, *Doctor in Tanganyika* (1955), 236. White, an Australian medical doctor in government service in southern Tanganyika, set off a tempest in a tea cup when he declined such an invitation without, according to protocol, explaining the reason. (He was ill).

66 "Son of Kibo," 9-page manuscript, author and date unknown (perhaps Emeroy Johnson, ca. 1954), GACA.

67 This event is drawn from two accounts, from "The Masai" manuscript, 28, and *Nüremberger Evangelisches Gemeindeblatt*, 4 April 1954, 2.

68 W. E. F. Ward, L. W. White, *East Africa: A Century of Change*, 1870-1970 (!972), 220.

69 Thomas Spear, *Mountain Farmers: Moral Economies of Land and Agricultural Development in Arusha and Meru* (1997), 222.

70 "Trusteeship Council's Study of Progress in Tanganyika," *UN Bulletin*, vol. 13 (1 August 1952), 144.

71 "Council Regrets Forcible Eviction of African Tribe," *U. N. Bulletin*, v. 13 (1 August 1952), 146.

72 Spear, 225.

73 E. Reusch, diary, 19 November 1951.

74 E. Reusch, diary, 28 November 1952.

75 B. J. J. Stubbings, District Officer of Arusha, "Operation Exodus," 17 December 1951 (CO 822-430-45), PRO.

76 Elmer R. Danielson, *Forty Years with Christ in Tanzania, 1928-1968* (privately printed, 2nd ed., 1996), 127.

77 *Forty Years*, 128.

78 *Forty Years*, 130.

79 Kirilo Japhet and Earle Seaton reproduced documents and recounted their experience and t estimony at the UN in *The Meru Land Case* (Nairobi: East African Publishing House, 1967).

80 "Committee Calls for Restoration of Lands to Evicted Tribe," *UN Bulletin*, vol. 13 (15 December 1952), 595.

81 Sir Alan Burns, quoted by Spear, 228.

82 Document UN-II, p. 467, cited by Anton Nelson in *The Freemen of Meru* (1967), 3.

83 E. B. David, Colonial Office, letter to Bruce Hutt, Dar es Salaam, 15 August 1953 (CO 822-517-35), PRO.

84 Bruce Hutt, British Secretariat in Dar es Salaam, confidential letter to E. B. David, Colonial Office, London, 10 October 1953 (CO 822-432-245), PRO.

85 Sir Edward Twining, confidential letter to W. L. Gorell-Barnes, Colonial Office, 23 October 1953 (CO 822-517-39), PRO.

86 Secret Extract from Political Intelligence Summary, August 1953 (CO 822-432-231), PRO.

87 Fredrik A. Schiotz, letter to Bruce Hutt, 9 November 1953 (CO 822-517), PRO.

88 Nelson, *The Freemen of Meru*, 31.

89 George Hall, from the author's notes of an interview, 17 July 1998.

90 Copy, "Form of Application to be filled out by Persons of Alien Nationality Desiring to Undertake Missionary, Educational or Philanthropic Work in British Territory," signed by R. Reusch, 9 September 1922, AELML.

91 E. Reusch, diary, 27 November 1950.

92 Diary, 20 July 1953.

93 Diary, 7 February 1953.

94 Diary, 11 February 1953.

95 Japhet, Seaton, *The Meru Land Case*, preface.

96 Notes, Colonial Office (CO 822-461), PRO.

97 Richard P. Gale, "British Have Mau Mau 'on Run,'" *Minneapolis Star*, undated clipping, GACA.

98 Sir Edward Twining, Secret telegram to the Colonial Office, London, 27 October 1952 (CO 822-731), PRO.

99 "Masai Give Mau Mau a Thrashing," *Tanganyika Standard*, undated clipping, GACA.

100 "Immoral Mau Mau," *Daily Telegraph*, 6 January 1953, clipping, GACA.

101 Sir Edward Twining, Secret Outward Telegram to Secretary of State for the Colonies, London, 29 September 1953 (CO 822-502), PRO.

102 Sir Edward Twining, secret letter to Sir Evelyn Barring, Nairobi, Kenya, 31 December 1953 (CO 822-806), PRO.

103 Donald C. Flatt, "World at the Cross-roads," *Lutheran Companion*, vol. 98 (21 January 1953), 10.

104 Sir Edward Twining, Despatch No. 85 to the Colonial Office, 5 February 1954 (CO 822-806), PRO.

105 Henry S. Wilson, *The Imperial Experience in Sub-Saharan Africa Since 1870 (1977)*, 304-305.

106 "Climbs Kilimanjaro Again; Missionary Reusch Leads British Expedition to Summit," *Lutheran Companion*, vol. 97 (15 October 1952), 8.

107 E. R. Danielson, 1952 Annual Report to the Mission staff, 3, GACA.

108 David Simonson, from the author's notes of an interview at Ilboro, Tanzania, 10 January 1996.

109 Michel Ralinafere, letter to Reusch, 3 May 1953, GACA.

110 Hall and Esbjornson interviews.

111 E. Reusch, diary, 2 January 1953, GACA.

112 "Dr. Reusch Comes Home," *Lutheran Companion*, vol. 99 (12 May 1954), 21.

113 Tanganyika Game Permit dated 3 August 1953, GACA.

114 R. Reusch, "A Leopard Hunt," undated manuscript (ca. 1954), GACA.

115 E. Reusch, diary entries for 24 September and 18 November 1953.

116 Member for Lands and Mines, letter to R. Reusch, 16 February 1953, GACA.

117 Member for Lands and Mines, letter to R. Reusch, 4 April 1953, GACA.

118 Sir Edward Twining, letter to R. Reusch, 30 April 1953, GACA.

119 Erik Modean, news release, National Lutheran Council, 16 October 1953 (R. Reusch file), AELCA.

120 Peter Wilkinson, letter to R. Reusch, 26 July 1953, GACA.

121 Sir Edward Twining, copy supplied to Reusch as it appears in his foreword to Reusch's *A Short History of East Africa* (1954), 7-8.

122 "Mountaineering in Tanganyika," *Tanganyika Standard* (27 April 1962), clipping, GACA.

123 "Dr. Reusch Says Farewell to Kibo," *Tanganyika Standard* (undated clipping), GACA.

124 M. B. Wirth, "The Mountain Club of East Africa," *Mitteilungen des Deutschen und Osterreichen Alpenvereins*, undated clipping, 285-86, GACA.

125 John Millard, letter to R. Reusch, 21 October 1953, GACA.

126 Stanley Benson, interview.

127 R. Reusch, notes, untitled, ca. 1954, GACA.

128 "Theologie-Professor war Kosaken-Offizier...," Nürnberg *8-Uhr-Blatt*, (25 March 1954), clipping, GACA.

129 "65 mal auf dem Kilimandscharo," *Nürmberg Zeitung*, 4 March 1954, 5.

130 "Von Innerafrica nach Nürnberg: Dr. Reusch," *Nürnberger Stadtspiegel*, 4 March 1954, clipping, GACA.

131 "From the High Plains of Central Africa to Nuremberg: an Interview with Dr. Reusch, One of the Most Important Missionaries — On the Search for a Mission Sister for His Masai" (translated from the German), *Nürnberger Evangelisches Gemeindeblatt*, 4 April 1954, 2, GACA.

132 Bruce Hutt, letter to R. Reusch, 24 June 1939 (reviews of East African history manuscript enclosed), GACA.

PART III

The Minnesota Years

(1954-1975

Dr. Reusch was the featured speaker at numerous Midwestern summer Bible Camps and youth conferences in the summer of 1954.

Gustavus Adolphus College Archives

Professors Reusch and Emmer Engberg taught in the Christianity (Religion) Department at Gustavus Adolphus College. Reusch was a conservative and member of the Republican Party; Engberg was a liberal and social activist.

Chapter Fourteen

ST. PETER, MINNESOTA
College Professor, 1954-1964

We Masai are thankful for the workers you have sent to us, but we are
urgently asking you to bring back our Father Reusch to us, to the
Masai. Every part of the country is shedding tears.

— Masai Elders at Longido[1]

Dr. Reusch was anxious about the future of the work among the Masai, which he had championed for the past six years. He landed at New York City on the 11th of April 1954, haggard and thin due to the lingering effects of malaria and a viral lung infection. Nevertheless, he went straightaway to National Lutheran Council headquarters to lobby members of the Commission on Younger Churches and Orphaned Missions. Then he boarded a train for Minneapolis where he appealed directly to the Augustana Board of Foreign Missions. Only after seeking to influence those two bodies on behalf of the Masai did he join his wife in St. Peter.

A pile of letters from missionaries and Masai Christians awaited his attention, some seeking advice and others reporting small victories along with seemingly intractable problems. Wrote Stan Benson, "I now know the troubles you had, and they are mighty heavy."[2]

The Synod office was soon inundated with requests from parishes seeking to reserve a place in his schedule of appearances. And so Reusch repacked his bags and set out on a breathless round of speaking engagements. His fame preceded him, and throughout the Midwest, Western Canada and the West Coast, audiences waited to hear more about his adventures in Russia and Africa.

Not only did he understand church audiences, he also knew the kinds of story elements that interested reporters and made for arresting copy. "One of Lutheranism's most fabulous missionaries, lion-shooting, mountain-climbing Richard Reusch, is back in Minnesota, supposedly to retire," Willmar Thorkelson reported in the Minneapolis *Star*.[3] The headline in the Los Angeles *Times* marveled, "Missionary Tells of Fabulous Feats; Ex-Cossack Shot the Bolsheviks and Baptized Tribes in Africa." In the religion editor's words, "His life sounds like something out of Richard Harding Davis, and maybe he is, although his Lutheran colleagues vouch for him, from Cossacks to Kilimanjaro."[4] The editor may have been skeptical of Reusch's colorful past, but he could not resist repeating the exotic details that by 1954 had become a familiar litany, a mixture of fact and embellishment not unlike Richard Harding Davis's reports from the front during the First World War. As in Tanganyika and Germany, an interview with Dr. Reusch guaranteed fascinating copy.

"Not every parish was alive to the cause of world missions," said Gustavus Adolphus College professor emeritus, Rev. Clair Johnson, "but after Reusch held them spellbound for an hour the people vowed to sponsor a missionary — even after all those bloody stories."[5] After his appearance at Elim Lutheran Church in Duluth, a Sunday school teacher wrote, "I can't help but comparing you to [the Apostle] Paul. I'm sure he was just like you. I know, too, the joy the early Christians felt when Paul made his return trips to the early Churches."[6]

The courtly behaviors that Dr. Reusch had absorbed as a second lieutenant in the cavalry of Tsar Nicholas II had become ingrained in him, rules of etiquette that he retained through the decades. They were part of his idiosyncratic charm that endeared him to British colonial officials and visiting royalty. In America, however, when he clicked his heels, bowed and kissed a woman's hand, the effect was electrifying. Alyce Carlson recalled his visit to the Lutheran Church at Pennock, Minnesota: "As I reached out to shake his hand he lifted mine to his lips and kissed it. You can imagine how surprising to a Mid-western middle-class woman this might be."[7] All women who were introduced to him received the same treatment. Said the secretary to the Augustana Synod president, "Goodness gracious, I couldn't concentrate on a thing after he did that!"[8]

First Lutheran Church in Worthington, Minnesota, was first to fete the Masai Missionary at a homecoming banquet in June 1954. "What a shotgun!" Reusch beamed in appreciation for the gift made famous by *Time* magazine. In Arusha it had saved gardens from ruination by baboons, eliminated many nasty hyenas, and claimed the lives of marauding lions and leopards. Unfortunately, because of famine, he had sold the weapon to buy food for starving children. But the Jeep provided by the young people of the parish, "the Iron Missionary," was now famous throughout the region because it could go through sand and mud 16 inches deep and used less petrol than his truck. The Masai called the Jeep a "he," which is to say, a warrior.

Reusch had sold his gun collection, along with other personal effects, including the gold and diamond medals awarded by the Mountain Club of East Africa, to raise cash for the Masai mission. The Worthington congregation presented him with the proceeds of yet another special collection — which Reusch promptly forwarded to Africa. "Thank God for those people who are giving for the Masai work," wrote Clarence Budke from Arusha.[9]

Jack Dozier, the college student whom Reusch had guided to Kibo Peak in 1937, learned that the "greatest friend" he had made while circumnavigating of the globe was coming to California for two weeks in July, and insisted that the Son of Kibo be his guest. Reusch accepted, and Jack and his wife took him climbing in Yosemite National Park.[10] In his few spare moments that summer, Dr. Reusch began preparing for the fall semester at Gustavus Adolphus College.

Dr. and Mrs. Reusch bought a modest home in St. Peter south of Swede Park just five blocks from First Lutheran Church. The pastor, Rev. Millard J. Ahlstrom, first met the Russian Cossack on the front steps of his church one Sunday morning. Reusch clicked his heels, saluted his "earthly cap-i-tan" and promised to serve as a loyal member of the congregation. The pastor remarked that he was immediately attracted to the Masai Missionary "because he was such a flamboyant and colorful character." His new parishioner did not wait to be asked to serve on the church council — he volunteered.[11]

The academic year was underway at Gustavus, but Prof. Reusch continued to honor requests for weekend appearances throughout the region. The Board of Foreign Missions tried to manage Reusch's schedule, but sometimes requests were sent directly to the former missionary in St. Peter, and mix-ups and conflicts ensued. Frustrated Synod officials begged the president of Gustavus to take on the task. Dr. Edgar Carlson agreed, deftly explaining to Reusch, "The purpose of this arrangement is not to prevent you from accepting off-campus opportunities as much as your time and strength allow, but to provide some protection for you against the great number of requests for your services, which may properly be anticipated."[12]

Senator Joseph McCarthy's campaign to unmask American Communists and their sympathizers had run its course by the time Dr. Reusch came to live in St. Peter. However, the threat of nuclear annihilation in the cold war with the Soviet Union continued to weigh upon daily life. Reusch felt duty-bound to accept invitations to speak before civic organizations, veterans' groups and officers' clubs where his dramatic account of Lenin's rise to power, the Russian civil war, and Stalin's terror more than satisfied his audiences. But his speeches were not superficial anti-communist diatribes. His analysis included references to Plato's *Republic*, the Tsin Dynasty, Sir Thomas More's *Utopia*, the French Revolution, and Lenin's own words.[13]

"Former Cossack Says Soviet Smile Is False," the Minneapolis *Star* reported after Reusch spoke to a group at the city's Athletic Club in 1955.[14] He was in Edmonton, Alberta, at the time of Premier Nikita Khrushchev's visit to the United States in September 1959. "Former Cossack Officer Says Khrushchev 'Coming to Spy,'" ran the headline in the Edmonton *Journal*.[15] On such occasions Reusch never spoke of his family in the Soviet Union, even though such stories would have added potent emotional appeal. Their safety was his foremost concern, and he did not want to jeopardize their welfare — or his own. After all, Gus Hall, the head of the Communist Party USA, was a Minnesotan, and party members were active in the Midwest. Only after Khrushchev's denunciation of Stalin in 1956 did Reusch occasionally refer to family members in the USSR.

At the same time, American pacifist groups had organized to try and stop the escalation of nuclear weapons. Some wondered how a missionary and religion professor could advocate a pro-militaristic position. Reusch's rationale included four points:

1. Democracy makes everyone equal before the law, and private initiative, private property and private enterprise make each citizen responsible for the wellbeing and prosperity of family, community and state. That sense of responsibility encourages altruism instead of egotism, and idealism instead of materialism.

2. Communism provides equality and freedom only for Party members. All property belongs to the state. There is no incentive for private initiative and enterprise. The farmer in Russia, a member of a collective, works eight hours a day and objects to overtime work. Therefore, the people are often hungry.

3. "If you have a poisonous Cobra in your house and you have little children, what would you do? Will you compromise, believing that *co-existence* is preferable? There is only one way: Either the Cobra clears out or it must be killed."

4. Jesus said to turn the other cheek. "HE meant that we should do this as long as there is hope that our adversary might convert to our ethical view. But when the SAVIOUR saw that HIS words had no effect HE took a whip and drove the evil-doers out."[16]

The Reusches' move to the United States yielded many benefits. Elveda was relieved to live on the same continent as her daughters and their families. For the first time in her life she set up housekeeping in her own home, and she continued her professional practice at the state hospital at the edge of town, where she was a charge nurse. Richard enjoyed college teaching. The University of Tartu had originally been named for King Gustav Adolph II, and now in America he taught at another institution named for same seventeenth-century Swedish defender of the Lutheran faith. "To Gustavus Adolphus College I was privileged to come and to find a new home," Reusch told a group of YMCA Hi-Y students at a retreat in mid-September 1954. "And my prayer is: 'God help the sons and daughters of this College that they may carry out the tasks which CHRIST [would have them accomplish] in our age!"[17]

But Reusch was sorely missed in Masailand. "Is Dr. Reusch returning to Africa?" asked Lasioki Ledawa, the native teacher at Naberera. If not, the teacher warned, five native teachers and evangelists would probably resign at the end of that same year.[18] Missionaries also missed Richard and Elveda. After a visit to Nkoaranga, Elmer Danielson wistfully wrote, "It seemed like we could hear your voices, see your smiles, and share your hospitality."[19]

The National Lutheran Council's Commission on Younger Churches and Orphaned Missions met in Chicago just before Christmas in 1954. Dr. George Hall, who had replaced Dr. Schiotz as chairman, invited Reusch to attend and "tell us something of the work among the Masai."[20]

After outlining the history of mission work among the Masai, Reusch reported that as of January 1954 there were more than 2,000 baptized males and 900 catechumens in Masailand. Those results, he argued, warranted the creation of an independent Masai mission.[21]

Commission members were sympathetic to Reusch's argument, but not with his conclusion. Instead of voting to establish an independent Masai mission, they discussed two alternatives: find another synod mission board to assume responsibility for the Masai mission, or place it entirely in the hands of the African Church.

Reusch was angry. Did his years of nurturing the work among the Masai count for nothing? How could his adopted Church seriously consider such alternatives? Stan Benson and Clarence Budke were leaving to enroll in seminary, which meant that there would be even fewer missionaries in Masailand than when Reusch left. And how could the Commission even think of giving responsibility for the Masai fields to Chagga church leaders? Did they not understand that tribal biases would jeopardize the work among the Masai?

Commission members finally voted several resolutions, one asking the National Lutheran Council for emergency relief assistance and additional personnel for the Masai fields, and another expressing their hope that "Dr. Richard Reusch return for another term of work on the Masai field."[22]

In Reusch's judgment, the Committee resolutions failed to address the essential issue, the unique characteristics of the Masai culture, which called for an independent Masai mission. Despite the enthusiasm for the Masai that Reusch generated in American congregations, it was apparently insufficient to influence Church policy. The African Church was moving quickly toward full independence, and Reusch had alienated its leadership during the Meru Land Case turmoil. Therefore, the American Church would not implement Reusch's plan even if it were so inclined. The Masai Missionary was in a state of depression when he returned from Chicago just in time to celebrate Christmas with his family.

Elmer Danielson and George Anderson continued to urge Reusch to return for a fifth term, but George Hall was convinced that the Masai Missionary ought not to return to Africa. Several days after the CYCOM meeting, Hall sent letters cautioning Commission members that "although Dr. Reusch is specifically mentioned in [our] resolutions, we must make our arrangements about the Masai work in a completely impersonal manner" and must not "make our arrangements tailor-made to any particular person."[23] Hall explained to Danielson that Reusch had made a down payment on a home in St. Peter. If he remains at Gustavus, Hall explained, "he will have a home and be well established when he retires; if he returns to Africa he will return to the USA a retired man with no employment and no home. Under these circumstances I cannot conscientiously urge him to return to Tanganyika, but at the same time, I will not urge him to remain in the USA."[24]

Toward the end of the Christmas holiday a letter arrived in Reusch's mailbox from Eliyahu Sayoloi, a teacher, and six Masai chiefs:

> May it be read to all the responsible pastors, this letter to the pastors and great ones in America.
> We greet you in the name of the Saviour, and we thank you for all the help you have given to us to do the work of God here in Masailand and to show the Masai the way of salvation. The Lord our Father bless you all.
> Ye pastors and great ones, we Masai are thankful for the workers you have sent to us, but we are urgently asking you to bring back our Father Reusch to us, to the Masai. Every part of the country is shedding tears because our beloved leader and our brave friend, a friend of every man and every child. Well, we urge you, bring back our beloved shepherd.[25]

George Anderson also urged Reusch to come back to Africa: "You are the only one who can actually handle the problems which we have in the Masai area."[26]

Reusch resolved to stand his ground: He would return to Africa only as superintendent of an independent Masai Mission. Discouraged by the stalemate, Clarence Budke wondered if the Missouri Synod might have work for him in New Guinea.[27]

"I have heard from Dr. Carlson that you have accepted the contract to teach at Gustavus next year [1955-56]," Hall wrote in April 1955, "but that you have told him that there might be an emergency assignment to Tanganyika which you will be bound to accept." The Commission, Hall admitted, was of the opinion that the work would suffer a great loss if

Reusch did not return. Was it true? Was Reusch still considering a fifth term?[28]

Reusch's furlough came to an end in June 1955. He had Masai support and that of his peers, but the Commission would not accede to his demand for an independent Masai mission. It was a stalemate, and so the Augustana Board of Foreign Missions voted to grant him indeterminate leave.[29]

Dr. Reusch spoke about the famine in Masailand at a chapel service at Gustavus just before Christmas vacation in December 1955. A note, slipped under his office door, read, "After listening to your inspirational chapel speech I would like to extend this small contribution to your work. May this help to provide food for some starving child. I am sure that this will be the most gratifying gift that I shall give this Christmas, and the returning joy shall be the happiest gift received — A Student."[30] So compelling was Reusch's rhetorical style that a local campus fraternity, Epsilon Phi Alpha (known as "Eppies"), proceeded to raise $500 and make Dr. Reusch an honorary member during a ceremony at the end of January 1956.[31]

In October 1956 Missionary David Simonson wrote to Reusch, seeking advice about several matters. But then came these words:

> Now I come to the main reason for this letter. We need a man who knows the Masai, who knows their language and their hearts. We need a man with the strength of Samson, the leadership of Gideon, and the wisdom of Solomon. There is only one man who can fill these shoes and you know the one I am thinking of. I beg of you again, before the Throne of Grace, to consider your return to your people.[32]

One month later the Board of Foreign Missions inquired one last time if Reusch would consider another term.[33] Despite his love for the Masai, Reusch replied that under present conditions he had no choice but to decline. Instead, he decided to generate support for the Masai among the churches in the United States.

THE "CRUMBS FOR AFRICA" CAMPAIGN

Masai tears, entreaties from missionaries and Simonson's prayer were to no avail. Reusch had failed to persuade church leaders to separate the Masai mission from the Northern Tanganyika Diocese or to adequately staff and fund the work. Therefore, like a Don Quixote — but without a Sancho Panza — he single-handedly launched his own "Crumbs for Africa" campaign. Its purpose was two-fold: raise money, and recruit new missionaries for Masailand. Unlike Don Quixote, however, Reusch's passion was based on decades of experience, and his efforts shaped by pragmatism. Dr. Reusch accepted speaking invitations with a renewed sense of purpose, and Midwestern Lutherans responded to his stories, honoring him with generous contributions. He was in St. Paul on Friday night and Saturday morning, the 11th and 12th of March, and Sunday morning at Calvary Lutheran Church in Minneapolis; on Wednesday night, Trinity Lutheran Church in St. Peter, and again on Sunday morning, the 20th; and on Thursday night, the 24th, at Grace Lutheran Church, Mankato.[34] At the same time he taught a full load of courses at Gustavus and began working on a series of manuscripts about foreign missions and his experiences in Africa. His weekly schedule would have caused most other men his age to weep from exhaustion, but it restored Dr. Reusch to physical health and optimistic vigor. As in Tanganyika, he had important work to do.

In 1956 Dr. Reusch devoted his Easter vacation to a Bible conference at Winger, Minnesota, where he was the featured speaker. His topics were listed in a special bulletin: "From an Officer of the Emperor to an Officer of the Saviour," "The Mission Work in East Africa," "Pioneer Work among the Wild Masai," "His Name Above All Names," and on Good Friday, "The Blood Brotherhood of All Christians in His Name," his scholarly treatise on the cultural context of the Lord's Supper.[35]

Summer vacations were no less strenuous as he traveled by train or bus to Bible conferences and youth camps. He spoke to Luther Leaguers at the Red Willow Bible Camp in Binford, North Dakota, in July 1957. Dr. Reusch anchored his speech in the Gospel of John 15:16: "I have chosen you and ordained you that you should go forth and bear fruit." Each person has been given talents, he said to the young people, some more than others; but regardless of the number, each remains a "zero" until the "One" is put in front of them — the Lord Jesus:

The Royal Prince and His Father, the King

In ancient times there was a prince in my homeland whose greatest desire was to earn his father's praise. He was diligent in his studies, and as an athlete he was famous. With his accomplishments, he becomes proud and asks his father, the King, "Father, am I great?"

"No, sonny. In the eyes of the people, yes, but not in the eyes of God."

"But look at what I have done!"

"You have done it to get a great name from the people." And the boy disappears.

A few years later comes a terrific epidemic into the land. Thousands of people sick and dying, dying, dying. No help. Suddenly appears a great young doctor, and he builds hospitals, and he takes care of the sick and gives injections, and he stops the plague, his name in everybody's mouth. It is the prince. A few nights later he appears before his father. "Daddy, I have saved the people from death. Am I great now?"

"You are great in the eyes of the people, but not in the eyes of God. You have done it to get a great name and fame from the people." And the boy goes sadly away.

Enemies enter the country. With the sword they kill the people, they burn the towns and villages, they capture the people and sell them by thousands into slavery. No help, the whole country crying. But out there in the mountains appears a young man, a master of arms, and he collects around himself other young men and like lightning he comes during the night, and he strikes the enemy here and there, and his army grows. Finally, the decisive battle: He routed them and fought the arch enemy leader to his knees, and forced him to return all the slaves, all that he has robbed, and to pay a great sum of money as a fine.

On a white horse with a laurel wreath on his helmet he rides down into the liberated capital of his country. Young girls in white clothes come throwing roses before his horse. And he jumps out of the saddle and bends the knee.

"Father, am I great, great in the eyes of God? I have risked my life to liberate my country."

And the father says, "Great you are in the eyes of your country, but not yet great in the eyes of God. For you have done it to get a great name in the eyes of the people." And the young warlord jumps into the saddle and disappears.

Months later comes the news from the greatest enemy, from the king of Persia himself, who has captured the young prince's brother and, in revenge, intends to torture and crucify him. The Persian king is no more afraid, because the famous young prince who routed his army has disappeared. And there appears before the king one afternoon, just before the execution, the heroic young prince. "King of Persia, I offer you all my riches, all my estates. Let my brother go. He has a wife and six children. They will suffer."

The enemy says, "No, never. I can only let him go if you will be his substitute."

The young warlord, after a moment: "I shall take his place, for I am alone. My life is not of much worth, but he has a wife and six children. Let him go."

And he was tortured and crucified. And died.

His aged father heard about it. He came down and said, "My son, my son, now in the eternity you are great in God's eyes, for you have sacrificed your life for your brother. Great you are in God's eyes."

Well, all of you have a lot of gifts, maybe not the same as this young prince. Maybe you are not expert swordsmen or sharpshooters or hunters or writers, but everyone has his gifts.

To the Young Ladies

I went once through Italy, not so long ago, and there I came upon a grove of trees. My guide said, "It is those trees from which the famous Stradivarius took his wood to make his violins." Such violins are more precious than gold.

I saw there a woman collecting this precious wood, a whole arm full, and she went home and cooked a pot of coffee. What was the price of the wood? I could have bought for 10 cents so much firewood. And there came a carpenter, and he cut out fine planks of this precious wood, and he made a table and a chair. What was the price? Maybe $20.00. And there came an organ builder, and he made from the same wood thin marvelous planks to build an organ. And you know the price of an organ is $10,000 and more.

Then comes Stradivarius, and takes such a little piece, and he makes a violin of it — and the price is hundreds of thousands of dollars and more. I cannot distinguish two notes one from the other; but when I was a young officer 5,000 of us were invited by the Emperor to listen to Guggermann, how he plays his Stradivarius. Oh, we were tough fellows! We were accustomed to fight. But the Stradivarius violin, it moved us to tears — old, scarred, battered warriors sitting there and crying. The Stradivarius violin gave us an inspiration: We jumped up and took out our swords: "Long live our Emperor!"

Young ladies, girls: God has chosen you, and appointed you, to be such violins. Develop your gifts. Use them in the right way, putting the Savior just at the head of all your gifts. Wherever you will appear, you will become a source of inspiration. You will inspire the man to high deeds of self-sacrifice and heroism. You will spread sunshine around you and those who were with you; and after you have parted, they will say, "Whenever Mary or Karen or Marilyn was with me, I had the impression of the semblance of the Paradise on earth; but if you will use them in flirting and such stuff, nobody will say, "Whenever she was with me, *there* was a semblance of Paradise."

You know now what you are worth in God's eyes. All your gifts are zeros unless you put Christ, the "1," before it.

To the Young Men

And you, young men, not many years will pass, and you will go to the college, and you will become engineers, maybe bank directors, maybe professors, maybe lawyers or doctors or great politicians. God has chosen you, appointed you, to bring fruit. Develop every gift which you have. And don't forget to put Christ before all the long line of your gifts. Then it will be a great sum. Words alone mean nothing unless you endorse the words with your deeds. If you reflect Christ in your work, in your life, it works overwhelmingly.

You know as well as I know from the history that in France one day came to the throne a great king, Henry the Fourth, who tried to help the lower classes, the peasants. And the aristocracy did not like him. And they made a conspiracy to kill the king. All the great Catholic names of the country — the Duke of Anjou, he should become the new king, another the field marshal, another the minister of finances, and another a banker and whatnot — sixty-four conspirators, were part of the plot. And they came together for a banquet, and the presiding duke asked everyone, "Yea, the King has to be killed, we must replace him, for he thinks only about the peasants and the lower classes."

At this moment someone knocks on the door, and a young captain of the Guards comes in — the youngest son of this chief conspirator — and clicks his spurs, salutes. "Daddy, I have two days' furlough. I came to visit you."

"Well, Johnny," said the king, "sit down beside me. We are discussing very, very important business here. The king must be overthrown; you will get big estates, become a baron," and so on. And they went around, and all agreed. And the father looks at the young captain and says, "Now, Johnny, you heard it. He who overthrows the king, he will be rewarded — that one over there, he will become field marshal and will have big estates; and that one, a bank director. Now what do you say, Johnny?"

The young captain stood up, his face white like a piece of chalk. "Father, Sir, I heard it all. I heard if I joined your conspiracy, break away from the king, I can become a field marshal, and the bank director, and get big estates. But, Father, Sir, I chose to serve my king because I have learned to know and to love him." And he turned and went away. He did become a field marshal, but for the rightful king.

It will not be a moment exactly the same for you, but propositions will come before you, and you can become the director of the bank, maybe gifted for it, and make a tremendous fortune. But you will drift away from Christ. You can become head of a great industry, a great mathematician; you will become rich and influential, but it will be nothing if you drift away from your King.

You can become a great political leader if you have the gift for it — but if you will have to drift away from your King? You will be a great social lady, popular and famous, but when this question will come before you, Luther Leaguers, what will be your answer? Will you say, "Yes, but what Christ taught is old-fashioned, for the older generation"? Or will you click your heels and proudly straighten up and stiffly salute and say, "I have heard it all, but Sir, I chose to serve my King."

Conclusion

The question will be put before all of you. You have heard that the Lord says this day to you, "I chose you, appointed you to go out into life and bring fruit." The question of temptation will be put before you. What will be your answer then? God help you to stiffen up, and to salute, and answer proudly, "I have chosen to serve my King, and to follow Him. For I have learned to know Him and love Him in the Red Willow Camp."

God help you to choose the right way; God help you to develop all your gifts; God help you to put Christ before the long line of your talents. God help you to give the right answer, that you girls might spread sunshine and a semblance of Paradise wherever you are; and you boys, that you may become proud fighters for Christ and His kingdom whom nobody can dent, nobody can persuade, nobody can bribe; who will always salute and say, "But I choose to serve my King — for I have learned of Him and I love Him." God bless you all and protect you until we shall meet again.

(*Sustained applause.*)[36]

Reusch's speech reveals much about the speaker: ancient stories from the Caucasus, the formation of his patriarchal character as a military cadet, and the orthodox evangelical Lutheran tradition he absorbed at Tartu. His narrative tales, emanating from the mists of ancient history and times long forgotten, were delivered with consummate skill. The sixty-five-year-old's presentation at another Bible camp prompted this response from a recently graduated high school girl:

> I've never met anyone as interesting as you are. I do hope you won't mind me saying this but your [sic] the only person I've ever met that I would call a Saint. I believe I have come to know God more last week because of you then [sic] ever before in my life, so thank you.
>
> I'm sorry I couldn't give more money to the Africans, but maybe if I pray for them that might help some too.
>
> I'm praying for you, just like you asked me to. I think I better ask you to pray for me to [*sic*], because I need God's help in everything I do, and nothing seems to work out right for me.
>
> I'll write again, if its [sic] okay with you, for I like to write to you and I like to be around you.

In July 1957 Dr. Reusch received a letter from a discouraged missionary in Masailand, Rev. Kermit Youngdale. "It is a desperate picture you have painted in your letter," Reusch wrote in reply,

> — Donald sick, your dear wife in a hospital, the Church without a president, the staff of the Masai field shrinking, the RCs [Roman Catholics] invading everywhere, the Masai budget in the 'red' — a picture that could not be worse! But the Old GOD is still living, and HIS mercies are still enduring!!! I shall double my efforts to obtain money for Masailand as well as workers for it.

Reusch explained to Youngdale that he had sent Simonson $1,200, some of the "crumbs" collected during his missionary journeys. "Please," he begged Youngdale, "do not mark these dollars on your books, otherwise the New York office will [subtract] the money from the Masai budget." Money contributed from the British Lutheran Council, he instructed, "goes directly to Masailand, not to the Chagga Church." In the hope that the money he had recently collected would reach Simonson before Christmas 1957, in July of that year Reusch sent Youngdale a check for $400, and a week later another for $500. Empty my account in Africa, he instructed, transfer all the money to Simonson in Masailand. Then followed specific instructions:

> Please find out in which districts the food shortage is most acute. Buy sufficient "posho" [corn meal] and distribute it generously among the school children, their needy parents, all crippled peoples and all those I used to support. . . If some money is left over, please buy some "lawa-lawa" [candy] and distribute it on Christmas among the children.
> Tell the Masai and every devilish critic that this is a present from me and my friends and has nothing to do with the mission. The money comes from circles outside of the Augustana church and from me.
> Tell the Masai, also, that those satans [sic] of Roman Catholics are spreading a 100% lie when they claim to be my sons.[37]

In October 1957, Simonson again appealed to Reusch: "I hesitate to write of the situation in Masailand because I understand what it will do to you," he confessed, knowing at the same time that his mentor would welcome a firsthand report. In the southern region "the people had lost confidence in us," the budget was in deficit, "and all this time the RCs [Roman Catholics] had been making hay off our mistakes." Simonson's plan of action? "Get this Church to realize its responsibility to the Masai" by improving the schools and staffing them with Grade II teachers, making the congregations self-supporting, training more Masai evangelists, and mimeographing the Gospels in Ki-Masai. Simonson also reported that he and two assistants had built a new school in Engesmet in only ten days, and because of their efficiency "the people thought Reusch had returned." Again Simonson urged the Son of Kibo to come back to Africa: "Day after day I can see the work done by another, and often hear of him from the Masai. They are looking for another like him — pray God that they will get him — his name was Reusch."[38]

The college professor continued to seek support for Simonson and other missionaries in Masailand. A physician sent him $100; the Women's Missionary Society, $500; Grace Lutheran Church in La Grange, Illinois, $231 and a month later $1200; in Tanganyika his South African friend, Willy DeBeer, donated arable land worth $800, and Governor Twining released hundreds of bags of corn meal to assist the Masai. Said Reusch, "The LORD takes 7 breads, blesses them as he blesses our harvests every year, and there was sufficient for the multitude of hungry people. HIS blessing multiplied those few dollars 7 fold & 7 fold & 7 fold!"[39]

From Elim Lutheran Church in Duluth, Edna Anderson sent $490 she had earned by selling home-baked bread and cakes. She also enlisted the Sunday School children in a campaign to help support Simeon, a Masai evangelist. "I told the children all the stories you shared with us," she said in one of several letters to Reusch. "I told them how much you loved your King, and your Masai children, about your gentleness, humility and your faith." From his speech at Elim, she added, "I learned for the first time the meaning of the words, 'The Compassionate Christ.'"[40]

The busy professor and successful fund raiser received a letter from Synod headquarters that must have caused him to shake his head: "In checking our records we find we do not have you listed as a member of the Minnesota Conference ministerium, nor have we received a letter of transfer for you from any other conference." If he wished to be so listed he should please look into the matter.[41] Had the bureaucracy forgotten that he had been a missionary in Africa for thirty-one years and had never been directly affiliated with any Augustana conference in the United States?

Student members of the Lutheran Student Association at the Duluth campus of the University of Minnesota invited him to speak as part of their annual Faith and Life conference. It was February 1958, and Reusch was tired and dispirited. He left Duluth feeling as if he had given "the most lousy speech of my life." A few days later he received a check for $500 contributed by Lutheran, Episcopalian, Presbyterian, and Methodist students in Duluth. Said Reusch, "I could again hear that whisper: 'MY Spirit will guide you and blessings will follow.'"[42]

In a chapel sermon at Gustavus Adolphus College that same month Reusch told the "Gusties" about the depression he had experienced as an exile in Denmark, confessing that he had recently again succumbed to a feeling of hopelessness in his attempt to aid the Masai. However, the contribution he had recently received from students at the University of Minnesota, Duluth, reminded him once again of God's faithfulness. Again now, as in Copenhagen, he heard "that whisper: 'MY Spirit will guide you and blessings will follow.' Having substantially exceeded the allotted time, he concluded,

> Young friends, you will have to make the decision before leaving this college. Make it, looking up into the Saviour's face, on your knees. Only then will you be able to see HIS face, HIS good, sad, compassionate, suffering eyes. Then HIS Spirit will guide you in your decision, and HIS blessing will follow you and abide with you forever.[43]

Some weeks later at the conclusion of a daily chapel service, a college basketball star, Jim Springer, presented Dr. Reusch with a check for $500. Deeply touched, Reusch enthusiastically declared that the gift would feed his Masai for three years. Later, over cups of coffee in the canteen, several professors ruminated over what had transpired minutes earlier in chapel. How many Masai were there? asked one. How could $500 feed the Masai for three years? wondered another. Kyle Montague, a doctor of jurisprudence who delighted in exposing inconsistencies of every kind, tamped his pipe and snorted, "What do those Masai eat — hay?!"[44]

THE PROFESSOR

Said Dr. Reusch's former student, Rev. Jim Anderson, "It took some time before we became accustomed to his accent, but he was the kind of professor who gave us intangible treasures that we took with us, things for the soul."[45] Another, Dale Bosch, was influenced by Dr. Reusch to serve as a missionary in Tanzania. Forty years later he was still of the opinion that Dr. Reusch's course in World Religions was "the most unusual class ever offered by any department at Gustavus."[46] Bishop Roger Munson recalled that Reusch would apologize to the girls in the class — "I am sorry that I must say this, but pleeze excuse me" — and then proceed to graphically describe the ancient ritual of the Mother Cult in which virgins heaved themselves onto the ivory penises of idols. Such frankness was shocking to Midwestern college students in the 1950s, and "I remember thinking at the time," said Bishop Munson, "that he probably apologized so as to appear a pietist — but he certainly wasn't one of those."[47]

Jim Peters was an agnostic when he came to study at Gustavus. His mother was Jewish, and all her relatives perished in the Holocaust. What made Reusch's courses unique, Peters said, was that the professor had counted as friends whirling dervishes, Zoroastrians, Jews, Arabs, Hindus, and pagan sorcerers, and had come to understand their religions from having lived among them. "He had a passion for contrasting other religions with Christianity," said Peters, "but he never disparaged other religions. Unlike Christianity, many other religions make sex an integral part of their spirituality. That was not easy for some of us to deal with, but Reusch understood that component." Peters, the former agnostic, became a Lutheran pastor and taught at Marangu, Tanzania, where Reusch had taught in the 1930s.[48]

Eighteen-year-old freshmen in his Old Testament course had never before heard the story of Samson and Delilah as rendered by Professor Reusch: "And so, Delilah, zee desert flower with zee beautiful long hair, comes into Samson's room. [Pause.] She walks slowly to him and sits down on his bed [pause], holds his head in her lap and strokes his muscular arms and chest. And Samson?" Reusch began stroking the edges of the lectern: "He purrs like zee tom cat." All eyes in the lecture hall were on Reusch. Not one student was taking notes.[49]

Professor Reusch's Old Testament lectures were peppered with contextual references to the ancient historical record, archeological evidence, and personal experience that enabled him to render the familiar Bible stories of Sunday School and Confirmation in a new way. Two examples illustrate his style:

The Bible reports that the Ark rested on the mountains of Ararat (Gen. 8:4). Recently was discovered a [Babylonian] map engraved on a large brick on which Urartu, Mt. Ararat, is [marked]. It has the river Araxes and Lake Van, the sources of Euphrates & Tigris [Rivers], & is very accurate. It dates from the days of Abraham. It is close to my homeland & is inhabited today by the Christian Armenians [who] have many ancient traditions about the ark. One of them dates back to 810 B.C. It mentions the Ark on the slopes of Mt. Ararat below the snowline & also that the inhabitants went up to scratch some tar off & make amulets which brought good luck. The Yezidis, or devil-worshippers, living close to it now have the same tradition. They will show you some of these rings which they wear on a little chain on their necks.

The "Sea of Reeds" are the Bitter Lakes to the north of Miktol-Migdol. Ancient fords can actually be traced in the Bitter Lakes. One was used by Alexander the Great in 330 B.C. He crossed it with his whole army, including the heavy siege-machinery. They are well known to the Bedouins. I crossed one of them, called al-Kantara (the Bridge) immediately after a strong easterly storm in 1930. It seems the Israelites crossed the Sea of Reeds on one of these sand-bank fords. In Ex. 14:21 we read, "And the LORD caused the sea to go back by a heavenly east wind which lasted all that night, and made the sea a dry land." A detachment of the border-guards from Migdol tried to stop and capture the Israelites. Only 600 war-chariots are mentioned in Ex. 14:7, but Egypt had thousands of them. The bulk of them were on the northern frontier.[50]

"If a student went to visit Dr. Reusch in his office wearing his Eppie fraternity jacket it was believed he'd get an 'A,'" said Anderson, "but I don't think that was necessarily true."[51] Others believed it was true, including some of Reusch's colleagues. Rather than return exams in class, Reusch required students to pick up their exams in his office so he could talk with each one. A day or two after an exam, professors in North Hall noticed young men milling in the corridor outside his office, each wearing the magic article — a few wearing Eppie jackets borrowed for the occasion.

The anecdotal evidence seems to have had a basis in fact: The registrar's analysis of depart-mental final course grades for 1947-48, the first year that Reusch taught at Gustavus, confirms that he did substantially contribute to grade inflation. It shows that 12 percent of the student body earned course grades of "A"; in contrast, 35 percent of Reusch's students did.[52]

Perhaps Dr. Reusch was an easy grader, but decades later many of his former students could cite material from his lectures verbatim. A miracle, Sandra Bottge Lipke recalled, occurred when a need and a solution converged, "God using his existing world, not changing it for the occasion." (She also gained the impression that the downfall of many male characters in the Old Testament was caused by scheming women, "desert flowers," as Reusch described them, many of whom apparently were blondes.)[53]

More than test grades were the subject of discussions in the professor's office, however. Richard Leider came to Gustavus to play hockey, but academically he was just going through the motions, in his words, "taking the tests and forgetting about it the next day while having a great social life being away from home and trying to grow up." At the end of the first semester, and in danger of failing his courses, he went to talk with Dr. Reusch before final exams: "I can still smell the pipe smoke, can still see him there in his office surrounded by all that stuff, his African artifacts. 'I'm really lost,' I told him. 'I want to stay here, but I've really screwed up my life. What should I do?'"

Dr. Reusch didn't ask about his courses but simply asked the boy to tell him something about himself. "About *myself?* No other professor had ever asked me that!" Said Leider, "He's been on a planetary odyssey through his whole life, weaving his way in and out of one culture after another. He was his message. And I want his essence."[54]

Each campus fraternity and sorority sponsored a spring banquet, occasions when a faculty member was invited to give an after-dinner speech. Later there was dancing, but the College had only recently lifted its ban on that activity, so the collegiate "proms" were still called "banquets." The Eppies annually invited Dr. Reusch to be their guest of honor. Recalled Rev. Craig Johnson, "Somehow Reusch made the social event almost a worship service, and we all knew something magical was afoot, as if he had lived through all of recorded history."[55] Dr. Reusch first handed out cigars to the members of his "regiment," as he referred to the Eppies, and proceeded with a speech typically seasoned with references to ancient Greeks, the Koran and chivalric medieval knights.[56]

'A Semblance of Paradise'
A Composite Fraternity After-dinner Speech

I recently asked a somewhat sophisticated man, "How do you do?" His answer was, "I do as I please as long as my wife is not around." "Well, and if she is around?" His expression reminded me of Socrates, who said, "If you are well-married you are happy; if badly married you become a philosopher."

Everywhere in the world the opinion of the ladies concerning the opposite sex is just about the same: the male likes to eat like a hog, and when his tummy is full he likes to be caressed by tender experienced fingers until he purrs like a tom-cat. Then you can twist the guy around your little finger like Delilah twisted Samson. Yet those silly males are convinced they are the crown of creation!

When Allah created the earth, says the Muhammedan tradition, HE gave to man robust strength, courage and determination; but to the woman HE gave gracefulness, mildness and the bewitching light of the full moon. As graceful as a Gazelle HE made her, as sweet as wild honey.

Well, here tonight are a number of those bosses of the creation. And do you know how they think of you? Atomic weight, 120; consumes an incredible amount of choco-late and sweets; turns green when placed beside another specimen better looking and better dressed; highly explosive if treated by inexperienced hands, strongly objects to being left alone at a dinner or, even more, at a dance.

If both sexes would have only the above-mentioned opinions, by Jove, life would be very unpleasant and every male would turn into a philosopher like Socrates. But there is still another, a mysterious side to both sexes, and it can make this very room and this very banquet into a semblance of Paradise!

It is perfectly true that a pretty lady can move not only the individual to perform extraordinary deeds, but even a whole nation. As his blond-haired, blue-eyed beauty said to Sultan Ibn Tulun, "Brave one, I love you. But I can be yours only if you show yourself worthy of me!" Ten years later he was a Sirdar and a year later King of Egypt. His soldiers used to say, "Ibn Tulun takes booty from between the horns of satan!"

Xantippe turned the earthly life of Socrates into a hell because she did not use her sunshine in the right way. Delilah brought Samson to a fall. Two sides: on one, to make a hell, on the other to inspire to extraordinary deeds. A great power, and much sunshine is given to them, the beauties with the long hair and luminous eyes.

Everyone of us present here has only one life. What has passed has passed forever. It will never come again. You have only one youth. If it is filled with sunshine, the memory of it will go with you until the end of your life.

Gentlemen! The Middle Ages and chivalry have passed. But the traditions survive! Behave as Knights towards your ladies! Treat them as ladies and they will awaken in you everything which is good, honourable and noble!

You are future businessmen, will be in leading positions in a few years. You will face hardships, difficulties and disappointments that can embitter you. May this evening of your youth leave a bright memory with you, a memory summarized in these words: "Whenever my girl, my date, my sweetheart was beside me, there was a semblance of Paradise."

And may the memory of this evening stay with you and inspire you, strengthen you, and comfort you. That is my sincere wish, my friends. Thank you.[57]

The record does not reveal if sororities invited Reusch to speak at their banquets, but as Craig Johnson said, "'Zee Eppies' had become his regiment, and I think he enjoyed his relationship with the fraternity to the hilt."[58] That relationship continued long after Dr. Reusch retired, and to this day new pledges must memorize a biographical sketch.

Geology Professor Chester Johnson once made the mistake of showing Reusch an American Civil War saber purchased at the end of the conflict by one of his forebears. "Reusch grabbed it right out of my hands, and I didn't get it back until he retired," Johnson exclaimed with a Charlie Brown smile. On at least one occasion, clad in a white sheet to simulate a Bedouin tribesman, Reusch brandished Johnson's Civil War saber while riding on the Eppie float in a Homecoming parade,[59] a spectacle that was noted by some of his peers.

Reusch also taught fencing in the physical education department, not with effeminate French foils — *Nyet!* — but with sabers. "Hack zem into cabbage!" he bellowed at his recruits.[60] The sabers were war surplus weapons he had ordered from Australia. They were delivered to his home on the day his daughter Betty arrived with her three boys for a summer holiday. Naturally, the youngsters were delighted to find Grandfather in the living room with swords scattered about. But that afternoon Betty and Elveda were horrified when they looked out the kitchen window. Richard had shaved his grandsons' heads, and like the young Cossacks of his youth, swords tied with cord around their waists, they were whooping and hollering as they ran around in the backyard on imaginary horses.[61]

Reusch's fencing students left the class knowing arcane but fascinating information: the differing characteristics of straight and curved blades and the historical contexts in which each was developed; the difference between a scimitar and a saber; how to deliver basic saber strokes and how to parry those strokes; how Roman soldiers used the straight sword; and why a triangular blade is more lethal than a plain blade.[62]

Reusch's chivalric behavior, heroic tales, and kindliness were accepted and appreciated by most of his students, a generation about to dissolve into post-modernity. In 1959 he was presented with a handmade certificate: "The Senior Class proudly announces Dr. Reusch as the 'most courteous' professor at Gustavus." The class president, Paul Youngdahl, had signed the document.[63]

MODERN BIBLICAL SCHOLARSHIP

None of Reusch's colleagues doubted that he was well educated, but some questioned his theological scholarship — interrupted as it was by the First World War and thirty-one years in Africa. For instance, during a discussion with colleagues in North Hall, Reusch referred to a theological work by Theodore Zahn. Clair Johnson was unfamiliar with that name, so he went to the library, where he discovered that the volume in question had been published in 1906. Zahn had been one of Reusch's professors at Dorpat.[64]

Reusch's years at Tartu had deeply influenced his theological perspective. The function of theological inquiry, according to the Dorpat School, was to aid in preaching the Gospel — not to deconstruct Holy Scripture. In Reusch's judgment, the only legitimate Biblical scholarship was described in a simple syllogism: Here is the scripture verse, and there is the archeological evidence; therefore, it is true.[65] He had no patience with form criticism.

Professor Bernard Erling, a scholar who had studied at Augustana Seminary, the University of Chicago, Princeton and Yale Divinity School joined the Gustavus faculty in 1957. One afternoon the Masai Missionary wandered into Erling's office. The conversation turned to biblical criticism — which Reusch regarded as so much intellectual debris floating in outer space. Sometime later Reusch poked his head into another colleague's office and confidentially whispered, "I have been to see zee Sputnik!"[66]

At a department meeting toward the end of the fall semester, Chairman Robert Esbjornson asked each professor to list the texts he planned to require for the spring term. "And for Christian Doctrine?" he asked, looking at Reusch. As if he were an Eastern Orthodox archimandrite, the associate professor listed three texts: Holy Scripture, the Nicene Creed, and the writings of Polycarp and the early church fathers. Casting his dark-eyed gaze upon his peers, Reusch asked evenly, "What else is there?"

Dr. Reusch was anything but timid in defending orthodox Lutheran evangelical faith. One morning after daily chapel, a group of professors and the new college chaplain were having coffee and discussing the homily of the day in which the speaker had praised the work of the modern theologian, Rudolf Bultmann. The new chaplain, Richard Elvee, added his opinion to the mix, suggesting that New Testament criticism made a valuable contribution toward understanding the historical Jesus. A dark look came over Reusch's face. Slowly he put down his pipe, the cigar stub smoldering in the bowl, and rose to his feet.

"Chaplain," he glowered in a commanding tone that arrested the attention of each person at the table, "that is utter nonsense! You will apologize, *now*, to our Lord and Savior, Jesus Christ!" Reusch's flashing eyes drilled into the young cleric. No one stirred. It seemed to Elvee that time had stopped.

"What did you do?"

"I stood up — and apologized."[67]

Reusch had no interest in modern biblical scholarship, and realized that some on campus regarded him as hopelessly outdated, even anti-intellectual. One day before leaving North Hall to conduct a chapel service, Reusch stopped by Professor Clair Johnson's office and asked with a wry grin, "Would you please come to chapel today — I need to see at least one friendly face!" Reusch had prepared a meditation on John 4:24: "God is Spirit, and they that worship him must do so in spirit and truth." Man must worship something, Reusch said in his homily, if not the true God then an idol — national power, science, or his own intellect. But, he concluded,

> Two world wars and the atomic bomb have left in their aftermaths maladjusted broken lives, social and economic tensions, a wild brew of hate, blood and sorrows. There is only one way out of this misery — to lift our fear-filled eyes to the FATHER of the universe WHO has revealed HIMSELF through CHRIST. Our spirit looks beyond the limits of the visible into the invisible world where our FATHER's word is law and where peace abides. Only then will we be able to say with a happy smile in our last hour, "Into YOUR hands, my FATHER, I bestow my soul." And HE will take our soul and bring it to its eternal home of love and light! Amen.[68]

As part of the dedication of Christ Chapel in 1962, the College invited Professor Anders Nygren, Bishop of Lund, Sweden, and President of the Lutheran World Federation, to give a series of lectures. Reusch had hosted Nygren at Nkoaranga and was asked to say a few words at the closing banquet. In his tribute to Nygren, Reusch noted that the Swedish missionary with whom he had worked during his first term in Africa, John Steimer, had introduced him to Nygren's book, *Agape and Eros*:

"Here was a man," said Reusch, indicating Nygren, "who recognized the Majesty of GOD'S Amnesty-proclamation. . . . What his book said to me was: Explain, proclaim & reflect this LOVE once embodied in the person of CHRIST JESUS your KING to WHOM you have sworn allegiance."

Then, to the surprise of the assembled guests, Dr. Reusch hefted one of the three leopard skins he was permitted to take with him when he left Tanganyika, explaining how he had shot the animal in mid-air as it leapt at him, and fell dead at his feet. Turning to Nygren he said, "I salute you, my friend! Take it, but not for under the feet — on the wall with it, for it is a royal beast!"[69]

When Professor Erling visited Bishop Nygren in Lund some years later he saw the leopard skin mounted on a wall in the Bishop's study.[70]

Dr. Reusch (right) presents Swedish Bishop Anders Nygren with a leopard skin.

Gustavus Adolphus College Archives

TRUTH OR FICTION?

A pastor remarked after Reusch's visit to his windswept North Dakota parish, "Either he was the world's best storyteller or the most unusual man alive in the world."[71] An Augustana missionary who had worked with Reusch said with a chuckle, "No one could describe some minor marketplace skirmish and transform it into a tale of heroic and epic proportions like Richard Reusch."[72]

Dr. Reusch was the consummate storyteller, but some of the sober rationalists in the Gustavus community grew suspicious of his narratives, especially his stories about the Russian civil war. For example, Reusch had always implied that he was a witness to the carnage in Tartu during the Russian civil war:

> When we came to the basement prison we had to smash the oak door with axes. The whole basement was filled with bodies. Some of them were literally torn to pieces by the hand-grenades, which the Bolsheviks had thrown into the basement through the windows. Many others were still alive. We brought them out and revived them. Among

them were Pastor J. Sedlatschek and his fiancé, Count R. Berg, etc. On the walls one could see spots of blood, a handful of brains hanging there, or an eye hurled onto the wall by the explosion — the whole scene looked like bloody hell! [73]

But had he, in fact, organized and led the 250 volunteers and driven the Reds from Tartu as he sometimes claimed? Had he actually fought with Field Marshall Mannerheim during the three-month Finnish civil war in 1918? With General Nikolai Nikolaiovich Yudenitch's campaign to retake Petrograd in September and October 1919? With Major General Johan Laidoner who served in the Imperial Russian army in the Caucasus before organizing and leading the Estonian army to victory over the Reds in 1919? These and other claims seemed implausible.

If his critics had searched the historical record they would have learned that, while Reusch may have witnessed the bloody events in Tartu, he did not, in fact, lead the volunteers. The Estonian partisan, Kuperjanov, accomplished that feat. The names of the volunteers are known, but Reusch's name is not among them. [74] Did he fight with Mannerheim during the three-month Finnish civil war? No, because his signature appears on parish baptismal records in Tartu during those three critical months. [75] Did he fight with General Yudenitch who led the failed campaign to take Petrograd in September and October 1919? No, because Reusch swore in a statement to British authorities that he left Estonia in January 1919. [76]

Did he fight with General Laidoner in Estonia? Maybe. Several thousand White Russians served with the Estonian volunteers, and Reusch could have joined in pursuing the Reds as they retreated from Tartu. However, individual fighters, volunteer units and private armies were in constant flux. Records were not kept. Therefore, his assertion cannot be verified.

Perhaps Reusch fought with the Landeswehr Army that was organized by the Baltic barons as the German troops withdrew in December 1918. Perhaps Baroness Anna von Liphart introduced him to one of her relatives, three of whom organized or led detachments of volunteers — Baron Heinrich, and Hans and Georg Manteuffell. [77] Careful Landeswehr records were kept, and the names of the volunteers are known. But Reusch's name is not among them. [78]

The Finnish government banished the White Russian officers after the civil war, so Mannerheim found refuge elsewhere in Scandinavia for the former Imperial Russian officers who had aided his cause. A neatly penciled list in the Finnish National Archives bears the names of Russian officers who passed through Customs at Nikolaistadt (Vaasa) on their way to Sweden. That is how Reusch claimed to have gotten to Denmark. But his name is not on that list, either. [79]

Much of what Reusch said about the civil war was factual. And some of what he claimed was truthful — but not factual. For example, although only his brother was arrested and shot by the NKVD, Reusch often said that his family in Russia was dead. The Russian dissident, Pavel Litvinov, explained why exiles often felt that way: "I thought that when I left the country it was forever and that I would never see my parents again. This was a typical experience for many people. You left, and for you the people you were leaving behind were as good as dead. They were alive, but you lost them the way you lose people when they die." [80] Only after Reusch learned of their fate in 1963 did he publicly refer to them by name.

Had Reusch actually witnessed 3,000 people being shot in Petrograd? No. But the canals of Petrograd were full of decomposing bodies, and in one month alone the population fell by 100,000 due to the Red Terror and emigration.[81] Had he personally "waded through the blood" of 11,700 Imperial army officers in Moscow? No. But thousands of Imperial officers were executed after the 1917 revolution. But the Reds never dragged a guillotine into the Dorpat town square.

Perhaps Reusch did not participate in the civil war at all; perhaps he left Tartu with the von Lipharts. No, because they were issued Danish visas on December 13, 1918; Reusch did not apply for a Danish visa until May 23, 1919. He said that he left Rostock, Germany for Copenhagen in May 1919. Indeed, Danish immigration records note that he crossed the border on May 26, 1919.[82]

There are two more pieces of evidence that support Reusch's claim that he fought against the Bolsheviks in the civil war. First, Baron E. Schilling, the White Russian representative in Copenhagen, stated in an affidavit dated March 3, 1921 that Richard Gustavovich Reusch "is personally known to this Consulate-General," and left Russia "owing to the present conditions in that country, fearing bolshevik [sic] prosecution."[83]

Second, for more than fifteen years after the civil war Soviet security agents tried to locate Richard Gustavovich. By whatever means, Soviet agents finally tracked him down in 1937 and dispatched two agents to Marangu, Tanganyika Territory.[84] Therefore, although such evidence does not exist in Moscow archives, it appears that Reusch must have been regarded as an enemy of the Soviet State.[85]

What are we to make of the Lutheran pastor and missionary who told such tall tales? Maybe he was both "the world's best storyteller" *and* "the most unusual man alive in the world."

First, it is important to remember that Reusch was shaped in part by the culture of the Caucasus where the guardians of oral tradition occupy an important place in community life. Storytellers throughout the Middle East narrate their stories and epic ballads as if they were eyewitnesses — whether weaving a tale of Alexander the Great in the third century B.C. or celebrating a recent raid on a Russian military depot in Chechnya. According to that tradition, Reusch was permitted to cast himself as a participant in past epic events, thereby making history more accessible to contemporary imagination. His skill delighted British colonial officials in Tanganyika and impressed Africans and Americans alike.

Second, Reusch's rabid anti-Bolshevik attitude was shaped by the three deep structures of culture: History, religion and family. He always defined himself as a loyal subject and imperial Russian cavalry officer; his deeply held religious convictions were antithetical to "scientific" Marxism; and perhaps the most potent of the three, the Reds had martyred his friends and continued to threaten his family in the Soviet Union. In addition to his experiences and knowledge of historical facts and events, he also drew from the experiences of others to shape his dramatic stories. As Pastor Seidel noted in 1922, Reusch used powerful, descriptive, vivid, and lively language *"according to the Russian style."* [Emphasis added.]

"We were all aware that, regardless of everyone's affection for [Reusch], some of his stories had a credibility problem," the retired Leipzig missionary, Ernst Jäschke, admitted. However, through the liberties permitted by that kind of storytelling, "the tale came to life [while some-times creating] the impression that he himself was the hero. He could fascinate hundreds of people, making them shed many a tear. We all enjoyed his story-telling gift and never doubted his scientific findings, which were verified."[86] "When he was in the story-telling mood," wrote his friend, Emeroy Johnson, an Augustana Synod historian, "a part of the listeners' fun was in trying to discern where facts ended and tongue-in-cheek Oriental exaggeration began."[87]

According to one of Reusch's more outrageous fables, he had once served as escort for one of the tsar's daughters in St. Petersburg. It was a bitterly cold winter night, but the grand duchess insisted on attending a grand ball elsewhere in the capital. Snow was falling heavily as the carriage departed from the Winter Palace. Turning onto the Nevski Prospect, they saw a crowd of demonstrators carrying red banners demanding bread, peace and land. "Why are the people angry?" the grand duchess asked. "Because they are hungry," Reusch answered. The young princess gazed silently out of her window at the sullen faces in the street. Then she wondered aloud, "If they have no bread, why do they not eat cake?"

Reusch never served with the Cossack Imperial Guard in St. Petersburg. Neither did Marie Antoinette leave that bread-and-cake line to history.

Said Jäschke, "We all loved him very much."

PROMOTION DENIED

However, there were those who doubted not only Reusch's stories but also his legitimate experience and accomplishments, even his academic degrees. How many languages, *exactly*, had he mastered — 12 or 20? And how many times, *precisely*, had he climbed Kilimanjaro — 50 or 65 times? Reusch's world of Oriental dreams, storytelling and heroic Christianity collided head-on with some in the College community. Among the skeptics were some students.

Reusch often alluded to his skill as a sharpshooter, so an older student decided to put him to the test. One Sunday afternoon he invited Reusch to do some target shooting. The young man shot first, hit the bull's eye, and handed the rifle to his companion. But Reusch declined to take it. "I never shoot on Sundays," he said by way of explanation.[88]

However, most of the faculty and student body at Gustavus held Dr. Reusch in high regard. Dr. George Forell, a published scholar and theologian, was familiar with some of the ancient vocabularies to which Reusch often referred in casual conversation and never once noted an error. Forell dismissed attempts to entrap the little giant from the Caucasus as wrongheaded. If Reusch sometimes embellished the facts, he contended, it should be understood as Oriental hyperbole. Forell and President Edgar Carlson, among many others, valued Reusch's presence on the campus. After all, Reusch knew the ancient texts and languages and understood the cultural contexts better than most. "But more important," said a colleague, Robert Esbjornson, "his contribution was that of a holy man who lived his faith, moved mountains, as it were, and taught by example."[89]

In keeping with academic expectation and his own desire, Reusch submitted a number of manuscripts for publication. He became discouraged because American publishers were not interested, even about the Masai. The Augustana Book Concern, the Synod's publishing house, rejected his monograph on the historical and cultural context of Holy Communion. "Unless thorough documentation for some of the unusual statements that Dr. Reusch makes can be furnished," the editor wrote, "I doubt that there would be any likelihood of its acceptance." He added, "I cannot venture that it will be acceptable even if it is documented."[90] In 1959 Henry Holt and Company rejected his text on world religions.[91] And in 1961, the University of Minnesota Press declined to publish an English language edition of his East African history.[92]

Dr. Reusch would turn seventy years old in 1961, and it depressed him that, owing to College policy, he would soon face compulsory retirement. He was in excellent health and could still bench-press 220 pounds. Associate Professor Reusch decided to apply for promotion so he could at least end his academic career as a full professor. He had a doctorate from Tartu University; *Der Islam in Ost-Africa* (1931) was praised in Europe, and *A Short History of East Africa* (1954) was source material in African studies at European and Russian universities. But the promotion process required him to submit his publications for peer review.

Reusch was indignant. Since no one save he had witnessed the secret rites of the whirling dervish, what good was peer review? And who were his peers? Who could evaluate more than twenty books, monographs, and articles in Ki-Swahili that he had written in Africa — biblical commentaries, translations and educational materials?

Reusch applied for promotion but refused to submit to peer review.

His application for promotion was denied.[93]

Apparently, he concluded, his scholarly, educational, pastoral and church leadership in Europe and Africa counted for nothing. Angry and embittered, he begged George Hall to find him a position at another Lutheran college.[94]

Meanwhile, drought continued in the Longido region, and in the summer of 1961 Stan Benson wrote to thank Reusch for another contribution from the Eppie fraternity.[95] But the Son of Kibo was powerless to do anything substantial to aid the Masai mission.

A few days after receiving the bitter news about his promotion, Dr. Reusch honored his commitment to speak at a foreign missions conference at Wartburg College. Missionaries, he asserted, must understand the people they have come to serve, their culture, their psychology. "Do not try to Americanize them or they will become estranged from their tribe. Preserve what is good in their customs" and "honour, do not scorn their views. Their ways of witnessing are different from our ways." The missionary, he declared, must think of himself as an officer of Christ, "not a paid agent of a Mission Board or Church."[96]

Dr. Reusch felt betrayed by both Church and College. Frederick Ungar decided to publish an English edition of *A Short History of East Africa* later in 1961, but it was too late to affect his application for promotion. The volume can be found today in many university libraries.

Associate Professor Reusch had marked his 70th birthday on October 31, 1961, and retired at the end of the 1961-62 academic year. But simply to fade away was contrary to his nature.

Despite the indignity of forced retirement and his failed bid for promotion, he continued to teach part-time as professor emeritus.

A LETTER FROM KAZAKHSTAN

Reusch had learned in 1953 that Baron Reinhold von Liphart had died in 1940, son Gotthard was dead, and their home near Munich had been bombed in 1945; son Reinhold had emigrated to New York and Paul to Caracas.[97] A year later Reusch received word of the death of Baroness Anna von Liphart-Rathshof.[98]

In 1963, a decade after Stalin's death, a letter arrived in St. Peter with a postmark stamped Alma-Ata, Kazakhstan, USSR. It was from Richard's sister, Aurelia. "Many, many years have passed since we last saw you, our dear Richard!" she wrote, recalling that they had last seen each other in 1913. Then came the tragic accounting, "every death so hard on us" — their father, dead in 1938 of a stroke; their brother, Albert, of tuberculosis in 1940; their mother in 1941 of lung disease; and brother Erich, a cardiac specialist, in 1960 of a fatal heart attack while examining a patient. Mindful of the censor, Aurelia was afraid to reveal that Emil had been arrested and executed in 1937. All she said was, "Poor Emil, well, either he was killed in an accident or something." Neither did she dare to describe the details of their sister Olga's tragic death in the firebombing of Dresden because the Soviet censors might think the information carried political implications. She wrote instead,

> We have waited impatiently for a word from Benno [Olga's son], such as where are his mother, father and Ninotchka [Olga's daughter]. Suddenly there is tragic news that Olga, Arthur, and Ninotchka are not alive. We are so shaken by this news that we still cannot calm down. We could not have expected that so soon our dear Olga, Ninotchka, and Arthur would pass away from us to eternity so soon. Poor, poor creatures. We are so sorry for them.

Richard had learned from the International Red Cross in 1945 that Olga and her daughter, Ninotchka, had perished in the Allied fire-bombings of Germany. But news of the other family deaths came as a shock. Aurelia also wrote that their sisters, Marie and Vallie, were well and also living in Alma-Ata. "Meena is a doctor, and Vallie is an accounts clerk and typist. Ellie [Aurelia's daughter] is a teacher, and her husband too. I was also a teacher, since 1956 in Alma-Ata and before that in Siberia."[99] Why in Siberia she did not explain. No mention was made of Emma, but she and her family had made their way back to Rostov-on-Don.

The news of so many deaths took a toll on the seventy-two-year-old man, already saddened by personal disappointments. The following year, 1964, Reusch gave up part-time teaching. Dr. Reusch spoke to his Eppies for what he thought would be the last time at their spring banquet in 1964. The fraternity reluctantly conceded that the time had come when they "must soon give the salute of farewell to its revered friend and constant inspiration." A fraternity member wrote in tribute, "But we, Dr. Reusch, the members of Epsilon Phi Alpha, 'remember thee with reverence' for the loyalty, devotion, and 'friendship thou hast taught us.'"[100]

Dr. Reusch thanked them for the kindness and friendship they had shown to one who had lost his homeland, and Africa, now so distant — how much he "would like to hear once more the lions roaring and to see my mountain." In their company he had "found the continuation of my regiment," and he concluded his farewell with these words:

> Continue to cultivate the high ideals of our brotherhood! You have shown that in supporting hungry children in Masailand, in far-off Africa. . . . Faith, hope and love! And love is the greatest! You have shown it as long as I had contact with you. Continue to cultivate these virtues, and our brotherhood will be a shining symbol of goodness, honesty and helpfulness for the generations to come. GOD bless you!

1964 was the year that one of Reusch's successors in Masailand, David Simonson, was dismissed by the Chagga bishop, Rev. Stephano Moshi. As Reusch had predicted, an independent African Church did not allocate sufficient funds for the work in Masailand. That is what Masai elders believed, and so did Simonson, who intervened on their behalf. Bishop Moshi fired Simonson. But since, in the Bishop's words, one never meets a charging elephant head-on but steps aside and lets him barge past, he permitted the "elephant" to serve independently at his own expense at Loliondo.[101]

The compassion Reusch had demonstrated in Africa was returned to him in retirement. Mary Nelson, a Gustavus student who went to Africa in 1963, reported that after morning worship at the Ashira parish "a whole group of the old men came around and wanted to know how you were, how your children were, and what you were doing. . . . There are also numerous stories about your frequent treks up the mountain and other feats still circulating around here. Your name won't be forgotten!"[102]

"Very many people, especially the Africans, remember you with gratitude like ourselves," wrote Aristotle P. Matsis, the Greek owner of a coffee plantation and member of the new independent Tanzanian parliament. "We hope you are well and that you might come over to see us."[103]

"My editors have assigned me to write an article about Mt. Kilimanjaro," wrote the free-lance writer, Gordon Gaskill, from Rome, Italy, "and I spent several weeks in Moshi, Marangu, etc. Of course I ran across your footsteps everywhere . . . [and] found, of course, that *everybody* knew you, or about you."[104]

Dr. Reusch remained in St. Peter from 1964 to 1967, working on his manuscripts and substituting on Sunday mornings for clergy who were ill or on vacation. Reusch reminded the president of the Minnesota Synod, Dr. Melvin Hammarberg, that he stood ready to serve full-time any parish in need of a pastor, however small.

St. John's Lutheran Church in Stacy, Minnesota was suddenly left without a pastor.

And so Dr. Reusch began a weekly commute to the small village along the shoulders of U.S. Highway 61 north of St. Paul where he conducted Sunday morning worship services. Although there were differences between Baratayevka and Stacy, both were small rural communities where, like the Masai, folks worked hard to earn their daily bread.

Gustavus Adolphus College Archives

Dr. Richard Reusch, on the occasion of his retirement dinner at Gustavus Adolphus College in the spring of 1962.

CHAPTER 14

1   Masai elders at Longido, letter, 2 January 1955, GACA.
2   Stanley Benson, letter to R. Reusch, 14 March 1954, GACA.
3   Willmar Thorkelson, "Mountain-Climbing Missionary Retiring — Unless Africa Calls," Minneapolis *Star* (22 April 1954), clipping, GACA.
4   Dan L. Thrapp, "Missionary Tells of Fabulous Feats; Ex-Cossack Shot the Bolsheviks and Baptized Tribes in Africa," *Los Angeles Times*, 27 June 1954, sec. IA, 10. Richard Harding Davis, an author (editor of *Harper's Weekly* and a World War I correspondent), was responsible for the heroic but inaccurate account of Teddy Roosevelt's charge up San Juan Hill during the Spanish-American War. Like Reusch, Davis was a champion of "muscular Christianity" who was said to begin his day with "shrapnel and chivalry." — *Dictionary of National Biography* and *Dictionary of American Biography*.
5   Clair Johnson, interview, 17 February 1997.
6   Edna Anderson, letter to R. Reusch, 10 February 1957, GACA.
7   Alyce Carlson, letter to the author, 21 August 1995.
8   Lorraine Bergstrand, from the author's notes of an interview, 5 June 1994.
9   Clarence Budke, letter to R. Reusch, 10 June 1954, GACA.
10 Jack Dozier, from the author's interview, 5 March 1995.
11 Millard J. Ahlstrom, from the author's interview, 8 March 1997.
12 Edgar M. Carlson, letter to R. Reusch, 1 October 1954, GACA.
13 R. Reusch, various outlines, GACA.
14 "Former Cossack Officer Says Soviet Smile Is False," Minneapolis *Star* (6 October 1955), 24.
15 "Former Cossack Officer Says Khrushchev 'Coming to Spy,'" Edmonton *Journal*, undated clipping (ca. 1959), GACA.
16 R. Reusch, letter to Miss Zakariasen, undated, GACA.
    Reusch never capitalized the "s" in Satan. It is ironic that in the Soviet era editors of Dostoevski's works capitalized the "s" in Satan, but the "g" in God was rendered in the lower case.
17 R. Reusch, notes for a speech at a Hi-Y (YMCA) Camp, 12 September 1954, GACA.
18 Arthur H. Anderson, letter to R. Reusch, 17 June 1954, GACA.
19 E. R. Danielson, letter to Richard and Elveda Reusch, 14 December 1954, GACA.
20 George Hall, letter to R. Reusch, 7 December 1954, GACA.
21 R. Reusch, "Memorandum about the Masai Work," GACA.
22 Hall, letter, "Copies to all parties concerned," 6 January 1955, GACA.
23 Hall, "Copies to all."
24 Hall, letter to E. R. Danielson, 7 January 1955, GACA.
25 Eliyahu Sayoloi and six Masai chiefs, letter to R. Reusch (translated by R. Reusch), 2 January 1955, GACA.
26 Anderson, letter to R. Reusch, 18 April 1955, GACA.
27 Clarence Budke, letter to Richard and Elveda Reusch, 1 February 1955, GACA.
28 Anderson, letter to R. Reusch, 18 April 1955, GACA.
29 S. Hjalmer Swanson, letter to R. Reusch, 28 June 1955, GACA.
30 "A Student," note to R. Reusch, 17 December 1955, GACA.
31 Epsilon Phi Alpha document, GACA.

32 David Simonson, letter to R. Reusch, 23 October 1956, GACA.
33 Melvin Hammarberg, letter to R. Reusch, 30 November 1956, GACA.
34 R. Reusch's entries in his appointment book for 1955, GACA.
35 Bible Conference Program, 25-29 March 1956, Winger, Minnesota, GACA.
36 Transcript of an audio tape made by Rev. Arland Fiske, Binford, North Dakota, July 1957.
37 R. Reusch, letter to Kermit Youngdale, 31 July 1957, GACA.
38 Simonson, letter to R. Reusch, 7 October 1957, GACA.
39 R. Reusch, undated sermon notes based on Mark 8:1-9, and other documents, GACA.
40 Edna Anderson, letters to R. Reusch in 1956, GACA. (Anderson later felt called to dedicate her life as a deaconess, sold her possessions, and moved to the Lutheran Deaconess mother house in Omaha, Nebraska.)
41 Secretary to Leonard Kendall, President of the Minnesota Synod, letter to R. Reusch, 16 April 1957, GACA.
42 R. Reusch, sermon notes, 27 February 1958, GACA.
43 R. Reusch, sermon notes.
44 Clair Johnson, from the author's transcript of an audio taped interview, 17 February 1997.
45 Jim Anderson, from the author's transcript of an audio taped interview, 17 February 1997.
46 Dale Bosch, "Richard Reusch Tales" (23 May 1995), 4, GACA.
47 Roger Munson, from the author's transcript of an audio taped interview, 23 June 1994.
48 Jim Peters, from the author's transcript of an audio taped interview, 22 June 1999.
49 The author's recollection of Reusch's Old Testament course, fall semester, 1960.
50 R. Reusch, excerpts from two lectures prepared for a course in the Old Testament, which he taught every fall semester to first year students, GACA.
51 Jim Anderson, interview.
52 Registrar, "First Semester Analysis of Final Grades, 1947-48," GACA.
53 Sandra Bottge Lipke, letter to the author, 8 March 1997.
54 Richard Leider, from the author's transcript of an audio taped interview, 13 June 1995. (In 1983 Leider found himself thousands of miles from Gustavus, atop Kibo Peak on Mount Kilimanjaro, looking down into Reusch Crater. "Why is it called that?" he asked his companion. Derrick Pritchard of Outward Bound didn't know the answer. When Leider later learned that it was named for his mentor he took it as a sign. The once floundering student went on to help people discover new directions for their lives by guiding them on treks through Masai-land to gain wisdom from the people who had made Dr. Reusch one of their own. Leider earned a graduate degree in psychology and in 1994 received the Gustavus Distinguished Alumni Award. His acceptance speech was framed as a tribute to Dr. Reusch.)
55 Craig Johnson, from the author's notes of an interview, 17 February 1997.
56 Bosch, "Richard Reusch Tales."
57 R. Reusch, excerpts from undated manuscripts, "A Semblance of Paradise," "Sailing in Moonshine or Moonlight," and "Knights and Daze," GACA.
58 Craig Johnson, interview.
59 Chester Johnson, letter to the author, 1999.
60 Carol Eide, "'Touchez!' Dr. Reusch Teaches Fencing Art," *Gustavus Weekly* (3 March 1961), 4.

61 Neil and Mark Anderson, Reusch's grandsons, letters and interviews.

62 R. Reusch, fencing exam, GACA.

63 Paul Youngdahl, senior class president, certificate, GACA.

64 Clair Johnson, interview.

65 Robert Esbjornson, from the author's notes of an interview, 17 February 1997.

66 Clair Johnson, interview.

67 Richard Elvee, from the author's notes of an interview, 17 February 1997.

68 R. Reusch, excerpt from an undated manuscript for a chapel sermon, GACA.

69 R. Reusch, Bishop Nygren testimonial, notes, GACA.

70 Bernard Erling, from transcript of an audio taped interview, 17 February 1997.

71 Arland Fiske, from the author's notes of an interview, 12 August 1996.

72 Stan Benson, interview.

73 R. Reusch, undated manuscript, "Lenin's seizure of power and how he handled it," GACA.

74 Eero Medijainen, History Faculty, Tartu University, in an e-mail letter to the author, 14 June 1996.

75 *Dorpater Kirchenbucher*, 130.

76 R. Reusch, copy, visa application for entry to Tanganyika Territory, 9 September 1922 (R. Reusch file), ELMLA.

77 Claus Grimm, *Vor Den Toren Europas 1918-1920: Geschicte der Baltoschen Landeswehr* (1963), 116, 226-27.

78 N. Rizhov, Director, Latvian State History Archives, letter to the author, 21 September 1999.

79 "Militära uppgifter," Gustaf Mannerheim Arkivet, Kartong 8, Handlingar 5, n. 1-70, Finnish National Archives.

80 Pavel Litvinov, quoted by David Remnick in *Lenin's Tomb: The Last Days of the Soviet Empire* (1993), 21.

81 Robin Bruce Lockhart, *Reilly, Ace of Spies* [reprint, 1983], 127.

82 Danish border visa registration card for Richard Reusch (1353 Rigspolitichefen/Lb. nr. 631), DNA.

83 E. Schilling, Consul-General of the White Russian Embassy, Copenhagen, affidavit No. 169, 3 March 1921, GACA.

84 Elveda Reusch told her daughters about the agents' visit; from the author's notes of Reusch family interviews.

85 V. P. Gusachenko, archivist, letter dated 21 March 1996, Central Archive, Federal Security Bureau, Moscow.

86 Ernst Jäschke, letter to the author, 25 August 1995.

87 Emeroy Johnson, "Dr. Richard Reusch 1891-1975," copy prepared for the *Greater Gustavus Quarterly* (December 1975), GACA.

88 Clair Johnson interview.

89 Robert Esbjornson, interview.

90 Victor E. Beck, letter to Rev. H. E. Sandstedt, 11 September 1958, GACA.

91 Henry Holt and Company's rejection letter, 12 November 1959, GACA.

92 John Ervin, Jr., letter to R. Reusch, 17 January 1961, GACA.

93 Reusch's claimed academic degrees were also questioned because, according to his own reports, they seemed to change over time:

His 1949 Augustana Biographical Data form: B.Ph., B.D., B.A., Lic. Theol and M. Phil. (Dorpat, 1915); Mag. Theol. (Dorpat, 1921); S.Th.D. (Dorpat, 1930); D.D. (Dorpat, 1931) and D.D. (Augustana Seminary, 1948).
In 1960: B.A., B. Milit. Sc. & B.Ma. (Imperial Cadet Corps, Vladikavkaz), B.Phil., B.D., B.Sc., Lic. Theol., M. Phil. and M.Theol. (Dorpat, 1915); S.Th.D. (Dorpat, 1922); D.D. (Dorpat, 1930); and D.D. (Augustana Seminary, 1948).

94 Reusch's College personnel file was unavailable to the author. The account presented here is drawn largely from the Hall interview.
95 Stan Benson, letter to R. Reusch, 9 July 1961, GACA.
96 R. Reusch, notes for an address on foreign missions at Wartburg College, 11 February 1962, GACA.
97 Anna von Liphart, letter to R. Reusch, 12 March 1953, GACA.
98 Notice of Anna von Liphart's death, GACA.
99 Aurelia Reusch, letter to the R. Reusch family in St. Peter, dated 1963.
100 "Eppies bid farewell to Dr. Reusch," *The Gustavian* (1964 yearbook), 103.
101 Jim Klobuchar, *The Cross under the Acacia Tree* (1998), 89-90.
102 Mary Nelson, letter to R. Reusch, 20 January 1963, GACA.
103 Aristotle P. Matsis, M.P., letter to R. Reusch, December 1963, GACA.
104 Gordon Gaskill, letter to R. Reusch, 3 June 1964, GACA.

Betty Anderson

Dr. Richard Reusch, Pastor of St. John's Lutheran Church, Stacy (1975).

Chapter Fifteen

STACY, MINNESOTA
Village Pastor, 1967-1975

Be you loyal unto death and I shall give you the crown of life.

— Revelation 2:10

"We were desperate to find an interim pastor," said Carolyn Frenning, a member of the parish council of St. John's Lutheran Church, "because our membership had declined to the lowest number in the fifty years." One pastor retired after his wife died, and his replacement had to resign for health reasons only six months later. "That's when the Synod recommended Dr. Reusch as an interim pastor, and since he wanted to come to a small parish we hired him."

For more than a year, the loyal cleric made weekend trips by bus from St. Peter to Stacy, and after Sunday lunch the Frenning or Capanni family drove him the 90 miles back to St. Peter. "On his first Sunday," said the former councilwoman, "people were a little confused. He was hard to understand because of his accent. But his charisma drew everyone to him." In the following months the little congregation learned about Cossacks, the Russian civil war, and Africa. "He used those stories to draw people back again to hear more of the Word of God," Mrs. Frenning explained, "and when he spoke to us about the Masai we could see that they were more his people than his birth people. He had a tremendous amount of respect and love for them."[1]

"It was just fantastic, the life he lived," exclaimed Ralph Skow, another parishioner. "And yet he always had time for the kids. When he was greeting them he'd get down and shake hands with the little ones. Oh, he was great with them!"[2]

The parish needed a full-time pastor if it were to survive, but even without Reusch's pastoral leadership during the week, attendance at Sunday morning services grew from less than a dozen people to more than a hundred. After two years, the church council insisted that the seventy-five-year-old Reusch be named their full-time pastor. The Synod president finally gave his permission for the little parish to issue a call:

> To Dr. Richard Reusch: Grace to You and Peace from God Our Father and from the Lord Jesus Christ. At a meeting of the members of St. Johns Lutheran Church held on the 12th day of March, A.D. 1967, you were duly chosen to become its pastor. By authority and on behalf of said church we, the undersigned, do hereby now extend you a formal call, and earnestly urge upon you the acceptance of the same.[3]

Dr. Reusch regarded the call to duty as a commission from his Heavenly King. He no longer had a role to play in an independent Tanzanian Lutheran Church, among the members of the Board of Foreign Missions, or at Gustavus Adolphus College. But now he had a mission among people who loved him and wanted him in their midst. In April 1967 he and Elveda happily sold their house in St. Peter and moved into the parsonage attached to the small Stacy church.

Throughout the spring and summer the energetic village pastor worked at rebuilding the parish. In September Dr. Reusch received a form letter from his former church home in St. Peter, First Lutheran Church, asking for his 1968 pledge. Dr. Reusch replied,

> When I was here in April, there came 7-8 people to the Sunday services, the financial position was miserable, and the Church Council in despair. All they could offer was 350 dollars per month. Now in September the church is again full, some new members have already joined, and a new group is preparing to join in October. We have already a fine and active Bible class, a good Confirmation class, and hope to have a choir before Christmas. New life is coming into the congregation with GOD's help. I feel that my first obligation is to this congregation, which my Heavenly King has entrusted to me, and my help has to be dedicated to this flock of CHRIST. I cannot divide the little financial help I am able to give among two congregations. More I cannot do financially now. All I can do will go to this little congregation as long as the LORD allows me to serve it.[4]

On Sunday, October 29, 1967, two days before Dr. Reusch's seventy-sixth birthday, the council president invited the congregation to bring their offerings to the altar in thanksgiving for "our wonderful pastor, Dr. Reusch, a most humble man, and as Dr. Hammarberg, the president of our Synod said, 'the most colorful and influential Lutheran in the state of Minnesota.'" He thanked the volunteers who had painted the church and parsonage inside and out and re-shingled the church roof; he congratulated the thriving Sunday School, the active women's groups, "beyond a doubt the backbone of our congregation," and the new members received into membership that day.[5] As it had been in Loliondo, so it was in Stacy.

"Friends in CHRIST!" Dr. Reusch greeted the group of new members clustered around the small altar, and proceeded to restate the theme of his ordination sermon, one that permeated his homilies from 1917 to 1975:

> CHRIST is love. Love is an invisible power which activates, controls and guides our actions, a power which helps us to do GOD-pleasing deeds. Such deeds of love reflect CHRIST's love. That unselfish love is a spark from GOD's love. Wherever it exists there is present GOD's holy influence. It unites us with our SAVIOUR here on earth and in eternity. If we have a spark of HIS love we will love HIM and one another. Such a love makes us to be a family of CHRIST, and that is all we want to be. A closely knit family is a power physically and spiritually. Its members know to whom to turn in need of help and comfort in distress, and know their obligations to support and help one another. As new members of our family we welcome you. May you feel at home in our midst here on earth and may we continue to be HIS family in eternity! Welcome in our SAVIOUR's name![6]

Mrs. Reusch "never intruded into his pastoral life, but she was a marvelous woman, always there *with* him, always there *for* him," said Mrs. Frenning. "I've never seen anyone walk like Elveda, even at her age, a stride like no one else around here. Just imagine the countless miles she must have walked in East Africa."

By January 1968, St. John's counted 160 members, 60 children enrolled in Sunday School, and a functioning Luther League for the young people. Dr. Reusch had made 34 hospital visits in the past year, and performed one marriage ceremony, nine baptisms, and six funerals. Their commanding officer wrote in his annual report for 1967, "Our Church Council has begun to sing a *new song unto the Lord* [emphasis his]. Let us follow their lead! If we sing such a new song, then our debts will melt away, we shall recover and be able to help the needy."[7]

Ralph and Irene Skow and their six children moved to the Stacy area in 1967. They were still searching for a permanent church home when in the spring of 1968 they decided to visit St. John's. Said Irene, "Our oldest daughter told a friend at school that she didn't much care for the church we were going to, and so her friend said, 'Why don't you come to our church sometime and listen to this guy, Dr. Reusch?'"[8]

The Skows chose to attend a mid-week Lenten service as a test: If the pastor made nothing special of the Wednesday night worship service, and if it were not well attended, they would continue their search. Said she, "All our kids wanted to go to St. John's after that."

The family more than filled a pew the following Sunday, and a few days later Ralph called Dr. Reusch to tell him that he and his family wanted to join the parish. Lary Skow, who was eight years old at the time, recalled what happened next:

> Dr. Reusch said to come over to the parsonage. I had to go with because none of my older siblings were around. The main door to the church was open, and we went inside and knocked at his office door. A voice farther back called, "Well, come in." And so we did, but saw nobody. "I'm in the back," came his voice again, and so we went through the other door that opened into the attached parsonage and found him in the back bedroom where he was bench-pressing weights.[9]

It took a while for Lary to get used to Reusch's accent, and at first he was not keen about going to church and Sunday school. But he was taken by Reusch's sermons because the pastor always told an interesting story. It was those stories that drew Lary to sit alone in the pew directly below the pulpit "so I could absorb every word he said."

At the end of the service Dr. Reusch always recessed down the center aisle during the singing of the last hymn. If there were enough verses to the hymn, he had time to remove his alb in his office. "And," Lary recalled with a grin, "if there were a few moments more he'd cut the end off a cigar and stuff it in his pipe so that when all the parishioners were gone he could have a smoke."

Dr. Reusch greeted the men with a hearty handshake. "But," said Mrs. Frenning, "it was not a handshake with Dr. Reusch for the ladies. Oh, no! He *kissed* our hands. He even kissed the hands of the little girls. And, of course, he always had a cigar for the men — whether they smoked or not!"

"If the young children were waist high he'd stuff you behind him and through the door into his office," Lary recalled. After Reusch had greeted the adults "he'd come into his office, go to his antique desk, and take out a piece of candy for each of us kids. He was always the gentleman, and ladies he treated delicately. As for the little girls, well, if you wanted to see his eyes light up, send in a well-dressed little girl!"

The congregation wanted to share their remarkable pastor with a wider public, and so during the spring and summer of 1968 they sponsored a weekly Sunday radio broadcast on WCMP-AM in nearby Pine City. On May 5th the parish announcer opened the week's program with these words:

> For the benefit of those of you who may have missed our earlier broadcasts, we would like to take this opportunity to say a few words about the regular speaker on this program — the pastor of St. John's congregation. Dr. Reusch is the author of 27 books and speaks fluently in 20 languages of the world. He is very widely travelled and has been in the Holy Land on many occasions and speaks from personal knowledge and acquaintance with holy, historical Biblical places.
>
> In addition to having taught in Europe he also served as professor of religion at Gustavus Adolphus College for 12 years after a missionary career in Africa spanning 34 years. Prior to his ordination he was a career officer in the Imperial Russian army and saw military action in the war of independence for Finland.
>
> From his wide background, his multiple professions, and his deep personal piety, and the burning conviction of his faith, we know that you will be blessed as you listen from Sunday to Sunday to this radio ministry.[10]

"The children were drawn to him," said Mrs. Frenning, "and so were the adults. But we didn't put Dr. or Mrs. Reusch on a pedestal. He was a wonderful, wonderful teacher, and that was what we were so blessed with in this community for ten years."

So successful was Dr. Reusch that in August 1968 President Hammarberg asked him to take responsibility for Salem Lutheran Church in nearby Oxford.[11] Reusch agreed to do so, heartened that at his age his service was valued.

"We can thank God for our Church and our Pastor and his wife," wrote Eugene Anderson, the chairman of St. John's church council, in October 1968. In addition to the radio broadcasts, parish organizations were flourishing and the debt had been reduced.[12] The essential challenges of parish leadership in America were not all that different from those in Africa.

Ralph and Irene Skow took on the responsibility for leading the youth activities. "One time we were stumped for a program," said Ralph, "so we asked Dr. Reusch to talk to the young people for fifteen to twenty minutes."

Irene interjected, "He wanted to know what subject, and I said, 'You pick it.'"

Ralph nodded, adding, "And you know, he talked for over an hour. The kids just sat there, spellbound."

"They were stunned," Irene agreed. But the stories of Cossack regiments and African leopards were more than tales of adventure. They illustrated God's love and mercy, and made the case for loyalty to the storyteller's Heavenly King.

The St. Croix District pastors met at Stacy in November 1968. "Upon arrival at St. John's," it was reported in the minutes, "Dr. Reusch greeted us at the door, led us to the coffee table, and gave cigars to those desiring them."[13] Rev. Dan Buendorf, one of the district pastors, said, "We just plain loved him because he was so gracious, a gentleman whose behavior and kindness changed the atmosphere wherever he appeared."[14]

THE "GREENING OF AMERICA"

Dr. Reusch apparently did not speak out on the issue of civil rights, from the desegregation crisis in 1957 at Little Rock, Arkansas, to the assassination of Dr. Martin Luther King in 1968. In 1971 the former imperial subject did express his opinion about the Watts Riots in Los Angeles, "with their burnings, lootings, killing and cries of 'burn baby, burn.'" He linked civil disorder of any kind, whether on behalf of racial equality or protesting the war in Vietnam, to Communist agitation, and was repulsed by the youth culture of drugs, sex and rock 'n roll.[15] His teenage grandson, Richard, came to visit one summer wearing bell-bottom jeans, his long hair hanging over an embroidered work shirt. "What are you, a hippie?" his grandfather growled.

"I felt as if I had betrayed him," said Richard.

One evening a few days later Reusch heard a knock at the church door. There stood a soldier in uniform, clutching his duffel bag, on his way home after a tour of duty in Vietnam. He had made his way as far as Stacy, he explained, but had no money to buy a bus ticket for the final leg of his journey. Could the pastor help him get home?

The former imperial officer welcomed the young private into the parsonage. While he assembled a late supper for his guest, Dr. Reusch telephoned a parishioner for assistance. After he had eaten, the soldier was put in the front seat of the neighbor's car, and Dr. Reusch and his grandson climbed into the back seat. "I don't remember where we went," Richard recounted, "but I remember pulling into a farmyard somewhere north of Stacy, getting the duffel out of the trunk, and watching as the family came running out of the house to greet their son and brother."[16]

Civil disorder in America led Reusch to look more closely at the Book of Revelation. The creation of the state of Israel in 1948 seemed to fit with some interpretations of prophetic literature, including the Apostle John's apocalyptic vision. In the late spring of 1969, Eugene Anderson, the church council president, helped to arrange a visit to the Holy Land. The church bulletin made the announcement: "Dr. Reusch, Mr. Gene Anderson and Rev. R. Landeen will leave on Tuesday for an extended trip to the Holy Land. We pray God's blessing upon them and may He bring them safely home to us."[17]

The Orientalist returned from his trip with trinkets for everyone and, of course, many stories. When visiting the Tomb of the Patriarchs at the Hebron mosque, for example, he was told that only Muslims could gain access to the cenotaphs of Abraham and Sarah, and so he disguised himself in Palestinian clothing and went inside.[18] Apparently, since his adventures in the Middle East in 1929, the danger of appearing in disguise appealed to Reusch. While in Jerusalem in 1963, he unexpectedly ran into a Gustavus colleague, Robert Esbjornson and said, "If you should see me in the bazaar and I am in disguise, pretend you do not know me. It could be dangerous!"[19]

In the autumn of 1970 Dr. Reusch held a series of Wednesday morning Bible classes on the Book of Revelation. "He thought the Second Coming would occur near the millennium," said one of his students, "and he would always say, 'Oi, I wish I could be here for that!' But he certainly wasn't obsessed with the topic. He was one of those old-time pastors who preached the Gospel. Despite his education and experience, even I could understand — even with all the Aramaic, Hebrew, and Greek vocabulary," she said, leafing through her worn Bible, the margins filled with notes from her pastor's Bible studies.[20]

However, Dr. Reusch did not always entertain, comfort, or instruct his flock. In his letter to the congregation at the end of 1969 he closed with an admonition that addressed an issue central to the mission of any Christian community:

> One thing hurt me, namely, that our benevolence contributions are still only 480 instead of 942 dollars. Our LORD said: "What you have done to one of these little ones you have done unto ME." Let us dig today into our pockets and make up the difference as good as we can! In CHRIST's family every one should be a supportive member, for it is the community that heals the wounds of others.[21]

At the March 1970 meeting of the St. Croix District pastors, Dr. Reusch presented his monograph on Holy Communion. His peers voted to mimeograph the paper and send copies to every pastor in the district.[22] Their enthusiastic response prompted the author to submit the paper for publication in *Christianity Today*. The editorial committee was "impressed with the article but indicated it was too long for our magazine."[23] Undaunted, Dr. Reusch continued to work on another manuscript, "Let These Stones Speak," an outline of archeological discoveries that corroborated biblical history. That subject had first drawn his interest at Tartu University in 1911 and continued to motivate his study and journeys until the end of his life.

In June 1971 Reusch made his last visit to Israel, a rigorous journey for a man a few months short of his eightieth birthday. Arriving in Tel Aviv on June 9th, he and Eugene Anderson went to Haifa and from there to the northern Galilee region; on the 16th he was in Eilat, and then to Jerusalem for an international conference on biblical prophecy, promoted by American evangelical Protestants. "The Prophetical Conference was nothing spectacular," he wrote on a postcard to his congregation, "but the Holy Places are as impressive as ever."[24]

Reusch and Anderson traveled south from Jerusalem to the Sinai Peninsula, the Timna Valley, and then through the wilderness to St. Catherine's Monastery at the foot of Jebel Musa, where Moses received the Ten Commandments. They left the monastery at 3:30 in the morning for, in Anderson's words, the "hard climb" to the summit. It was the last mountain that Reusch climbed. As he boarded the El Al flight for New York, Dr. Reusch had but one regret:

The daughter of his mentor at Tartu University was scheduled to be in Israel in August, and he missed seeing Sophie von Bulmerincq by only two days.

The village pastor's luggage was again stuffed with small gifts for his congregation, items made by the children at a Roman Catholic orphanage in Jerusalem — rosaries, bracelets and tie tacks for the adults, and flaky almond candy for the children.

Rosaries?

"Yes, *rosaries*," affirmed the Lutheran Mrs. Frenning as she held up the one she had received. "He bought them to help the children."

During his years in Stacy, Dr. Reusch continued to receive invitations to speak about Africa or the Communist threat, but only from nearby communities. He spoke at Our Saviour's Mission Family Night in Soderville (East Bethel) on September 19th, 1967. "You will want to meet Dr. Reusch," declared a note in the church bulletin, "short of stature but great in devotion." And so the good people of Our Saviour's heard his story: Imperial Russian cadet, his regiment's battalion decimated in Persia; the Russian civil war; his call to Africa where Missionaries Ovir and Segebrock had been murdered and where he was poisoned three times; his initiation as a Masai warrior; and the spears at Longido. Of course, he also used the opportunity to pitch the work among the Masai: "If a few crumbs are left over," he concluded, "for these crumbs I beg!"[25] And so another contribution was sent to his friends in Masailand. As always, his stories had a purpose.

The last speaking invitation came in January 1975: "We would like to have you present a 1/2 hr. program on the Star of Bethlehem at our next Lutheran Church Women's meeting at 2:00 p.m. on Thurs. Jan. 9th. The meeting will include a lunch at the Fish Lake Lutheran Church. If you need a ride, let me know."[26] The request must have taken him aback because the writer had confused him with his friend and colleague at Gustavus, Dr. Karlis Kaufmanis. It was the Latvian astronomer, not Reusch, who had developed a popular and provocative presentation on the Star of Bethlehem.

Dr. Reusch was the featured speaker at the Russian History Dinner sponsored by the Fort Snelling Officers' Club in May 1973 where he spoke on the topic, "Personal Reminiscences of Czarist Russia." In April 1975 he spoke to the American Conservative Citizens Assembly on the topic, "Joseph Stalin: Apostle of Evil,"[27] and a month later was asked to give the same speech at Isanti, Minnesota.[28]

Some who saw him infrequently noted that in his last years his accent became heavier and his energy had begun to flag. He was moved to clip and save the lines of doggerel that spoke to his stage in life:

> The reason I know my youth is all spent,
> My get up and go has got up and went.
> But I really don't mind, when I think with a grin
> Of all the grand places my get up has been.

Members of St. John's realized they would not have Dr. Reusch with them forever, and so in the autumn of 1974 some parents took the unusual step of placing their younger children in the Confirmation class to receive the benefit of Dr. Reusch's instruction. Preparation for the Rite of

Confirmation was a two-year process, and the young people met for two hours once a week during the school year. During the first hour Dr. Reusch told stories about Old and New Testament characters, lacing his experiences and contextual knowledge into the narratives: King Balak of the Moabites; Balaam, "the famous Seer who knew and worshipped the GOD of Abraham"; Og, the Giant of the Northern Kingdom; and Melkizedek.

"As an adolescent, when life is starting to make sense," Lary recalled, "there was always something in Dr. Reusch's stories that applied to my life." After a break the students took out their spiral-bound notebooks and took Dr. Reusch's dictation, which prepared them for the final public examination.

Meanwhile, Tartu University professor, Pent Nurmekund, was working on a monograph about Dr. Reusch, one of the institution's illustrious alumni. Working from a list of graduates, he found Reusch's academic file in the Estonian State Historical Archives and learned of Reusch's connection with the Leipzig Mission. "Your last letter [to the Leipzig Mission] dates from the 28th of December 1961," the Estonian professor wrote in 1974. "Obviously, more data are needed for writing your monograph." But Estonia was a Soviet satellite. Dr. Reusch did not reply.

Professor Nurmekund wrote a second letter: "The contemporary Tartu State University endeavours to get acquainted with its past history. . . Considering your being a former student of our university, your subsequent activity in Africa cannot be passed over in silence." He added, "I assure you that my request follows a strongly scientific aim."[29] Reusch filed the letter without a reply, and therefore the Tartu professor prepared a biographical sketch of Reusch drawn from the available data and presented it at a conference of African historians at Leningrad in 1975.[30] Ironically, even as his reputation as a scholar and African missionary was fading in America, it was being revived in his homeland.

FADING AWAY

Not only was Reusch's robust health in decline, but also Mrs. Reusch had, as the Lakota Indians would have put it, "turned inward to live in another country." Her driver's license was not renewed in 1971 because of Alzheimer's disease.

Thereafter, the Reusches were homebound, depending on others for transportation. Dr. Reusch would call and politely ask if one or another might drive him and Elveda to Forest Lake, where cigars were five cents cheaper than in Stacy. On the way home Dr. Reusch always suggested stopping somewhere for cherry pie. "Of course, it had less to do with a better deal on cigars and a piece of pie," Mrs. Frenning noted, "than it was a way to take Elveda out of the house and to socialize."

The community tried to be of help. Nevertheless, the hour-to-hour burden fell upon Richard. His children begged him to place their mother in institutional care but he would not hear of it. He had promised to remain loyal — for better and for worse. The frail couple's eldest daughter, Betty, spent most weekends driving from Ontario, Canada, to Stacy in order to assist with her mother's care.

African clergy occasionally came to study at Luther Seminary in St. Paul. They and their families always made the short trip to Stacy for a visit with Dr. and Mrs. Reusch. Early in 1973 the Masai Missionary learned that the General Synod of the Northern Diocese had accepted the requests of the Masai/Mbulu and Pare Church Districts to withdraw from the Northern Diocese. The Masai were finally independent — for the same reasons that Reusch had argued some twenty-five years earlier. Vindication must have brought him some sense of satisfaction. But he was now preoccupied with the burdens of caring for his wife and the decline brought on by his own advancing age.

The Reusch family gathered at Stacy for Easter, 1975. "We were watching the Easter story on television," recalled Neil, one of Reusch's grandsons, "and as the camera zoomed in on Christ on the cross, Grandfather turned to me and, with tears in his eyes, said, 'If I'd been there with my Cossacks, the Romans wouldn't have crucified Him.'"[31]

On Sunday, May 11th, the eighty-three-year-old Reusch fainted after finishing his sermon, but insisting there was no cause for alarm he received the offering and concluded the liturgy. Mrs. Frenning remarked that her pastor never allowed anyone to see any weakness. "He was always the strong person, not just for our sakes but for Elveda's sake. He never wanted to concern her about his health."

The following Sunday, May 18th, the little church was filled to capacity for the Rite of Confirmation, the day that the Lutheran Church Women also were collecting clothing and bedding for the needy. Lary Skow had prepared to respond to Dr. Reusch's question about Holy Communion, and his answer that morning earned an "excellent" from his pastor.

Gustavus Adolphus College Archives

Dr. Reusch and his last group of confirmands at St. John's, May 1975.

FAREWELL

On June 8th there was no service at St. John's because Dr. Reusch was attending the annual Minnesota Synod conference. He was back in the pulpit the following Sunday, June 15th, but it was clear to everyone that he was not well. Like the wheat that springeth green and withers after a season, Dr. Reusch had come to recognize that he could no longer adequately serve his parish. Neither could he continue to serve as the primary caregiver for his wife. Two days later, on June 17th, he submitted his resignation, effective July 1st. It was agreed that he and Elveda would go to live with their eldest daughter in Ontario, where Richard would volunteer as an assistant to the local Lutheran pastor in ministering to elderly immigrants from the Baltic countries.

But on June 22nd, five days after tendering his resignation and little more than a week from retirement, Dr. Reusch again fainted during the liturgy. Again he revived and insisted on concluding the worship service. However, when he collapsed a second time, despite his protestations several men gently carried him from the church. It is remembered that as they did so, the aged pastor pulled on the sleeve of one of the deacons and said, "Do not forget to take up zee collection!" He was transported from his beloved St. John's to the Chisago Lakes Hospital.

Dr. Reusch fully intended to be in his pulpit the next Sunday to give his farewell sermon. The 29th was Youth Sunday, and his Luther Leaguers would be providing special music and reading the Epistle and Gospel lessons. Between medical tests in the hospital during the early part of that week, he carefully typed his farewell sermon.

Betty was with her father when the diagnosis was delivered on Wednesday. Dr. Reusch had cancer. It was terminal. She called her sisters, and the family began gathering at the patriarch's bedside.

Irene Skow was shocked to learn on Friday, the 27th, that Dr. Reusch's condition was rapidly deteriorating. "If I cannot make it on Sunday," her pastor had said, "I want Lary Skow to read the sermon." The final draft of a two-page manuscript lay on his bedside table.

The telephone rang at the Skow residence on Saturday morning, shortly before 15-year-old Lary had planned to leave for the hospital to visit Dr. Reusch. A church council member informed Lary that their pastor had died at 12:08 that morning. The boy was overwhelmed with grief. Said Lary, "Dr. Reusch was one of those people who is bigger than life, and you don't expect he will ever die. I mean, he was old when he came to Stacy, but where were the signs that he was about to *die?*"

That same morning, between planes at Winnipeg, Reusch's grandson, Richard, called the parsonage in Stacy. That is how he learned that his hero had already died. The young man later bought a cigar and at the funeral home placed it in his grandfather's hand. "I'm not my grandfather," Richard admitted, "but I've always striven to be like him."

"The Reverend Richard Reusch, D.D., departed this life on June 28, 1975," the Synod president, Rev. Melvin Hammarberg, informed the Minnesota clergy. "Funeral services will be held on Tuesday morning, July 1st, 11:00 a.m. at St. John's Lutheran Church, Stacy, Minnesota."[32]

On Youth Sunday, the 29th, the church was packed with grieving parishioners. Lary Skow faced the most daunting task in his life that morning as he stepped into the pulpit to read Dr. Reusch's sermon. "I concentrated only on keeping my composure," he recalled. "If I looked up I had to look above their heads because if I made eye-contact with those weeping and sobbing people it would be all over for me." And so he began to read the words of farewell that Dr. Reusch had typed earlier that week:

John 6:37: "And he, who comes to ME, I shall not cast out!"

Dear friends in XP! I am thankful to the LORD that HE allowed me to come here to say good-bye to you. I longed for this before going home. The doctor gives me about a year to live. With your help I regained confidence in mankind, which I had lost, and I am very thankful to you for it.

As my farewell text I have chosen these words of XP: "He, who comes to ME, I shall not cast out!" A day after HE had fed 5000 with 5 breads a huge crowd came to XP on the west side of the lake. The feeding of the 5000 was still fresh in their mind. HE had refused yesterday to become their earthly King, but they still hoped to persuade HIM to accept the Crown, because HIS power would protect them from famine and every disaster. HE knew their thoughts and told them that HE brought them more than earthly bread, namely bread from Heaven which gives them eternal Salvation.

They said that Mose[s] gave them also Heavenly bread, namely Manna. HE said that it was not Mose but GOD, WHO gave them Manna to sustain their spiritual life and bring them to eternal Salvation. The bread that Mose gave them sustained only their physical life, the bread HE brings them will sustain their spiritual life!

They said: "LORD, give us this bread always!" HE said: "I am the bread of life; he who comes to ME shall not hunger; he who believes in ME shall never thirst; and he who comes to ME I will not cast out!"

What does it mean to come to HIM? It means: to believe in HIM and pray to HIM! To believe alone is not sufficient. To believe can mean to be convinced that HE exists. Well, does it help you to believe that electricity exists but not to use it for light and warmth? Does it help you to know that medicine exists, but not to use it when you are sick? Does it help you to know that there is water but not use it when dying of thirst? There are many who believe in the existence of XP, but they do not come to HIM to ask for help. Their belief is useless!

Another meaning of belief is to have trust. If we trust a person we will talk over with him our needs and follow his advice. Our trust produces friendship and love which is best expressed by the word, *faith*. The following ancient story illustrates this.

There were 2 friends who trusted one another fully. One of them was innocently accused of having murdered the King's son and condemned to death. He had only days before his execution. He wanted to say good-bye to his old parents, but it was a long way. He asked permission, promising to return in time. The King did not trust him and said: "I shall give you those six days, if your friend will substitute for you. He will be crucified if you do not return in time." His friend said, "I will substitute for you," and went to prison. He ran the long way to his parents, found them, said good-bye to them and started to run back. A heavy rain delayed him. The next day he ran with double speed because the time was short. Approaching the city, he had to cross a river where he was attacked by 2 robbers. He knocked them down with his club. Looking at the sun, he knew that the time of execution was nearing. He ran with his last strength and arrived when they were ready to crucify his friend. He cried in a loud voice: "Stop! I am here. Let my friend go!" The King heard this, ordered to stop the execution and bring both before him. With tears in his eyes he said: "I have never seen such a friendship, such a trust. I pardon you, and please, bestow your friendship upon me. I need it!" They agreed. A short time later it was discovered that he was innocently accused. The real murderer was found. And the 2 friends saved the life of the King in battles more than once!

Such a friendship can only be characterized with the words: "They had faith in one another." And such a faith XP, WHO died for us, expects from us! Whosoever comes to HIM will not be cast out! Such a faith produces trust and loyalty. HE died for us to show us how much HE loves us. If we have real faith in HIM, we will recognize that HE is our best friend to whom we can come explaining our needs in prayer.

We can be sure that HE will not cast us out, but help us and do what is best for us during our earthly life. And when our last enemy, death, will approach, HE will stretch out HIS hands, take our tired soul and bring it safely into HIS Kingdom of love and light. As HE helped the hungry, sick and crippled during HIS stay in the Holy Land, so HE will help us. As he called back to life the daughter of Jairus, the son of the widow in Nain and Lazarus in Bethany, so HE will call us back to life and bring us safely home. He has promised: "He who comes to ME I will not cast out," and HE will fulfill what HE has promised because HE is our best friend. Therefore, come to HIM, as long as there is time; and our time is limited! Amen.

LOYALTY

Tuesday, July 1st, 1975, dawned without a cloud in the sky, and by eleven o'clock the temperature had become uncomfortably warm. Said Lary, "I'd never seen so many people in town, so many cars, so many people — dignitaries from foreign lands and Africa, Synod officials, a delegation from Gustavus — the sheer number of people who knew this man! I'll never forget the rows of chairs in every aisle. The fire marshal would have been horrified." Mourners spilled out of the sanctuary into the narthex, down the steps and onto the lawn outside. Lary's parents were lucky to find a place to sit in the church basement.

The Scripture reading was taken from I Corinthians 3: 21-23: "For all things are yours, whether Paul or Apollos or Cephas or the world or life or death or the present or the future, all are yours; and you are Christ's; and Christ is God's."

The first hymn, "Nearer My God to Thee," brought tears to the eyes of many, but the familiar ritual and ancient words of the Order for the Burial of the Dead — the *Kyrie*, and reading from the Psalms and New Testament Lessons — restored order to personal grief and provided comfort. After Lary's Confirmation class sang "How Great Thou Art," Pastor Jessie Stephano from the Lutheran Diocese of Northern Tanzania and Professor Robert Esbjornson from Gustavus Adolphus College spoke in tribute. But Lary, the boy who had just finished ninth grade, drifted off into his own reverie, "still reeling from all that had happened."

As in Africa, the church windows were wide open. For the final hymn the assembly turned in their hymnals to Reusch's favorite, number 551, "Stand Up, Stand Up for Jesus, Ye Soldiers of the Cross." It seemed to some that a Heavenly Host had descended upon the congregation as they joined in lifting their voices in thanksgiving for the life of Richard Reusch.

Then followed the *Nunc Dimitis* and the benediction. Dr. Reusch's five grandsons served as pallbearers and carried the coffin down the aisle and tenderly placed it in the hearse. A long procession of vehicles proceeded slowly from the church along Highway 61 to the village graveyard a mile north of town.

The Son of Kibo — "whose life," according to a reporter in the local *Chisago County Press*, "reads like some sprawling Russian novel," who had "walked with African natives, American college students, and Minnesota farmers"[33] — was buried neither on Mt. Elbruz in the Caucasus nor on the broad chest of Father Kibo in East Africa but in rural Minnesota where, on that bright summer day red-winged blackbirds and meadowlarks called from nearby marshes and fields.

Two years later, on the 10th of October 1977, his family gathered again in the quiet cemetery to bury Elveda Bonander Reusch alongside her husband.

Gustav Otto Richard Reusch's tombstone faces directly onto the highway, the only marker in the cemetery etched with an outline of the African continent.

On the occasion of his retirement as a college professor, Richard Gustavovich had written a simple and personal confession that summarized his life and faith:

> Eventide is coming for me, and the call to the last parade is at hand. An empty place awaits me in the regiment. Even as St. John was loyal to his Saviour, loyal unto death, so the men of our regiment. Loyalty is what counts in life: "Be you loyal unto death, and I shall give you the crown of life!" Weak and sinful, I have tried to be loyal to HIM. And this gives me the courage to pray in my last hour, "LORD, remember me."[34]

V. Eugene Johnson, Archives of the Evangelical Lutheran Church in America

"It is time for me to take my leave of 'my mountain.' Good has been Kibo to me, a constant source of vigor and health, a place where I forgot my sorrows and troubles, where I was nearer to my God." — *Richard Reusch*

CHAPTER 15

1 Carolyn Frenning, from the author's transcript of an audio taped interview, 10 August 1999.
2 Ralph Skow, from the author's transcript of an audio taped interview, 10 August 1999.
3 Document, "Official Call," signed by St. John's Council Chairman Willard J. Knutson and Council Secretary Melroy L. Aslakson, 21 April 1967, GACA.
4 Richard Reusch, letter to First Lutheran Church Council, St. Peter, ca. September 1967, GACA. Dr. Reusch accepted a salary of $4200 a year plus a $600 car allowance. That was less than the annual wage a newly licensed public school teacher with a bachelor's degree would expect to earn during the first year of employment.
5 John Knutson, letter to St. John's members, 14 October 1967, GACA.
6 R. Reusch, "New Members," undated manuscript, ca. 1967, GACA.
7 R. Reusch, 1967 Annual Report and Letter to the St. John's congregation, 21 January 1968, GACA.
8 Irene Skow, from the author's transcription of an audio taped interview, 10 August 1999.
9 Lary Skow, from the author's transcription of an audio taped interview, 31 July 1999.
10 Michas M. Ohnstad, radio announcer's script, 5 May 1968, GACA.
11 Melvin Hammarberg, letter to R. Reusch, 12 August 1968, GACA.
12 Eugene L. Anderson, letter to the congregation, 29 October 1968, GACA.
13 Dan Buendorf, minutes of the St. Croix District Pastors meeting, 21 November 1968, GACA.
14 Buendorf, from the author's notes of an interview, 15 July 1994.
15 R. Reusch, "World Events and Bible Prophecy," undated speech notes (ca. 1971), GACA.
16 Richard Anderson, interview, 7 March 1995.
17 St. John's Church Bulletin, 29 June 1969, GACA.
18 Lary Skow, interview.
19 Robert Esbjornson, from the author's notes of an interview, 17 February 1997.
20 Carolyn Frenning interview.
21 R. Reusch, "Annual Report for 1969," GACA.
22 Dean Gevik, acting secretary, report of the district pastors' meeting, 2 March 1970, GACA.
23 Irma E. Peterson, secretary to the editor of *Christianity Today*, letter to R. Reusch, 19 August 1970, GACA.
24 R. Reusch, postcard to the St. John's congregation, 19 June 1971, GACA.
25 R. Reusch, notes for his missions speech at Our Saviour's Lutheran Church, 19 September 1967, GACA.
26 Fish Lake Lutheran Church, LCW president, letter to R. Reusch, January 1975, GACA.
27 American Conservative Assembly program, Stacy, program for 10 April 1975, GACA.
28 R. Reusch, outline for his speech at Isanti, Minnesota, 26 May 1975, GACA.
29 Pent Nurmekund, letter to R. Reusch, December 1974, GACA.
30 Nurmekund, "Vklad Rexarda Reesha v Afrekanesteku," paper delivered at Leningrad State University, 1975 (Nurmekund Papers, V 30-8), Tartu University Archives.
31 Neil Anderson, letter to the author, 9 March 1999.
32 Melvin Hammarberg, notice to Minnesota clergy, undated, GACA.
33 "Dr. Richard Reusch Dies at 83," *Chisago County Press*, 2 July 1975, clipping, GACA.
34 The following paragraph has been condensed from R. Reusch's retirement speech, "From the Cavalry to Calvary," undated, GACA.

NAME INDEX

SUBJECT INDEX